PEACE, PROFIT
OR
PLUNDER?

INSTITUTE FOR
SECURITY
STUDIES

*This publication was made possible by the Swedish Government,
the MacArthur Foundation and the Government of Canada*

**Canadian Council for
International Peace and Security**

**Conseil canadien pour
la paix et la sécurité internationales**

ISBN: 0-620-23834-8

First published by the Institute for Security Studies,
P O Box 4167, Halfway House 1685, South Africa

Cover photograph: Jesper Strudsholm/iAfrika Photos

Design by Madhatter Image Design
Language editing and layout by Euníce Reyneke
Printed by Dando & van Wyk

PEACE, PROFIT
OR
PLUNDER?

The Privatisation of Security in
War-torn African Societies

Jakkie Cilliers and Peggy Mason (eds)

AFRICA

Contents

Abbreviations

ACDA	Arms Control and Disarmament Agency
ACRF	African Crisis Response Force
ACRI	African Crisis Response Initiative
ADFL	*Alliance des forces démocratiques pour la libération du Congo* (Alliance of Democratic Forces for the Liberation of Congo)
AMF	American Mineral Fields
ANC	African National Congress
APC	All Party Congress
APSG	African Peacekeeping Support Group
ARMSCOR	Armaments Corporation of South Africa
BICC	Bonn International Center for Conversion
BMATT	British Military Advisory and Training Team
BP	British Petroleum
CAMEO	Canadian Association for Mine and Explosive Ordnance
CAR	Central African Republic
CCB	Civil Co-operation Bureau
CDF	Civil Defence Force
CEO	Chief Executive Officer
CIS	Commonwealth of Independent States
CRL	Consolidated Rutile Ltd.
CSC	United Nations Supervisory and Control Commission
DCC	Directorate of Covert Collection
DIA	Defense Intelligence Agency
DRC	Democratic Republic of the Congo
DSL	Defence Systems Ltd.
DTAP	Democracy Transition Assistance Program
EC	European Community
ECOMOG	Economic Community of West African States Monitoring Group
ECOWAS	Economic Community of West African States
EO	Executive Outcomes (Pty.) Ltd. or Executive Outcomes CC or Executive Outcomes Ltd.
EOD	Explosive Ordnance Disposal
EU	European Union
FAA	*Forças Armadas Angolanas* (Armed Forces of Angola)
FAF	Bosnia-Herzegovina Armed Forces
FALA	*Forças Armadas de Libertação de Angola* (UNITA's armed wing)
FNLA	*Frente Nacional de Libertação de Angola* (National Front for the Liberation of Angola)
GAAP	Generally Accepted Accounting Practice
GNP	Gross National Product
GRAE	*Gouvernement révolutionnaire angolais en exil* (Revolutionary Angolan Government in Exile)

GSG	Gurkha Security Guards, Ltd.
GURN	Government of Unity and National Reconciliation
HRW/A	Human Rights Watch (Africa)
ICRC	International Committee of the Red Cross
IDAS	International Defence and Security, Ltd.
IFOR	Implementation Force
IMF	International Monetary Fund
ISC	International Security Consultants
JHQ	Joint Headquarters
JPMC	Joint Political-Military Commission
KMS	Keeny-Meeny Services
MISAB	Inter-African Mission to Monitor the Implementation of the Bangui Agreements
MK	*Umkhonto we Sizwe* (Spear of the Nation)
MNF	Multinational Force
MPLA	*Movimento Popular de Libertação de Angola* (Popular Movement for the Liberation of Angola)
MPRI	Military Professional Resources, Incorporated
MPWD	Maggie Peacock Working Dogs Limited
MSP	Military Stabilisation Program
MTS	Military Technical Services
NATO	North Atlantic Treaty Organisation
NCACC	National Conventional Arms Control Committee
NCO	Non-commissioned Officer
NEC	National Electoral Commission
NGO	non-governmental organisation
NPFL	National Patriotic Front of Liberia
NPRC	National Provisional Ruling Council
OAU	Organisation of African Unity
ONUMOZ	United Nations Operation in Mozambique
OSCE	Organisation for Security and Co-operation in Europe
PDD	Presidential Decision Directive
PESC	public enterprise security companies
PNG	Papau New Guinea
PSI	private security industry
RDMHQ	Rapidly Deployable Mission Headquarters
RECAMP	*Renforcement des capacités africaines de maintien de la paix* (Reinforcement of African Peacekeeping Capabilities)
RENAMO	National Resistance Movement of Mozambique
ROTC	Reserve Officer Training Corps
RPF	Rwandan Patriotic Front
RSLMF	Republic of Sierra Leone Military Forces
RUF	Revolutionary United Front
SAAF	South African Air Force
SADC	Southern African Development Community
SADF	South African Defence Force (before April 1994)

SANDF	South African National Defence Force (after April 1994)
SAP	South African Police (before April 1994)
SAPS	South African Police Service (after April 1994)
SAS	Special Air Service
SDM	*Sociedada de Desenvolvimento Mineiro de Angola* (Mining Development Society of Angola)
SFOR	Stabilisation Force
SGS	Special Gurkha Services, Ltd.
SHIRBRIG	Standby High Readiness Brigade
SIPRI	Stockholm International Peace Research Institute
SLPP	Sierra Leone People's Party
SPS	Special Project Service Ltd.
SRC	Strategic Resources Corporation
SRL	Sierra Rutile Lit.
TeleServices	*Tele Service Sociedade de Telecomunicaçoes, Segurança e Servicos*
ULIMO	United Liberation Movement of Liberia for Democracy
ULIMO-J	United Liberation Movement of Liberia for Democracy (Roosevelt Johnson faction)
ULIMO-K	United Liberation Movement of Liberia for Democracy (Alhaji Kromah faction)
UN	United Nations
UNAMIR	United Nations Assistance Mission for Rwanda
UNAVEM	United Nations Angola Verification Mission
UNCTAD	United Nations Conference on Trade and Development
UNDP	United Nations Development Programme
UNHCR	United Nations High Commissioner for Refugees
UNITA	*União Nacional para a Independência Total de Angola* (National Union for the Total Independence of Angola)
UNITAF	Unified Task Force (Somalia)
UNMOGIP	United Nations Military Observer Group in India and Pakistan
UNOMIL	United Nations Observer Mission in Liberia
UNOSOM	United Nations Operation in Somalia
UNPROFOR	United Nations Protection Force
UNRISD	United Nations Research Institute for Social Development
UNTSO	United Nations Truce Supervision Organisation
UXO	Unexploded Ordnance
VORGAN	*A Voz Resistencia do Gala Negro* (Voice of the Black Cockerel)
WHO	World Health Organisation

About the Contributors

Jakkie Cilliers is the Executive Director of the Institute for Security Studies in Pretoria, South Africa.

Sean Cleary is the Director of Strategic Concepts (Pty.) Ltd. in Johannesburg, South Africa.

Richard Cornwell is the head of the Africa Early Warning Programme at the Institute for Security Studies in South Africa.

Ian Douglas is a retired Brigadier-General from the Canadian Army and member of the Canadian Council for International Peace and Security in Ottawa, Canada.

Douglas Fraser is the Executive Director of the Canadian Council for International Peace and Security in Ottawa, Canada.

Peter Lock is the executive co-ordinator of the European Association for Research on Transformation in Hamburg, Germany.

Mark Malan is the head of the Peace Missions Programme at the Institute for Security Studies in South Africa.

Peggy Mason is Director of Development for the Canadian Council for International Peace and Security in Ottawa, Canada, and a former Canadian ambassador for disarmament.

Khareen Pech is an independent journalist, based in Johannesburg, South Africa, who specialises in the study of mercenary and private security companies in Africa. She is writing a book on Executive Outcomes.

Yves Sandoz is Director of Law and Policy, at the International Committee of the Red Cross in Geneva, Switzerland.

Alex Vines works for the Arms and Africa Divisions of Human Rights Watch in London and is a Research Associate of Queen Elizabeth House, University of Oxford.

The authors wrote in their individual capacities. The views expressed in this book do not necessarily reflect those of the Institute for Security Studies, the Canadian Council for International Peace and Security, Human Rights Watch, the Government of Sweden, the Government of Canada or the MacArthur Foundation.

ISS contact details:
P O Box 4167
Halfway House
1685
South Africa
Tel: +27 11 315-7096
Fax: +27 11 315 7099
E-mail: iss@iss.co.za
http://www.iss.co.za

CCIPS contact details:
300-1 Nicolas Street
Ottawa, ON K1N 7B7
Tel: +613 562-2736
Fax: +613 562-2741
E-mail: ccips@web.apc.org
http://www.web.net/~ccips

Preface

The papers on which this book is based, were first presented at a conference in Pretoria, South Africa during March 1998 with the title <u>Profit and Plunder: The Privatisation of War and Security in Africa</u>. Rather than analysing the trend toward an increased role for the private security industry in Africa from a theoretical or ideological perspective, considerable care was taken in the choice of contributors to ensure that the issues would be discussed and presented from different angles. Subsequent months saw the authors conduct independent research on three continents prior to the finalisation of the book early in 1999. This final product is considerably expanded and updated from the original conference papers. As the study progressed, opinions changed and others were refined.

The conference and this book have been collaborative projects between the Institute for Security Studies based in Pretoria, South Africa and the Canadian Council for International Peace and Security in Ottawa, Canada.

The ISS is an independent policy research institute which aims to enhance human security in Africa. With offices in Pretoria and Cape Town, the Institute does extensive work in Africa on areas related to, among others, corruption and governance, crime, policing, arms management, early warning, peacekeeping, regional security, defence, justice, and civil-military relations.

CCIPS comprises Canadians who have a common interest in presenting an independent, informed and reliable voice in Canada on issues of peace and security. The Council seeks to assist in developing and advancing innovative Canadian policies on issues of international peace and security in keeping with Canada's internationalist tradition. It promotes public debate and dialogue by providing independent views and sources of information to the Canadian government and public.

The ISS and CCIPS gratefully acknowledge the financial contributions to the joint project by the Swedish government, the MacArthur Foundation and the Canadian government who have all been patient in awaiting the conclusion of this project.

We would like to express our gratitude for the co-operation and support of the various authors who worked long and hard over an extended period of time on this publication and, in particular, to Richard Cornwell of the ISS who assisted extensively with the publication.

Jakkie Cilliers, ISS and Douglas Fraser, CCIPS
Pretoria and Ottawa
January 1999

Chapter 1: Private security in war-torn African states

Jakkie Cilliers[1]

Much has been written about the modern private security industry – particularly about 'corporate mercenaries'.[2] Until fairly recently, the approach to mercenaries within international law was explicitly associated with the process of armed opposition to decolonisation. This view is substantiated by even a cursory reading of the 1977 OAU Convention for the Elimination of Mercenarism in Africa and the 1989 UN International Convention against the Recruitment, Use, Financing and Training of Mercenaries. In the latter half of the 20th century, the term has taken on a pejorative tone – often recalling the image of the foreign white mercenary brutally suppressing or intervening in African politics at the behest of corrupt politicians or exploitative businessmen.

Although the debate on mercenaries *per se* has been substantial, research into the context in which this phenomenon occurs, as well as into the much broader continuum of private security and private military companies, is still fairly scarce. It is to address the wider spectrum of this complex problem that we have undertaken the writing of this book. Even though the problem of private military and security companies seems to have global characteristics and implications, we have chosen to demonstrate the connections by referring to one particular continent: Africa.

In Africa, private security companies are increasingly supplanting the primary responsibility of the state to provide both security for its peoples and for lucrative multinational and domestic business activities. Globalisation, the failure of African countries to achieve sustainable development, concomitant with the general weakening of the African state and Western peacekeeping disengagement from Africa after the Somali debacle, all provide a new context within which one should view historical mercenary patterns.

Before launching into the first substantive chapters of the book, brief reference must be made to the status of the global security industry in the 1990s and those factors that assist in transforming this 'old' problem into a uniquely contemporary phenomenon. These factors consist of the following:

- the relationships between private security companies and their countries of origin;

- the relationships between private security companies and countries receiving their services;

- prevalent trends in outsourcing core national security obligations in some parts of the world;

- the links between private security companies and the mining industry; and

- the difficulties in exercising national controls over these types of operations, particularly in regions such as sub-Saharan Africa.

Current status

The global security industry is a multibillion dollar business. Companies are relatively small in international terms (average annual turnover of US $5 million), highly specialised but undercapitalised, and tend to serve finite geographical regions.[3] Entrance barriers in the industry are low, fuelling the rapid entry and equally rapid demise of dozens of companies attempting to access a potentially lucrative market. Depending on how they are defined, companies provide anything from competitor intelligence and risk assessment, to personal and asset protection, to the sale, installation and maintenance of basic protection equipment, to high-technology protection and surveillance measures. They provide passive, defensive equipment and services, or offensive, intrusive and aggressive technology and services. Although companies like the recently disbanded Executive Outcomes had some assets, the most important are contacts, a network of possible employees and ready cash in the bank as start-up capital for new projects.[4]

In many countries, the industry is most obviously present as watchmen, often augmented by rapid reaction units armed with handguns and shotguns. In more turbulent countries, private security personnel take on a more paramilitary nature and are armed and equipped accordingly. Some can even be described as private armies. According to this view, a company such as Executive Outcomes was a radical form of the privatisation of security in Africa, not an anomaly, and was an extension of more legitimate personal protection services.

Companies such as Executive Outcomes and Sandline International transcend the role of traditional security consultants – they are, in fact, private paramilitary organisations which style themselves as 'military consultants'. They employ former soldiers and, in many of their activities, act in a manner indistinguishable from classic mercenaries at the behest of their economic or political paymasters.

Tim Spicer's definition of 'private military companies' goes far beyond even that of Executive Outcomes whose principals have vehemently argued that they do not participate in combat. Private military companies, Spicer argues,

"... are defined as those organisations which do more than provide passive assistance in areas of conflict. They may provide training and equipment to extend the capabilities of their client's military resources, providing them with the strategic or operational advantage that is necessary to suppress their opposition or, going even further, play an active role alongside the client forces, as force multipliers, deploying their own personnel in the field of conflict, but with the strict caveat that they are acting within the chain of command of the client's military hierarchy."[5]

Relationships with countries of origin

Some private security or military companies, like Sandline and Military Professional Resources, Incorporated (MPRI), have close ties to their home governments, in this case Britain and the United States. In the US, for example, there is strict federal and state legislation which requires that any company has to obtain government sanction before any commitment may be made which involves the provision of security or military goods and services to a foreign client, albeit a multinational corporation or a government. Since companies such as MPRI regard themselves as normal and legitimate business concerns, they must comply with such regulations.

Although the British government is on record as saying that the growth of private mercenary companies is a source of serious concern, its actions show that expediency may replace principle. In fact, British actions under a Labour Party government have made many analysts question the commitment of Britain, and other former colonial mother countries, to curb mercenary activity. Sandline International is one of a small number of private security companies employing former special force and intelligence officers that provide 'hard' security services. In a relationship in some ways similar to that between MPRI and the government of the US, Sandline claims close links with the British government.

The now disbanded Executive Outcomes, arguably the most well-known of these companies, was the odd one out in this regard. It drew its recruits from former apartheid armed forces – although this changed in recent years – and had its roots in a dirty tricks, covert front company for the South African Division of Military Intelligence. These origins would ensure that Executive Outcomes retained the mortal hostility of a South African government under Nelson Mandela after the African National Congress came into power in 1994. As a result, it was neither trusted nor apparently used by the Mandela government – a factor that undoubtedly played an important role in the decision to terminate its operations.

Following the passage of ineffectual but symbolically important extraterritorial legislation by the South African Parliament during 1998 – aimed at outlawing mercenary activity and regulating private foreign military assistance – Executive Outcomes announced that it would be winding up its affairs with effect from 1 January 1999. While this may bring one chapter in the saga to an end, there can be little doubt that most, if not all of its assets, knowledge and operations will continue under a different name or names. Already, the former CEO of Executive Outcomes has established a new security company, while many of the former senior managers of the company remain active in the field.

Relationships with recipient countries

There is often also a network of personal and financial connections between the heads of state/government members, multinational corporations and private security companies. The economic stakes are high. The host government, in many instances, is poorly equipped, corrupt and faced with internal armed political opposition. According to <u>Africa Confidential</u>,[6] for example, former Executive Outcomes head, Eeben Barlow, established a joint-venture security consultancy company with Raymond Moi, the son of Kenya's president, in 1995. Moi and Barlow are apparently also linked through Ibis Air, which is partnered with Simba Air in Kenya, partly owned by Moi. Ibis Air has often provided air transport for Executive Outcomes and was generally considered to be part of the same network of companies.

In neighbouring Uganda, Saracen Uganda (a former Executive Outcomes subsidiary) guarded the gold mining operations of Branch Energy (Uganda). Saracen Uganda was established in co-operation with the recently disgraced half-brother of President Yoweri Museveni, Major-General Salim Saleh. Saleh owns 45 per cent of Saracen Uganda and 25 per cent of Branch Energy (Uganda). During December 1998, Saleh resigned as presidential advisor on defence and military affairs after confessing that he engineered the improper take-over of the recently privatised Uganda Commercial Bank through a firm in which he has a significant shareholding, Greenland Investments.[7] In this manner, political power, nepotism, economic interests and security profits coincide in a common thread that seems to pervade much of Africa.

In a country such as Angola, mercenary activity appears to have become endemic to the war. During the nineties, mercenaries played a crucial role in the reverses that *União Nacional para a Independência Total de Angola* (UNITA) suffered on the battlefield. The impact of foreign soldiers, however, did not end once Executive Outcomes allegedly left the country on 11 January 1996.[8] As recently as March 1998, South African mercenaries were reportedly hired by the Angolan government to man SAM-14 ground-to-air missile systems in the Bailundu and Andulo area as part of an effort to isolate the UNITA forces about 150 kilometres north of Huambo. In January 1998, fighter aircraft allegedly flown by foreign pilots forced down a DC-4 cargo plane trying to land at Andulo, an area controlled by UNITA. The plane was carrying a cargo of diamond mining equipment and munitions. Executive Outcomes subsequently denied its involvement, stating categorically that it had no operatives in Angola at the time.[9] This incident also demonstrates the difficulty in isolating fact from fiction and rumour in an industry that guards its secrets as effectively as it does its clients. In the case of Executive Outcomes, it would probably be true to state that its reputation and alleged involvement in most countries far exceeded its actual activities. The legend that became Executive Outcomes was, in fact, as powerful a marketing tool as it was an impediment to the legitimisation of the company in the eyes of the South African government.[10]

The extreme case of a territory so thoroughly privatised that the slightest semblance of statehood has disappeared, must be Somalia, where warlords are most plausibly regarded as commercial operators, each with a private military force recruited largely on a clan basis and dealing in straightforward looting, arms trade, narcotics, and the considerable profits to be made out of humanitarian relief and, most ironically, international peacekeeping.[11]

Outsourcing

The trend towards the outsourcing of core national security obligations is not limited to Africa, nor is it necessarily viewed negatively, particularly in the West. In developed economies, this trend is largely driven by market forces – ever in search of less expensive and more effective ways of using scare resources. During the second half of 1998, the US contracted a private security company, DynCorp, to provide supplies to its contingent for the civilian verification mission of the Organisation for Security and Co-operation in Europe (OSCE) in Kosovo. DynCorp won the contract against stiff competition from MPRI which is involved, among others, in military training in Croatia and the Federation of Bosnia and Herzegovina.

Yet, while security outsourcing and even commercialisation are common practices in countries such as the US, Britain, France and others, it is often core functions of statehood that are contracted out in Africa – due to the inability of the state to fulfil such functions. The purpose is therefore not to enhance cost-effectiveness, but to fill a vacuum left by the effective collapse, partisan nature or inefficiency of the national forces – or to make money for a small political élite, often connected by marriage or other personal ties. By far the most important case was the former Belgian Congo, where the collapse of discipline in the *Force publique* led, within days of independence, to UN intervention. When some form of order was established, it paved the way for the most ruthlessly privatised of all African armies under the patronage (rather than command) of Mobutu.

The case of the Belgian Congo was in no way a unique occurrence. According to Clapham, *"[i]n the three East African states of Kenya, Tanganyika/Tanzania and Uganda, the mutinies of early 1964 were suppressed by instant British intervention, but led to rather different political responses on the part of the three governments concerned: in Kenya to a small professional army under a measure of continued colonial tutelage; in Tanzania to something close to a citizen army, in association with the ruling party; and in Uganda, most dangerously, to the buying off of the mutinous elements who were permitted to remain within the military."*[12]

In recent years, the political élite have been responding in a variety of ways to the security dilemma in African states, but these have increasingly been characterised by the trend towards the privatisation of security as former colonial links became ever distant. In 1994, for example, the Israeli company Lev'dan signed a $50 million contract with the government of Congo-Brazzaville to train the local army and presidential bodyguard.[13]

Links with mining

The relationship is not limited to internal actors, however. Often, private security companies are in the service of multinational mining interests or closely associated with high risk international base mineral exploration companies. Mining still represents one of Africa's few real areas of progress – and companies have no alternative but to go where the rich mineral deposits are to be found. Africa already provides most of the world's gold and gem diamonds, as well as platinum and palladium. Most of the world's cobalt, copper, chrome and titanium dioxide are also mined in Africa. The US Bureau of Mines estimates that deposits in Southern Africa alone hold nearly ninety per cent of the world's platinum and palladium, 85 per cent of the chromium, 75 per cent of the manganese, fifty per cent of the gold and fifty per cent of the vanadium.

Cash-strapped African governments, that once treated international mining groups with deep suspicion, now compete for their favours. Many have watered down or abolished foreign ownership restrictions or punitive taxes that had previously discouraged companies from exploring for mineral deposits. From Algeria to Zimbabwe, more than thirty African countries have made substantial changes to their mining codes. As a result, poor governments pay for services and favours by granting mining concessions – or mortgage future profits to purchase arms or line the pockets of the governing élite as is the case in Angola.

The amount of foreign funds spent on mining exploration in Africa has increased rapidly in the 1990s despite the fact that low commodity prices are forcing mining companies to cut exploration budgets. Planned capital expenditure, as distinct from exploration spending, has also jumped significantly in recent years, most of it for gold and copper mining.[14] This kind of mining requires vast investments and therefore a stable environment – in contrast to diamond mining in much of Angola and the Democratic Republic of the Congo, for example, which is much less capital intensive.

The reality of weak African states creates an environment within which foreign companies must provide not only their own infrastructure, such as roads and medical facilities, but also private security forces capable of protecting their property and employees. As a result, mining companies argue a strong case when it comes to the costs of doing business in Africa, where mining can be a dangerous and very expensive activity. During January 1999, four employees of the *Sociedada de Desenvolvimento Mineiro de Angola* (SDM), which mines diamonds in Angola's Lunda Norte province, were killed when their vehicle was ambushed by an armed band. At the time, SDM was reported to employ 500 security guards to protect the 200 people on its mining site. Some months earlier, the Yetwene diamond mine, also in Lunda Norte, was attacked. Eight employees were killed, 24 injured and ten abducted. Speculation at the time was that the alleged UNITA attack may have been targeting the part-owner of the mine, DiamondWorks, given the close relationship between DiamondWorks, Branch Energy, Executive Outcomes and the *Movimento Popular de Libertação de Angola* (MPLA). Yetwene was protected by TeleServices, a company within which senior members of the Angolan armed forces hold significant shares.

Apart from paying off local politicians, warlords and often the military, mining companies have to employ teams of security 'advisors' at enormous cost to protect their staff and property and to alert them to impending conflict. The personnel at hand are also often of doubtful efficiency. For example, following the attack on the Yetwene mine mentioned above, the local TeleServices guards decided to loot the mine. Mining companies must also draw up elaborate evacuation plans, usually involving special teams on standby, chartered aircraft and so on. To reduce psychological stress, companies such as De Beers rotate their Angolan field staff every three months. As a result, the security costs to protect the extended operations and capital investments of a large mining operation can be enormous. As the war in Angola escalated during January 1999, the Canadian company SouthernEra Resources reported that it was closing its two operations in the Lunda Norte province since security costs had made mining there only marginally profitable – and highly dangerous.[15]

Official harassment and the lack of security in the granting of government licences are other factors that increase mining costs in Africa. The result is, inevitably, that mining companies concentrate on gaining the highest returns in the shortest time possible. In an article that appeared in the <u>Financial Mail</u> of 15 January 1999, the South African company Anglo

American alleged that it was awarded a 20 000 square kilometre prospecting concession in 1996 by the then government of Zaire. Anglo was lucky to have its concession area reduced to 13 000 square kilometres by President Laurent Kabila's new government. Kabila annulled the contracts of American Mineral Fields (AMF) and Banro Resources Corporation.[16]

The extent to which a government such as that of President Mobutu of the former Zaire lacks control over its own territory and the extreme lengths that mining houses are prepared to go to in order to secure contracts, are evident from another example involving American Mineral Fields. During April 1997, AMF signed agreements worth about $1 billion with Laurent Kabila, then still a rebel, to buy the Kolwezi copper and cobalt project. On assuming power, Kabila cancelled the agreement.[17]

The result of these often complex arrangements is a trilateral relationship between the government, the mining company and the private security company. Such a special relationship is often removed from public or governmental scrutiny and characterised by 'special' methods of payment and secrecy. In this manner, the governing élite regain control over those areas that provide private and public resources, the mining company is ensured of a captive and malleable government that enables it to exploit its concessions, while both benefit from the stability provided by the security companies. In a small country such as Sierra Leone, the services of a private security company like Executive Outcomes can become crucial to the survival of the government. As is so often the case, the losers are the communities that occupy the land where mineral exploitation occurs and the population at large.

The difficulties of control over the activities of private security companies

One of the most obvious characteristics of the private security and military industry is that it presents a confusing and misleading maze to the outside observer. Companies sometimes form part of giant inter and transcontinental concerns, making it difficult to establish where they begin or end. Some of these concerns are often registered as businesses in other territories which complicates issues such as governmental control over their activities. Moreover, contracts are often obtained on a subcontracting basis, that diverts the locus of control and responsibility. Large sections of this book will look at exactly these issues as part of an attempt to dissect the nature of the problem. The final chapter addresses the regulatory challenges.

A guide to the book

In an attempt to illustrate these trends, this book will first deal with globalisation and the growth of the private security industry in Africa (Peter Lock); the crisis in external response (Mark Malan); and the collapse of the African state (Richard Cornwell). These chapters are followed by case studies of three companies: Executive Outcomes (Khareen Pech); Military Professional Resources, Incorporated (Cilliers and Douglas); and Gurkha Security Guards Limited (Alex Vines). The case studies serve to highlight the nature of the operations and the impact of such experiences on particular countries which are discussed in subsequent chapters, namely Angola (Sean Cleary); and Sierra Leone (Ian Douglas and Richard Cornwell). The second last chapter (Yves Sandoz) places the increased prevalence of the private security industry within the context of international humanitarian law. The final chapter (Cilliers and Cornwell) attempts to identify the underlying causal themes evident in Africa and to provide a broad policy response to the growing trend towards the privatisation and commercialisation of security and war in Africa.

We trust that this book will contribute to an understanding of the trend towards the privatisation of security – and even of war – in Africa within its wider context. We hope that it will encourage additional research on the subject and will provide information necessary to establish a regulatory framework and oversight over such activities. The latter are urgently required, if anything, because of the negative trends tying weak states and private security companies together on this troubled continent.

Endnotes

1   I would like to acknowledge the advice, counsel and assistance of Richard Cornwell, Virginia Gamba, Mark Malan, Sarah Meek and Jakkie Potgieter.

2   The common understanding of a mercenary is probably that of a 'hired soldier in foreign service', essentially working for money or other reward.

3   A Vines, *Security for a Few: Privatisation of Security in Africa in the 1990s*, paper read at a conference on The Privatisation of Security in Africa, South African Institute of International Affairs, Johannesburg, 10 December 1998, p. 1. According to Vines, the combined US and international security market has estimated revenues of $56,6 billion in 1999 and is growing at a compounded rate of 7% annually.

4   For example, in Angola and Sierra Leone, Executive Outcomes flew two second-hand Boeing 727s as supply planes (bought for $550 000 each from American Airlines). It also regularly flew Soviet Mi-17 armed transport helicopters, Mi-24 Hind gunships, MiG-23 jet fighter-bombers and a squadron of Swiss Pilatus training planes converted to fire air-to-ground rockets. Yet, even at its height, the true potential of Executive Outcomes probably pales in comparison with US companies such as Military Professional Resources, Incorporated. (MPRI), Vinnell Corporation and Betac Corporation, given the backing that companies such as these receive from the US government. See K O'Brien, *Freelance Forces – Exploiters of Old or New-age Peacebrokers?*, Jane's Intelligence Review, August 1998, p. 42

5   Private Military Companies – Independent or Regulated?, <www.sandline.com/company/index/html>, 31 December 1998.

6   Anon., *Militias and Market Forces*, Africa Confidential, 38(21), London, 23 October 1998.

7   Apparently, EO also helped to secure import licences for military hardware brought into Uganda by Branch Energy and Saracen. In a facsimile to Jane's Intelligence Review dated 21 August 1997, Branch Energy stated that *"BE Uganda is a separate legal entity to BE."* See Branch Energy (BE), <www.eo.com/presrel/press.asp?series=30>, 31 December 1998.

8   A number of 'former' EO personnel stayed on in Angola, redeployed to companies linked to BE such as Branch Mining, Shibita Security, Stuart Mills Associates, Saracen and Alpha 5. Vines, op. cit., p. 5.

9   BE, <www.eo.com/presrel/pressrel.asp?series=73>, 31 December 1998.

10   Tim Spicer writes: *"The extent of Active Private Military Companies (APMC's) involvement in ... conflicts ... has been heavily dissected by the press. However, there has been almost as many different versions of reported events as stories published or broadcast. The speculation about the motivations of an APMC to accept an assignment, their long-term goals in a particular country, inter-relationships with mining companies and other commercial entities, and the method of payment, to name a few issues, has been simply staggering."* T Spicer, Should the Activities of Private Military Companies be Transparent?, <www.sandline.com/home/index/html>, 31 December 1998, p. 3.

11   C Clapham, *The Changing Nature of Mercenary Activity in Africa: An Historical Analysis*, paper read at a conference on The Privatisation of Security in Africa, op. cit., p. 9.

12   Ibid., p. 5.

13   O'Brien, op. cit.

14   K Gooding, *Africa's Mineral Wealth Still Beckons*, Business Day, Johannesburg, 29 December 1998.

15   J Sikhankhane, *The Profits of Doom*, Financial Mail, Johannesburg, 15 January 1999, p. 33.

16   Ibid.

17   Ibid.

Chapter 2: Africa, military downsizing and the growth in the security industry

Peter Lock

Military downsizing: Background and context

*E*mpirical data[1] and theoretical reflections on the evolution of warfare[2] suggest that the outbreak of large-scale interstate wars are unlikely in the future. The sudden demise of the Cold War – clearly an interstate configuration – has reinforced this trend and provoked a widespread downsizing of military postures. The end of modern interstate wars has not only resulted in military downsizing, but also in the development of forms of military proliferation beyond the geographical area of the battlefield. One of the most important examples of this proliferation is the current growth in the private security industry. In order to contextualise this development, certain trends which occurred before, during and after the Cold War need to be highlighted.

Historical context

Military downsizing is not a 20th century phenomenon and has mostly been associated with the end of a war. As such, the Napoleonic wars saw the transfer of military personnel of losing parties to other theatres. Hundreds of aristocratic Polish officers who had placed their hopes on Napoleon to resurrect the Polish state, ended up fighting a slave rebellion in Haiti on behalf of France. The demise of Napoleon further marked the first large demobilisations in modern times. The new order designed by the Congress of Vienna reduced the demand for the military profession in Europe. Not surprisingly, the military histories of the newly independent Latin American states reflect a corresponding influx of military officers from Europe who sought and found employment in the New World.[3] The failed revolutions of 1848 and the subsequent repression led to the emigration of democratically-oriented military personnel, many of whom ended up in the US fighting in the Civil War. The Franco-Prussian War of 1870-71 pushed the defeated French into concentrating their military efforts on the conquest of what became the French colonial empire.

It was only after the two World Wars, however, that the full proliferation of military expertise, personnel, and hardware became evident in the aftermath of a conflict. As the losing party in both wars, Germany became a major source of legal and illegal, governmental and private proliferation. Most of Germany's military hardware was confiscated and either destroyed or distributed as reparation among the members of the extensive winning alliance. After World War I, strict limitations were imposed upon force strengths and equipment, which resulted in large-scale demobilisations, including that of an outsized officer corps. After World War II, Germany was totally demilitarised, a policy that was only reversed after the Korean War gave rise to the intensification of the Cold War.

It is beyond the scope of this chapter to describe the post-conflict proliferation of German military expertise and personnel in detail. However, the largely private involvement of German military personnel in Chiang Kai-Shek's China – which was at first tacitly and later openly supported by the German government – displays a number of features that can also be observed today.

In 1927, Chiang Kai-Shek expelled sixty Soviet military advisors and, in a clear political shift, attracted a large group of demobilised German officers to work for him instead. Good salaries were offered and officers with revolutionary ideals had the opportunity to be politically active. Some maintained close contacts with the German arms industry in particular. Colonel Max Bauer, was one officer who made use of this opportunity. He served for some time as armaments advisor in the USSR, and also consulted in Spain and Argentina. In 1927, he was invited by the Chinese leadership to inspect the military, and immediately became an economic advisor.

"Bauer arranged economic contacts [and] arms deals and eventually enlisted 20 more civil and military specialists ... Faced with the civil war the advisors became ... involved in military affairs, they organised a battalion of instructors, taught at war schools and laid the foundations for intelligence and counter-espionage ... In 1929 ... lieutenant-colonel Wilhelm Kriebel became leader of the consultants. He was a follower of Hitler and had participated in Hitler's failed insurrection of 1923 ... The consultants took part at the side of Chiang in the fights against disloyal warlords in Northern China and in the campaigns against the communists."[4]

As this originally private scheme of military consulting expanded, it developed into a brokerage in which officers earned lucrative commissions, set up trading companies and finally managed to first get the *Reichswehr* and later the German government involved in China. Increasing numbers of Chinese officers, including Chiang's son, studied at the German general staff college. Eventually, the brain behind the post-1918 *Reichswehr*, Hans von Seeckt, became the 'general manager' of the China connection. He initiated barter trade, supplying raw materials such as large quantities of wolfram, for Germany's demanding rearmament programme.[5] The German arms industry also won lucrative orders from Chiang's government to make use of idle capacity.

But the foreign activities of demobilised German military personnel were not restricted to China. In violation of the prohibition of foreign military relations imposed by the Versailles Treaty, German officers travelled as private citizens and were hired as military consultants throughout South America, and even adopted local citizenship to provide better cover for themselves. Most importantly, they received covert support from the Ministry of the *Reichswehr*. This undeclared foreign military policy was effective in creating markets for the German arms manufacturers. In South America, it also led the general resurgence of Germany as a trading partner.[6] In Argentina, Chile, Bolivia and Peru, demobilised officers from Germany were particularly influential. Ataturk's new Turkey also contracted German military personnel in their private capacity.

This brief survey of the consequences of earlier post-war demobilisations suggests that the privatisation of foreign military and security relations pursued by companies such as

Executive Outcomes, Military Professional Resources, Incorporated (MPRI) and the like is not new. Their link to economic interests and access to raw materials are also not novel. However, it reflects a pattern where the demobilisation of qualified military personnel without appropriate civilian job alternatives, in combination with weak states and civil wars creates a demand for external military and strategic support.

The Cold War and its aftermath

After 1945, the Cold War and colonial wars absorbed most of the military surplus in personnel and hardware. In the case of personnel, some settled in the remaining colonies, as in the case of British officers in Kenya. Many young men from *Waffen-SS* formations of various national origins joined the French Foreign Legion, ending up in Indochina and later in Algeria. In the early 1950s, 80 000 Germans were believed to be serving in Indochina and Algeria, though many of these were younger than the *Waffen-SS* generation.[7] Dutch members of the *Waffen-SS* were sent with the Dutch contingent to the Korean War as a precondition for regaining their citizenship. Some World War II veterans formed the first generation of mercenaries who became notorious in the early post-independence years in Africa.[8] Only the US managed to reintegrate their World War II military personnel into a booming post-war economy. In contrast, the Vietnam War produced a number of unintegrated former soldiers who floated around the world and undertook such jobs as piloting aircraft in risky operations, transporting illegal commodities and drugs and providing logistics for right-wing insurgencies.

In the Middle East, nations such as Saudi Arabia, Oman and others have been employing foreign military specialists on leave from their national armed forces, among them Pakistani pilots flying Saudi Arabian fighter aircraft. Britain pioneered these arrangements in Oman in the 1970s for reasons of 'stealth' accountability, and many military functions have been outsourced to private American and British companies, making the Middle East the precursor of a general and increasingly pervasive privatised security phenomenon.

The end of the Cold War marked the end of a period of hypermilitarisation that affected almost the entire world. In many countries, the downsizing of the military sector had already begun by 1985 as a result of the protracted economic and financial crisis which brought the first Reagan administration's rearmament bonanza to an end. Gorbachev's propagation of global disarmament was part of a misguided attempt to save the Soviet economy by reducing its military burden. However, the implosion and dissolution of the Soviet Union set off a chain reaction of military downsizing which eventually reached most parts of the world. The process was somewhat slowed by the Gulf War, and the trend became only apparent in South-East Asia when the region was hit by the present regional economic crisis.[9]

In Africa, the implications of the end of the Cold War are clearly shown in arms procurement figures. They reflect the downgrading of sub-Saharan Africa on the foreign/military policy agendas of the leading powers who were the main suppliers to and paymasters of the region's military posture. At the height of the Cold War, sub-Saharan Africa absorbed military equipment worth more than US $5 billion in some years, or up to fifteen to twenty per cent of the value of the region's exports. By 1995, recorded values were estimated at only US $270 million for arms transfer deliveries.[10]

The diminishing volume of arms procured by the region indicates that the military went through an internal and external repositioning. With the exception of South Africa, military equipment is increasingly confined to cheap infantry weapons, with air forces and navies merely equipped with the essentials, if at all. No government seems to be able to draft more than minimum budgets which cannot provide for the regular replacement of existing stock. Other influences were also clearly at work, as the reversal of trends precedes the end of the Cold War.

Belligerents in the region will have to manage with the equipment inherited from the Cold War period, with the exception of small arms which are affordable and readily available on the black market. Since the volumes of hardware supplied during the 1970s and 1980s were unequally distributed throughout the region, the military level of warfare will be determined largely by what remains in operational condition in each conflict arena. Angola and Ethiopia alone absorbed almost two-thirds of the regional arms imports calculated at US $33 billion between 1984 and 1994. While Ethiopia virtually ceased to import arms after 1990, Angola's arms imports alone since 1991 comprise almost half of the regional total.[11]

One of the most profound effects of the end of the Cold War has been the reduction of, among others, direct US government involvement in African affairs. *"The United States ... switched to policies which emphasised the role of non-state activities such as those of private companies or civic associations."*[12] Direct US aid moulded Africa's political landscape throughout the Cold War, and not necessarily in a favourable way, as is documented by the main countries receiving aid at the time: Sudan, Zaire, Kenya, Somalia, Ethiopia, and Liberia.[13] Africa had suddenly lost its strategic significance for the great outside powers; the Soviet Union disappeared altogether. This state of affairs was further exacerbated by the general displacement of state-to-state relations as a result of globalisation.

The end of the Cold War also saw new transnational organisations acquiring significant power resources as the industrialised countries themselves underwent a process of institutional restructuring. These organisations took over the external relations with Africa. Foreign aid is a case in point: it became mostly privatised even though United Nations agencies started to play a larger role in the provision of aid. This hardly represented a small-scale retreat by the state, for aid generally amounted to roughly ten per cent of regional GNP. Transnational corporations such as Lonrho and Bridgestone became direct political players in East Africa and Liberia respectively, while external non-governmental organisations (NGOs) were effectively privatising diplomacy and acting as mediators in armed conflicts, such as the Catholic groups in Mozambique in 1992.[14]

Africa and demilitarisation in the 1990s

Throughout the Cold War, much of the military build-up in sub-Saharan Africa, including that of insurgent forces, was the product of non-requited arms transfers from outside the continent, if only as credits that were written off. Today, military spending in sub-Saharan Africa accounts for less than one per cent of global military expenditure and continues to fall.[15] South Africa alone still spends more than forty per cent of the regional total, although cuts and general downsizing have reduced South Africa's military expenditure during the last ten years from 4,6 per cent to less than two per cent of gross national product (GNP).[16] Since military transfers into the region have become purely commercial transactions, diminishing military budgets reflect only part of the actual military downsizing.

On a global scale, the manpower absorbed by military activities is also declining. The Bonn International Conversion Center (BICC) has calculated that the world's armies shrank by more than six million soldiers from the peak in 1987 to 22,7 million at the end of 1996.[17] Sub-Saharan Africa failed to follow this trend, however, and maintained some 1,1 million soldiers under arms during the 1990s. In some countries, South Africa in particular, part of the armed forces has been demobilised, while numbers have apparently increased in regions afflicted by continued armed conflict.

In the sub-Saharan military context, such aggregated figures explain little, however. Not only are the available statistics notoriously unreliable, but more importantly, the delineation of what should be considered as armed forces is ambiguous, as many countries have seen a proliferation of a variety of armed formations in recent years. Presidential guards, often better paid and equipped, are a case in point.[18] Sometimes, it is also unclear whether state formations have been appropriated for private interests or whether private formations have come to substitute government functions. In any case, the functions of the military in sub-Saharan Africa do not reflect the clear separation between internal and external security which is normally represented by the police and the military respectively. The logistical capacities of the national armed forces often do not cover the entire national territory, and operational equipment seldom amounts to more than small arms and the most basic infantry equipment. Many observers attribute the relative absence of interstate wars in sub-Saharan Africa to the inability of most armed forces to conduct such operations.[19]

In general, the attrition of weaponry exceeds replacements by a large margin. Imports of major conventional arms in sub-Saharan Africa in 1997 amounted to 0,5 per cent of the world trade in weapons. On average, the region imported weapons to the value of US $243 million each year during the period between 1993 and 1997, the lowest average figure since 1960. Only Angola, South Africa and Nigeria imported major weapons valued at more than US $100 million during the last five years, with Angola leading the group with US $185 million. SIPRI claims that, between 1993 and 1997, 144 tanks, 352 armoured vehicles, eight combat aircraft, eleven helicopters, 54 pieces of artillery and fourteen transport aircraft or helicopters at most were imported by countries engaged in conflicts in the region. All of the imported systems were relatively unsophisticated and most were second-hand.[20] According to SIPRI, however, these imported weapon systems did not play a significant role in the conflicts.

In South Africa, the armed forces of the apartheid regime constituted the dominant military in Africa. They fought permanently undeclared interstate wars, based on a doctrine designed to pre-empt the assumed 'total onslaught'. As a result, the current downsizing of South Africa's military has not only released experienced military personnel with intimate knowledge of other countries in the region, but the country also has to cope with an oversized intelligence apparatus that covered much of the continent. This heritage is both a burden and a boon for the ANC post-apartheid government as it tries to come to terms with its new role on the continent. On the one hand, the intelligence assets inherited from the apartheid state could assist in the country's self-assumed role as conflict mediator and peacebuilder. On the other, these persons, contacts and their activities are uncontrollable, with intelligence networks potentially abusing their knowledge and networks throughout sub-Saharan Africa. The result could be practice that is clearly not in South Africa's best interests or even commensurate with its declared policy.

The continuing French military reforms are also contributing to regional military downsizing. The more than 8 000 prepositioned troops present in six countries until recently – Senegal, Côte d'Ivoire, Djibouti, the Central African Republic, Chad and Gabon[21] – are being reduced by a further 2 000 soldiers. Given the superior equipment of the French troops in an African context and their linkage to rapid reaction forces stationed in France, the reduction of the French posture in sub-Saharan Africa represents a substantial alteration in the African military equation. However, the often miserable state of many armed formations in sub-Saharan Africa has been illustrated whenever the intervention of a hundred or so French soldiers has sufficed to quell disturbances[22] and to shift the balance of power mostly in favour of the entrenched Francophone élite.

The downsizing of the military sector in sub-Saharan Africa, therefore, has a quantitative and a qualitative dimension. Taken together, these have resulted in what is effectively a military vacuum across large parts of sub-Saharan Africa. In addition, states have often yielded the monopoly of legitimate violence, because police forces are in an equally disastrous condition. Yet, the evolution of a political consensus and the availability of the necessary means to rebuild legitimate and efficient forces are clearly not in prospect.

Downsizing is not a one-way process. External intervention supported by a moderately efficient military force becomes a tempting option in the context of a relative military vacuum, especially if a clear and realistic objective is at stake and a new coalition of external and internal interests can be forged. Angola's partisan support in neighbouring countries, which aims at cutting off the logistics lines of UNITA, is a case in point. In this context, it should also be noted that the training of officers at military academies in France, the US, Britain and Israel, among others, continues unabated, with at least 2 000 officers receiving advanced education and training abroad every year.[23] In addition, the rapidly increasing number of joint military exercises between the US and individual African states indicate that there is a tacit competition between outside powers seeking to link up with African armed forces by planting potential liaison officers. Finally, the option of filling the military vacuum selectively with an emerging private security industry is a possibility, not least because the US and other Western governments are condoning, if not actively supporting, the acquisitive strategies of the private security industry in sub-Saharan Africa.[24]

A further consequence of the strategic relocation of Africa, which heralded major changes in the region, is the reduced significance of international borders. After thirty years of tacit agreements sanctifying the arbitrary borders of African states inherited from colonial times, there are many indications of future changes in the borders within the region. The secession of Eritrea may just have been the harbinger of a new geopolitical order.

Unlike the Eritrean case, any possible restructuring of the region's political geography will not necessarily follow the European model, where most actors worked towards forming homogeneous nation-states throughout the late 19th and early 20th century. Instead, in the age of globalisation, control over commerce has become the key demarcation of political power, especially when trading in the global market.[25] The classical nation-state may therefore be relegated to a back seat in the reorganisation of Africa's political economy and the ensuing new continental map. The major powers are not likely to defend the territorial *status quo* provided that their interests are not endangered by the changes.

In purely military terms, large parts of sub-Saharan Africa now constitute such a vacuum into which the infusion of a small well-organised external force can tip the balance in ongoing confrontations. However, state structures have collapsed in many cases to such an extent that a military victory is unlikely to have any impact on levels of social violence, social fragmentation and the criminalisation of the economy. Nevertheless, in the absence of an alternative, the hiring of external military force to achieve political ends always remains a temptation in the destitute environments which make up so much of the region.

The economic crisis in Africa and the downsizing of the state

The outside world seems to have come to terms with Africa's economic plight. Until recently, increasing volumes of humanitarian aid compensated for the lack of a more serious commitment to overcome the economic crisis – represented by ever-mounting arrears in debt repayments – which afflicts most of the states in sub-Saharan Africa. Even in cases where gross human rights violations occur, the outside world has opted to ignore these, and refuses to intervene. Almost twenty years of structural adjustment programmes, sponsored by the World Bank and the International Monetary Fund (IMF), have failed to alleviate Africa's economic plight, which continues to be characterised by extreme levels of aid dependency, insupportable levels of foreign debt, and decaying infrastructure.

However, it would be wrong to conclude that there were no changes, based only on the obvious fact that very few, if any, economic improvements were achieved in some countries, and that many countries have experienced a steady deterioration. On the contrary, the character of the sub-Saharan state has changed in response to the pressures of structural adjustment policies and the paradigmatic changes of development aid.

The first long period after independence saw an élite retaining power by means of systems of patronage which incorporated a self-defeating logic of continued expansion.[26] By the second decade of independent statehood, available resources were exhausted and development aid and its manipulation became the main sources of patronage. Not surprisingly, such political systems revealed a strong link between the disposition of economic benefits and the achievement of political stability. The élite remained the absolute arbiter over external economic relations, which allowed them to exploit not only the Cold War competition, but also the political rivalries among donor nations. In Francophone Africa, it was also possible to call on French troops to quell opposition forces and protect the incumbent élite.

The increase in foreign debts during the 1970s paved the way for international pressure on African governments to accept structural adjustment programmes designed by the IMF and the World Bank. It was held that inflated and inefficient state bureaucracies were the main causes of Africa's economic malaise and that allowing market forces to operate freely would set the continent's economies on the right path. After more than a decade of these programmes and debt rescheduling exercises, however, most low income countries still face inaffordable debt obligations.

While these failed restructuring programmes were in progress, African states still needed the resources to govern their own territories, despite the fact that they were losing their legitimacy in international and domestic spheres.[27] The ensuing downsizing of the state also did not necessarily eliminate the incumbent élite. They were often able to manipulate the enforced privatisation of the most valuable assets and acquire them at bargain prices,[28] in a process similar to the notorious *nomenclatura* privatisation in Russia. The expected elimination of corrupt systems did not materialise. Instead, an empirical survey on the state of corruption concluded that, *"... we discovered the rise of a 'new corruption', rooted in the logic of economic and political liberalisation, reflecting the activity of rapacious local elites no longer subject to the domestic and international constraints of the Cold War era and increasingly pervaded by criminal or 'mafioso' forces."*[29]

Most importantly, this period was characterised by a cumulative externalisation of state functions. Some observers have called the process 'recolonisation', although the ideologies behind this transformation are distinct from the motives behind Africa's conquest in the 19th century. Numerous aid agencies also adopted this new paradigm. They boldly bypassed the arbitration of the recipient state and imposed their own respective philosophies, often in collusion with former bureaucrats turned into non-governmental receptacles of aid. *"The capacity of African governments to manage the connections between their own societies and the outside world was consequently reduced or even extinguished, and instead such connections were taken over, to the extent that they were sustained at all, by external agencies operating on their own account."*[30] These NGOs were active in every field, from famine relief and human rights monitoring to wildlife protection.[31]

The important political implications of this change are often conveniently overlooked. In the first place, external actors should share the responsibility for the continued regression of most economies in the region.[32] Failed development projects, the accumulated debt burden, and the grip of the élite over valuable assets to the detriment of the population at large are the products of decisions which were long since predominantly externalised or in which external actors at least had a veto. Secondly, as the United Nations Conference on Trade and Development (UNCTAD) correctly points out, economies in regression are prone to state failures or even collapse, as well as internal conflicts. These can result in complex emergencies, which are highly contagious and not restricted by borders.[33] Thus, any complex emergency can no longer be dealt with as an isolated case, as an entire region is often in danger of being drawn into a downward economic spiral.

Finally, while liberalisation and democratisation continue to be offered as panaceas, the state is virtually being hollowed out with little or nothing left for democratically-elected politicians to decide, because the major state functions have long since been externalised. As a result, African states are in a process of being steadily converted into hollow façades, behind which international agencies and actors are running the economy, mostly in collusion with the local élite-turned-entrepreneurs. This process has been dubbed 'the project of external governance'.[34] Military functions and security services are simply the latest additions to the list of state functions that are increasingly being externalised and often privatised.

Privatisation and the criminalisation of the state

Most states in sub-Saharan Africa appear to be moving along similar paths in varying degrees, at the brink of state failure. The inherent expansion of clientelistic political systems requires a steady flow of additional resources which the élite must appropriate in order to stay in power. Hence, clientelism carries steadily increasing costs. This trap, which constantly confronted the élite in control of the state, was reinforced by international pressures to accept the need for the structural adjustment of economies burdened by inaffordable debts.

Under pressure of adjustment, the incumbent élite often abandoned their social obligations and concentrated on safeguarding their economic fiefdoms, while duly paying lip service to the imposed financial regime.[35] As more and more core functions of the state were outsourced to foreign contractors in order to comply with the dictates of the international financial institutions – such as the profitable trade certification to the *Société générale de surveillance* – the incumbent élite expanded their activities into informal parallel networks with the aim of maintaining their controlling stake. This move, labelled as the *"creation of a shadow state,"*[36] has provided the élite with continued control over exploitable resources. An American scholar's assessment is even harsher: *"In a number of countries, the state is slowly being merged into a web of informal business associations instituted by rulers who have little interest in carrying out the traditional functions of the state and who do not recognize or respect boundaries, while enriching themselves through trade."*[37]

The failure of the formal state as a normative authority made the informal settlement the norm, arbitrariness the rule, corruption a political philosophy, and shrewd double-dealing the only means of existence.[38] The *nomenclatura* privatisation of the state sector demonstrated that market forces were incapable of taking over the regulation of the economy from the well-entrenched informal networks. Privatisation simply reallocated the *"economy of pillage"* into less accountable, by definition almost shady or illegal spheres.[39] In search of new resources, these economic networks expanded into international criminal dealings and transformed parts of sub-Saharan Africa into an important hub of the global drug trade.[40] Money laundering and financial fraud became viable industries in the region.[41]

The élite networks maintained their leverage at the price of relying increasingly on violent coercion, while the cannibalisation of all public goods became the rule.[42] Rent-seeking continued to expand alongside the growth of illegal activities and an influx of dirty money. Violence as a mode of economic regulation penetrated an increasing number of economic spheres and thus prepared the ground for an escalation of armed conflict and anarchy.[43]

The ensuing structure of economic, financial and political power increasingly deprives the formal state of the means with which to carry out even its minimum functions. The extensive community of public servants which expanded under the patrimonial state is now being denied and relieved of its income. The state fails to pay salaries regularly, if it does so at all. Rampant inflation, often caused by criminal fiscal manipulation such as bringing printed money into circulation on behalf of kleptocratic leaders, has devalued public salaries to such an extent that office-holders must either extort illegal fees for their services or moonlight in the private sector or the informal economy. As a consequence of structural adjustment policies, the formal state has lost its attraction for the rent-seeking élite; they withdraw their allegiance and abandon their former power base without remorse.

The police and the military are not spared from this absolute weakening of the state and the resulting privatisation of its functions. In all but name, the effects on all armed agents of the state in many countries can be described as demobilisation in slow motion. The rules on which a market economy is based, are no longer enforced. On the contrary, the public security forces either sell their services to an oligarchic group or live on some form of extortion themselves. In response to the resulting general insecurity, all social actors take up their own defence against criminality. This privatisation of security polarises society, because security is converted into a commodity. It can either be purchased in the regular economy from a private security company, in a grey area by buying off state agents, in the informal sector by militianisation, or in the criminal sector by paying a racketeer. Once violence has begun to regulate economic transactions, the search for security becomes a major occupation as it is a functional precondition to the successful conclusion of any transaction. An escalation in private security providers is the logical consequence, which eventually takes on the dimension of an internal arms race encompassing mainly small arms. The productivity of the economy, including the criminal and informal sectors, rapidly contracts further because of cumulative transaction costs related to security.

It is but a small step from such a condition in a society to the outbreak of armed conflict, from a criminalised economy to a war economy. In both cases, security is the major concern and violence a principal means to achieve mainly economic objectives. While demobilisation is typically associated with the end of armed conflicts, it is argued here that many weakened states are faced with the *de facto* demobilisation of their armed agents even without an open armed conflict coming to an end. In the process, security personnel, both military and police alike, transform themselves into private instruments of violence, offering their services to the highest bidder either as moonlighters or full-time, notwithstanding the criminal character of the services required.[44] Alternatively, they enter into the world of pillage, looting and extortion. Thus, post-conflict demobilisation is not so much a unique circumstance. This should not come as a surprise, because the principles of economic circulation in most of the sub-Saharan region remain the same in war or peace.[45]

The organisation of security in weak states:
The case of sub-Saharan Africa

"The notion that Africa was ever composed of sovereign states classically defined as having a monopoly on force in the territory within their boundaries is false. Most colonial states did not make any effort to extend the administrative apparatus of government much beyond the capital city ... After independence, African countries did try to extend the administrative reach of the state, but were always more focused on the urban populations."[46] The façade of sovereignty was maintained throughout the Cold War and held up by the unconditional support for essentially dysfunctional states whose territorial composition was neither based on economic or ethnic cohesion, nor on a democratic consensus.

The armed forces played an important role in maintaining this façade either as arbiters over élite factions or the foot-soldiers of entrenched leaders. But the 'military balance' between the state and society has changed profoundly. At independence, the state was basically in full control of all the weapons on its territory. This is no longer the case, because states have atrophied further[47] and weapons spilling over from armed conflicts throughout the region have begun to circulate virtually uncontrolled, allowing societies to arm and challenge the incumbent élite.

As Africa's armies seem to melt into a new privatised security order dominated by oligopolistic groups, a short review of the evolution of armed forces will help in understanding the process.

Africa's armed forces are basically colonial institutions which served to police the empires, but were also enlisted as cheap cannon fodder during the two World Wars and, in some cases, in colonial conflicts elsewhere. The pattern of colonial recruitment exploited existing group rivalries, so that the respective territorial populations were never proportionately represented in the colonial regiments. At independence, the colonial military personnel formed the army of the newly independent state. They became the most visible expression of sovereignty. Underrepresented groups, however, could not identify with this national 'symbol'. Furthermore, the armed forces were burdened by their image of colonial coercion.

Post-colonial interests and the dictates of the Cold War opened the military academies of the foremost military powers, such as the People's Republic of China and Israel, for African officers. Eventually, competition among the major powers to dispose of military surplus and new arms extended to the procurements of Africa's armed forces as well. But these weak economies hardly permitted the operational maintenance of the cascading surplus of equipment, except for the large stock of rugged light weapons.

The incumbent élite had a strong interest in leaving the inherited borders untouched, since their position depended on the maintenance of the *status quo* and the pretence of heading a nation-state.[48] This predilection combined with resources that were too limited to maintain armed forces capable of fighting cross-border wars.[49] However, if an armed internal conflict was dubbed to be a surrogate war, the fighting parties were stocked with military equipment, often beyond realistic requirements. This left huge surplus stocks at the end of those wars which were bound to be offered on black markets, because the regimes were unable to sustain an orderly demobilisation. Instead, armed formations often fragmented into autonomous units that appropriated the military property of the government to generate income wherever an outlet could be found. As already mentioned, these weapons now flow freely throughout Africa in search of effective demand; the prices are volatile, but arms often sell well below the production price.

In general, the armed forces of sub-Saharan Africa were eager to adopt the role of symbolic guardian of the nation, charged with the task of external defence. This explains the many jet fighter aircraft that were procured during the 1970s, despite the absence of any defence doctrine to justify such acquisitions. Sophisticated weaponry was seen as a way of not being drawn into internal security. However, the armed forces never managed to desert their colonial role and were often exclusively engaged in internal security, particularly as general economic conditions deteriorated. At the same time, professional standards declined along with the social status of the military, not least because military budgets were shrinking and often misappropriated.

The general economic decline led military personnel to seek additional sources of income to supplement their meagre and often irregular wages. Moonlighting in the private security industry is among the more benign alternative activities. However, rackets and other predatory behaviour turned the military institutions of a number of countries into a scourge permanently haunting the civilian population. Marchal depicts the ensuing confrontational dynamics between the dispersed military formations and the society at large as *"double militianisation."*[50] This reflects a process of de-institutionalisation which draws the procedures of hierarchical and bureaucratic functioning into question and transforms entire units of the armed forces into bands who receive the main part of their income not through their allegiance to the state, but through the confiscation of resources belonging to the public and through theft from civilians. This provokes a reflexive organisation on the civilian side and marginalises the authority of the state and its monopoly of violence in the national security equation.

Kleptocratic governments prolong their survival by proliferating the coercive forces of the state. The creation of a presidential guard is often the most visible step, but other specialised security services may also be created to keep any challenges to their power at bay. These formations are likely to be better equipped and paid than the usually neglected armed forces, but may also face sudden dissolution if they no longer fit into the security equation of the ruling élite.[51] In the terminal stages of state atrophy, special forces protecting the 'Big Man'[52] are sometimes remunerated out of the privy purse of the incumbent to ensure their allegiance.

In countries involved in protracted civil wars, the insurgent army has often also benefited from intensive military training abroad. This is not without some relevance for downsizing and demilitarisation procedures, because this training was based either upon Maoist guerrilla doctrines or right-wing destabilisation manuals, depending on the patron. In the northern part of the region, former volunteers from the war in Afghanistan are said to transfer what they learned during their destabilisation training with US special forces.

The final addition to the potential surplus of personnel with military experience are children. Thus, no matter whether large-scale demobilisation after conflict or a pervasive slow motion demobilisation characterises the scene, the emerging private security industry in Africa and the criminal sectors of the economy alike can draw from a labour market oversupplied with a wide range of military experience and expertise.

As if this were not enough, the continuing debate on how to cope with violence in Africa generally ignores the problem that police forces are also in a miserable shape. Social science has given surprisingly little attention to African police forces, in stark contrast to the large body of literature on the role of the military. *"When the police are discussed, it is usually in relation to the military, compared to whom they are seen academically as the poor relation: lower in status, educational level, resources and discipline, and less prone to political intervention."*[53] During the Cold War, the way in which political leaders were policing their country scarcely mattered, as long as the regime was not in danger of being overthrown.

The police forces in most African countries are of colonial origin and are run as quasi-military units.[54] They are therefore by definition badly prepared to function as a modern police force, in other words, acting pro-actively.[55] In spite of significant differences in the political evolution of African states after independence, their police forces share many characteristics.

"The salient features of policing across a number of African states are its low status, paramilitarism and propensity for violence. In turn, the features of existing African police systems are that they are generally organized as a nationally-unified, vertical body with a centralized force directed from the top, but whose divisional administration units are divided into regional, district, station, sub-station, and police-post levels."[56]

In spite of the marginal formation of their forces,[57] police officers are typically endowed with extensive discretionary power that serves, among others, as an invitation to treat different groups of citizens unequally. In fact, most police forces became notorious for corruption, greed, violence, weakness and partiality. The population have come to perceive the police as part of the (security) problem and not as a solution. Compared to the armed forces and other special coercive units, the police have been of little importance to the ruling élite. They have felt more threatened by the likelihood of an insurgency or a *coup d'état* and accordingly focused on the military and special forces in which they could have confidence. Proper policing of the society at large was not their priority.

The weak state structure and extremely low remuneration pave the way for the inevitable deterioration of policing in the context of fragmenting states. The police increasingly turn towards illegal but lucrative activities. What has been described as *"sobels"* in Sierra Leone[58] – soldiers who turn rebels at night – has its equivalent in *"pobers"* – police officers who turn into robbers at night and at other times. The syndrome of predatory policing is widespread in Africa and not restricted to war-torn countries. In Kenya, this expression of social fragmentation seems to fester in extremes.[59] Kenya provides a case of direct colonial lineage in the organisation of the police; it also demonstrates that extreme social fragmentation and formal democratic procedures can coexist.

The emphasis of policing systems in Africa is towards the order-and-control end of the spectrum of police functions rather than justice and crime prevention.[60] At the same time, the distinction between state and government has little tradition in African political systems. Security means principally regime security. Governments usually appropriate state organisations. Police and military functions are not properly separated, riot control and counterinsurgency are not distinguished. The control of resources, patronage, and the means of coercion come into the hands of privileged individuals, and are methods of political reward.[61] The next step – the quasi-privatisation of the state, as in the former Zaire[62] for example – is but a matter of degree: the path is prepared almost everywhere.

In fragmenting states, the coercive agents, mainly the police and the military, no longer provide security. Physical security often decreases dramatically, because the police and the military act locally on their own and become pobers and sobels, at least for part of the time. *"Some form of localised protection becomes necessary because physical force (rather than 'traditional' moral authority) provides the only possible basis for creating limited stability in conditions of societal breakdown."*[63] If the state fails, as was the case in Somalia or Liberia, there is no civil order to enforce or maintain, and consequently there is no role for the police.[64] Under these circumstances, police personnel will focus on personal reproduction and survival, which is not necessarily a predicament for increased violence. It merely marks the final dominance of a general private rearmament process which takes many different forms, from the local strongman who has the potential to become a warlord during conflict escalation to the international private security firm selling protection. The society turns into a web of competing militias. In the process, the perception of insecurity suffices to feed the escalation that explains the difficulties to reverse this dynamic and reinvent a state which commands the monopoly of legitimate coercion.

Thus, policing takes on new private forms. Vigilante groups and militias can be seen as a form of social adaptation to a major failure of the state security equation. The reconstruction of a legitimate state will have to account for existing social policing and transform this into accountable formations. But this requires an understanding that the absence of state policing is not identical with chaos and an absence of policing. Or as Hills emphasises – referring to the *"web of radically privatized, quasi-vigilante security arrangements [which] provide reasonable deterrents to crime ... policing exists in Somalia (as in most fragile and fragmented states) as an activity, rather than as an organisation."*[65]

The evolution of the private security industry: Its impact in the region

The apparent emergence of the private security industry is not entirely new. It has been pointed out repeatedly that international commerce itself was alone responsible for its security for long periods. The East Indian Company paid for its own 'army'. Only at the zenith of the imperial age did states begin to shoulder the cost of maintaining the public order required to exploit the colonies. In the 19th century, large business concerns were separate dominions with their own police forces. The eventual preponderance of public law is an achievement of the early 20th century. Finally, the worldwide mining and oil industries were always known to employ special protection forces, a fact which is not surprising, as they often penetrated into territories lying beyond the functional perimeters of modern states where traditional social formations were disturbed, if not destroyed. Although there are many parallels between the current activities of the private security industry in sub-Saharan Africa and private coercive forces in previous periods, they shall not be dealt with here except where they are directly related to massive demobilisation, as was the case with the German-China connection discussed above.

Instead, this analysis departs from the hypothesis that globalisation and the current global changes to the security equation – away from the state towards private spheres – are also bound to determine the security order in Africa. The debate about weakening states losing their legitimate monopoly of coercion juxtaposes ongoing changes and the regulation of violence in the constitutional welfare-state whose historical climax was represented by the social-democratic era in Western Europe during the 1970s. At no time and in no other region did social reality come as close to this ideal model of democratic equality.

It goes without saying that the prevailing security order in sub-Saharan Africa never came close to this European constitutional model, however much the leaders of the first hour of independence had copied and paid lip service to it. On the contrary, the dominant form of regulation in the region has been classified as neo-despotic.[66] The neo-despotic form of regulating violence is characterised by a state whose radius of influence is restricted to urban concentrations. Its jurisdiction over its subjects is rather limited. The resources of neo-despotic states have but two main sources: customs receipts and foreign aid. The state acts arbitrarily through local brokers; a rational bureaucracy does not exist. Instead, the bureaucracy turns into an unstable web of personalised relations. This implies that all political and administrative functions are based on personal relations forming a concentric circle around the 'big man of the day' or president. The state is effectively transformed into their booty and loses its legitimacy. The important feature of this form of regulation in the context of the privatisation of security is the absence of an efficient public control over violence. Hence, such systems are characterised by a complex web of security and self-defence arrangements, on the one side, and the pervasiveness of certain forms of violent crime such as arms smuggling, predation, and banditry, on the other. It is against this background that the impact of the trend towards the privatisation of security in sub-Saharan Africa must be explored.

The growth of the private security industry (PSI) gathered speed in the early 1980s and has accompanied the triumphant march of neo-liberalism. Since then the growth rates of the sector are well above the average in industrialised countries – eight per cent annual growth – virtually exploding in transitional countries – twenty per cent annual growth – and in most parts of the developing world – ten to thirty per cent annual growth.[67] So far, the growth of the sector has been counter-cyclic. In other words, economic and political crises fuel the demand.

The expansion of the PSI has three dimensions. Security activities which until now, have been the preserve of the state are being privatised – prisons, patrolling and so on;[68] citizens, economic actors in particular, are rapidly increasing their demand often for new types of security and intelligence services from the PSI;[69] and in a climate of perceived insecurity, the commodification of security through infrastructural investments and applications of modern high-technology is spreading pervasively.[70]

In this process, the state cumulatively loses its role as a guarantor of security, and individual security becomes a function of disposable income. The changes in the social fabric include major transformations of the social geography with deep social segmentation. Public space turns into commercial centres and private confines, sometimes in the guise of private business districts financed through 'private' taxes.[71] Gated communities spreading rapidly in the US, in capitals of the developing world, and in transitional countries are the most visible manifestation of this trend. While the well-to-do social strata opt for self-ghettoisation and give notice to the social contract of the constitutional welfare-state,[72] criminal energy directs itself against the poorer strata of the society living in an apartheid of poverty without the economic resources required to seek protection through the PSI. The polarisation between no-go areas for the public police and the appropriation of public security services by the middle and upper classes is also reinforced by corporate sponsoring of local police forces.

The boom in the PSI has a self-promoting effect. The visibility of its activities nourishes perceived insecurity, no matter what the real crime situation, which feeds back into the growth of the sector. Individual arming, permanent supervision, bodyguards and so on mark the escalation towards an oligopolistic-preventive regulation of security and a gradual end of the state monopoly of coercive violence.[73] The new order translates economic inequality into the social inequality of security.

Outside the barricades of the wagon laager, an order based on violence develops. Self-defence groups, youth gangs and drug cartels compete for territorial control. In the apartheid of poverty, violence becomes an integral part of the emerging cultural ideologies which claim to protect group identification and self-respect. Religious sects and reactivated or even invented ethnicity[74] are among the vehicles of communitarian defences in deeply fragmented societies. The sharp borderline between the segregated spheres reinforces the prevailing trends on both sides and promotes the ideological foundations of the internal security race which is, in fact, an arms race. Not unlike the former strategic bipolar arms race, it absorbs enormous economic resources and creates jobs in the regular and the illegal economy which, however, do not add to collective welfare. The extension of this race into the informal and illegal sectors of the economy marks a major difference between the former state-centred bipolar world and social polarisation in the age of globalisation with its neo-liberal privatisation and international externalisation of state functions.

The analysis so far clearly shows that the growth of the PSI is a civilian trend and that there is no direct causal linkage to the massive military demobilisation accompanying the end of the Cold War. However, the availability of trained personnel in certain contexts fitted perfectly into suddenly emerging markets. Russia is a good example where the PSI was allowed to move into entirely new fields much closer to military tasks than its traditional area of activity.

The PSI is not a capital-intensive sector; it works mostly with cheap labour. Until a few years ago, the sector was characterised by thousands of small companies. But a rapid transnational consolidation of the industry is presently taking place. Among the reasons for this concentration is the poor reputation of a sector which often brings crime from within.[75] Private security companies also present themselves as ideal covers for criminal organisations and racketeering.

The social capital of large international companies allowed them to increase their global market share rapidly. Borg-Warner, Pinkerton's Incorporated, Wackenhut, Securitas, Securicor, G-4, and ISI are among the big players. But other more specialised companies have arrived on the scene, taking advantage of new opportunities in strategic consulting, military training, operational support and logistics, armed protection and, in some cases, also military operations.

The latter category relies heavily on demobilised personnel from special forces and on specially qualified military officers. The former Executive Outcomes, Defence Systems Limited (DSL), and MPRI are the icons of this new category.[76] The present circumstances in Russia are a prism of all post-Cold War trends in the PSI. While the government recognises some 5 000 firms in the sector employing 155 000 people, independent estimates put the figure between 800 000 and 1 200 000 plus 200 000 employed by small companies without a licence. These figures compare with roughly 500 000 police-related personnel. On the basis of this estimate, conditions in Russia have caught up with the US where the ratio is three private security officers per one police officer. Inadequate pay and low prestige in the state sector have allowed the PSI to lure the brightest and the best from among the military police and the extended security apparatus. It is estimated that seventy per cent of officers of the infamous KGB who have quit before the age of retirement, have entered the PSI. Russian corporations and banks often have their own security branches, for example, Gazprom's security service alone employs 20 000 men. The Russian PSI provides all services from bodyguards, intelligence and counterintelligence to plant protection and the transportation of valuables.

Foreign firms said to have entered the market in partnerships are, among others, Kroll, Control Risks Group, International Security Services and DSL. A particular feature of the Russian PSI, typically found in weak states, are the government agencies which hire out their services to the highest bidder in an unending quest for resources and payment. And the PSI pays four to six times the salary of a government employed security officer.[77] Finally, many firms are front operations of the *Mafiya*, though some may be moving from open racketeering to formalised protection.

In Russia, a society fragmenting with frightening speed and a government with little legitimacy make it almost impossible to draw clear lines between the state and private sectors, and between crime and the wilderness of early capitalist appropriation. There are no indications, however, that the mushrooming of the PSI has contributed to an improvement of security or to a reduction in crime: armed violence booms and smuggling is rife. The PSI and crime seem to be interdependent variables heading for further growth.

One result of the impudent appropriation of state property in the former Soviet Union is a large number of air transport companies prepared to provide logistical support worldwide with military transport planes, not only in regular markets. The availability of cheap demobilised, but experienced personnel in combination with weak state controls make these companies, typically registered in some distant tax haven, the preferred choice for illegal transports worldwide, including the logistics for current conflicts in Africa. There are reports of other military services, for instance maintenance, being carried out by demobilised former Soviet military personnel. It is probably because of the cultural distance and the lack of international experience among demobilised Russian military personnel that Russian firms have not entered the market of comprehensive private military services until now, except as subcontractors for security firms operating in Africa.

Outsourcing of foreign military policy to military advisory and training companies appears to mark a trend which was led by the US and gained momentum after the end of the Cold War. This tendency will certainly also play a role in sub-Saharan Africa. MPRI, Vinnell and DynCorp are among the leading American contenders. According to Goulay,

"[t]he use of a private military contractor permits Washington to project its influence quite cheaply and very quickly to countries where it would be normally difficult to send troops because of political sensitivities. Moreover, the cost of cutting any links with a foreign regime is even less expensive, as MPRI protects Washington behind a potential screen of deniability."[78]

Elsewhere, in Colombia for example, DSL is contracted to protect oil wells and pipelines. The contract is extended to the training of special units of the Colombian armed forces, constituting an intriguing case of the corporate sponsoring of foreign armed forces by British Petroleum (BP) through DSL.

Based on the post-colonial African experience, the United Nations came to condemn mercenary activities, and still has a special rapporteur on the issue.[79] But the unanimity behind this condemnation is beginning to falter. It appears most likely that US interest in the military segment of the PSI is behind the surprising shift in opinion with respect to military support missions carried out by the private sector.[80] Thus, the interventions of Executive Outcomes in Angola and Sierra Leone might well be harbingers of future international military relations.

Against this background, it is not altogether futuristic to see political actors enhancing their military capability by internationally leasing military personnel and hardware from the private sector. In purely economic terms, such a move would resemble the rationalisation and restructuring of industrial production in the maelstrom of globalisation. But military restructuring affects the very core of the nation-state and this trend is therefore likely to see many modifications and manifestations.

If the likely impact of global trends on the privatisation of security in Africa is considered, the similarities between urban African conglomerations and their counterparts in Russia are obvious. Particularly striking are the similarities with respect to the *de facto* privatisation of state agents and the loss of the monopoly over legal coercion, the slow motion demobilisation (in Russia, in addition to large-scale demobilisation), and the fatal role of violence as a means of economic regulation which makes the position of bank director a high risk profession in Moscow. The PSI in sub-Saharan Africa is a booming business. The traditional, individually employed watchman was more a symbol of social prestige than an efficient protection against crime. He is being replaced by security firms modelled after the industry in developed countries, partly because many international firms have branched into the African security market.[81] These PSI companies only operate in the regular economy and depend on the monetarisation of the respective economies, which is always linked to the viability of their export sectors. The demand derives from a high concentration of incomes and valuable productive assets. Reports of demobilised military personnel in post-conflict situations, or of slow motion demobilisation in failing states where public security personnel moonlight as part of security companies in the private sector, always refer to countries or regions which produce and export a commodity. Alternatively, the demand is fuelled by expatriates involved in externally-financed development projects or humanitarian aid.[82]

Thus, more than anything else, the massive presence of the PSI in African countries is an indicator of the insertion of a viable economic sector into the global economy. Putting it differently, in contrast to the dismal economic performance of the region as a whole, one can argue that the expansion of the PSI in Africa indicates the resilience of Africa's participation in the global economy. The context, however, is of otherwise polarised and deeply fragmented societies, further propping up the demand for the PSI. Africa's difference consists in the extensive informal economy and its high proportion of rural populations which are only marginally integrated into monetary economic circuits. It is estimated that about half of the region's transborder trade is not part of the regular economy,[83] a fact which defies the presumption of national sovereignty. This large segment of African societies also relies on differentiated, though informal security systems of its own. From a sociological point of view, it mirrors the PSI in the modern sector. It provides roles which demobilised soldiers are just as likely to take up, if the circumstances do not allow them to cling to the modern sector.

To the extent that the fragmentation of African societies progresses and state functions are being hollowed out, the role of violence in the confrontation between the different security arrangements in the modern and informal sectors will increase and eventually become the dominant mode of economic regulation. The escalation along this path will eventually be recognised as civil war. Similar to the situation in Russia, it is difficult to prove that the massive growth of the PSI contributes to national security outside the limited confines of its customers.

Economic zones or states?
The economy of security in sub-Saharan Africa

The kleptocratic exploitation of exportable resources by a corrupt élite for their own benefit seems to have exhausted the necessary recourse of power. This is not least because the steady flow of external support stopped after the end of the Cold War – except for humanitarian aid. The brokerage of these, often voluntary transfers provided the central tool that kept the prevalent regimes in power or, alternatively, kept an armed conflict going, as has been the case in Sudan.[84] Humanitarian aid has often turned into an innovative asset fuelling the economy of continuing wars by creating humanitarian sanctuaries.[85]

The persistence of armed conflicts and the pervasive absence of government control over the national territory provide room for violence. Rufin[86] takes a detached view and interprets the violence and the ongoing armed conflicts in the region as part of the process of sub-Saharan Africa finally taking possession of its own history. He supports Bayart's interpretation which sees the present turmoil as a mode of political production whereby sub-Saharan Africa finally and autonomously plays out a new political economy of the region. Most of the armed conflicts are about repositioning African resources in the world market. Reno believes that warlords who manage to be recognised as heads of state will be the central figures in the new political economy of the continent.[87] He predicts that the international community will rush to give recognition to those new rulers, just as the dictators of the quasi-states were recognised without demur during the Cold War period, Mobutu being one example.

Alternative political projects are evolving that have abandoned the Western model of a democratic state. In parallel to the decay of the quasi-states, the regular segment of most economies has been shrinking, in many cases dramatically. However, dynamic parallel and illegal economic circulation across the region and often connected with the global economy is also an important part of the African reality. This is not statistically evident and by definition is organised outside the legal order, corrupted as that may be. In the absence of any law-based regulation, this circulation therefore operates permanently under the menace of blackmail, racketeering and violence. The dynamics of this situation are the origin of the profound destating and privatisation of security in the region, which eventually leads to a militianisation of the entire society.

The joint articulation of the parallel and illegal sectors results in a pervasive arming of the economic actors that are involved. This cumulatively affects all layers of the society and the regular economy. Though markets are also at the centre of parallel economies, no legal arbitration controls the battles over predominance. Coercion and intimidation rule over the access to these markets, and force is often used to deny access to unwelcome competitors. However, as battles over access escalate, the mobilisation of politico-ideological group identities is often applied to dominate specific markets in the parallel economy. This step has great potential to eventually escalate into armed conflict, because the original economic motive of excluding others from a specific marketplace readily converts into a general enemy image triggering violence no longer related to the originally limited intention. The large numbers of internally displaced persons and refugees in the region are a tragic manifestation of such exclusion strategies.[88]

Such armed conflicts are no longer civil wars, where two or more parties fight over the hegemony of a traditional state. Instead, the battles are over economic sectors, regions, trade routes, preferably over those allowing access to the world market. In these cases, the established term 'intrastate' war is somewhat misleading, because the conflict is over the creation and control of a new local-global economic space, which is no longer burdened with the ballast of an exhausted territorial nation-state. And most importantly, new alliances are being formed during ongoing armed conflicts between the substate, international, and supranational actors which labour in the midst of fighting to develop competitive production locations for the global market, no matter whether the access routes are legal or criminal. With the local monopoly of coercion being the precondition to advance such projects, successful warlords become indispensable partners. All this is possible because substate units are able to interact with the world market on their own, and in defiance of a formal state, without fearing sanctions in this era of deregulation. Additionally, there are many shady actors in the international financial markets eager to loan the necessary capital in exchange for exploration titles. It remains attractive, however, for a warlord who controls an economically viable territory to strive for control over the formal state, because this provides a legal cover for the ruthless appropriation of state enterprises and property titles. It becomes feasible for a warlord in the position of formal head of state to contract military services from the international PSI to bolster his position without running into international opposition.

The US is among the countries that have come to consider interventions by the PSI as an acceptable way of ending destabilising conflicts by tilting the balance of power and allowing one side to take all. What is needed, according to the proponents of this qualitatively new form of mercenarism, are internationally accepted rules to make sure that certain standards of humanitarian law will be respected.[89]

Contrary to the political rhetoric of warlords-turned-presidents, such as Liberia's Charles Taylor, there is no longer a vision of creating an integrated territorial state which provides, or promises to provide a social infrastructure, education and so on. The externalisation of state functions, such as customs and the certification of trade, merely continues to expand, as does direct control over resources by international capital. The inclusion of security into the externalised sphere marks a new step in the process of the externalisation of political accountability. The open private militarisation of security accelerates the destating process in the region, though it is portrayed as stabilisation. Therefore, these contexts become acceptable areas for the international emergency aid industry which regularly moves to alleviate the worst excesses of social polarisation and the ensuing apartheid of poverty. There is no easy solution to the dilemma of aid agencies becoming useful partners of the new political economy that separates *Afrique utile* from *Afrique inutile*.

While the evolution of Africa's new political economy will be marked by many contradictory trends, it is possible to outline the parameters of the PSI in this process. The PSI will thrive in the monetarised export-oriented pockets of Africa's economies. Its services will be instrumental in positioning these sectors competitively in the world market, because security is a fundamental precondition to attract the foreign capital required to realise the potential wealth in the region. The economic logic of these pockets places a premium on keeping the rest of the society at bay, in order to remain profitable. To the extent that the excluded sectors contest their marginalisation, the demand for the services of the PSI is bound to diversify and escalate up to levels at which the industry prices itself out of the market because the competitive advantage of the respective economic zone is lost.

Military downsizing and demobilisation provide a large pool of trained labour for the PSI. While demobilisation is usually associated with the end of a conflict,[90] this chapter argues that the actual demobilisation of security-related personnel is a pervasive phenomenon in the region and produces an oversupply of dislocated labour as result of slow motion demobilisation in imploding states, and post-conflict demobilisation. It is not likely that the PSI, however thriving it may be, will absorb more than a small proportion of this oversupply.

This comes as no surprise, since the PSI proliferates because it provides a rationalised and effective, though rather selective form of security replacing the failed-state security institutions. For the time being, international firms run by expatriates dominate the market of the PSI. One might speculate about what will happen when the many foreign-trained African officers turn to become entrepreneurs and begin to create an African PSI.

Because of the general economic conditions in the region, few of the demobilised will be absorbed by the regular economy. The majority will join the ranks of the parallel economic circulation and the informal sectors in the context of weak or failing states. The resulting fragile security equations in most African states are permanently in danger of flaring up into open armed conflict. In addition, the post-Cold War demobilisation outside the region has facilitated the easy rearmament of such conflicts, because huge black markets emerged, stocked with surplus weaponry from the weakly controlled arsenals of the Cold War. But in this marketplace, dollars are the only currency. Thus, conflicts will concentrate on 'glocal' spots on the continental map where the local economy can be linked to global demand.

Endnotes

1   M Sollenberg & P Wallensteen, *Major Armed Conflicts*, in Stockholm International Peace Research Institute (SIPRI), <u>SIPRI Yearbook 1998: Armaments, Disarmament and International Security</u>, Oxford University Press, Oxford, 1998.

2   M van Creveld, <u>The Transformation of War</u>, The Free Press, New York, 1991; I Freedman, <u>The Revolution in Strategic Affairs</u>, Adelphi Paper 318, Institute for International Strategic Studies, London, 1998.

3   J Schäfer, <u>Deutsche Militärhilfe in Südamerika</u>, Ekon-Verlag, Düsseldorf, 1974; P Keegan, <u>The Armies of the World</u>, Macmillan, London, 1983.

4   G Krebs, *Die deutschen Militärberater in China und der japanisch-chinesische Krieg 1937/38*, <u>Militärgeschichte</u>, 8, 1998, p. 12 ff.

5   Ibid., p. 13.

6   Schäfer, op. cit., p. 193.

7   J P Cahn, *La République Féderale d'Allemagne et la question de la présence d'Allemands dans la Légion etrangère française dans le contexte de la guerre d'Algérie (1954-1962)*, <u>Guerres mondiales et conflits contemporains</u>, 186, 1997, p. 96.

8   H G Burmester, *The Recruitment and Use of Mercenaries in Armed Conflicts*, <u>American Journal of International Law</u>, 72(1), 1978, pp. 47-50.

9   SIPRI, 1998, op. cit., pp. 187-198.

10 Two timeseries taken from SIPRI and ACDA unambiguously reflect the trend, in spite of the differences in data as a result of methodological variances in the definition of weaponry included and in price estimates. Ibid.; Stockholm International Peace Research Institute (SIPRI), <u>SIPRI Yearbook 1996: Armaments, Disarmament and International Security</u>, Oxford University Press, Oxford, 1996; US Arms Control and Disarmament Agency (ACDA), <u>World Military Expenditures and Arms Transfers 1995</u>, Government Printing Office, Washington DC, 1996.

11 ACDA, 1996, ibid., pp. 104, 111; SIPRI, 1998, ibid., pp. 301, 318.

12 C Clapham, <u>Africa and the International System: The Politics of State Survival</u>, Cambridge University Press, Cambridge, 1996, p. 256.

13 A de Waal, *Democratizing the Aid Encounter in Africa*, <u>International Affairs</u>, 73(4), 1997, p. 625.

14 Clapham, 1996, op. cit., p. 260 ff.

15 Ibid., p. 195.

16 Bonn International Center for Conversion (BICC), <u>Conversion Survey 1998: Global Disarmament, Defense Industry Consolidation and Conversion</u>, Oxford University Press, Oxford, 1998, p. 34.

17 Ibid., p. 39.

18 S W Meditz & T Merill (eds.), <u>Zaire: A Country Study</u>, Government Printing Office, Washington DC, 1994, chapter 5.

19 P A Ela, *La coopération militaire franco-africaine et la nouvelle donne des conflits en Afrique*, <u>Relations Internationales & Stratégiques</u>, 23, 1996, p. 184; A Kacowicz, *Negative International Peace and Domestic Conflicts: West Africa 1957-96*, <u>The Journal of Modern African Studies</u>, 35(3), 1997, p. 384.

20 SIPRI, 1998, op. cit., pp. 302-305.

21 A Dumoulin, <u>La France militaire et l'Afrique</u>, Editions GRIP, Bruxelles, 1997, p. 113 ff.

22 Ibid.

23 Ibid., p. 121 ff.; Demilitarization for Democracy, <u>Fighting Retreat: Military Political Power and Other Barriers to Africa's Democratic Transition</u>, Demilitarization for Democracy, Washington DC, 1997, p. 14.

24 H Howe, *Private Security Forces and African Stability: The Case of Executive Outcomes*, <u>The Journal of Modern African Studies</u>, 36, 1998, pp. 307-331; D Shearer, <u>Private Armies and Military Intervention</u>, Adelphi Paper 316, Institute for International Strategic Studies, London, 1998.

25 W Reno, <u>Warlord Politics and African States</u>, Lynne Rienner, Boulder, 1998, p. 71; W H Reinicke, <u>Global Public Policy: Governing Without Government?</u>, Brookings Institution, Washington DC, 1998, p. 54 ff.

26 J F Médard, *Le Big Man en Afrique: Esquisse d'analyse du politicien entrepreneur*, <u>Année Sociologique</u>, 1992, p. 188.

27 Clapham, 1996, op. cit., p. 186.

28 Ibid., p. 250; Reno, 1998, op. cit.

29 B Harris-White & G White, *Corruption, Liberalization and Democracy*, <u>IDS-Bulletin</u>, 27(2), April 1996, p. 4.

30 Clapham, 1996, op. cit., p. 186.

31 C Clapham, *Discerning the New Africa*, <u>International Affairs</u>, 74(2), London, April 1998, p. 265.

32   UNCTAD, <u>The Least Developed Countries, 1997 Report</u>, United Nations, Geneva, 1997, pp. 126-148.

33   Ibid., p. 127.

34   Clapham, 1998, op. cit., p. 265.

35   R Marchal & C Messiant, <u>Les chemins de la guerre et de la paix: Fins de conflit en Afrique orientale et australe</u>, Karthala, Paris, 1997, p. 32.

36   W Reno, *African Weak States and Commercial Alliances*, <u>African Affairs</u>, 96(383), April 1997, pp. 165-185; or the *"dédoublement de l'Etat"*, according to B Hibou, *Le* capital social *de l'Etat falsificateur ou les ruses de l'intelligence économique*, in J F Bayart, S Ellis & B Hibou, <u>La Criminalisation de l'Etat en Afrique</u>, Editions Complexe, Paris, 1997, pp. 105-158.

37   J Herbst, *Responding to State Failure in Africa*, <u>International Security</u>, 21(3), Winter 1996/97, p. 124 ff.

38   T Vircoulon, *Au coeur des conflits, l'Etat,* <u>Afrique Contemporaine</u>, 180, October-December 1996, p. 205.

39   Hibou, op. cit.

40   *Observatoire géopolitique des drogues,* <u>Atlas mondial des drogues</u>, Presses Universitaires de France, Paris, 1996, pp. 188-191.

41   J F Bayart, S Ellis & B Hibou, *De l'Etat kleptocrate à l'Etat malfaiteur?,* in: Bayart, Ellis & Hibou, op. cit., p. 26.

42   Vircoulon, op. cit., p. 205.

43   Hibou, op. cit., p. 146.

44   D Keen, <u>The Economic Functions of Violence in Civil Wars</u>, Adelphi Paper 320, Institute of International Security Studies, London, 1998, p. 31 ff.

45   M Duffield, *Post-modern Conflict: Warlords, Post-adjustment States and Private Protection*, <u>Civil Wars</u>, 1(1), Spring 1998, p. 98; ibid., p. 23 ff.

46   Herbst, op. cit., p. 122.

47   Ibid., p. 123.

48   Kacowicz, op. cit. p. 382.

49   Ibid., p. 374.

50   Marchal, op. cit., p. 33.

51   A de Waal, *Contemporary Warfare in Africa*, <u>IDS Bulletin</u>, 27(3), 1996, p. 7.

52   Médard, op. cit.

53   A E Hills, *The Policing in Fragmenting States*, <u>Low Intensity Conflict & Law Enforcement</u>, 5(3), Winter 1996, p. 339.

54   M A de Montclos, <u>Violence et sécurité urbaines en Afrique du Sud et au Nigeria: Un essai de privatisation</u>, Editions L'Harmattan, Paris, 1997.

55   R Midgeley & G Wood, *Community Policing in Transition: Attitudes and Perceptions from South Africa's Eastern Cape Province*, <u>Low Intensity Conflict & Law Enforcement</u>, 5(2), Autumn 1996, pp. 165-181.

56   E A Hills, op. cit., p. 340.

57   A Hills, *Towards a Critique of Policing and National Development in Africa*, The Journal of Modern African Studies, 34(2), 1996, p. 289.

58   A Hills, *Warlords, Militia and Conflict in Contemporary Africa: A Re-examination of Terms*, Small Wars and Insurgencies, 8(1), 1997, p. 47.

59   C Majtenyi, *In Your Face: Kenya's Police Act More Like an Occupying Army*, New Internationalist, August 1996, p. 22 ff.

60   Hills, 1996, op. cit., p. 278.

61   Ibid.

62   Meditz, op. cit., pp. 279-327.

63   Hills, 1997, op. cit., p. 35.

64   A E Hills, op. cit., p. 343.

65   Hills, 1997, op. cit., p. 36.

66   T von Trotha, *Ordnungsformen der Gewalt oder Aussichten auf das Ende des staatlichen Gewaltmonopols*, in B Nedelmann (Hg.), *Politische Institutionen im Wandel*, Kölner Zeitschrift für Soziologie und Sozialpsychologie, Sonderheft 35, Westdeutcher Verlag, Opladen, 1995, p.136 ff.

67   *Nachrichten für den Außenhandel, Markt für Sicherheits- und Schutzdienste boomt*, Nachrichten für den Außenhandel, 7 September 1994.

68   N Christie, Crime Control as Industry, Routledge, London, 1994.

69   M Wrong, *Fear Drives Africa's Boom Business: Security Companies Trade on Lawlessness and Crime*, Financial Times, 8 May 1996, p. 4; M Galeotti, *Policing Russia: Problems and Prospects in Turbulent Times*, Jane's Intelligence Review, special report 15, 1997; M Galeotti, *Boom Time for the Russian 'Protectors'*, Jane's Intelligence Review, August 1997, pp. 339-341.

70   D Nogala, *Le marché de la sécurité privée: Analyse d'une évolution internationale*, Les Cahiers de la Sécurité Intérieure, 24, 1996, pp. 121-142; D H Bayley & C Shearing, *The Future of Policing*, Law & Society Review, 30(3), 1996, pp. 585-606.

71   A Pike, *A Private Tax for Cleaner Streets*, Financial Times, 9 January 1997, p. 10.

72   E J Blakely & M G Snyder, Fortress America: Gated Communities in the United States, Brookings Institution, Washington DC, 1997.

73   Trotha, op. cit., p. 153 ff.

74   E Dorier-Apprill, *Guerres des milices et fragmentation urbaine à Brazzaville*, Hérodote, 86/87, 1997, pp. 182-221.

75   R Redmond, *The Security Industry Poor Image?*, Intersec, 7(3), 1997, p. 82 ff.

76   Radio National, *We Don't Do Wars*, 1997, <abc.net.au/rn/talks/bbing/stories/s10592/htm>; Y Goulet, *MPRI: Washington's Freelance Advisors*, Jane's Intelligence Review, July 1998, pp. 38-41.

77   Galeotti, August 1997, op. cit.

78   Goulay, op. cit., 1998, p. 41.

79   E B Ballesteros, <u>Report on the Question of the Use of Mercenaries as a Means of Violating Human Rights and Impeding the Exercise of the Right of Peoples to Self-determination</u>, UN Commission on Human Rights, 1994, E/CN.4/1995/29.

80   Shearer, op. cit.; Howe, op. cit.

81   Wrong, op. cit.

82   International Federation of Red Cross and Red Crescent Societies, <u>1997 World Disasters Report</u>, Oxford University Press, Oxford, 1997, chapter 2.

83   F Constantin, *L'informel international ou la subversion de la territorialité*, <u>*Cultures & Conflits*</u>, 21/22, 1996, p. 326.

84   Duffield, op. cit.

85   J C Rufin, *Les économies des guerres dans les conflits internes*, in F Jean & J C Rufin (eds.), <u>*Economies des guerres civiles*</u>, Hachette, Paris, 1996, p. 27.

86   J C Rufin, *Les conflits en Afrique: Décadence et risorgimento?*, <u>Relations Internationales & Stratégies</u>, 23, 1996, p. 80; ibid., pp. 19-59.

87   Reno, 1998, op. cit., p. 222.

88   United Nations High Commissioner for Refugees, <u>The State of the World's Refugees: A Humanitarian Agenda</u>, Oxford University Press, Oxford, 1997, p. 51 ff.

89   Howe, op. cit.

90   K Kingma & K Gebrewold, <u>Demilitarisation, Reintegration and Conflict Prevention in the Horn of Africa</u>, BICC, Bonn, 1998.

Chapter 3: The crisis in external response

Mark Malan

Introduction

*T*he international system, through the United Nations Security Council, has been unable to act effectively in enforcing international humanitarian law, ensuring stability, or in providing security for the provision of humanitarian assistance for those in dire need. The Security Council is also reliant on the voluntary contributions of member states to provide the material and human means for enforcing its mandates, but national actors have had little stomach for enforcement actions, unless their parochial national interests have been threatened.

In particular, the UN and the rest of the international community face seemingly insurmountable hurdles in trying to bring stability to conflict-ridden African states. The problem of effective intervention is almost as complex as the type of conflicts that demand efforts at amelioration, and the obstacles are conceptual, contextual, political, and practical in nature. In the absence of political will and public support, of financial and other resources, and of a 'recipe' for success that is acceptable to their own populations and to Africa, lukewarm donor commitments to the continent are fast growing cold.

On the other hand, a number of Western countries that have been major troop contributors to international peacekeeping have been promoting the idea of 'privatising' peacekeeping, albeit behind closed doors – especially in Africa. The basic thrust of their argument is that there can be no peacekeeping without peace, and that the international community has failed to provide a viable recipe for Boutros-Ghali's ill-conceived concept of 'peace enforcement'. Other actors may therefore be far more suited to the task than multinational forces under UN command.

This chapter will explain how the absence of legitimate and effective international responses to African crises has created a potential 'niche market' for the purveyors of a particular brand of private security.

The international community's response mechanisms

Article 1(1) of the United Nations Charter clearly states that the primary purpose of the UN is "*... to maintain international peace and security, and to that end: to take effective collective measures for the prevention and removal of threats to the peace ...*" Article 24 confers upon the Security Council primary responsibility for the maintenance of international peace and security, and directs it to act in accordance with the Purposes and Principles of the UN, according to the specific powers granted in the relevant chapters of the UN Charter.

For example, Chapter VI of the UN Charter deals with *The Pacific Settlement of Disputes*. It empowers the Security Council to "*... investigate any dispute, or any situation ... in order to* *determine whether the continuance of the dispute or situation is likely to endanger the maintenance of international peace and security."*

Apart from empowering the Security Council to determine which disputes would endanger peace and security, if allowed to continue unresolved, and to recommend 'appropriate' measures to resolve such disputes, Chapter VI provides a weak and vague basis for conflict resolution. It does suggest, however, that keeping the peace will require negotiation, mediation, conciliation and arbitration.

Chapter VII deals with *Action With Respect to Threats to the Peace, Breaches of the Peace, and Acts of Aggression.* It empowers the Security Council to decide on measures to be taken to **restore** peace, and is essentially coercive – allowing for political and economic pressure, as well as the use of force (Article 42). Importantly, Chapter VII requires all members of the UN to "... *make available to the Security Council, on its call and in accordance with a special agreement or agreements, armed forces, assistance, and facilities ... necessary for the purpose of maintaining International peace and security."*

The will of the Security Council to use its full powers under Chapter VII obviously depends on the means at its disposal. Unfortunately, the military forces envisaged in Chapter VII never materialised. As early as 1947, the UN's Military Staff Committee abandoned all hope of securing military contributions to the Security Council.[1] In the absence of sufficient resolve and adequate means to enforce international peace and security, the UN thus had to rely extensively on Chapter VI of the Charter, and the instrument of consensual peacekeeping.

Despite the lack of coercive power, most peace operations established during the Cold War were entirely military in composition and mandate. There were therefore a limited number of actors involved in international efforts to keep the peace through the insertion of impartial military observers or forces to monitor cease-fires – the UN Security Council, the UN Secretary-General, a limited number of troop-contributing member states and, of course, the belligerent member states.

Compared to early peacekeeping missions, those conducted since 1989 have often had a substantial or predominantly non-military mandate and composition.[2] Where the UN has been called upon to oversee the implementation of detailed peace agreements, a much larger and more complex agenda for operations has been required, which includes such non-military functions as: "... *verification, supervision, and conduct of elections; supervision of civil administration; promotion and protection of human rights; supervision of law and order and police activities; economic rehabilitation; repatriation of refugees; humanitarian relief; de-mining assistance; public information activities, and training and advice to governmental officials."*[3] This continues to be the norm for most new missions.

The growth in such civilian tasks implies that contemporary operations face enormous problems in staff provision, logistics, and co-ordination among tasks and actors. A plethora of UN agencies and non-governmental organisations (NGOs) are to be found in the contemporary mission area. Transnational corporations have also become major players in conflict-torn areas, while the media obviously remain an important part of the international community. So do individuals such as retired statesmen, scholars, philanthropists, and others.

However, amidst the proliferation of actors in the international community, it is still the national governments that contribute the military forces which remain essential to operations aimed at ending conflict.

States are the foundation of the international community, but also the cause of severe limitations on its ability to intervene in conflicts to restore peace and security. The UN consists of member states – with the Permanent Five members of the Security Council having a disproportionate say in what is to be done, or not to be done in the maintenance of international peace and security. But the whole UN system is dependent upon the payment of financial contributions from its member states. Most of the major NGOs that provide essential humanitarian assistance in zones of conflict are also funded by a variety of governments.

Limits to international intervention

The end of the Cold War signalled the demise of ideologically-based and motivated conflicts between capitalism and socialism. It allowed a new, co-operative mood for the management and resolution of African conflicts. There was progress toward a peaceful transition to democratic governance in Namibia, Ethiopia, Angola, Mozambique and South Africa.

At the same time, subregional, ethnic, and religious conflicts flared up in countries such as Liberia, Sierra Leone, Rwanda, Sudan, Somalia, Congo, and the former Zaire. In fact, since the turn of the decade, the UN Security Council has had to react to growing international demands for intervention in a number of 'complex emergencies' on the African continent. These have often been characterised by the combination of an internal or international conflict with serious human rights violations and large-scale suffering among the threatened civilian population, which has inevitably resulted in large numbers of refugees and displaced persons. *"In many African emergencies ... beleaguered governments ... have lost control over substantial parts of their territories. Their monopoly of power at state level becomes eroded, proliferating downwards into the hands of warlords."*[4] Under such circumstances, the *"... civil population becomes the principal target of violence, its control, division, relocation and extermination the war aims of opposing factions."*[5]

Many of these conflicts have deep-rooted causes, such as a lack of coincidence between nation and state, ethnic tensions and the suppression of minorities; corrupt and dictatorial regimes; support for such regimes by international arms traders; chronic poverty and underdevelopment, and a grinding debt burden. The international community has struggled to resolve such conflicts, exactly because the causes are numerous, complex and often deeply entrenched. Conflict prevention is a long term business and there are no quick fixes.

However erroneously, the resources and energies of the international community tend to be mobilised around the symptoms, rather than the causes of conflict – particularly when these include genocide or civil war. The situation is further complicated by the fact that most of Africa's actual and potential conflicts are internal ones within the state, which impedes international attempts to broker peace for a number of reasons.

In the first place, the jurisprudence and methodology of conflict prevention, management and resolution have mostly been established in the context of conflict between independent sovereign states. There are far fewer rules to go by in the case of internal conflict.

Secondly, one of the parties in an internal conflict is likely to be an internationally recognised government, and third parties who want to help, are more likely to be blocked by objections based on interference in the internal affairs of countries.

Thirdly, the causes of conflict in internal situations are often politically sensitive issues: the quality of governance; the way law and order is maintained; the equity of the economic and social systems; and issues such as ethnic discrimination. These issues are particularly sensitive where external involvement is concerned, and governments will understandably resist such attempts.

In the fourth place, the nature of the other party to the conflict also hampers attempts at brokering peace: it is normally an insurgent movement or movements, amply supplied with arms, obsessively secretive, inexperienced in negotiation, without transparent lines of authority, undisciplined, violent, and unfamiliar with the norms of international behaviour, including humanitarian law.

Finally, civilians tend to suffer much more than they do in interstate conflicts. Where civilians are a target of aggression, it is impossible for international agencies to respond to their humanitarian needs without being drawn into the politics of the conflict, as has clearly been demonstrated both in Central Africa and in Bosnia.[6]

Despite such limitations, graphically reported and portrayed humanitarian tragedies still move the international community to act in Africa – but through humanitarian assistance, rather than UN peacekeeping. However, international aid agencies and NGOs lack the power and organisational structure needed to conduct operations in situations of ongoing conflict, and the aid which they provide often becomes a resource which further serves to fuel, rather than resolve armed conflict.

During March 1997, in the former Zaire, for example, Kabila's rebel forces obtained the fuel needed to airlift troops for an attack on the key southern city of Lubumbashi from a depot maintained by the UN High Commissioner for Refugees (UNHCR) in Goma. More than 15 000 gallons of fuel were seized to ferry 300 troops and their weapons southward for the successful assault on Lubumbashi on 9 April 1997. In addition to stolen aid fuel, Kabila's army also relied on stolen aid trucks for transport and stolen aid food for sustenance. Likewise, Mobutu's army hijacked UN-chartered aircraft to transport weapons for its futile fight against the rebels. The planes flew into UN-run refugee camps, where the arms were distributed to Rwandan Hutu refugees who had become Mobutu's first line of defence.[7]

Humanitarian assistance also has a significant indirect impact. When international agencies and NGOs meet the needs of civilian populations, this frees warring governments and opposition forces to use their resources for warmaking. Intergroup tensions are also increased when NGOs provide external resources to some groups and not others, or where they hire workers from certain groups to the exclusion of others.[8] Food and money, in the absence of troops and diplomatic pressure, have become important components in the tactics of local belligerents, as the UN and other aid agencies increasingly operate in a political, military and diplomatic vacuum,[9] Burundi and Sudan being examples.

Where the UN Security Council has indeed intervened to restore peace and security in Africa, it has been through stretching and mutating the concept and conduct of classical UN peacekeeping, which was used with varying degrees of success for the limited purpose of monitoring cease-fire agreements (mainly in the Middle East) during the Cold War-era. A degree of success was achieved with 'expanded peacekeeping' interventions in countries such as Namibia (1989) and Mozambique (1992-1995), where regional and global changes had enabled an escape from an impasse and where conflicts had run their course to the point of exhaustion.

In Mozambique, the UN intervened after nearly thirty years of ruinous war which had claimed the lives of tens of thousands of people, driven millions from their homes and destroyed much of Mozambique's economic and social infrastructure. After President Chissano and Afonso Dhlakama signed a General Peace Agreement on 4 October 1992, the Security Council authorised the United Nations Operation in Mozambique (ONUMOZ) – the first UN peacekeeping operation to incorporate a large humanitarian component.

ONUMOZ was able to withdraw with honour after the staging of democratic elections at the end of 1994. In the final analysis, it was a successful political and humanitarian mission, rather than a successful multinational military intervention. The political leadership of the two Mozambican parties remained committed to the end-state of the process, and they were helped along by a population exhausted by war and drought.

However, the general perception of success in Mozambique reinforced an international preoccupation with the idea of establishing peace and democracy in a war-torn society in one fell swoop. ONUMOZ provided a Utopian blueprint against which other operations would be judged as failures. Indeed, virtually in tandem with the Mozambican peace process, the involvement of the international community in Somalia heralded both the high watermark and the subsequent abandonment of Africa.

Armed conflict in the collapsing state of Somalia exploded in November 1991, with heavy fighting in the Somali capital of Mogadishu between armed elements allied to General Mohamed Farah Aidid, those allied to Ali Mohamed Mahdi (the appointed interim president), and a number of other armed factions. The violent conflict coincided with a serious drought, which proved disastrous for the population.

By 1992, approximately half of the nine million people of Somalia were threatened with starvation, severe malnutrition and related diseases. An estimated 300 000 people actually died from disease and acts of violence, while some two million people were displaced from their home areas in an attempt to flee the suffering.

In March 1992, the warring parties eventually agreed to a cease-fire, to be monitored by UN observers. They also agreed to the deployment of UN security personnel to protect assistance agencies responding to the humanitarian disaster. The subsequent United Nations Operation in Somalia (UNOSOM) had an authorised strength of fifty military observers to monitor the cease-fire, and a 500-strong infantry unit to provide escorts for UN convoys of relief supplies. A 90-Day Plan of Action aimed to provide food and non-food supplies to some 1,5 million people immediately at risk and to help an additional 3,5 million people with food, seeds, drinking water and basic health supplies.

In the absence of a government capable of maintaining law and order, relief organisations experienced increased hijacking of vehicles, looting of convoys and warehouses, and detention of expatriate staff. On 3 December 1992, the Security Council was moved to welcome a United States offer to help in creating a secure environment for the delivery of humanitarian aid and authorised, under Chapter VII of the <u>Charter</u>, the use of "... *all necessary means*" to do so. The US responded with a decision on 4 December to initiate Operation Restore Hope, under which it would assume the unified command of the new operation in accordance with Resolution 794.[10]

By March 1993, UNITAF had deployed a total of approximately 37 000 troops in southern and central Somalia, covering approximately forty per cent of the country's territory. Although UNITAF had a positive impact on the delivery of humanitarian assistance, incidents of violence continued. There were still no effective functioning government in the country, no organised civilian police and no disciplined national army. On 3 March 1993, the Secretary-General submitted recommendations to the Security Council for changing the UNITAF mission into UNOSOM II which, endowed with Chapter VII enforcement powers, was to establish a secure environment **throughout** Somalia.[11] The mission took over from UNITAF in May 1993.

It soon became apparent that Aidid's faction would not co-operate. Attempts by UNOSOM II to implement disarmament led to increasing tensions which culminated, on 5 June 1993, in a series of armed attacks by Somali militia against UNOSOM II troops throughout south Mogadishu. The attacks resulted in 25 Pakistani soldiers being killed, with ten reported missing and 54 wounded.

UNOSOM II subsequently initiated military action on 12 June 1993, conducting a series of air and ground operations in south Mogadishu. The objective of the action, according to the Secretary-General, was to restore peace to Mogadishu "... *so that the political reconciliation, rehabilitation and disarmament process can continue to move forward throughout Somalia.*"

In support of UNOSOM's coercive disarmament programme, the US deployed Rangers and Quick Reaction Forces (under US command and control) in Mogadishu. On 3 October 1993, the Rangers launched an operation aimed at capturing a number of key aides of General Aidid who were suspected of complicity in attacks on UN personnel and facilities. During the operation, two US helicopters were shot down by Somali militiamen. Eighteen US soldiers lost their lives and 75 were wounded. The bodies of the US soldiers were subjected to public acts of outrage, and the humiliating scenes were broadcast around the world.

Within days, President Clinton sent reinforcements and set a pullout date for American troops. *"No single event has done as much to influence peacekeeping in the post-Cold War world as the Somalia intervention. In the five years since the humanitarian mission dissolved into combat, Somalia has had a profoundly cautionary influence on American foreign policy."*[12] By 28 March 1995, the complete withdrawal of UN peacekeeping troops had been effected, with few of the mandate objectives of UNOSOM II achieved.[13] A Comprehensive Seminar on Lessons Learned from UNOSOM later concluded that the operation's mandate was vague, changed frequently during the process and was open to myriad interpretations.

The three-year UN intervention in Somalia cost the international community over $1 685 million. Furthermore, 150 peacekeepers died – 114 as a result of hostile acts. The death of the US Rangers in October 1993 had an indelible impact on US policy on multilateral peace operations. In May 1994, the Clinton Administration's Presidential Decision Directive 25 (PDD 25) decreed that the US would not intervene in future crises unless American national interests were clearly at stake, and the mission had clear and limited objectives, including a well-defined exit strategy.[14]

UN officials involved in the mission were left with the conviction that the use of force should be avoided in future peace operations, as the degree of destruction in Somalia was not matched by the achievement of overall (political) mission objectives. The US, on the other hand, ascribed mission failure to the fact that not enough force was used. The UN Secretary-General was faced with the black and white options of either defensive peacekeeping or high-intensity enforcement. Somalia was thus the turning point at which the international community lost all desire to experiment further with 'middle ground' operations in Africa.[15]

Nowhere was the 'Somalia effect' so dramatically and tragically demonstrated as in the tiny nearby country of Rwanda.[16] Fighting between the (Hutu-dominated) Armed Forces of the government of Rwanda and the (Tutsi-inspired) Rwandan Patriotic Front (RPF) first broke out in October 1990 across the border between Rwanda and its northern neighbour, Uganda. After nearly three years of fighting, and a number of broken cease-fire agreements, a comprehensive peace agreement between the Government of Rwanda and RPF was successfully concluded on 4 August 1993. Both parties called for a neutral international force to assist with implementing the agreement.

On 24 September 1993, the Secretary-General recommended to the Security Council that a United Nations Assistance Mission for Rwanda (UNAMIR) should be established, with the purpose of *"... contributing to the establishment and maintenance of a climate conducive to the secure installation and subsequent operation of the transitional Government."* The mandate of UNAMIR resembled the ONUMOZ blueprint, and envisaged a sixteen-month, four-phase plan which included the demobilisation and integration of the various armed forces and *Gendarmerie*, and concluded with the monitoring of democratic elections and the installation of a new government.

UNAMIR was established on 5 October 1993 by Security Council Resolution 872, and the deployment of the first UNAMIR battalion in Kigali was completed in the first part of December 1993. However, the government and the RPF continued to drag their feet in setting up the transitional institutions in terms of the peace agreement. The security situation in the country deteriorated steadily until, on 6 April 1994, an aircraft carrying President Habyarimana of Rwanda and President Ntaryamira of Burundi crashed (or was shot down), killing all those on board.

This sparked a civil war that led to country-wide massacres of the Hutu opposition and intelligentsia, as well as members of the Tutsi minority and other RPF supporters. Within two weeks, tens of thousands had been killed. Victims of the violence included ten Belgian members of UNAMIR. Following the murder of the Belgian soldiers and threats to Belgian nationals, the Government of Belgium unilaterally decided to withdraw its battalion from Rwanda.

By the end of April 1994, it had become patently obvious that the much weakened UNAMIR had neither the mandate nor the strength to take effective action to halt the continuing massacres, and would be unable to protect threatened people in Kigali if a new wave of massacres were to start. UNAMIR had been reduced, by 13 May 1994, to 444 personnel in Rwanda – essentially consisting of a battalion from Ghana. The Secretary-General recommended to the Security Council that it provide a new mandate to create UNAMIR II, consisting of 5 500 troops to support and provide safe conditions for displaced persons and other groups in Rwanda, and to help with the provision of assistance by humanitarian organisations. Despite offers from over fifty potential troop-contributing countries, the Secretary-General calculated that the deployment of the first phase of UNAMIR II could not occur before the first week of July 1994.

On 22 June 1994, the Security Council, acting under Chapter VII of the <u>Charter</u>, authorised the Government of France to lead a multinational operation to assure the security and protection of displaced persons and civilians at risk in Rwanda, until such time as UNAMIR was brought up to strength. While expressing its strong opposition to the French move, the RPF did not seek confrontation with French forces and, on 18 July, unilaterally declared a cease-fire, effectively ending the civil war. On 19 July, a broad-based government of national unity was formed, two weeks ahead of the scheduled French withdrawal from Rwanda.

The French withdrawal effectively heralded the end of international engagement in Rwanda in pursuit of peace and security. The UNAMIR II mission never really got off the ground. On 1 August 1994, it had fewer than 500 soldiers deployed. The RPF had established military control over most of the country, and about 1,5 million (mainly Hutu) Rwandans had sought refuge in the former Zaire out of fear of retribution. It is estimated that, of a total population of approximately seven million, as many as 500 000 had been killed, three million had been internally displaced, and more than two million had fled to neighbouring countries. As the UN Secretary-General observed, the international community's delayed reaction to the genocide in Rwanda "... *demonstrated graphically its extreme inadequacy to respond with prompt and decisive action to humanitarian crises entwined with armed conflict.*"

The inability of the international community to cope with crises such as those in Somalia and Rwanda, is often explained in terms of a lack of political will on the part of third parties to become embroiled in someone else's civil war. This lack of will is not surprising, given the absence of a clear concept for enforcing the peace in situations where peacekeepers and humanitarian agencies cannot operate effectively as a result of crumbling consent and co-operation by the conflicting parties. Although former UN Secretary-General Boutros-Ghali proposed the idea of peace enforcement in <u>An Agenda for Peace</u>, he presented it as an activity that would possibly require separate and distinct forces to that of a peacekeeping operation:

"Cease-fires have often been agreed to but not complied with, and the United Nations has sometimes been called upon to send forces to restore and maintain the cease-fire. This task can on occasion exceed the mission of peacekeeping forces and the expectations of peacekeeping force contributors. I recommend that the Council consider the utilisation of peace-enforcement units in clearly defined circumstances and with their terms of reference specified in advance."[17]

While the Secretary-General coined the phrase 'peace enforcement', he subsequently had to admit that he did not provide a universally accepted definition or concept for its implementation.[18] In fact, 'peace enforcement' has since existed solely in the realm of theory, where peace enforcement units intervene impartially in a civil war in order to compel the warring parties to peace talks, so that a peacekeeping operation can be established. In reality, forces such as UNOSOM in Africa (and UNPROFOR in Europe) were unable to maintain impartiality. They either took sides openly, or were perceived as favouring one side, thus becoming the allies of one faction, and the 'legitimate' target of others. Mixing the use of force with the principles of impartiality and consent has largely discredited the notion of intervening in intrastate conflicts. According to Mackinlay,[19] *"[r]eliance on the military doctrines and humanitarian relief conventions of a previous era, as well as political short termism have disabled international interventions."*

Peace enforcement has failed, not just because of a lack of support or finances, but also because the concept itself is unsound. Peace enforcement bears little similarity to peacekeeping, where the military's primary role is that of a support force, not an active combatant. As yet, there is no coherent body of military doctrine explaining the conduct of peace enforcement operations. No one is even sure what is meant by 'peace enforcement'. UN 'peace enforcement' operations have been combat operations in which the Rules of Engagement governing the use of force have been only slightly adapted from 'classical' peacekeeping rules.

It is thus clear that the UN *" ... still lacks the capacity to implement rapidly and effectively decisions of the Security Council calling for the dispatch of peacekeeping operations in crisis situations. Troops for peacekeeping missions are in some cases not made available by Member States or made available under conditions that constrain effective response. Peacemaking and human rights operations, as well as peacekeeping operations, also lack a secure financial footing, which has a serious impact on the viability of such operations."*[20]

The utility of new mechanisms being developed to enhance UN reaction time – such as the Standby Arrangements System, the Standby High Readiness Brigade (SHIRBRIG) and the Rapidly Deployable Mobile Headquarters (RDMHQ) – will depend on effective political direction and the will to put such capacity to good use. However, there is no international mechanism in existence (beyond military alliances such as NATO) for the effective formation and management of Chapter VII operations. Secretary-General Kofi Annan has stated categorically that the UN "... *does not have, at this point in its history, the institutional capacity to conduct military enforcement measures under Chapter VII. Under present conditions,* ad hoc *Member States coalitions of the willing offer the most effective deterrent to aggression or to the escalation or spread of an ongoing conflict.*"[21] Annan, of all people, should know that this is easier said than done – and that the Security Council is still haunted by the Somalia syndrome, for his efforts to end the civil war in the Republic of Congo came to naught.

Fighting began in the Congo capital of Brazzaville on 5 June 1997, when President Pascal Lissouba's forces tried to disarm the private militia of Denis Sassou-Nguesso, the country's former military dictator and an opponent of Lissouba in the presidential elections that were scheduled for 27 July 1997. An estimated 3 000 people, most of them civilians, died in the first major clashes between the rival militias, and many more were forced to flee the city – joining the ranks of Africa's millions of displaced people.

Initially, French troops based at the international airport had managed to keep the opposing sides largely at bay. But on 20 June 1997, ignoring pleas from Lissouba and the UN for them to stay, France pulled out the last of its 1 250 soldiers from Brazzaville, after they had helped to evacuate nearly 6 000 French and other foreign nationals. As the civil war in the Republic of Congo threatened to engulf neighbouring countries, the Security Council authorised the Secretary-General, on 21 June 1997, to consult with potential troop-contributing countries about sending in a force to secure the airport, pending wider deployment at greater strength.

Annan originally estimated that the initial size of the force should be no fewer than 1 600 to 1 800, plus support units and UN military observers. He looked especially to the countries of the region to provide soldiers "... *to try and stabilise the situation and ensure that there is a cease-fire."* Togo and Senegal volunteered to provide troops for the operation, while UN/OAU envoy Mohamed Sahnoun looked to Paris for the provision of logistic support. However, former president Sassou-Nguesso objected to the proposed force – perhaps because Lissouba reportedly made the mistake of offering the UN $1 million towards launching the mission.

In the absence of any type of co-ordinated international response, the Republic of Congo soon became a battlefield on which Angolan troops, soldiers from the Democratic Republic of Congo, and various mercenary forces were all involved. The UN Security Council continued to vacillate on dispatching advance elements of a peacekeeping mission to Libreville in accordance with an urgent request by the Secretary-General. All that emerged was a statement to the effect that *"[t]he members of the Security Council strongly urge the neighbouring countries and other external parties involved to withdraw any forces they may have sent to the Republic of Congo and to refrain from intervening in that country's internal affairs."*[22]

With Kofi Annan still pleading with the Security Council about sending a peacekeeping force, Brazzaville fell to the forces of General (again President) Sassou-Nguesso on 15 October 1997. This concluded the presidency of democratically-elected Lissouba, and crowned yet another violent and unconstitutional regime transfer in Central Africa. While West African states had indicated a willingness to provide intervention forces, the Security Council had supplied neither the mandate nor the means to save the democratic experiment in the Republic of Congo.

Congo-Brazzaville also highlights another facet of international engagement in African conflict resolution – that of single-nation guarantors. Since 1988, the major military powers have largely withdrawn from direct involvement in African conflicts, while even former colonial powers have become far more subtle in their military engagement on the continent. In particular, the withdrawal of France from its role as external guarantor for the stability of regimes in its former colonies has left a gap in the traditional repertoire of external responses to African conflicts.

Until the 1960s, France controlled more than a third of the African continent (22 of the 53 OAU member states were previously under some form of French administration), and its military presence in Africa has been a pillar of its international status. Independence from France in the early 1960s was, in many respects, a charade. However, French control in Africa has now lost its Cold War imperative, politics in Paris has become focused around issues of European unification and, with domestic economic reform a top priority, France's quasi-imperial role in Africa is untenable. Moreover, with the introduction in 1997 of an all-volunteer army, France will no longer have the personnel to maintain large military bases in Africa. Premier Lionel Jospin's socialist-led government has therefore decided to rationalise French defence operations on the continent.

In July 1997, Paris announced military cuts in Africa which involved, most dramatically, a pull-out of its 1 400 troops in the Central African Republic. Over the next five years, France is expected to cut its total forces garrisoned on the continent from 8 000 to no more than 5 000.[23] It plans to fill this gap by a concerted Africanisation programme, by helping to establish military academies and to train armed forces and national police forces.[24] The official military policy towards Africa has thus shifted from zone of influence policing with garrisoned soldiers to a 'multilateral approach'[25] towards security problems on the African continent. While maintaining existing defence agreements with African countries, France now *"... refuses to be brought into the internal conflicts or to intervene in the interior affairs of its African partners."*[26] Military co-operation will become increasingly focused on the training of African contingents for participation in 'peacekeeping' operations.

France's new policy is but part of a broader international response which aims to solve the dilemmas of intervention in Africa by devolving responsibility for peacekeeping to Africans themselves – an idea which has crystallised into a confusing and contentious mix of foreign 'peacekeeping' capacity-building initiatives.

The devolution of peacekeeping responsibilities

It has also become readily apparent that Boutros-Ghali's <u>An Agenda for Peace</u> and the related definitions are no longer relevant to the realities of intrastate conflict. There can no longer be a clear distinction between 'peacekeeping' and 'peace enforcement', and the UN is reluctant to contemplate anything with a Chapter VII mandate. This reality is reflected in the declining number of UN missions and peacekeepers worldwide. While the number of troops deployed on UN operations ballooned from 10 000 in 1989 to 70 000 in 1995, this number has dwindled over the past two years to some 19 000 by 1998, and will probably stabilise around levels more common in the eighties.

On the other hand, the dwindling statistics belie the fact that the number of non-UN 'peacekeeping' missions are increasing. Substantial and forceful missions have been conducted since 1990 by the Economic Community of West African States (ECOWAS) in West Africa, and, since July 1992, by Russia and the Commonwealth of Independent States (CIS) in Georgia, Azerbaijan and Tajikistan. However, it is since the 40 000-strong North Atlantic Treaty Organisation's (NATO) Implementation Force (IFOR) took over from the overextended UN Protection Force (UNPROFOR) in the former Yugoslavia at the end of 1995, that the idea of regional peace operations has steadily gained ground. In 1997, a 6 000-strong Italian-led multinational force intervened in the civil turmoil in Albania, with a UN mandate to deliver emergency humanitarian aid. The relative effectiveness, as well as constraints on the use of force by NATO in Bosnia and the force of the Organisation for Security and Co-operation in Europe (OSCE) in Albania, have lent credence to the argument that regional capacities for conducting peace operations would allow for multinational intervention where the UN lacks the capability or the will to act.

After a brief experiment with large-scale, multifunctional peacekeeping and 'peace enforcement' operations (1989-1995), the UN seems to have settled into a phase of conducting much smaller and more specialised monitoring missions, while delegating the large-scale, personnel intensive functions to regional organisations and arrangements.

The precedent for devolving 'peacekeeping' responsibilities in Africa was set when ECOWAS[27] intervened in a conflict which began in Liberia late in 1989. A small force of Charles Taylor's National Patriotic Front for the Liberation of Liberia (NPFL) invaded from Sierra Leone in an attempt to bring down the then president Samuel Doe. This incursion soon degenerated into a many-sided factional war that split the country into fiefdoms with no overall control. By early 1990, several hundred deaths had already occurred in confrontations between government forces and fighters of the NPFL. The civil war subsequently claimed the lives of between 100 000 and 150 000 civilians and led to a complete breakdown of law and order in the tiny country of some 2,3 million inhabitants. It displaced thousands of people, both internally and beyond the borders, resulting in approximately 700 000 refugees in the neighbouring countries.

From the outset of the conflict, ECOWAS undertook various initiatives aimed at a peaceful settlement – including the creation of a Military Observer Group (ECOMOG) in August 1990. ECOMOG initially comprised about 4 000 troops from The Gambia, Ghana, Guinea, Nigeria and Sierra Leone (as ECOMOG became drawn into the fighting, the force was later to reach a maximum strength of nearly 12 000). ECOWAS efforts to achieve a peaceful settlement in Liberia included the mediation of a series of agreements that became the basis for the shifting mandates of ECOMOG. On 30 October 1991, ECOWAS brokered the Yamoussoukro IV Accord which outlined steps to implement a peace plan that included the encampment and disarmament of warring factions under the supervision of an expanded ECOMOG, as well as the establishment of transitional institutions to carry out free and fair elections. However, the West African force lacked the capacity, resources and credibility to implement this ambitious peace plan.

The impartiality of the force has always been questionable. From the outset, Taylor regarded ECOMOG as the tool of Nigeria, which had assisted former dictator Samuel Doe, both economically and militarily. Taylor was convinced that Nigeria's military regime intended to use ECOMOG to frustrate his attempt to achieve power and was forcing other countries participating in the operation to toe the Nigerian line. This obviously played a key role in Taylor's sabotage of a number of peace agreements, and led to divisions within the ECOMOG mission itself. The tortuous relationship between Taylor and Nigeria, on the one hand, and Nigeria and its ECOMOG partners on the other, illustrates one of the key difficulties with the concept of 'backyard peacekeeping'.[28]

Although a small United Nations Observer Mission in Liberia (UNOMIL) was established in September 1993, it played a definite second fiddle to ECOMOG and Nigeria. In its four years of deployment, UNOMIL suffered no fatalities, while the only significant outside assistance for the West African effort, before the establishment of UNOMIL, was about $30 million from the US. By contrast, ECOMOG cost Nigeria more than $1 billion – and 500 lives. Even in the diplomatic field, ECOMOG took the lead in brokering an astonishing number of failed agreements among the belligerents.

The force initially managed to secure the greater Monrovia area, allowing it to act as a safe haven from the fighting up-country, but was never really able to establish its authority in the hinterland. Moreover, ECOMOG troops were accused of various misdeeds, including extensive looting. At times, they turned brutal in the face of resistance to their authority, particularly from Taylor's NPFL.

It took ECOWAS five years to broker a thirteenth peace agreement in August 1995, which was widely believed to have a real chance of success. It was the first accord to involve all the factions (by this stage, there were nine major belligerent parties), and it also had the support of other political organisations and civic organisations.[29] However, on 6 April 1996, Monrovia erupted in bloody conflict when police attempted to arrest Roosevelt Johnson, a former leader of a faction of the United Liberation Movement for Democracy in Liberia (ULIMO) known as ULIMO-J. The carnage involved civilians and children, and forced the evacuation of virtually all the humanitarian relief workers from the former safe haven which had provided shelter for up to one million people. ECOMOG stood by helplessly as warlords looted their offices and supplies. When ECOMOG troops eventually managed to separate the armed factions and gain a measure of control over the city in June 1996, health workers recovered more than 1 500 bodies from shallow graves.[30]

In the wake of this catastrophe, Taylor reached a *rapprochement* with the Nigerian ruler, General Sani Abacha, and attended a peace conference in Abuja that finally paved the way for elections to be held on 19 July 1997. In an ironic outcome, Charles Taylor won the presidential vote hands down. The UN, of course, welcomed the success of the elections and the Security Council called upon all parties to abide by the results and to co-operate in the formation of a new government. It also called upon the new government to protect the 'democratic' system and to promote human rights and fundamental freedoms under the rule of law.[31]

The ECOMOG initiative represents the first time that a regional body had intervened to stop a conflict in its own region, and there is little disagreement that the military and political actions of ECOWAS saved many lives – at considerable cost to the member states. The operation was one of the largest in the world, and from 1990 to the end of 1995 (when the NATO-led IFOR took over from UNPROFOR in Bosnia), the only major peacekeeping effort not run by the UN. For the people of Liberia, however, only time will tell the difference between Taylor the former warlord and Taylor, the President of Liberia. It has also been said that the same result could have been achieved with less bloodshed and at far less cost if Taylor had simply been allowed to seize power in 1990.

The Liberian experience challenges the assumption that an African capacity for conducting peace operations would allow for effective multinational intervention where the UN lacks the will or capacity to act. However, key players in the international community continue to cite ECOMOG as a success story, and remain intent upon resolving the crisis in external response to African emergencies through a strategy of African empowerment for participation in future peace operations.

Building peacekeeping capacity in Africa

The international community is steadily moving towards a reliance on Chapter VIII of the UN Charter, in the aftermath of the failure of consensual peacekeeping in Africa. However, such an approach requires capable forces and effective regional structures for directing operations. By January 1995, the OAU Secretary General observed that there was a proliferation of initiatives from outside Africa, all with the aim of supporting OAU efforts in the area of peacekeeping. He noted, in particular, that the British government had convened peacekeeping seminars in Camberly, Accra, Cairo and Harare, in order to examine various ways of enhancing the OAU's capabilities to prepare and deploy African peacekeepers.[32]

In parallel with the British initiative, a French proposal for an African intervention force had emerged from the Biarritz Francophone Summit of 1994. In essence, the French proposal aimed at the creation of a modest standing force, with possible contributions from African countries, which could be utilised during times of crisis. It was further proposed that this force would be mobilised under the auspices of the OAU and its member states. The French initiative included plans for an assessment of the capacity of member states in a particular subregion to intervene during crisis situations, the training of contingents in peace maintenance, and the training of a high command staff.[33]

The main thrust of both the British and French initiatives related to the setting up of a Multi-National African Rapid Deployment Peace Force. These initiatives, which enjoyed European and American support, further envisaged the prepositioning of equipment at logistics bases situated strategically in Africa, with Europe, the US and others providing logistics while Africa would supply the personnel.[34]

The US soon joined the clamour to 'capacitate' Africans. In October 1996, former US Secretary of State, Warren Christopher, travelled to Africa to promote a proposal for the setting up of an all-African military force. This African Crisis Response Force (ACRF) was to be used to deal with African crises where insurrections, civil war or genocide threaten mass civilian casualties. The intermediate objective of the ACRF was to develop a rapid reaction capability for such contingencies. It was hoped that the ACRF would be used for humanitarian intervention in Burundi. However, this 'quick fix' solution met with widespread scepticism, and the US transformed the idea of an African intervention force into a longer term capacity-building initiative. By mid-1997, the original ACRF idea had evolved into the African Crisis Response Initiative, or ACRI.

According to the State Department, "[t]he African Crisis Response Initiative (ACRI) is a training program which envisions a partnership with African and other interested nations to enhance African peacekeeping capacities, particularly the capacity to mount an **effective, collective response to humanitarian and other crises.**"[35] The transformation of the US initiative caused confusion and some annoyance in Africa, and exposed the lack of donor co-ordination in the realm of African capacity-building.

This moved the major players to announce the launching of a 'P3' initiative, which presents the ACRI as the US component of a joint initiative by the UK, the US and France. The French element of the P3 initiative is known as RECAMP (Reinforcement of African Military Peacekeeping Capacity), while the British element is known as the UK African Peacekeeping Training Support Programme.

The P3 further envisages the creation of an African Peacekeeping Support Group (APSG), open to all interested states, which would meet regularly under the aegis of the UN and the OAU to facilitate international co-ordination on peacekeeping training activities in Africa. It was also envisaged that smaller *ad hoc* co-ordinating groups would be set up to deal with more specific issues pertaining to the reinforcement of African peacekeeping capacities.

However, the great flaw in the whole P3 (or APSG) initiative arises from the very element that was meant to make it more politically acceptable – the **failure to establish a credible linkage between capacity-building and capacity utilisation**. An inordinate amount of resources are spent worldwide on military training including, latterly, peacekeeping training. But this has not solved the problem of the lack of political will to act on the part of the UN Security Council and potential troop-contributing countries in the face of man-made crises in Africa.

In other words, the P3 may make a contribution to potential peacekeeping capacity, but potential capacity in the form of more infantry battalions is clearly not the problem at hand.[36] There is, theoretically, an abundance of infantry battalions already available on standby for peacekeeping deployment – but there is no way of putting these together in any meaningful way when faced with a risky intervention which may involve the use of force and exposure to hostile acts.

This factor was graphically illustrated by events in the former eastern Zaire towards the end of 1996. The humanitarian crisis which captured the international media limelight during 1996 clearly had its origins in the Rwanda genocide of 1994 and the subsequent exodus of hundreds of thousands of Hutu refugees and militia when the RPF took control of the country. However, once UNAMIR had withdrawn from Rwanda, the focus shifted squarely onto the emerging genocide in Burundi and to US efforts to create an African Crisis Response Force to resolve the problem. Although it had been patently clear that the entire Great Lakes region remained highly volatile, and that the refugee camps in the former Zaire were one of the principal causes of instability, the international community was unable to take any concerted action to ease the plight of refugees or to avert the eight-month civil war which raged through Zaire from October 1996 to May 1997.

The problem was not one of a lack of warning, but one of a lack of political will among those with the necessary capacity to organise a coherent and effective multinational response, and to accept the sacrifices that this would entail. When help was eventually offered, it was not from 'newly empowered' African peacekeeping nations; it was a Canadian proposal to lead a multinational force with the limited humanitarian objective of ensuring the peaceful repatriation of refugees to Rwanda. Although the proposed multinational force (MNF) proved to be too little and too late, it did highlight some of the weaknesses of relying on multinational 'coalitions of the willing' – even those involving Western powers – for dealing with African crises.

The envisaged operation involved the insertion of armed forces into an area where the parties were still engaged in combat. Perhaps largely because of the potential for combat involved, almost all troop-contributing countries, including Canada, made the presence of US ground forces a precondition for their participation.[37] Given the stipulations of US PDD 25, this meant that the planned intervention could only occur in pursuit of the US national interest. While Canada and the US continued to wrangle over the exact timeframe and mandate of the mission, the issue was decided by default. Elements of the Rwandan army attacked the positions of former Zairian government forces and refugee camps thought to be sheltering Hutu militia who had been involved in the 1994 genocide.

Attacks by (soon to be President) Laurent Kabila's surrogate forces from Rwanda on refugee camps near the border led to the precipitous return of 600 000 refugees to Rwanda. Requests by the UNHCR for military forces to assist in an operation to rescue the hundreds of thousands of others who fled westward into the forests of the former Zaire, remained unheeded. Together with other humanitarian organisations, the UNHCR was left to its own devices in searching for and rescuing refugees, often inside conflict zones. Access to refugees was frequently limited, obstructed or denied, and makeshift refugee sites were subjected to attacks and other atrocities by the military forces of both Mobutu and the agglomeration of forces loyal to Kabila's *Alliance des forces démocratiques pour la libération du Congo* (ADFL). Although the aid workers managed to help with the evacuation of some 250 000 Rwandans, many others perished either of starvation, disease, or at the hands of the belligerents.[38]

Despite the failure of the Canadian initiative in the former Zaire, contemporary thinking still sees the solution to the 'overload' on UN peacekeeping in increasing recourse by the Security Council to Chapter VIII of the UN Charter.[39] This notion was stretched to its limits on 6 August 1997, when the Security Council retrospectively authorised the 800-member Inter-African Mission to Monitor the Implementation of the Bangui Agreements (MISAB).[40] Mission costs would be borne by each of the participating countries, the government of the Central African Republic, the French government, and the OAU. The African countries were required to provide limited vehicle support and personal equipment, while the provision of tactical and support vehicles, including fuel and maintenance, was left to the French government.

However, in one of its regular reports to the UN, MISAB has warned that, without financial support, African nations will continue to lack the capability to resolve conflict on the continent. Paragraph 56 of the fourth MISAB report states that "... *owing to the insufficiency of the African countries' own resources, logistic support from the international community, along the lines of the support which France has provided to MISAB and which remains open to contributions for all other States, is still needed.*"[41]

By the end of 1997, the term 'coalition of the willing' had become common UN parlance, and MISAB was increasingly being touted as another fine example of subregional peacekeeping on the African continent in the wake of ECOMOG. However, while both the ECOMOG and MISAB interventions may provide lessons for the development of regional responses to conflict in Africa, they also demonstrate major shortcomings in the field of peacebuilding. If, despite the shortcomings and disparities, these two African interventions are considered worthy precedents for adopting Chapter VIII of the UN Charter as the panacea for conflict resolution in Africa, then the credibility of the international system must be seriously questioned.

The privatisation of peacekeeping?

The crisis in external response is closely related to the notion that international intervention must produce peace and democracy from conditions of abject human misery. However, it is "... *difficult, if not impossible, to secure the higher, more dynamic aspects of peace before the lower aspects of law and order are met.*"[42] Third-party intervention in civil conflict must thus necessarily (and primarily) be aimed at the restoration of order, which inevitably involves the imposition of power.

According to Mackinlay,[43] "*[u]nless a monopoly of violence can be achieved, any attempt to disarm will expose the vulnerable ... Recentralising the power within a state may require recognising and dealing with 'power brokers' or war lords ... Achieving real success may mean a tougher trade off between maintaining the moral high ground and the advantages of involving local power brokers in the stabilisation process ...*" Thus far, international interventions have been based more on morality (whether this be false or real) than on effectiveness.

Early and concerted action requires a multinational rapid deployment capability for intervention in communal conflicts. The very concept of rapid deployment under such circumstances negates the use of a complex multinational system of standby arrangements. The latter necessarily involves the mobilisation of national contingents from a variety of countries, lengthy wrangling over the nature and scope of the mission mandate, and the right of contributors to withdraw support for particular types of missions. Indeed, the existing UN standby arrangements system is based on an understanding that specifically excludes 'peace enforcement' operations.

The future of international responses to conflict-induced crises thus seems to be reduced to two scenarios. In the first, the Security Council passes a resolution (and the responsibility) to authorise *ad hoc* member states' coalitions of the willing to 'do something' about the problem. In the second, the UN essentially turns a comfortable blind eye – even where international law is flouted as was the case recently when South Africa effectively intervened militarily in Lesotho. The fundamental issue of political will has therefore been devolved from the level of the UN to anyone or anything capable of initiating some sort of action.

While common wisdom (and, perhaps, decency) has led the world to believe that only national, multinational and intergovernmental actors should be involved in such undertakings, there is no practical or objective reason why other roleplayers cannot enter the intervention 'market'. In fact, these new actors may have a greater degree of 'success' in fulfilling the needs outlined above – especially in the African context. Already, the various humanitarian agencies and NGOs are in the field long before a peace operation is deployed. This trend is therefore likely to continue.

Humanitarian agencies cannot function in anarchic conditions, and they have an understandable preoccupation with security. However, the multinational forces of the international community have not excelled in the provision of such security. In 1995, for example, the UN had to hire two battalions of Zairian soldiers to provide military security at its refugee camps in Rwanda.[44]

The national military contingents of UNAMIR proved an unwieldy humanitarian instrument because of their preoccupation with 'force protection'. Of all the humanitarian functions fulfilled by international troops, they were least available and least effective in providing security (which was precisely their area of comparative advantage over the other humanitarian actors). Moreover, the military were not free agents, but had to subordinate their potential efficacy to political decisions, priorities, and timetables.[45]

During the UN intervention in Somalia, some national contingents refused to carry out what they considered to be dangerous operations. When assigned such tasks, contingent commanders sought to circumvent the chain of command by turning to their national governments for clarification – thereby effectively paralysing the operation concerned.[46] Aid agencies and NGOs were often forced to enlist the services of armed Somali gangs in an attempt to ensure their security. The privatisation of the security function for humanitarian workers has already become common practice in a number of other UN missions across the world, perhaps reflecting a broader trend towards the privatisation of the humanitarian function itself. According to Walker:

"[t]he burden of caring is being privatised ... A growing 'contract culture' may be drawing humanitarian agencies away from their core values ... today there is a plethora of agencies, UN, bilateral, international NGOs, national NGOs, and human rights groups, operating on the ground, all believing they have a legitimate right to provide their unique brand of assistance and protection to those in need ... slowly but surely commercial enterprises see a new product – relief aid – and a new market – donors hungry for profile – into which they can step."[47]

Humanitarian assistance has indeed become big business, with global figures for 1994 indicating that developed nations provided 4,2 million tonnes of food aid and $3,4 billion to crisis areas.[48] In an *"... all-but-unregulated multi-billion dollar global industry of life and death,"*[49] there is obviously a niche for a cost-effective provider of decent standards of security for those who dispense humanitarian aid in situations of conflict or minimal law and order. Such services would resemble the radical end of the guarding and cash-in-transit sector of the private security market in functioning states.

At a higher level of analysis, the problem is not so much that of security (defined in terms of an enabling environment for the conduct of a specific task such as providing humanitarian aid), but one of stability. Stability is a condition in which a whole variety of tasks can be executed as part of daily life, without undue threat to life and limb. It is this **essential and elementary aspect of law and order** that the international community has been unable to provide in African countries afflicted by civil strife and armed conflict. It is unlikely that this situation will improve simply through the devolution of responsibility to lower level multinational 'coalitions of the willing'. When the going gets tough, such coalitions become unwilling to take risks, unless their collective core interests are directly threatened.

It is not inconceivable, therefore, that a further stage of outsourcing and privatisation may see the emergence of entrepreneurial actors who are willing to take such risks to enforce stability within the state, as long as there is a reasonable chance of outperforming the competition. In the failing states of Africa, the competition faced by the would-be stabiliser may not be too stiff. Originally armed and trained by the major powers, rebel movements now typically rely on lightly-armed foot soldiers, and their ability to mobilise local populations to join their cause through persuasion or coercion. They often have no access to more sophisticated weaponry than assault rifles, light machine guns and mortars.

For example, Charles Taylor's invasion of Liberia in 1989 was conducted by a lightly-armed, Libyan-trained force numbering only about 100 men. If even a modest intervention force with tactical aviation assets had been in place, this incursion may easily have been halted. And such an action would not have been beyond the capability of a small private army of specialists. It is the proliferation of such scenarios that presents a possible niche for private security entrepreneurs. These would obviously have a far greater military focus and weight than the police-type guarding and escort service providers for humanitarian assistance.

However, where opposing forces are larger and better armed and equipped, there is a limit to what a private intervention force of fairly modest size can achieve through direct participation in combat operations. The greatest potential for maximising the impact of such a force lies in the co-option and reorientation of local military forces. This, in turn, would require that a private intervention force consists of a high percentage of specialist instructors, who are capable of retraining and re-educating local forces to high standards of combat proficiency and professionalism – and who are willing and able to lead them in effective 'conflict termination' operations.

The morality of such an approach may be debatable, but there is a certain logic to it. Where the means of orchestrated coercion has devolved, without legal authority, into the hands of a number of factions in a failing state, the stability function has already been 'privatised' – for it is beyond the ambit of state control. Under such conditions, it is extremely difficult for other state actors to intervene within the framework of state-centric international law. However, the private security or stability practitioner may thrive in such a 'free enterprise' environment.

There is not necessarily a contradiction in this logic when the end-state of the contract is the 'remonopolisation' by the state of the means of orchestrated coercion. The practitioner is a transnational and transitional actor, and proven success in one contract soon leads to lucrative contracts in other countries. The privatisation of the stability function is also in line with US pressure to streamline the UN system – among others, through 'outsourcing' – and perceptions that private industry is always more efficient than public bureaucracies.

However, even the strongest is never strong enough to rule indefinitely by might alone. Stability will soon revert to anarchy if it is not followed by a process of peacebuilding. Peacebuilding requires the mobilisation and engagement of the international community. If the privatisation of the stability function is to succeed, it must be linked to the higher-order notions of peace and integrated with longer term programmes of development. This clearly did not happen in the recent cycle of war and peace in Sierra Leone – a spectacular example which demonstrates the limits to private security involvement (and may soon serve to highlight the folly of 'backyard peacekeeping').

A further limit to the privatisation of security within peace processes is that of legality. Morally, there can be no doubt about the repugnance of mercenary activity (which is ineffectually proscribed under international law), or any other form of private activity which makes a direct contribution to ignite or prolong violent armed conflict. The decision to intervene and to take sides in an armed conflict should be a political one, whether it is made by an international organisation, a regional organisation, a coalition of states, or a single country. However, this has not been the case in many instances of humanitarian assistance which have unintentionally served to fuel a number of conflicts where aid workers and their agencies have fallen prey to unscrupulous belligerents in an insecure environment.

It is thus possible (and probable) that professional private contractors will increasingly provide security services to humanitarian agencies and NGOs in situations where the state cannot ensure law and order. It is also possible (but less probable) that private companies which provide cost-effective stability services may eventually be accredited by the UN as legitimate actors in peace processes. The most likely scenario in this regard is, however, the outsourcing of the stability function through 'mission creep'. In other words, private companies may continue to be contracted by the UN or powerful member states to provide services related to humanitarian demining or military transformation ('professionalisation'), which places them in an excellent position to expand their mandate – and in the process also their profit margin.

Endnotes

1   A Roberts, *From San Francisco to Sarajevo: The UN and the Use of Force*, <u>Survival</u>, 37(4) Winter 1995-96, p. 9.

2   S R Ratner, <u>The New UN Peacekeeping: Building Peace in Lands of Conflict After the Cold War</u>, St. Martin's Press, New York, 1995, pp. 22-23.

3   Ibid.

4   J Mackinlay, *International Responses to Complex Emergencies*, <u>International Peacekeeping News</u>, 2(5), 1996, p. 36.

5   Ibid.

6   M Goulding, *The Case for an Integrated Approach to Peace and Security*, paper presented at an <u>ISS/Zimbabwe Staff College Seminar on Multinational Peace Operations: The Evolution of Policy and Practice in Southern Africa</u>, Pretoria, South Africa, 4-6 November 1997.

7   J Pomfret, *Aid Dilemma: Keeping it from the Oppressors*, <u>Washington Post</u>, 23 September 1997.

8   D R Smock, *Humanitarian Assistance and Conflict in Africa*, <u>Journal of Humanitarian Assistance</u>, <www-jha.sps.cam.ac.uk/a/a016.htm>, reposted 4 July 1997, p. 2.

9   For a more detailed description of how aid agencies assisted the belligerent parties in the civil war in the former Zaire (October 1996 – May 1997), see Pomfret, op. cit.

10   Quoted in United Nations (unofficial document), <u>United Nations Operation in Somalia I</u>, <www.un.org/Depts/DPKO/Missions/unosomi.htm>, 25 November 1997.

11   Ibid.

12   M Bowden, quoted in G Constantine, *Death of 18 US Troops Haunts American View on Peacekeeping*, <u>Washington Times</u>, 22 January 1998.

13   J Chopra, Å Eknes & T Nordbø, *Fighting for Hope in Somalia*, <u>Peacekeeping and Multinational Operations</u>, 6, Norwegian Institute for International Affairs, p. 2.

14   See <u>PDD 25: Key Elements of the Clinton Administration Policy on Reforming Multilateral Peace Operations</u>, US Department of State, released 22 February 1996, <ccnet.com/suntzu75/pdd25.htm>

15   Chopra, et al., op. cit., p. 40.

16   This chronology of events is summarised mainly from <u>Rwanda – UNAMIR</u>, an unofficial record of events prepared by the United Nations Department of Public Information, September 1996.

17   B Boutros-Ghali, *An Agenda for Peace: One Year Later*, <u>Orbis</u>, 37(3), Summer 1993, p. 329.

18   Ibid.

19   Mackinlay, op. cit., p. 37.

20   UN Report on Reform, released 16 July 1997, <www.un.org/reform/track2/part2.htm>

21   Ibid.

22   J Aita, *UN Reassessing Plans to Help Congo/Brazzaville* USIA, AEF302, 15 October 1997.

23   J Rupert, *Free of France but Still Dependent*, Washington Post, 31 August 1997.

24   J Benamisse, *France Announces Closure of Military Base in Central African Republic*, Associated Press News Agency, 8 January 1997.

25   Unless there is a strong military alliance such as NATO involved, 'multilateral approaches' are notoriously inadequate and unsuitable for applying enforcement measures. Witness the (albeit failed) US role in Somalia, the French role in Rwanda, the Nigerian role in Sierra Leone, the Russian role in the CIS, etc.

26   B Dufourcq, *La politique africaine de la France*, address to South African parliamentarians and academics, Residence of France, Cape Town, 9 September 1997.

27   ECOWAS membership comprises Benin, Burkina Faso, Cape Verde, Côte d'Ivoire, The Gambia, Guinea, Guinea-Bissau, Liberia, Mali, Mauritania, Niger, Nigeria, Senegal, Sierra Leone and Togo.

28   C Duodu, *'Rent-a-Mob' Threat Haunts Intervention Plans*, Gemini News Service, 12 September 1997, <www.oneworld.org/gemini/sep97/africa.html>, 25 November 1997.

29   Anon, *Liberia: More US Support Needed*, Washington Office on Africa, 22 October 1995, <www.sas.upenn.edu/Arican_Studies/Urgent_Action/DC_2210.html>

30   Anon, *Liberia: WOA Update/Alert*, Washington Office on Africa, 29 July 1996, <www.sas.upenn.edu/Arican_Studies/Urgent_Action/DC_2210.html>

31   United Nations Press Release, SC/6402.

32   OAU Secretariat, Report on the OAU's Position Towards the Various Initiatives on Conflict Management: Enhancing OAU's Capacity in Preventive Diplomacy, Conflict Resolution and Peacekeeping, Central Organ/MEC/MIN/3 (IV), Addis Ababa, July 1995.

33   Ibid.

34   Ibid.

35   Texts of a briefing by Ambassador Marshall McCallie on the African Crisis Response Initiative (ACRI), US Department of State, Office of the Spokesman, Washington DC, 29 July 1997.

36   Data of standby personnel resources which could be made available to the UN, are included in UNDPKO, United Nations Standby Arrangements: Status Report, <www.un.org/Depts/dpko/rapid/str.htm>

37   J Appathurai & R Lysyshyn, *Lessons Learned from the Zaire Mission*, unpublished report, June 1997, pp. 2-3. Although, respectively, members of the Canadian Department of National Defence and the Department of Foreign Affairs and International Trade (and members of the Interdepartmental Task Force to co-ordinate Canada's participation in the crises in the former Zaire), the report was written in their personal capacity.

38   Excerpts from a Statement by Mrs Sadako Ogata, United Nations High Commissioner for Refugees, to the Third Committee of the General Assembly, New York, 3 November 1997.

39   Article 52 of Chapter VIII of the UN Charter outlines the concept of 'regional arrangements' as they deal with "... *matters relating to the maintenance of international peace and security as are appropriate for regional action, provided*

that such arrangements or agencies are consistent with the Purposes and Principles of the United Nations." Article 53 refers to enforcement action by regional bodies, but requires that *"... no enforcement action shall be taken under regional arrangement or by regional agencies without the authorisation of the Security Council ..."*

40   The force, which had been operating without international approval since early 1997, consisted of voluntary troop contributions by Burkina Faso, Chad, Gabon, Kenya, Senegal, and Togo. Under Chapter VII of the <u>UN Charter</u>, MISAB was entitled to use force in order to implement its mandate, which included the disarmament of rebellious factions of the CAR military. The wording of Resolution 1125 speaks for itself:
"The Security Council, ... [d]etermining that the situation in the Central African Republic continues to constitute a threat to international peace and security in the region,

1.   *Welcomes the efforts of the Member States which participate in MISAB and of those Member States which support them;*

2.   *Approves the continued conduct by Member States participating in MISAB of the operation in a neutral and impartial way to achieve its objective to facilitate the return to peace and security by monitoring the implementation of the Bangui Agreements in the Central African Republic as stipulated in the mandate ... including through the supervision of the surrendering of arms of former mutineers, militias and all other persons unlawfully bearing arms ..."*

41   <u>Fourth Report to the Security Council Pursuant to Resolution 1125 (1997) Concerning the Situation in the Central African Republic</u> (29 September 1997), <www.un.org/Doc/sc/letter/1997/s1997759.htm>

42   M W Doyle, *Peacebuilding in Cambodia*, <u>IPA Policy Briefing Series</u>, December 1996, p. 3.

43   Mackinlay, op. cit., p. 37.

44   Smock, op. cit., p. 5.

45   L Minear, *Humanitarian Action and Peacekeeping Operations*, <u>Journal of Humanitarian Assistance</u>, <www-jha.sps. cam.ac.uk/a/a024.htm>, posted 4 July 1997, p. 6.

46   M Rupiah, *Peacekeeping Operations: The Zimbabwean Experience*, <u>Journal of Humanitarian Assistance</u>, <www-jha. sps.cam.ac.uk/a/a061.htm>, posted 25 February 1996, p. 4.

47   P Walker, *Chaos and Caring: Humanitarian Aid Amidst Disintegrating States*, <u>Journal of Humanitarian Assistance</u>, <www-jha.sps.cam.ac.uk/a/a020.htm>, posted 13 October 1996, p. 3.

48   P Walker, *Whose Disaster is it Anyway? Rights, Responsibilities and Standards in Crisis*, <u>Journal of Humanitarian Assistance</u>, <www-jha.sps.cam.ac.uk/a/a019.htm>, posted 13 August 1996, p. 1.

49   Walker, October 1996, op. cit.

Chapter 4: The collapse of the African state

Richard Cornwell

*T*he state has been the most prominent feature of the international political system for so long that it is easy to take the permanence of its role in the organisation of society for granted. Lately, however, a growing body of literature has appeared, dealing with the erosion of the power of the sovereign state. Usually, this centres upon the impact of what is generally referred to as globalisation, and the emergence of major transnational economic and financial actors, able to shift their operations almost at will and answerable to no one nation's political masters. This has signified the removal of several instruments of economic sovereignty from the control of the state.[1] The establishment of regional groupings in parts of the world has also eroded state sovereignty.[2] At the other end of the spectrum, local particularisms challenge the authority of the nation-state,[3] and significant elements of the population even seek to evade or ignore the state's claims to authority. This latter phenomenon is also marked among the growing underclass in industrial and post-industrial societies, especially as the state's ability to fulfil its welfare function comes into question.[4]

In short, the end of this century sees the modern state, as structure, facing a number of serious challenges and a need to redefine its essential role and its relationship with its citizens. The question of state legitimacy, in the general sense, has probably not been as sharply posed since the emergence of the modern international system, and though there are few who see any other structure emerging to replace the state system as the skeleton of the international order, there can be little doubt that the state of the mid-21st century will bear only a superficial resemblance to that of the mid-20th.[5]

The world is afflicted by a growing number of intrastate conflicts, apparently of racial, religious and ethnic derivation. A growing number of civilians, as opposed to armies and security forces, are becoming involved in this violence, often for no obvious or clearly articulated political reason. Ethnic and racial cleansing combined with acute religious extremism, intolerance or pure criminality suggest a growing social crisis in the international system.[6]

These instances of turmoil are the local and particular manifestations of a common crisis of individual and group identity in the context of deepening social inequality and fragmentation. The combined effects of the weakened state administrative and policy apparatus, the current cessation of bipolar ideological competition and the accelerating and unaccountable process known as globalisation, have called some of the more fundamental and familiar premises upon which our lives and our sense of security are based into question. Prominent among these is the nation-state project. Globalisation and the expansion of economic scale have implications not only for state capacity and legitimacy, but also for society at large, as various groups and individuals seek to redefine themselves in a rapidly changing domestic and individual environment.[7] It is scarcely surprising when, in such circumstances, other certainties suddenly become negotiable.

Turning to Africa, and some other parts of the world's margins: the end of the Cold War has seen not only the dissolution of the bipolar world order, but, in some cases, the collapse of individual states. As Zartman points out in his recently edited work on the subject, the phenomenon of state collapse goes further than the overthrow of a regime. It reflects the disintegration of structure, legitimate authority, law and political order within the confines of the state. This does not imply, however, that anarchy reigns. Other actors move into the vacuum left by the collapse of the state.[8] If of local origin, these may be ethnic nationalists or simply warlords; if foreign, they generally take the form of international companies providing their own security. Zartman sees a period in which various rivals vie with each other and with attempts to re-establish central authority. During this period, the state itself, as a legitimate functioning order, is gone.[9]

Though the phenomenon of collapsed states is by no means confined to the post-Cold War environment or to Africa, it is here that it is most often encountered. Given that the modern African state is a relatively new creation, and of essentially foreign origin, this should not be surprising.[10]

It was during the period of colonial rule that modern Africa took on many of its most familiar characteristics. The imposition of alien rule, the colonial experience and the African reaction to these were by no means uniform, but, throughout Africa, the impact of these events was revolutionary, whether measured in political, economic or social terms.

Whatever the various reasons for, and the myriad local responses to the 'Scramble for Africa', one consequence was common: in Lonsdale's elegant formulation, *"... most Africans did not actually live in states until colonial rule fastened Leviathan's yoke upon them. Indeed the most distinctively African contribution to human history could be said to have been precisely the civilized art of living fairly peaceably together not in states."*[11]

In the brief historical space of eighty years at most – the period of effective colonial rule – the countless societies and cultures of Africa were incorporated into fifty or so states, with all that this radical transformation of political size, scale and doctrine implied. Traditional political and social structures, incorporating a moral universe often based on the assumption of the existence of kin and blood relationships with other members of the immediate community and its polity, were either overlaid or replaced by a new abstract colonial state whose extensive rights were founded on an impersonal doctrine of sovereignty quite alien to most African cultures. At the same time, they were drawn more closely into the global economy, and exposed to new technologies and ideas as never before.[12] Viewed from this perspective, it is to be expected that the modern state structure in Africa often forms little more than a thin carapace over the living social organism, and that the vital activity often takes place in the largely hidden realms of the informal economy and its companion polity. It is here that most of Africa's population struggle to make sense and to survive in a world in which crisis has become a state of being.[13]

What is interesting, in hindsight, is that the eventual leaders of the successful revolt against colonial rule made no attempt to overturn this imposed system of states or dismantle the alien political framework in favour of a return to the more 'natural' shape of pre-colonial African society. Instead, they sought to preserve the arbitrarily demarcated artificial boundaries of the colonial period virtually at any cost, in order to seize control of the colonial state as an operating system. Indeed, the successful preservation of the imposed state structures, if not their operating systems, was one of the more striking achievements of the statesmen of independent Africa.

Part of the explanation for the survival of African states as juridical units, for all their weakness, was their usefulness to other more powerful actors in the competition for global influence.[14] As Austin has pointed out, the "... *colonial legacy prevails today because an alternative map of traditional Africa in modern guise defies belief.*"[15] Most importantly, the new African states, however tenuous their administrative control over their defined territories, were received into the international system and were recognised in law as sovereign entities. It is worth noting that, even when groups and entire regions have successfully defied central governments and exercised *de facto* control over large areas, their claims have failed to win international recognition.[16]

The inherited state

Much is made in popular writing about Africa of the artificiality of its imposed boundaries. While it is true that these have created problems of a sort, it is not here that the essence of the difficulty lies, but in the nature of the state inherited by Africa's independent rulers. It is all too readily assumed that the European colonial powers simply transferred the political systems and ideas of the metropole to their African colonies. Though these concepts obviously informed the constitution-makers of independent Africa, this perspective is flawed in at least one important respect: the colonial state was **not** essentially a replica of the metropolitan power. It is in this context that the nature and internal structural problems of the African state have to be considered, for they go a long way towards explaining its brittle and essentially fragile nature.

It is true that the colonial powers transferred new concepts of statehood to Africa – some, indeed, relatively new to Europe itself – and imposed upon the continent a largely novel pattern of territoriality and sovereignty, but it should be noted that certain important parts of contemporary European state theory were not immediately transferred to Africa. For instance, the doctrines of European theory dealing with the limitations of the power of the state were not incorporated – a significant omission when one considers the subsequent move to authoritarian rule across much of independent Africa. Nor was the relatively new idea of nationhood, as complementary to the state, transferred by the colonial authorities, eager as they were to divide and rule. The trappings of independent statehood were introduced very late in the day, and sometimes not at all.[17]

It is important to bear in mind that, at root, the colonial state was based on domination, and on its ability to impose its hegemony upon the subject peoples to extract from them the taxes necessary for the maintenance of the colonial state apparatus. Even in those cases where constitutional reforms were introduced to limit the absolute power of the state, this happened only during the immediate approach to independence. Again, viewed from this perspective, it is less surprising that some of Africa's new rulers decided that these limitations could be dispensed with fairly quickly, though this was a development that helped to render the African state less flexible.

The control exercised by the colonial state was based upon its monopoly of power and its ability to use force – or the implied threat of superior force – to impose its will on people who were at odds either with the authorities or with each other. It is worth noting that the colonial administration maintained effective control over the whole state apparatus – military, police and communications systems included. In other words, there was no chance of any subordinate part of the state apparatus suddenly promoting itself as an alternative power base. There was also no chance of succession problems emerging to disturb the smooth continuity of personnel. Though there were acute differences of a personal and policy nature within the various colonial civil services, these rarely became public or were allowed to upset the routine running of the administrative machine. The colonial administration was expected, as part of the confidence trick that comprised colonial rule, to present a united, professional and assured face to its subjects.[18]

As Austin has pointed out, the accusations that many African governments are little more than continuations of the former colonial regimes, is abuse that misses the point in a singular way. *"The primary need of African leaders, in party or military uniform, has been how to keep the colonial state going ... how to recreate the mechanisms of colonial control has been a tough puzzle."*[19]

He remarks that one major difference between the colonial administrations and their immediate successors was that the former was an intrusion ruled by a foreign élite banded together under the governor by a code of behaviour, *"... a set of guardians whose strength lay in the pack."*[20]

"African governments have no such code of ethics or surety of racial solidarity. They are under party or military leaders who retain control by exercising power over their own kind. The difference can be sharply expressed at its extreme by noting that no governor ever hanged one of his colonial officers, whereas Nkrumah in Ghana imprisoned his own party colleagues, and Idi Amin in Uganda beat to death civil servants, judges, university teachers, and his fellow army officers alike.

The fundamental difference is that while the colonial state was essentially bureaucratic, the postindependence regimes have been ultrapolitical."[21]

Now the rulers of independent African states suddenly had to rely increasingly on their fellow nationals to maintain law and order, people who were full citizens of the new country – some with political ideas and ambitions of their own – for it soon became evident that the closer one was to the centre of the political apparatus, the greater the chances of material reward.

The dominance of the political

The state in 20th century Africa has been the primary arena for competition, power and influence over the distribution of scarce resources. As Jackson and Rosberg have noted:

"What the church was for ambitious men in medieval Europe or the business corporation in nineteenth and twentieth century America, the state is today for ambitious Africans with skill

and fortune. The political system in African states is more like a game or a market than a planning organization ... State power in African countries has been the major arena of privilege ... accessible to ambitious men of humble origin. The political capital of social standing and wealth has been useful but not essential to partake in the game or to win; personal strength, power, and popularity have been more important. In fact political activity has been seen by ambitious Africans as a way – indeed the most important way – of securing such capital."[22]

There was another important difference between the representative democracies of the 19th century and the new African independent states. The Western democracies emerged into a world in which they initially had to contend with a fairly limited number of government functions, and the management of fairly simple economic and political systems in a relatively spacious global system in which their technological achievements tended to give them the advantage. The new African states, on the other hand, emerged into a wholly new environment. They were asked to establish full-scale social welfare states with complicated mechanisms, at the same time as undertaking a complex drive for social and economic development, and this in a world of population explosion, widening technological and economic gaps, superpower competition and global tension and conflict. And if the resulting problems of social discontinuity, cultural strain and the pragmatic problems of development had not been sufficient to unhinge the strongest constitutional formula, there was still the additional business of national integration awaiting them.

Particularism and ethnicity as a challenge to the nation-state

Part of the problem was the difficulty experienced by many of Africa's new leaders in seeking to live up to the expectations nurtured during their fight against colonial rule. Indeed, with independence won, and the colonial power shifted from the centre of attention, it proved impossible to sustain the level of public political interest and cohesion within the new state. For many Africans, attention now reverted to the local levels in which their lives were rooted, and where the complex battle between the modern and older established values would continue to be fought. Yet, the local and traditional leaders who remained so significant to most Africans also represented an incipient threat to the would-be builders of the new nation and their tentative political legitimacy. New presidents and prime ministers regarded these local leaders with suspicion and, aware of the fragility of the machinery they had inherited, tended to regard any dissent or argument as disloyalty. It was thus hardly surprising that so many new African governments soon began to deal harshly with those whom they saw as opponents, and that human rights and political freedoms often became casualties of the new order. Accordingly, the old traditional institutions were either incorporated by the state, reduced in terms of their formal powers or summarily abolished. Sometimes the kings, chiefs and headmen were also derided as part of a backward tribal past, essentially ethnically divisive and often tainted by collaboration with the old colonial system.[23]

As the state took on the responsibility for nation-building, with all its centralising implications, the project tended to take on the characteristics of a narrow ethnic base which was identified as nationally authentic. From here it was expanded, even though this implied the denial of concomitant status to other ethnic identities, which were given a narrow and negative tribal connotation. Not only was diversity seen as a source of dangerous weakness, but ethnic identity itself was interpreted as inimical to the state-building project. But from the perspective of a largely rural population, the idea of a common national culture made no sense, and lacked any content with which they could identify. As Laakso and Olukoshi note:

"Without an economic and social push towards the kind of national 'high culture' experienced in Europe, the idea of national unity came, paradoxically, to be reduced to an almost perfect negation of a common culture ...

Armed with the rhetoric of unity, the post-colonial African state, instead of enhancing its capacity to provide new economic and professional opportunities to all segments of the society, increasingly resorted to protecting itself against the populace. The idea of unity which leaders sought to impose on Africans ... together with the ideologies that underpinned them served increasingly to distinguish the state from society and to prevent any meaningful confrontation between the ruling élites and the masses. The character of the bureaucracy inherited by post-colonial state agencies and the persistence of the language of colonial governance exacerbated this cultural distance between the governors and the governed and further strengthened the position of those in power at the expense of the populace over whom they ruled and to whom, increasingly, they failed to account."[24]

Certainly, it seems evident that such feelings of belonging as most African peoples have, remain rooted in their local communities with their familiar bases of kinship and allegiance. No parallel community has been created at national level, and the unity of the nationalist movements evaporated soon after independence.

Nevertheless, cultural pluralism, or tribalism, or ethnicity, or whatever other label is chosen, is a far more complex and dynamic concept than many realise. The phenomenon that is addressed, is not simply a hangover of pre-colonial identities. Cultural pluralism refers to a complex and shifting interaction of affinities based on common language, ethnicity, religion and region. The simple static tribal map with its stable, distinctive and defined categories is quite inadequate to explain a complex amalgam of communal identities in a constant process of change. These group identities are fashioned and reshaped by the subjective perceptions of their members, and therefore depend to a great extent on what the members are opposed to at any given time. In Young's explanation, *"... particular categories are defined according to characteristics that differentiate them from relevant others ... [These identities are] ... not defined by innate, permanent culture characteristics."*[25]

Colonial and post-colonial policy itself has had an important modifying effect on ethnic and regional consciousness. Since colonial times, the emphasis on export-oriented production has sometimes created severe regional imbalances, which may exacerbate the effects of an uneven distribution of natural resources. The siting of administrative centres and the unequal distribution of educational and health facilities and employment opportunities have exercised a profound influence on the life chances and social mobility of groups. The migration of an individual away from his traditional milieu may even have the effect of enhancing ethnic identity in a strange environment where competition for scarce resources and employment is intense. Even education may have the effect of heightening social consciousness and lead to a more articulated cultural identity.[26]

In the political arena, ethnic consciousness also has a special importance. Aspirants to political office naturally begin by mobilising their own local clientele before casting the net wider. As a consequence, rival networks of political bosses and their clients form an interlocking web of patronage and support, affecting all sectors of society. The security services, bureaucracy and trade unions are all vulnerable to infiltration by ethnic or regional rivals to the incumbents in office.[27] Austin describes the dilemma of many African governments:

"... one section or another of the elite is often in league with its own local community against the center. The search for votes pulls national leaders apart toward rival bases of communal or regional support. Governments therefore exist precariously, and their members grow distrustful of one another. They remain in office only because the possibility of change is held in check by the very plurality of forces that makes them precarious. The dilemma is aptly contained in Nolutshungu's description of Nigeria – applicable to many African states – as held together in an uneasy balance only by 'the conjunction of negatives': the elite is too feeble to dominate, but the masses are too divided to rebel."[28]

The attempts to marginalise certain regional and ethnic groups in the period after independence also had the perverse effect of politicising ethnicity. This was serious enough in times of relative abundance, when the state was able to dispense its patronage over a broad field, albeit differentially.[29] In the current conditions of exaggerated scarcity, ethnic and regional associations have taken on a particular significance in the survival strategies of many Africans.

The exclusionist strategies adopted by many of the leaders of independent Africa and the steady concentration of political power around a coterie surrounding the president himself also worked against any consolidation of systemic legitimacy in the state as structure. In a situation where rules-based competition in the political arena had been made all but impossible, and where the spoils of office were of absolute importance in gaining access to economic power, it was scarcely surprising when new political actors made their presence felt in an unorthodox fashion, with all the implications this had for systemic legitimacy. Before long, a number of African countries had experienced their first *coups*, as the soldiers took over the government, often ushering in a cycle of *coup* and counter-*coup*, with only brief returns to civilian rule.[30]

From boom to crisis

To compound matters, Africa's political problems interacted with inherent economic weaknesses aggravated by inappropriate and poorly executed policies. Of all the parts of what is known as the 'Third World', Africa's development problems seem the most intractable. On the economic front, of course, it has long been apparent to all but the incurably optimistic that many African countries are poor simply by virtue of their modest natural resource bases and their reliance on the vagaries of an unkind climate. From the colonial period, some inherited an overdependence on a narrow range of primary commodities for export and foreign exchange earnings, which rendered them excessively vulnerable to fluctuations in commodity prices.

African states also inherited from the colonial period a tradition of state intervention in almost every sector of the economy. Government administered price controls regulated or intervened in labour, mining, agriculture, manufacturing and financial markets. The public sector grew as various enterprises and institutions were brought under state control. In some countries, the mining sector was nationalised and in most marketing monopolies were given to parastatals. Foreign exchange and the import-export trade were centrally administered, and tax regimes were manipulated to favour the urban élite at the expense of the mass of rural producers.[31] Of course, this massive expansion in the activities of the state served the political élite well, providing it, in the days of relative plenty during the post-independence continuation of the post-World War II boom, with the wherewithal to create and sustain extensive networks of clients.[32]

Yet, interventionism, as it extended the state's reach throughout the economy, eventually outran the state's administrative capacity. Not only did judicial and regulatory functions deteriorate, especially because of arbitrary political interference, but the provision of public services became increasingly less efficient. As the urban bias of the state's economic and fiscal policies became more apparent, unskilled workers poured into the towns from the countryside, while expanding education services for populations growing at an unprecedented rate churned out qualified workers fully expecting to find jobs in the public sector.[33]

Even before the oil shocks of the 1970s turned global terms of trade so dramatically against agricultural exporting countries, many African states were already resorting to deficit financing to generate employment, regardless of existing capacity utilisation levels. Subsequent commodity price falls eroded the existing tax base, while heavy public investment in the boom years left governments with long term recurrent expenditure even after public spending was curtailed.[34]

Instead of allowing exchange rates to move in tune with the balance of payments crisis, most governments intervened even more strongly in currency markets, promoting the growth of parallel markets and economies, which further reduced the state's access to revenue.[35]

Growing budget deficits could be covered only by recourse to increasingly expensive foreign loans. Bureaucratic and political mismanagement, incompetence, corruption and even grand theft often compounded the problem, and most African states quickly found themselves entrapped in an ever-deepening pit of indebtedness.

As private capital inflows dried up, many African states found that their only recourse was to the International Monetary Fund (IMF) and the World Bank, which now designed new lending mechanisms. This was the beginning of a new phase in Africa's independent history which would see the imposition of monetarist philosophies that may be summed up crudely as 'the less state the better'.[36] The austerity policies which governments were required to implement also implied a resort to greater authoritarianism on the part of governments, further undermining the social contract upon which so much of the state's declining legitimacy rested.[37]

Though it was too early to describe the phenomenon as collapse, the symptoms of a wasting disease were already in evidence.

Take for example the picture being painted by Jackson and Rosberg in 1982:

"Black Africa's forty-odd states are among the weakest in the world. State institutions and organizations are less developed in the sub-Saharan region than almost anywhere else ... Most of the national governments exercise only tenuous control over the people, organizations and activities within their territorial jurisdiction ... Some governments have periodically ceased to control substantial segments of their country's territory and population ... there have been times when Angola, Chad, Ethiopia, Nigeria, Sudan, Uganda and Zaire have ceased to be 'states' in the empirical sense – that is their central governments lost control of important areas in the jurisdiction during struggles with rival political organizations."[38]

Writing at virtually the same time, the journalist and traveller, Marnham made the following trenchant observation:

"In many African countries the city limits mark the effective borders of the state. Outside the city official life evaporates: within is the favoured area, the place where all the money goes, the place where the entire educated community insists on living. It is the one lump of earth out of the whole inheritance which the fragile governments can make more than a pretence of governing."[39]

The transition from a chronic condition to one potentially terminal coincided with the end of the Cold War, and the bipolar rivalry that had made African states useful pawns.

'Choiceless democracy'

It was no coincidence that the debate about Africa's 'second liberation' took place once the major powers no longer needed to compete for Africa's international support. The East-West conflict had provided the first generation of post-colonial African élite with their means of survival. In the early 1990s, domestic support became more important than foreign patrons for the first time since independence. African leaders had to confront the inherent weaknesses of their regimes and consider sharing power with others. The early 1990s were uncomfortable times for Africa's rulers and their clients, for all this happened at a time of deep and structural economic crisis.

The driving force behind Africa's second experiment with democracy came both from ideological conviction and the growing impatience of an ever-bolder public consciousness, and from the related matter of the continent's prevailing economic crisis.

On the domestic front, the politically-conscious, urbanised, professional and student bodies began to rail against the continued failure of their rulers to match rhetoric and promises to economic progress. Indeed, much of Africa had suffered a steady decline in living standards through the 1970s and 1980s.

For their part, the World Bank, the IMF and other bilateral aid donors also made it quite clear that, if further financial assistance was to be forthcoming, Africa's governments had to pay urgent attention to their human rights' records. More specifically, they had to become politically more accountable to their people, and curb corruption. They were also required to adopt structural adjustment programmes and to allow market forces to send the major signals through their economies.

Structural adjustment entailed a number of things: the reduction of public expenditure, balanced budgets, economic liberalisation and currency devaluation. The course advocated, and even enforced in Africa by the apostles of the free market was not without a certain inherent paradox, however. On the one hand, structural adjustment programmes involved a sharp decline in living standards for most and a steep rise in the price of food and social services, especially in the towns. On the other, the democracy movement had locally been driven largely by popular demand for improved living standards. Structural adjustment programmes thus aggravated social welfare problems, diminishing the capacity of governments to cope with political demands. The contradiction between the imperatives of democratisation and structural adjustment soon became apparent: at the very moment when democratisation stimulated the popular demand for better social and welfare services, structural adjustment required that this be denied. In broad terms, this played a significant part in further undermining the state's claims to legitimacy in the eyes of its own citizens.

Simultaneously, the demand for government accountability and the reduction in 'corrupt' practices put severe pressure upon state-centred patronage networks. This meant that rulers had to try and build new constituencies based on consent. Inasmuch as structural adjustment created a drastic change in patterns of resource allocation, it eroded the clientelistic foundations on which most African state systems are based.

In essence, this structural adjustment/aid-linked movement towards democracy contained within itself not only the seeds of its own undoing, but a threat to the very existence of Africa's fragile state structures. It was all very well for an urban mob, a guerrilla army or a national conference to topple a dictator, it is quite another to construct a democratic polity, especially in a political environment pervaded by the intolerance and brutality of previous regimes, and by an acute shortage of material resources with which to sustain even the essential services usually associated with statehood.

The effects of the current economic and social crisis in Africa are so profound and pervasive that, in the view of Laakso and Olukoshi, they threaten to dissolve the cultural, economic and political glues that held the different elements of the African nation-state together, to such an extent that the future of the African nation-state may be in jeopardy. At the same time, structural adjustment policies undermine the basis of the social contract underpinning the foundation of the post-colonial state structures, depriving the state simultaneously of its capacity and of the last vestiges of legitimacy.[40]

Structural adjustment programmes also contributed to the growing informalisation of the economy, further reducing the state's revenue base and thus its capacity to deliver services even of a rudimentary type. Africa's states are increasingly dependent on foreign aid, and some need to rely on expatriate and donor personnel in a manner redolent of colonial days.[41]

"In the most extreme cases, the state has, more or less, been reduced to its coercive apparatuses (army, police and prisons), which are then employed, crudely, to safeguard the authoritarian political framework within which governments, faced with a host of donor conditionalities, attempt to abide by the neo-liberal agenda for the reform of the economies – and politics – of African countries."[42]

Meanwhile, in terms of the choices to be made between alternative policies, the political space available to African politicians was largely closed down by the Washington consensus. By emptying the political arena of ideas, competition for power was reduced to its bare essentials, personality and local/ethnic considerations became paramount, and the remnants of the state were likely to fall prey to the untrammelled competition for power.

Mkandawire has coined the term 'choiceless democracies' to encapsulate the paradoxes facing African political reformists in the context of globalisation. Structural adjustment policies, the manifestation of globalisation in the African context, he argues, constrain the actions of the formal institutions of democratic rule on at least three levels: that of objectives, of instruments, and of structural constraints. The choiceless democracy that emerges, is at best a technocratic husk of the real organism, unable to respond to the needs of its citizens.[43]

Pathway to the future: Escape from the state?

Faced with this situation, many citizens sought to find solutions outside the state arena. Of the survival strategies adopted by Africans in their confrontation with the harsh realities of their condition, one of the more common is 'avoiding the state'.[44] This strategy has obvious implications for the viability of the state project, politically as well as economically. It also raises the question whether the Western belief in creating room for and strengthening African civil society will have the expected consequences: that it will help to promote the consolidation of democratic structures that reinforce and legitimise the modern state. This is a matter for debate, and the argument about the future of the state in Africa has to take cognizance of the emergence of different and particularistic forms of civil society in Africa, sometimes as alternatives to, and sometimes as adjuncts of the state and its owners.

The term 'civil society' has only recently been extended in the literature on Africa to include ethnic associations, which, with other associations of similar type, have important political functions beyond the surveillance of state agencies. In the Western political science canon, the concept 'civil society' has generally implied the opening of opportunities for individual freedom. But one should be careful not to misapply Western political constructs to African circumstances. In Western history, the public realm has been shared between the state, other political organisations and civil society, all of which were assumed to have some concern for individual liberty, which simply is not the African historical experience. The pre-colonial African state rarely felt the need to justify its existence in terms of meeting the needs of individuals. Nor did the colonial state often include the security and welfare needs of ordinary Africans in its considerations. As Ekeh has argued, this heritage has been passed on to the post-colonial state and, as a consequence, the ordinary individual has sought to attain his security and welfare needs in ways and idioms different from those familiar in Western political thought. As has been suggested above, the principal structures with which the individual has sought alliance are kinship organisations which have expanded and developed along a path quite distinct from the European experience.[45]

*"... [T]he trend for several centuries in African history led to the creation of kinship as an alternative public institution, existing side by side with the formal state. They constitute two public realms that I identified some years ago as the **civic public**, operating on amoral codes of behaviour and using the apparatuses of the formal state, and the **primordial public** whose value-premises are moral, binding together members of the same natural and assumed (including ethnic) groupings. The complexity of African politics lies in the fact that they cover more diversified political space than that of the public realm in Western society. Accordingly, individual liberty and the problems of civil society in Africa pose sharply different issues from those we are used to in Western political thought. "*[46]

This primordial public has the ability to withstand the intrusions of the state. Africa has a wide variety of organisations and associations occupying this space, though this is seldom recognised.

Another author who has written on this subject is Abdou Maliqalim Simone. He argues that *"[t]he definition of civil society must be expanded to include the loosely configured social practices which make up a discourse of manoeuvres on the part of peoples shut out of official economies and forms of government. "*[47] He makes the point that African societies are not mere victims of Western domination, never having been fully captured, and that they are slipping further out of Western comprehension and control. They are opportunistic, but reconfigured in a sense of social connectedness. He finds it difficult to decide whether civil society's responses help empower on anything more than a symbolic level, however.

"They are certainly not revolutionary in any conventional sense, nor are they merely complicit in maintaining or revising existing forms of domination ... But they have in the past been forced to operate with relative invisibility – something which sustains the ability of civil society to resist domination but leaves it unable to socialize outlooks and behaviours explicitly within institutional contexts that are able to cohere diverse interests and agendas over the long term. Yet the responses of the civil sector do point to alternative spaces of political formation – never able to fully bring them about but, nevertheless, serve as indications that political life remains fluid and that the future in Africa is not over before it begins.

While it is clear that African states must find ways to maximize the participation of its peoples in the process of governance, the emphasis on multiparty democracy may simply solidify their capture in an international division of labour mediated by IMF and World Bank dictates."[48]

In addressing the all-too-common assumption made by Western observers that expanding the room available to civil society in Africa will lead to democratic consolidation, Ekeh argues that the state does not occupy the total active political space in Africa, which is segmented and only partially under state control. *"The sphere of the primordial public occupies vast tracts of the political space that are relevant for the welfare of the individual, sometimes limiting and breaching the state's efforts to extend its claims beyond the civic public sphere.*"[49]

Though Africa has a vast array of institutions and associations of civil society, it does not follow that these will be useful in the promotion of democracy. As Ekeh argues, African civil society is largely indifferent to the affairs of the civic public realm over which the state presides. Civil society in Africa is content to look after those affairs of the public over which the state shows little concern. This is a very important distinction between African and European society. When the African individual feels wronged in the public realm claimed by the state, he withdraws from it into the primordial public realm:

"Herein lies the problem for democracy in Africa, from the point of view of civil society. It is insufficient to argue that the mere presence and even further growth of civil society will help the development of democracy in Africa. What is needed is to search for ways that will enable the state and Africa's civil society to be mutually engaged in the public arena, lessening the claims of the state for total ownership of the political space of the public realm and encouraging the competence of the individual with respect to his view of who owns the public realm where the state operates."[50]

Ekeh warns that there are some distinctive features of these African civil society associations that have not helped in promoting democracy or in defining individual liberties or respect for the human person in abstract. Indeed, because kinship is intrinsically segmentary, they are precluded from doing so by their very nature. Many of these groups are concerned with the welfare of their 'own'. Those associations that operate in the civic public realm, such as trade and student unions, are relatively vulnerable to the state. There appears to be little sign of a reconciliation of these two types of organisation.[51]

Simone's conclusions are a little different, in that he sees a greater possibility of a creative interaction between the democratic movement and African civil society, whose variety he again emphasises.

"Democratic movements in Africa may not generate functional governance. But they may provide an opening that allows people to at least show what they are doing and how they are doing it; to be more conscious of the practices they have used to survive and, conversely, that have impeded a better way of life. Macro-level ignorance and micro-level resistance have combined to render much of what is significant in terms of how people actually govern themselves invisible – in the domain of households, neighbourhoods, institutions, dance halls, street corners, bars, shrines, churches, mosques and cafés. For it is in these places where the bulk of Africa is governed, the important decisions made.

Increasingly, African kin groups find themselves spread out over distance and continents, zones of activities and agendas, yet, in most cases, they seem to co-ordinate their efforts, come together as some cohesive body. Little is known about these efforts; given existing political climates their survival is probably predicated on little being known about them. Invisibility may have been the key to the continuation of thousands of local initiatives and organizations, but it precludes them from operating as provisional models for the generation of institutions on a larger scale."[52]

Simone concludes that the way forward may be the African state's recognition of the autonomy of the civil sector, which would imply that the latter was required to produce, mobilise and develop instead of merely acting as an escape from the state.[53]

Another, less optimistic or idealistic, view of the second polity and its links to the second economy is provided by Lemarchand. He points to the distinctions between approaches to and interest in the informal sector. Rational-choice theorists and proponents of the economy of affection approach the phenomenon of the informal economy from different directions, and view its potential from different perspectives. Whereas rational-choice theorists urge the introduction of market incentives to reduce the informal sector as a step towards restructuring Africa's economies, the supporters of the economy of affection see the informal sector as suggesting the potential for co-operation in traditional modes of production.[54]

Lemarchand also distinguishes between activities supposedly under state control but which evade the state or involve illegal use of state position, and activities which ignore the state and operate beyond its reach. The former transform the state into a market, the latter represent the withdrawal from state and market, and are quite distinct.[55]

He is also at pains to dispel certain fallacies about what is broadly described as the informal sector. One of these he describes as the convivialist view, in which the emphasis is on the capacity of individuals to beat the system with their imagination and resourcefulness. Lemarchand has some misgivings about the rosy picture painted here and tends to agree with a more depressing view of some of the informal economic arrangements which have drawn such praise. He also disputes the idea that informal economies are a transitional phenomenon which will disappear as capitalism develops. Arguing that the evidence contradicts this, he points out that the informal sectors are not only expanding in proportion to capitalist development, but they have already reached a degree of institutionalisation that makes their anticipated demise highly unlikely.[56]

The relationship between the second economy and the state is by no means clear-cut, or universal in nature. Clientelism in its most oppressive forms can enter and use the informal system. There is a seamy and sometimes violent side to this, and the penetration of society by the state may be reversed. *"What some see as evidence of new social configurations is sometimes better understood as a reconfiguration of pre-colonial social formations, whose renewed vitality stems from their partial insertion into the formal apparatus of the state."*[57] Sometimes control of the informal sector, therefore, may also derive from access to the state.

Sklar rejects the popular obsession with the need for a transition to democracy as essentially unscientific, assuming as it does the idea of a continuum of political practices.[58] He then goes on to examine the co-existence in Africa of sovereign and traditional authorities, finding here a prospect for political innovation.

"In Africa, one finds a Janus-like relationship of back-to-back dimensions of authority. The two dimensions are not symmetrical, since all but a few African countries consist of several, or many separate and distinct traditional polities. In every African country an overwhelming majority of citizens have dual political identities, but in no case does the second dimension vie with the sovereign dimension for sovereignty. Yet, as a separate source of authority, embedded in tradition, it does help to maintain social stability during the current era of turbulent changes."[59]

"The evidence ... indicates a growing propensity in African statecraft to use the troubling legacies of multiple sovereignty and dual political identity for constructive purposes. The existence of a multiplicity of states is conducive to political experimentation, including innovations influenced by custom, while dual authority is compatible with the idea, and practice, of constitutional government. To be sure, the connotations of dual authority in Africa are frequently (but not always) undemocratic, because they imply deference by citizens to traditional hierarchies. However, democracies have never been viable without substantial admixtures of oligarchy which functions to mitigate the less desirable effects of popular power."[60]

None of the above should be interpreted as subscribing to an interpretation of African political life as in some sense atavistic. Most of the associational life of Africa is essentially recent in origin, a reaction to the stresses of modernity expressed often in pseudo-traditional terms.[61]

The defence of the state's shrinking laager

The avenues of escape open to African publics are not likely to recommend themselves to those who earn their living in the wealthier parts of the economy. Certainly, there will be an interaction between the formal and informal, in economics as in politics, and in certain circumstances, various parties may seek to benefit from a condition of 'controlled chaos'. Nevertheless, a modicum of order and predictability are demanded by those who seek to hold on to the limp reins of state power, and those who seek to take advantage of their claims to sovereign status in order to exploit such parts of the national resource base as may be secured.

But increasingly, the men with the guns – and Africa is awash with them after the conflicts of the 1980s – have become important players in the political arena. The reduction in global ideological conflict has decreased the political and military incentives for outside powers to intervene on the continent; and, contrary to some expectations, an Africa omitted from the calculations of external rivals has not become a more peaceful place. That local disputes are now less globalised means that outside powers have less influence on the conduct, termination and outcome of these conflicts. Local rivalries and antagonisms are given freer rein, being more remote from world centres of power and insignificant in terms of the global system.

African states could no longer rely on outside assistance to end local wars that are no threat to vital foreign interests.[62]

External non-state actors have increasingly stepped into the void left by the international community – sometimes as proxies, sometimes as independent agents. By virtue of their wealth and command of expertise, they are able to influence events to their local and often short term advantage. It is for all the world as if Africa has returned to the 1880s, and the age of the chartered companies, marking out their enclaves in an otherwise disorderly environment. Indeed, some of the colonial states of Africa owe their origins to such companies.

This is the reverse side of globalisation. Transnational companies, having demanded a new set of global rules which have effectively undermined the state in certain of the world's margins, are now able to provide just as much of the apparatus usually reserved to the state, to carry out their businesses in relative safety and at great profit, their bargaining advantage being apparent. Their worries now focus on their competition with others of their ilk, and their relative abilities to co-opt those parts of the state's political apparatus that still have some status in law.

In effect, Africa is again divided, between those under protection and those without. The implications for the political and economic future of Africa are profound. For most of Africa's peoples, the state has long since ceased to be the provider of security, physical or social. Only the 'useful bits' will be recolonised by the forces of the outsiders.

Endnotes

1   R J Barnet & J Cavanagh, Global Dreams: Imperial Corporations and the New World Order, Simon & Shuster, New York, 1994; G J Millman, Around the World on a Trillion Dollars a Day: How Rebel Currency Traders Destroy Banks and Defy Governments, Bantam, London, 1995; D C Korten, When Corporations Rule the World, Kumarian, West Hartford, 1995; W Grieder, One World, Ready or Not: The Manic Logic of Global Capitalism, Simon & Shuster, New York, 1997.

2   K Ohmae, The End of the Nation State: The Rise of Regional Economies, Free Press, New York, 1996

3   G Gottlieb, Nation Against State: A New Approach to Ethnic Conflicts and the Decline of Sovereignty, Council on Foreign Relations Press, New York, 1993; M Horsman & A Marshall, After the Nation-state: Citizens, Tribalism and the New World Disorder, Harper Collins, London, 1994

4   A de Haan & S Maxwell, *Poverty and Social Exclusion in North and South*, IDS Bulletin, 29(1), 1997. For a broad discussion of the consequences for employment and democracy in a globalised economy, see H-P Martin & H Schumann, The Global Trap: Globalization and the Assault on Democracy and Prosperity, Zed Books, London, 1997.

5   A particularly alarming prognosis is provided by R D Kaplan, The Ends of the Earth: A Journey at the Dawn of the 21st Century, Random House, New York, 1996. Kaplan fails to take account of the positive implications of some of the survival strategies now being employed by the least fortunate of the planet's inhabitants. It is too early to decide on the balance to be struck between the optimistic and pessimistic interpretations of local manifestations of civil society. No doubt this is also coloured by the peculiarities of particular cases. A more sober assessment of the effects of the reform of the state as a global phenomenon is to be found in *The Nation-state is Dead. Long Live the Nation-state*, The Economist, 23 December 1995-5 January 1996, pp. 17-20.

6 United Nations Research Institute for Social Development (UNRISD), States of Disarray: The Social Effects of Globalization, UNRISD, Geneva, 1995.

7 Ibid.

8 I W Zartman, *Introduction: Posing the Problem of State Collapse*, in I W Zartman (ed.), Collapsed States: The Disintegration and Restoration of Legitimate Authority, Lynne Rienner, Boulder, 1995, p. 1.

9 Ibid.

10 Ibid.

11 J Lonsdale, *States and Social Processes in Africa: A Historiographical Survey*, African Studies Review, 24(2/3), 1981, p. 139.

12 R Hodder-Williams, An Introduction to the Politics of Tropical Africa, George Allen & Unwin, London, 1984, p. 10.

13 A Mbembe & J Roitman, *Figures of the Subject in Times of Crisis*, Public Culture, 7, 1995, pp. 323-352.

14 R H Jackson & C G Rosberg, *Why Africa's Weak States Persist: The Empirical and the Juridical in Statehood*, World Politics, 35(1), 1982a, p. 14.

15 D Austin, *Things Fall Apart*, Orbis, Winter 1982, p. 932. Basil Davidson has argued that by taking on the form of the colonial state, Africa's leaders opened the way for the 'vampire state' smothering the life-support systems of the African peoples. He quotes the Nigerian Dele Owolu as saying that *"... what will get Africa out of her present food and fiscal crises is not the clamping down of more government controls, but the release of the people's organizational genius at solving community problems."* B Davidson, The Black Man's Burden: Africa and the Curse of the Nation-state, James Currey, London, 1992, p. 314.

16 Jackson & Rosberg, 1982a, op. cit., pp. 18-24.

17 C Young, *Patterns of State Conflict: State, Class and Ethnicity*, Daedalus, Spring 1982, pp. 74-75.

18 D A Low, *Lion Rampant*, Journal of Commonwealth Political Studies, 2, 1963, pp. 246-247.

19 Austin, op. cit., p. 928.

20 Ibid., pp. 928-929.

21 Ibid., p. 929.

22 R H Jackson & C G Rosberg, Personal Rule in Black Africa: Prince, Autocrat, Prophet, Tyrant, University of California Press, Berkeley, 1982b, p. 14.

23 Hodder-Williams, op. cit., pp. 88-112.

24 L Laakso & A O Olukoshi, *The Crisis of the Post-colonial Nation-state Project in Africa*, in A O Olukoshi & L Laakso (eds.), Challenges to the Nation-state in Africa, Nordiska Afrikainstitutet, Uppsala, 1997, pp. 14-15.

25 Young, op. cit., pp. 73-74.

26 Ibid., pp. 88-89.

27 D Austin, Politics in Africa, Manchester University Press, Manchester, 1978, p. 17.

28 Austin, 1982, op. cit., p. 932.

29   Laakso & Olukoshi, op. cit., p. 15.

30   N Chazan, R Mortimer, J Ravenhill & D Rothchild, <u>Politics and Society in Contemporary Africa</u>, Macmillan, Basingstoke, 1988, pp. 127-216.

31   J Aron, *The Institutional Foundations of Growth*, in S Ellis (ed.), <u>Africa Now: People, Policies and Institutions</u>, Ministry of Foreign Affairs, The Hague, 1996, p. 98.

32   R Sandbrook with J Barker, <u>The Politics of Africa's Economic Stagnation</u>, Cambridge University Press, Cambridge, 1985, pp. 112-127.

33   Aron, op. cit., p. 99.

34   Ibid.

35   Ibid., p. 100.

36   Ibid., pp. 100-101.

37   Laakso & Olukoshi, op. cit., pp. 19-20.

38   Jackson & Rosberg, 1982a, op. cit., p. 1.

39   P Marnham, <u>Dispatches from Africa</u>, Sphere Books, London, 1981, p. 145.

40   Laakso & Olukoshi, op. cit., pp. 9-10.

41   Ibid., p. 10.

42   Ibid.

43   T Mkandawire, *Crisis Management and the Making of 'Choiceless Democracies' in Africa*, paper read at the <u>African Renewal Conference on State, Conflict and Democracy in Africa</u>, Massachusetts Institute of Technology, Boston, 6-9 March 1997.

44   Sandbrook, op. cit., pp. 148-151. He also invokes the Gramscian dictum *"Pessimism of the intellect, optimism of the will"* as representing a balanced approach to the African predicament; ibid., p 145.

45   P P Ekeh, *The Constitution of Civil Society in African History and Politics*, in B Caron, A Gboyega & E Osaghae (eds.), <u>Proceedings of the Symposium on Democratic Transition in Africa</u>, Centre for Research, Documentation and University Exchange (CREDU), Ibadan, Nigeria, 1992, pp. 187-192.

46   Ibid., pp 192-193.

47   A M Simone, *Between the Lines: African Civil Societies and the Remaking of Urban Communities*, <u>Africa Insight</u>, 22l(3), 1992, p. 159.

48   Ibid., p. 163.

49   Ekeh, op. cit., p. 196.

50   Ibid., p. 197.

51   Ibid., pp. 207-209.

52   Simone, op. cit., p. 163.

53   A similar view is held by Laakso & Olukoshi, op. cit., pp. 29-33.

54   R Lemarchand, *The Political Economy of Informal Economies*, <u>Africa Insight</u>, 21(4), 1991, p. 214. See also the discussion in E Aryeetey, *Formal and Informal Economic Activities*, in Ellis, op. cit., pp. 119-135; J MacGaffey, <u>The Real Economy of Zaire</u>, James Currey, London, 1991; T L Maliyamkono & M S D Bagachwa, <u>The Second Economy of Tanzania</u>, James Currey, London, 1990; M B Brown, <u>Africa's Choices after Thirty Years of the World Bank</u>, Penguin, London, 1995.

55   Lemarchand, op. cit., pp. 214-215.

56   Ibid., p. 215.

57   Ibid., p. 218.

58   R L Sklar, *African Politics: The Next Generation*, paper read at the <u>African Renewal Conference</u>, op. cit., p. 3.

59   Ibid., p. 5.

60   Ibid., p. 14.

61   In a recent book on the politics of Chad, Sam Nolutshungu provided a very subtle and eloquent explanation of the interaction between identities with a 'traditional' orientation, and the modern political context. Though his description is specific to Chad, it also suggests ways of attempting to understand the complex political interplay in other African states.

"The rebellions under Tombalbaye's regime and the phenomenon of warlordism that followed its collapse had shown that Chad was characterized by a multiplicity of communities with varying degrees of political detachment from each other, sometimes represented by factional leaders in the central political competition, at other times more or less isolating themselves from national politics and authority or putting up a more or less protracted local resistance to them. The liberation movement had been little more than a coalition of militants from such semi-independent political communities. The faction leaders, when they were responsive at all, were representative of such groups. Political representation involved a dual recognition: the communities recognized themselves in their leaders, and judged their place in Chadian politics by the share of power their representatives enjoyed; on the other hand, coalition formation among leaders amounted to mutual recognition of spokesmanship of discrete community-constituencies within the shared discourse of common Chadian citizenship.

It would be misleading, however, to identify 'communities' with primordial tribes or ethnic groups, reifying such groups and imputing to them a political self-consciousness they have seldom shown. The communities in question are not coextensive with ethnic groups or clans, however defined, but consist of individuals within such larger groupings who are brought together by a common political orientation ... often no more than a combination of powerful individuals backed by a number of important, more or less closely related families. Each such community has the potential to mobilize, on a privileged basis, support from a wider group to which it belongs – in some sense – ethnically. But the boundary of belonging is an ever-shifting one defined by conflict with others and by quarrels and contentions within the group being mobilized. Success in mobilizing a wider following on ethnic grounds is not assured, nor is effectiveness in national politics, even when such support can be secured. For that reason, leading activists are always drawn toward personal alliances outside their ethnic groups, the ethnic element constantly being redefined – both as to the relevant level (tribe, clan, family) and as to the criteria of its contention (religion, language, culture or locality). Above all, in practice all the communities are fissiparous."

See S C Nolutshungu, <u>Limits of Anarchy: Intervention and State Formation in Chad</u>, University Press of Virginia, Charlottesville, 1996, p. 288.

62   An early realisation of this state of affairs is reflected in D B Dewitt, *Introduction: The New Global Order and the Challenges of International Security*, in D Dewitt, D Haglund & J Kirton (eds.), <u>Building a New Global Order: Emerging Trends in International Security</u>, Oxford University Press, Toronto, 1993, pp. 2-3. *"[T]he axes of conflict in*

the shadow of the cold war will probably be more complex, not less, and more difficult to manage, not easier ... Inevitably, global security will depend on the ability of the world's political processes to address the perceived needs, the articulated demands, and the felt insecurities of the majority of states and the majority of the globe's population, both of which lie outside the privileged group of advanced industrialized capitalist countries."

Chapter 5: Executive Outcomes – A corporate conquest

Khareen Pech

An old emperor in a new suit

*E*xecutive Outcomes (EO)[1] has been called a 'new' mercenary company – one which was different to any that preceded it – one which was more legitimate than the former armies raised by mercenary heroes such as Bob Denard, Jack Schramme and 'Mad' Mike Hoare – one which was less of a threat to regional stability than it was an enforcer of peace – one which functioned as a highly disciplined and organised military corporation – accountable to international and national leaders, which could even be a solution to African problems of insecurity.[2]

However, there is much that is not new about EO and the factors which give rise to the present proliferation of South African mercenaries and private security companies in Africa and abroad. Throughout history, professional soldiers have sold their military skills to foreign forces and private corporations in post-war periods. Prior to demobilisation that began in the early 1990s, the former South African Defence Force (SADF) had a combat capacity of roughly 40 000 soldiers out of a total permanent force cadre of about 120 000 men and women. About 3 500 men constituted the special forces regiments and covert military or intelligence units.[3] Most of these units fought for more than a decade in Africa, combating the African National Congress (ANC) and its allies. As a result, many of these troops are both feared and unwanted by the new political order in South Africa, are still hungry for combat in lawless lands where 'quick-rich' opportunities abound, and have few other marketable skills. The existence of major private security forces that are primarily staffed by the élite of the former SADF is therefore not surprising. They include former commanders and members of the Koevoet counterinsurgency unit (a police unit that co-operated closely with the SADF in northern Namibia), 32 (Buffalo) Battalion, 1 to 5 Special Forces Reconnaissance regiments, 44 Parachute Brigade, the offensive intelligence units of the Civilian Co-operation Bureau (CCB), former Directorate of Covert Collection (DCC), as well as Special Branch detectives and top-ranking officers of the former South African Police (SAP).

There is also little new in the fact that EO is the advance guard for corporate kings and their emerging corporate empires. Through the ages, mercenaries have been useful to imperialistic states and opportunistic individuals wishing to carve out a more prominent place in the world. As such, mercenary armies have shaped the history of warfare and, in part, the history of the world. For example, the armies of Rome in the 11th century, of Napoleon Bonaparte in the 18th century and of the small, wealthy states of Italy at the time of the Renaissance were all mostly composed of mercenary forces. The latter case is especially relevant. Small city-states in 14th century Italy used highly organised mercenary armies to conquer rich and strategic neighbouring states. In the course of plundering wealth and seizing land, they built their noble houses into larger, more powerful states. The captains of these forces were called *condottieri* because they signed a written contract – a *condotta* – with a feudal lord or a rich city for a mercenary army.[4] Interestingly, these *condottieri* used the rewards of their mercenary activities to found their own noble houses and, in time, became rulers of states.[5] These powerful states that emerged in 14th century Italy, in turn, sponsored and financed the development of a new age of Western learning and art – the Renaissance. The revival of science, literature, architecture and knowledge which began in Italy, soon spread throughout Europe.

The *condottieri* of the Italian Renaissance are worth noting in an attempt to make sense of the upsurge of mercenarism in Africa in the last six years and when looking at its most visible and powerful agent yet, Executive Outcomes (EO). This is important – not so much in the sense that the mercenaries and private security companies can be seen to be assisting (or resisting) the delivery of some sort of 'Renaissance' in Africa – but in the sense that they constitute an advance guard for the construction of new corporate empires. These corporate empires, in turn, are useful to the architects of a new order in two important ways. Firstly, EO and other private military companies are capable of forcing political change in strife-torn regions characterised by weak and crumbling states – as in West and Central Africa. The military companies are hired to play a direct role in controlling or changing the outcome of an emerging balance of power. Secondly, the corporate powers provide the bulk of the funds and are the key sponsors of the military companies – a fact that greatly assists the impoverished African client governments or rebel armies. In turn, the corporate sponsors win access to the strategic mineral and energy resources of the beleaguered countries.

When England defeated France during the 14th century, English soldiers refused to disband and return to their home countries. Instead, they formed large mercenary companies which pillaged France and laid its feudal system open to anarchy.

> *"They hired themselves out to feudal lords and princes, grew rich on protection money and ransoms ... squeezed the Pope at Avignon dry and even [opposed] a formidable feudal army sent to suppress them by the King of France ... Their power was so great ... and their military ability was so useful ... that the only way to be rid of them was, the feudal authorities discovered, to siphon them off elsewhere. Thus it was that ... with the Pope's blessing ... [mercenary companies hired by Lord Montferrat attacked] the Pope's [greatest enemy] and Europe's wealthiest and most populous city, Milan."[6]*

One state's problem was cleverly diverted to a rival, neighbouring state – a move that not only solved the first state's problems of insecurity, but allowed it to gain a political and economic advantage in Europe. For his services, the opportunistic procurer of the mercenary companies gained a vast personal fortune.

Throughout history, mercenary armies are a common factor found at the initial phase of building up an economic empire that later becomes a legitimate structure. They are also valuable to others who use their services at arm's length. Like the Pope at Avignon, these greater powers can reduce their own domestic security risks and, simultaneously, secure a strategic foreign victory through the activities of mercenary forces. In the same way, after independence was granted to African countries in the mid-20th century, mercenary forces such as those commanded by Denard and Schramme acted in the interests of European powers while backing African politicians. Mercenaries have thus covertly and in a deniable way, served their native state's foreign political agendas.

EO and the new mercenary companies are therefore modern manifestations of an old phenomenon. Instead of medieval battle dress, these new *condottieri* wear Savile Row suits and carry satellite telephones. In EO's case, they may even own major weapon systems such as attack helicopters. Key new developments in the private military business are: the wide range and sophisticated nature of the security-related services on offer; an apparent wide demand for their services; the transnational nature of their operations; a complex corporate and military organisation; a determined campaign to gain international credibility; and the diverse range of hidden corporate, financial and political powers that fund their operations. Determining the above are the new, global forces discussed elsewhere in this book by Lock, Cornwell and Cilliers.

Hired armies lessen the risks for petroleum and mineral companies with business interests in resource-rich Africa. While the high risks of exploration and mining in Angola, for example, are unattractive to large mining houses, who are sensitive to their public profile and to shareholder sentiment, the potential for earning quick and extraordinarily high profits make these risks worthwhile for an exploration company. The rules of the high-risk junior mining game lie in first procuring and then marketing the concessions in such a way that they are attractive to the larger mining concerns to whom the concessions can be sold. At the second and more legitimate tier of this commercial strategy, an established mining company with real investment potential moves in. Far from becoming obsolete, the private security company who partnered with the exploration company in securing the concession, can now win a follow-on contract with the mining group. The junior who has sold the concessions takes a percentage of the mining and, in some cases, also the security profits. In this way, the proprietors of military firms like EO, who are paid in cash by major strategic resource corporations and given rights to land and mineral concessions by political leaders, are not unlike the *condottieri* of the 14th and 15th centuries.

21st Century *condottieri*: A consolidated corporate army

A corporate army is defined here as a privately owned military group whose finances, personnel, offensive operations, air wing division and logistics are all handled within a single group or through interlinked companies and enterprises. In its most basic form, it would be managed by a common pool of directors and have a small permanent corps of staff, serving its own commercial interests and those of affiliated entities. Such a group of companies would typically be owned, organised, paid and deployed by the controlling shareholders of one or more private companies which, in turn, may be transnational conglomerates. As such, the traditionally state-owned powers and instruments for effecting political and social change through the use of force are transferred through privatisation to a corporate entity or group. These powerful entities function at both a corporate, suprastate and the transnational level thus transferring the powers of a global city-state to a corporate group that is essentially accountable only to laws of profit and those of supply and demand.[7]

This article will show how EO started out as a covert front company for its national defence force and was later used to recruit military personnel for Angolan support operations. Under the primary control of a group of British-based entrepreneurs (consisting of former élite British soldiers and foreign businessmen), a consortium of military-related and mineral companies was established. EO formed a key military component in this group and its directors became shareholders in a number of the affiliated companies. EO grew into a veritable private military giant between 1994 and 1997 whose operations in Africa were facilitated by these affiliated companies. As such, EO was only the most visible part of the consortium and press reports often confused the identity of the consortium with EO. In certain cases, it would have been more accurate to refer to the 'EO-related group of companies' or the EO group. In this article, the term 'EO group' refers to the consortium of security and mineral companies with common shareholders and paymasters whose day-to-day business was closely affiliated with EO's military operations. Between 1994 and 1998, this network included anything from thirty to fifty companies. Although EO has announced its closure, new military companies have taken its place and the consortium continues to do business.

Since its inception almost a decade ago, EO has shown itself to be an adaptive military entity that mutates and reincarnates itself when the political environment changes and when it encounters challenging or hostile influences. Underpinning this mutation is an aggressive and competitive marketing strategy to survive both as a private army and as a corporation. Key to its business strategy has been the drive to gain greater legitimacy in order to become an international peace enforcement agency

Phase 1: 1989 – 1992

Between 1989 and 1992, EO was a faithful agent of the former apartheid state and a privatised part of its 'total onslaught' war machine. It operated as a small closed corporation (cc) with only two directors and a fast-dwindling bank account after the CCB, the state's covert special forces organisation, was closed in 1990.[8] This secret unit targeted ANC leaders for surveillance and possible elimination. When these activities were exposed in the late 1980s, the CCB was officially disbanded.

EO was set up in 1989 as an intelligence training unit for SADF special forces. It was run by Luther Eben Barlow, previously a lieutenant-colonel with military intelligence and a senior CCB member.[9] Barlow was head of an external CCB cell that is allegedly tied to the murder of ANC activists in Europe. Barlow was also engaged in sanction-busting efforts in Europe which brokered the procurement of military equipment on behalf of the SADF. EO's origins, like many private security and intelligence companies operating in South Africa today, are therefore to be found in the complex and still shielded web of civilianised front companies set up by the former SADF.

The military services provided by this early version of the future EO giant are interesting, because it has consistently denied that such services are provided. In a 1992 proposal, EO offered the following:

- support services for "... *clandestine warfare operations*";

- training of "... *freedom fighters*" (in other words, insurgency forces);

- procurement of "... *any*" weapons and equipment;

- the conducting of "... *clandestine sabotage actions*"; ·

- conducting of "... *specific harassment operations within enemy rear-areas*";

- conducting of "... *political propaganda operations*"; and

- waging of "... *total guerrilla warfare behind enemy-lines.*"[10]

The EO proposal also states: "*The deployment of a well-trained, well-equipped and well-led element of Freedom Fighters can greatly assist a Sponsor in attaining the tactical and strategic advantage in an Area of Operations [sic].*"[11] During this early phase, EO developed a business relationship with the mining sector and, in particular, with the diamond world, including the Anglo American and De Beers conglomerate.[12]

Phase 2: 1993

In 1993, EO executed its first significant military operation and thereby led the charge of the new corporate brigades into Africa.[13]

Two former British special service officers with oil interests in Africa hired Barlow and a colleague to recruit a band of mercenaries for two month's work in north-western Angola in January 1993. The operation sounded simple – capture and defend valuable oil tanks at Kefekwena and then do the same for the oil town of Soyo which had been overrun by the troops of Jonas Savimbi's *União Nacional para a Independência Total de Angola* (UNITA). Barlow brought in Lafras Luitingh, a former CCB cell leader who had been touting for private security contracts in Luanda in 1992 while he evaded South African authorities who wanted him for questioning in connection with the murder of anthropologist and ANC activist, David Webster in Johannesburg in 1989.

Barlow and Luitingh recruited as many of their former 32 Battalion, CCB and 'Recce' friends as they could and departed for Soyo with half the numbers that had been requested. An operation that was regarded as a cinch turned into a pitched battle once the South Africans were deployed. Thousands of UNITA troops had moved into the area. Several mercenaries were wounded and three died in action. Over two dozen chose to terminate their contracts and were evacuated after just a few days. The remaining men – including Luitingh who led one of the three fighting groups – chose to stay on. For their perseverance, they were paid a bonus of $3 000 by their client, former British officer, Anthony Buckingham. Buckingham is a senior board advisor to several North American oil companies and the founder and chief executive officer of Heritage Oil and Gas in London.[14] Barlow and

Buckingham told the mercenaries that payment would be made by Buckingham from offices in London and would be deposited by Barlow into the men's local bank accounts.[15] After two months, the reduced force of EO mercenaries were extracted. Although UNITA subsequently reclaimed the area, EO did succeed in controlling it while deployed. Barlow and Luitingh had secured not only a sizeable sum of cash, but had also won the opportunity to sell EO.

In early 1993, UNITA troop columns were marching on the Angolan capital, Luanda. With its oil resources under threat and its back against the sea, the *Movimento Popular de Libertação de Angola* (MPLA) government was ready to accept outside assistance – especially from forces with a firsthand knowledge of UNITA. In the early 1980s, Barlow was the deputy commander of the long-range reconnaisance wing of 32 Battalion – a crucial component of the SADF's operations in Angola conducted in support of UNITA.[16] A deal was struck – negotiated by Buckingham and his colleague, former British Special Air Service (SAS) officer Simon Mann – whereby the state-owned oil entity SONANGOL would partly finance the mercenary support operations and, in turn, the project leaders of EO would work closely with their former enemy, the *Forças Armados Angolanos* (FAA) and its military chief, General João de Matos. EO set about planning a more thorough mission. They recruited more carefully and established a highly successful support operation in Angola that enabled the FAA government forces to claim a decisive military victory in late 1994. In November 1994, representatives of Savimbi and the Angolan president, José Eduardo dos Santos, signed the <u>Lusaka Peace Accord</u> and full-blown war was temporarily averted.

Phase 3: British principals and African commanders, 1993 – 1995

EO's two-and-a-half year contract with the Angolan government earned the company over US $40 million per year and several lucrative oil and diamond concessions. Angola gave EO the necessary capital and the wartime opportunity to establish itself as a powerful corporate army. Front-line combat operations of the cost, scale and level of sophistication that EO deployed in Angola are not commonly available. It used this military contract to diversify and establish a range of related companies.

Between 1993 and 1995, EO adopted several aggressive corporate strategies. It sought to align itself politically with the new ANC government.[17] It also expanded, diversified and reincarnated itself as a full-fledged private army. British operations were established under EO (UK) Limited, registered in London during September 1993.[18] Barlow registered EO as a private limited company in South Africa in 1994.[19] He also set up a holding company called Strategic Resources Corporation (SRC) which was registered in South Africa in 1995.

Corporate and military expansion occurred under two main branches: South African-managed operations conducted under the parent company SRC in Pretoria were controlled by EO directors; and UK-managed operations conducted out of London offices were controlled by Buckingham, Mann and a group of directors who ran Heritage Oil and a new company called Branch Energy, which served as EO's mineral counterpart until late 1996.

SOUTH AFRICAN WEB OF COMPANIES
1995 & 1996

STRATEGIC RESOURCE CORPORATION (SRC)

1 Executive Outcomes cc 1989 CC 1993, (Pty) Ltd 1995

2 Cross Swords Holdings (Pty) Ltd

3 OPM Support systems (crime & intelligence)

4 Saracen (security – Angola/Uganda/SA)

5 Ibis Air/Ibis Ltd

6 Capricorn Systems – 50%

7 Branch Mining Ltd (Angola – 40%)

8 RANGOL Medical (Pty) Ltd & Stuart Mills

9 Trans Africa Logistics (Pty) Ltd – 100%

10 Military Technical Services (MTS)

11 Gemini Video Productions (music & videos)

12 Advanced Systems Communication Ltd (telecommunications)

13 Shibata Ltd – 60% (demining)

14 New Africa Informatics (Pty) Ltd

15 Livingstone Tourists (tourism)

16 The Explorer (travel & tourism)

17 Steelpact & Falconer Systems (equipment)

18 Aquanova Ltd – 33,3% (Zambia, exploration equipment)

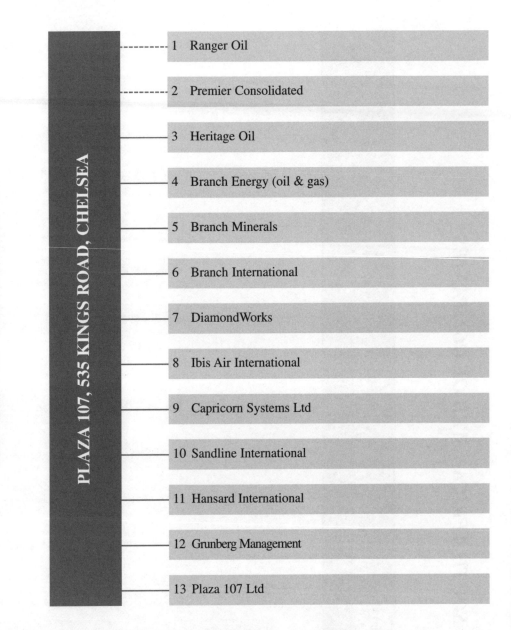

UK WEB OF COMPANIES AT:

PLAZA 107, 535 KINGS ROAD, CHELSEA

1 Ranger Oil

2 Premier Consolidated

3 Heritage Oil

4 Branch Energy (oil & gas)

5 Branch Minerals

6 Branch International

7 DiamondWorks

8 Ibis Air International

9 Capricorn Systems Ltd

10 Sandline International

11 Hansard International

12 Grunberg Management

13 Plaza 107 Ltd

As a military force, EO grew in size and operational capabilities. Its stock of military hardware increased. Entities within the EO group procured a private fleet of troop and cargo carriers and a light aircraft fitted with sophisticated surveillance equipment. On behalf of the Angolan government, they procured and deployed aircraft that included Soviet-issue Mi-24 helicopter gunships, converted Mi-17 troop-carriers and L-39 trainer jet fighters. They also set up a charter airline with several light aircraft and two Boeing 727 carriers that operated out of Johannesburg International Airport and Malta. These aircraft were owned by Ibis Air and Techline Resources Limited – based in Cyprus and the south of England.[20] The executive officers of Ibis included Buckingham, Mann, Luitingh and Barlow. Ibis-owned planes have had frequent access to airports in South Africa, England, the Middle East, Malta, Cyprus, and several African countries. EO also established and absorbed a multitude of other privatised military and civilian companies within the SRC holding company. The EO group's website has been reported to include between thirty to fifty affiliated or subsidiary companies, but an exact number has not been confirmed.

Ironically, while EO carefully concealed core aspects of its war business, it adopted a highly successful international media campaign between 1994 and 1997. In 1994, EO began conducting media tours of their operations in Angola, hosting many domestic and international media groups – including CNN, Sky and BBC, as well as foreign correspondents from many of the world's major newspapers. Journalists (no visas needed) were flown from Johannesburg directly to Angolan military bases. Once in Angola, they were briefed by Barlow and senior intelligence officers (who acted as media managers). and were shown EO/FAA training. Barlow and his men constantly refuted all reports of EO's active involvement in the war. They also denied having any relationship with mining operations and strictly controlled journalists' access.[21] Similar tours were conducted in Sierra Leone and later planned for Papua New Guinea. News coverage of its activities in Angola, Sierra Leone and even Papua New Guinea ensured that EO remained highly visible for four years and that it was seen to operate in several war-theatres. EO promotional brochures and a corporate video – produced by their in-house facility, Gemini Video Productions – were distributed to journalists to use in their reports. In the process, Barlow and Luitingh were established as experts in the private war business and the media attention they received, helped to sell EO as a global military brand and as the best-known transnational mercenary firm in history.

Buckingham and his London-based associates had established Branch Energy to manage the mineral concessions awarded to them. Branch Energy still operates out of a suite of offices at Plaza 107, Kings Road, Chelsea, and is formally incorporated in the Bahamas. In 1995, Branch Energy acquired gold, diamond and other mineral concessions in six African countries: Angola, Uganda, north-eastern Kenya, Sierra Leone, Mozambique and Tanzania – "... a portfolio of prime exploration properties covering an area of some 35,000 sq km."[22] A company inventory for the Branch group claims that, in 1996, it was considering mining ventures that would increase its property portfolio by more than double the number. In addition, the prospectus describes the Branch Energy group as having a significant competitive advantage over its rivals:

- It has a "... pan-African communication network" that enables it to bypass the logistical problems of operating in Africa. This includes the "... provision of aircraft for the transport of personnel and supplies and an established procurement infrastructure for the distribution of equipment and consumables."

- The mineral group is capable of operating in "... politically sensitive and high risk security regions [and] has the ability to secure its own and other's assets in extremely confrontational situations."[23]

During this period, Barlow, Luitingh and Nico Palm, a former weapons procurement manager at ARMSCOR, set up a number of corresponding companies and offices outside South Africa to facilitate this pan-African system.[24] The companies were each registered as a separate corporate entity – which Barlow and the other directors insisted were not directly connected to EO. The group's aviation firm, Ibis Air, was also registered in Angola and Kenya; the demining and security company, Saracen International was registered in Uganda and Tanzania; and Branch Energy was registered as a local company in Angola, Sierra Leone, Uganda and Kenya. In these local variants, partnerships were extended to local politicians and influential power-brokers to secure the group's business interests.[25] To further occlude matters, the key companies such as EO, SRC and their cornucopia of sister and affiliated companies are registered in offshore locations where their true directorships and financial details are concealed.[26]

In London, a similar web of companies can be found at the Heritage Oil and Branch Energy offices at Plaza 107. Over fifteen companies operate from this suite, share the same telephone numbers and the same UK-based directors and personnel. This clandestine approach to business enables EO and its British principals to operate and benefit from a hidden empire of corporate and military companies. In this sense, EO is only the visible tip of a great iceberg of interconnected and related corporations. The private companies function in the same way that the main support structures of a formal defence force would – only on a much smaller scale. They supply the mercenary component, namely EO, with all the services it needs to function as a private army. These include an air attack wing, logistical supplies, a small medical corps, weapons and equipment procurements, technical support systems, strategic, aerial, tactical and counterintelligence sections, infiltration of enemy or rival groups, sophisticated surveillance capabilities, demolition, demining and associated engineering services, recruitment of personnel and, of course, financing.

In addition to this military capability, EO's operations facilitated the granting of some of the richest diamond concessions in the world, valued at over US $3 billion.[27] EO directors also expanded into civilian sectors through trade, transport, construction, tourism and mining equipment companies. As well as tendering for civilian contracts through their civilian fronts, EO principals have also acted as local brokers for large transnational corporations wanting to secure contracts in the construction, aviation, telecommunication, information technology, financial, fuel and mining sectors.[28] As a result, EO was a vastly transformed organisation by the beginning of 1996, and could no longer be seen simply as an independent military company. It was a crucial unit within a greater military and corporate whole and its directors were dominant figures in a web of interconnected companies that shared directors, personnel, contracts and clients.[29] As Vancouver-based financial analyst, Adrian du Plessis said of the mining and military companies: *"[The directors] are always keen to say, 'You can't show there's a corporate relationship ... But it's just ... a word game because essentially you have the same people involved on both sides.*"[30]

Phase 4: Problems and solutions, 1996-1997

Between 1996 and 1997, EO encountered several commercial threats. International pressure resulting from its role in a country such as Angola, was rising, it experienced increasing cash-flow problems to fund its operations in Sierra Leone, and was confronted by the proposed legislation in South Africa, aimed at outlawing mercenaries and controlling the provision of security services.

In 1996, EO was forced to relinquish a lucrative contract with the Angolan government following pressure from the US government and calls from the United Nations for its withdrawal. To avoid pulling out entirely and to capitalise on the commercial opportunities that had opened up in the Angolan market, it utilised other private companies to protect and continue its interests. A few of these are:

- **Saracen International** – which tenders for a wide range of security and military contracts including the clearing of landmines. Saracen is registered and based in South Africa, as well as offshore. It operates in a number of African countries, including Angola, Uganda, Rwanda, Tanzania, and Mozambique.

- **Bridge Resources International** – which provides reconstruction and development services.

- **OPM Support Systems Limited** – a South African registered security and private intelligence company which is headed by senior former officers of the South African Police and which operates both internally and in African countries. OPM recruits both former SADF intelligence and police counterintelligence officers. It offers a wide range of services that range from offensive intelligence gathering, organised crime prevention projects, VIP protection and airport privatisation schemes.

- **Stuart Mills International** – a professional medical unit staffed by former SADF medical officers that provides field medical assistance to the EO group's fighting troops. It is also involved in developing medical care schemes in African countries, and has secured contracts to establish and equip clinics in Angola and Rwanda.[31]

- **Advanced Systems Communications** – registered in South Africa and England. It supplies satellite communications, designs and manufactures communication systems and has tendered for contracts to supply telecommunications systems in Africa.

- **Trans Africa Logistics** – provides logistical support to all the affiliated companies in Africa.[32]

Through companies like these, EO and the SRC group have established and retained a considerable grip on key sectors of the Angolan economy.[33]

In 1996, EO ran into further problems when it shifted its core military forces from Angola into Sierra Leone where Buckingham had secured a two-part deal with the ruling military junta.[34] This involved the deployment of mercenary forces to drive the Revolutionary United Front (RUF) rebels from strategic mining areas in the east of the country in return for significant diamond concessions.[35] However, during the eighteen months that EO operated in Sierra Leone, the company was paid less than a third of its total fee.[36] EO found itself strapped for cash and had to cut back on staff. The company reportedly used Angolan profits to fund the Sierra Leone military operations.

That same year, Buckingham approached a high-risk mining entrepreneur and, at the time, one of Canada's wealthiest men, Robert Friedland. A fast-talking penny stocks promoter,

Friedland had hit an unexpected jackpot two years earlier when his junior exploration company, Diamond Field Resources, discovered the richest nickel deposits in history in Canada's Voisey's Bay.[37] Friedland was paid $400 million for his stake in Diamond Fields and moved his office from Vancouver to Singapore where he set up a "... *dizzying array of high-risk mining ventures*" through his private holding company, Ivanhoe Capital Investments.[38] The move to Singapore saved Friedland and his new-found fortune from legal procedures brought against him by US authorities who were trying to recover the costs of a massive environmental disaster he had caused in Summitville.[39]

With ventures in China, Burma and Indonesia, Friedland was a known high-risk mining opportunist who "... *thrives in countries that have dodgy governments that are reputed to be corrupt.*"[40] Friedland and Buckingham came to an agreement whereby Branch Energy's diamond concessions in Angola and Sierra Leone were merged with Carson Gold Corporation which had gold mining interests in the Far East, Venezuela and North America. Friedland provided an injection of capital, at least $24 million, in exchange for Branch Energy's diamond concessions. As a result, a new company called DiamondWorks Limited was formed in late 1996 with Buckingham as the controlling member.[41]

A list of DiamondWorks' major shareholders provides a clear linkage between the two groups of military and mining companies. In 1997, in addition to Buckingham, the following were listed as shareholders:

- Tim Spicer, the head of the UK-based military company, Sandline International, who subcontracted EO to conduct military operations in Papua New Guinea in 1997;

- Michael Grunberg, a British chartered accountant who is head of finances for the group; and

- Eben Barlow, who bought his shares in February 1997.[42]

DiamondWorks quickly claimed that it was a prominent diamond producer in Angola – the richest diamond-producing state after Botswana.[43] In May 1997, it announced an expansion of its African properties and added prospecting rights in the Republic of Congo, Namibia, Botswana and Senegal to its growing portfolio.[44]

Interestingly, when its links with mercenary armies and disreputable governments were publicly disclosed in media reports in 1997, DiamondWorks did not suffer any serious setbacks to its mineral business. As Correy pointed out, "... *[mercenaries] are opportunists. It is problems with geology that drives down the cost of shares, not association with mercenaries. In fact when DiamondWorks' connection to mercenaries was made public in Canada, the share prices went up immediately. The risks may be high, but so are the potential profits.*"[45]

By early 1997, EO had proved itself militarily in both Angola and Sierra Leone, but it still had not secured international credibility for its operations. As a mercenary organisation, its continued presence in both Angola and, arguably, Sierra Leone hampered the conclusion of a peace accord. It also presented a problem to governments wishing to secure financial aid from international bodies like the World Bank and the International Monetary Fund (IMF). Despite having provided emergency evacuation services to UN staff members and escort services to humanitarian aid organisations in Sierra Leone, EO could not shake off its mercenary identity.

In 1996, British principals at the London offices formed a new military company, Sandline International. As the British equivalent to EO, Sandline provides the same military services, but it has a more sanitised image. It is commanded by a respected former British officer with a distinguished record, Lieutenant-Colonel Timothy Spicer from the Scots Guards battalion, who had participated in the Falklands campaign of 1982 and had received an OBE for service in Northern Ireland. In 1991, Spicer spent six months as a military assistant to General Sir Peter de la Billiere, the most senior British officer in the Gulf War. He also served in Bosnia as a senior aide to General Sir Michael Rose in 1995/96. Upon his retirement, Spicer began a new career as the head of Sandline International.[46] Sandline is registered in the Bahamas and is headquartered at the smart, glass-fronted offices of Branch Energy and Heritage Oil in Chelsea.[47] It also has offices and representation in the US, headed by Bernie McCabe, a former officer in the US Army Special Forces. Sandline claims to have engaged in six operations since 1993 and has admitted that it frequently subcontracted EO to do the work.[48] Curiously, Sandline was only incorporated in 1996 and its known operations have always been linked to the EO group. It would therefore appear that Sandline is a newer and more sanitised version of EO. A measure of the impact of these companies can be seen in the fact that both Sandline and EO were invited to a US closed-door conference sponsored by the Defense Intelligence Agency (DIA) in 1997. Both Barlow and Spicer attended the event and were generally regarded as the key protagonists of an "... *activity … [that] is going to greatly increase during the next few years.*"[49]

Sandline first drew public attention in the mineral-rich islands of Papua New Guinea where it secured a contract to quell a nine-year armed independence movement in 1997. Sandline claimed that it had subcontracted EO to provide the necessary armed forces and logistics for the military contract.[50] In February 1997, about seventy EO soldiers were deployed with a few British officers. At the time, Spicer and EO directors claimed that the contract only provided for strategic advisory and training services. They also claimed that there was no direct relationship between EO and Sandline. But the military group was destined to see a serious setback – described by one military analyst as 'EO's Vietnam'. Spicer and two senior EO officers were arrested and held for several days by military leaders who staged an army mutiny against the government. The mercenaries were later expelled from the Pacific island state and Spicer was charged with possession of a 9mm pistol and 41 rounds of ammunition. To make matters worse, the Papua New Guinea government was forced to resign. A confidential contract signed by Buckingham and the government was subsequently leaked to the press and quickly found its way onto the Internet.[51] The contract and resulting public inquiry into Sandline revealed direct corporate connections between Sandline International and Buckingham, on the one hand, and Sandline International and EO, on the other. It also revealed that the Papua New Guinea government made payment for the Sandline contract into a Hong Kong bank account owned by both Barlow and Buckingham.[52]

Shortly after the Papua New Guinea debacle, Sierra Leone was also seized by a paroxysm of war and destruction in the wake of a military *coup* staged by former National

Provisional Ruling Council (NPRC) officers early in 1997. Nigerian-led forces of the Economic Community of West African States Monitoring Group (ECOMOG) laid siege to and attacked the capital in a bid to oust the military junta. EO's former enemy, the RUF, joined sides with the *coup* plotters and a vicious eight-month battle ensued in the capital. In the wake of EO's involvement in both Papua New Guinea and Sierra Leone, both countries saw greater violence and unrest ensue.

In Sierra Leone, EO trained, armed and used traditional hunters known as the 'Kamajors'. In 1995, at an early stage of their involvement in Sierra Leone, EO identified the traditional hunters as a useful alternative to the Bushmen trackers used by the SADF in northern Namibia in the 1970s and '80s.[53] Not only could the Kamajors provide the necessary tracking skills to penetrate thick jungle, but the hunter society, which is spread across the strife-torn land, could also provide useful tactical intelligence to the South Africans. With their warrior cult beliefs and hunting habits, the Kamajors were eager to co-operate, since they were not highly regarded by the government military troops who were less interested in fighting than they were in commandeering. During 1995 and 1996, EO equipped the Kamajors with ammunition and radio communications and deployed them as part of their ground attack forces when carrying out air and ground offensives on rebel bases hidden in the tropical jungle.[54]

The chief of the Kamajors, Captain Hinja Norman was later appointed as the Deputy Minister of Defence under the new civilian president, Tejan Kabbah. After the military *coup* in May 1997, EO and Sandline were both involved in the training of thousands of Kamajors who fought alongside the Nigerian-led ECOMOG forces and who were instrumental in the ousting of the military junta in mid-1998.[55] It remains to be seen whether Sierra Leone will survive the meddling of foreign military forces in its mineral-rich and war-devastated land. The involvement of the EO group in Sierra Leone between 1995 and 1997 needs to be carefully examined in the light of its consequences. EO trained groups of inept soldiers to become far more capable fighters and some of these men later seized power after EO's departure. This in itself could not be blamed on EO, since Sierra Leone has experienced several military *coups*. The heavy air attacks that EO carried out on rebel-held areas and which killed both civilians and rebels fuelled the fury of the RUF leaders who were not easily overcome in their bases hidden in the rainforest. The role of 'peace-enforcing', which EO is so keen to claim for itself, cannot be achieved by operations that are primarily targeted at reclaiming strategic resources and which essentially service the commercial interests of mining companies.

A final problem for EO in 1997, was the drafting of new legislation by the ANC government to ban mercenarism and regulate foreign military support in South Africa. Under pressure from international human rights groups who had monitored five years of press reports on EO's activities, the South African government drafted a tough new Act to clamp down on mercenarism. The new legislation rules that any South African or permanent resident or any company registered or incorporated in South Africa that wishes to provide any type of foreign military assistance (including medical, logistical, advice, training, intelligence, support or any other action that has a military benefit) to a party that is involved in an armed conflict, must obtain authorisation from the National Conventional Arms Control Committee

(NCACC). Authorisation to supply foreign military assistance is a two-step process – first, the applicant must obtain permission from the NCACC to offer its services to foreign clients and, after the contract has been approved, the applicant must reapply for permission to supply its services. The penalty for operating without the state's approval is harsh and can result in the seizure of assets, as well as fines in excess of $150 000 (R1 million) or ten years in jail, or both.

Publicly, EO welcomed the legislation, stating that it was not a mercenary organisation and therefore had nothing to fear. Privately, it sought extensive legal advice. In addition, EO lobbied about fifty top resource corporations with interests in Africa to sensitise them to the broader implications of the proposed new Act and rally support for opposition to certain clauses.

As a result of the new legislation, EO began unbundling and restructuring itself. EO's top guns – Luitingh (operations manager) and Barlow (chairman) – announced their 'resignations' from the firm in mid-1997. Both Barlow and Luitingh admitted that they would continue acting as consultants to EO when necessary. Sources close to EO were sceptical about Barlow and Luitingh's departures. According to one former EO employee, *"... [t]hese moves are prompted by the new bill. They are simply removing the guts of the company to place it elsewhere where it can function in the same way."*[56]

Barlow was replaced by Nick van den Bergh, a former paratrooper with the SADF who had a less controversial history of military service with the SADF, since he had no known links to the CCB. Van den Bergh was a project manager for EO during the first Angolan contract and served the same role in Papua New Guinea where he was arrested and held captive with Tim Spicer. According to Van den Bergh, Barlow and Luitingh had not sold their shares in EO, but had awarded it to him as part of a remuneration package. There had therefore been no transfer or sale of shares or of company assets.[57]

Barlow retained ownership of SRC, the holding company, as well as EO (UK) and Advanced Communications Systems.[58] In addition to these, Barlow is still a registered director of several other companies attached to the EO complex. In late 1997 and early 1998, he moved his operations offshore and was reported to be working out of the Branch Energy offices in Chelsea.[59] He has maintained his business links with the Angolan and Ugandan governments where Saracen and other affiliates operate. Barlow has also retained the services of EO employees and former ANC intelligence officers to assist with his strategic planning operations in North Africa (Morocco and Algeria).[60]

Luitingh focused his business operations in Angola where tensions were rising between UNITA and the MPLA. In late 1997, he was reported to have secured a new deal with the FAA for a 'surgical operation' in UNITA territory and had deployed dozens of members of the core fighting group that EO previously recruited and deployed in Angola, Sierra Leone and Papua New Guinea.[61] Luitingh's team have also conducted air reconnaissance operations, one of which led to the forced landing of a UNITA supply plane and the arrest of its South African pilots in early 1998.

Phase 5: Recent developments and renewed attempts to win international legitimacy, 1998

EO underwent significant corporate changes in 1998, prior to the decision to close the company with effect from 1 January 1999. In response to both new legislation that has tightened South Africa's control of mercenarism and new developments in the mining and private military industry, the consortium reconfigured itself and altered its *modus operandi*. Several affiliates were closed or 'sold' and a number of key personnel moved to separate businesses. The web of entities was therefore dissected so that the most powerful components and shareholders remain hidden. By December 1998, EO still worked out of its suburban offices in Pretoria, but its permanent staff had been reduced to a mere handful. It was no longer the giant of earlier days and did not publicise any of its operations. Upon termination, Van den Berg has established a new company, NFD (Proprietary) Limited, which now operates from offices in Centurion, while a number of former senior EO staff are seeking alternative employment. Since EO is registered in the UK and offshore, it is likely to continue operating both as an international company and through Sandline.

EO was the first entity in the group to establish an Internet website in mid-1997. The website enables the military group to recruit soldiers discreetly in South Africa and around the globe. As Kader Asmal, the Minister of Water Affairs and Forestry and chairperson of the NCACC, pointed out when presenting the <u>Regulation of Foreign Military Assistance Act</u> in Parliament in February 1998: "... *[a] mere website on the Internet can raise an army, from a dirty dozen to a brigade far more effectively than any previous form of press gang.*"[62]

EO's most visible recent security contract was with farmers in the Eastern Cape in South Africa where it operated a rapid reaction helicopter service to protect assets and livestock in the Lesotho border region. In addition, EO admitted to having several smaller military projects in Africa that utilise small groups of men.[63] Contracts with such personnel are signed for short periods – usually three months – with the option of renewal. Employees are often not told where they are going and are unsure of the identity of the client. Strict secrecy is enforced and names of the new security fronts are not readily available. Contracts with clients are now secured by individual consultants – rather than a group of directors linked to a specific company. This ensures that corporate ownership remains hidden. The EO group's present activity in Africa is therefore hidden by a brokerage system and new fronts in a complex web of affiliated corporations.[64] Today, it is harder to identify where and what is still active, who their clients are, how they are organised and which corporate entities are involved than ever before. While EO may no longer formally exist in South Africa, the industry continues to expand and, as it grows in complexity and sophistication, is increasingly hard to monitor.

In 1998, EO's former CEO, Van den Bergh, pointed out that despite the new legislation, EO would still be able to operate in foreign countries.

"The crux of the new bill [is] to regulate foreign military assistance to parties involved in armed conflict. So, as far as I'm concerned, if I'm not going to support any party involved in armed conflict then I don't need to apply for permission or authorisation ... If a country like

the United States wants to contract me to provide a specific service for them, why would I need to ask the government's permission? Because that is not regulated by this bill."[65]

As seen recently in Sierra Leone, EO's military operations have increasingly been taken over by Sandline. As long as EO or an alternative entity within the EO group is subcontracted to Sandline, its services to foreign clients should escape legal scrutiny. In addition, it will be very difficult to enforce the Act since South Africa's notoriously high crime rate is already stretching law enforcement agencies and the judiciary beyond their capabilities. It is very difficult to police "... *mercenaries who are able to create offshore companies and simply shift the locus of their activity outside South Africa.*"[66]

In 1998, Van den Bergh expected EO to continue operating successfully and that it would secure official contracts with the UN, the Organisation of African Unity (OAU) and even the South African National Defence Force (SANDF).[67] "*It's part of our strategy to engage in discussions with the UN and tell them who we are and what we can do; and where and when we can provide a service for them which will be much cheaper than what they can do on the ground ... We can do a better job than the UN for about 10 percent of the cost.*"[68]

But EO's controversial and mercenary reputation prevented it from securing the legitimacy and confidentiality it needed since South Africa passed the <u>Regulation of Foreign Military Assistance Act</u> in early 1998. The consortium of companies described above as the EO group, therefore had to divest itself of this liability and over a period of about two years, its executives set in place the necessary corporate moves to achieve this. The consortium may have become smaller, but it has not closed its doors. Companies such as Sandline International, Saracen International, OPM, Bridge Resources and LifeGuard – to name a few – continue to sell their military-related services to clients in Africa. EO's rural operations that provide security to farmers will also continue, according to Van den Bergh.[69]

Overview of services provided by EO and its military-related affiliates in Africa

Since EO was part of a greater network of security and mining affiliates, it is perhaps more useful to describe its services in the context of the growing private security market. During its six years as a dominant player in this field, the EO group expanded and adapted its range of services to meet new demands in the market. When government clients requested a service that EO could not supply, its principals still tendered for the contract and then drew from a vast pool of military and security expertise in South Africa, Britain or any other country to supply these services. EO could therefore subcontract either a second firm or relevant experts to provide the necessary services.[70]

Offensive or mercenary operations contracted by governments

Very few of the prominent private military and security companies operating in Africa can deploy full-scale combat operations. In addition, contracts of the size, scale and cost that EO had with the MPLA government between 1993 and 1995, are very rare.

Military contracts of the type deployed in Angola, and to a lesser extent in Sierra Leone between 1994-1996, therefore constitute the smallest wedge at the extreme of the private security market. But such contracts are also the most lucrative – not only because of the high price-tag attached, but because they provide access to profitable mineral rights. Government contracts afford the mercenary leaders direct contact with the most powerful political structures in the client country. This allows them to:

- secure payment in the form of strategic mineral and oil concessions;

- earn greater, long term incomes from the concessions which are worth far more than the military contract fees;

- secure other business contracts with the host government;

- broker deals on behalf of transnational companies wishing to gain access to the indigenous economy; and

- act as agents of influence for foreign governments, non-governmental organisations (NGOs), business corporations and international or regional organisations like the OAU, the Southern African Development Community (SADC), ECOMOG and the UN.

Government contracts for mercenary services are therefore the key means by which a corporate empire is quickly developed. EO was clearly the recognised leader in this field – despite its insistence that it only advised and trained armed forces.

Sandline International is also included in this category and it frequently subcontracts South Africans from the EO group to provide the manpower and logistical services required by its clients. Sandline claims that it only accepts recognised governments and international organisations as clients.[71] In this category of services, Sandline advertises the following: *"Operations that provide reaction forces, special operations forces, and air operations ... [as well as] ... Combat Service support in hostile environments."*[72] In Papua New Guinea, Sandline agreed to purchase and deploy an air force of Mi-17 and Mi-24 attack helicopters, as well as 57mm rocket launchers and AGS-17 grenade launcher systems.[73]

Mercenary contracts are kept secret – unlike training contracts. EO and other private military companies have confidentiality clauses written into their contracts with both client governments and their hired forces. It is therefore difficult to ascertain how many offensive operations Sandline and the EO group have undertaken. What is certain is that there is an increasing demand for foreign military support in conflict-torn parts of the world, especially in Central Africa.

Newly emerging South African companies are increasingly entering this narrow end of the market. The former Stabilco – which secured contracts with the former Mobutu government in 1997 and which was almost entirely staffed by former EO soldiers – is one example. Many of these companies seemed to be both associated with EO and, at the same time, rivals. The exact nature of the relationships between these firms remains unclear and can at best be described as fickle – depending on the availability of work. Many other South African-based military companies have been set up by former EO personnel or were rejuvenated out of the past network of front companies set up by the former SADF. Another example is Military Technical Services (MTS) which was set up in 1989 under retired Major-General Tai Minnaar, and procures Soviet-issue helicopters and provides private military services. Although some companies, like MTS, have the same business interests, cross shareholdings and even shared personnel, EO directors denied that they were associated with these companies. In addition, they claimed that these companies were falsely using the name of EO in order to win contracts. This is yet another confusing aspect of the recent proliferation of private military companies in South Africa.[74]

An alarming factor is that many of these rival or formerly affiliated firms are selling military services and weapons to insurgent forces opposed to governments that have contracted the EO group. This is a concerning development, since South African soldiers who previously fought side by side in the SADF are now conducting offensives against one another in foreign battlefields. In Angola, South African-based military firms and former SADF special forces soldiers are supporting UNITA troops.[75] The MPLA government is also militarily assisted by South African personnel who formerly worked for EO, but who now fall under Luitingh's 'separate' employ. In early 1998, Luanda-based sources reported that mercenaries deployed by Luitingh were training for a joint government and mercenary forces operation against UNITA strongholds and its remaining rear bases. An L-39 trainer jet fighter procured by EO personnel in Angola in 1994 was deployed during this time to obstruct South African-flown aircraft delivering supplies to UNITA-held capitals.

Combat operations by South Africans against other South African mercenary companies are increasingly possible in Angola and Central Africa. At the time of writing, no significant offensive of this nature had yet occurred. But the longer term implications are worrying. Many of the South Africans who support UNITA, ally themselves to an apartheid regime ideology, while supporters of the MPLA government generally subscribe to the new order.

Private military companies like EO, who can and will conduct offensive operations, are extremely useful to governments and parties who cannot publicly disclose their support of a beleaguered government. EO is ostensibly unaccountable to a government, unlike its American equivalent, Military Professional Resources, Incorporated (MPRI) which is closely linked to the US government.[76] *"Corporate entities are used to perform tasks that the government, for budgetary reasons or political sensitivities, cannot carry out."*[77] As Silverstein of The Nation explains: *"The use of private military contractors allows the [foreign power] to pursue its geopolitical interests without deploying its own army, this being especially useful in cases where [services are] provided to regimes with ghastly records on human rights. It's foreign policy by proxy."*[78]

Training of defence force personnel

Military training contracts are not conducted as covertly as combat operations and there are a greater number of competitors to the EO group and Sandline. The nature of these contracts is well-illustrated by the EO promotional video which claimed to provide "*... the most professional military training related to land, sea and air warfare.*" In addition to the training of ground forces and naval or airborne special forces, EO and Sandline also provide intelligence training courses which equip foreign defence forces with surveillance, countersurveillance, interrogation and counterinterrogation skills. Competitors to EO would include:

- MPRI;[79]

- the full range of British-based companies, for example, Defence Systems Limited (DSL), Saladin and Omega Support Systems (which is partly South African);

- Israeli companies like Lev'dan and Silver Shadow;

- French companies like Paul Barril's SECRETS, ABAC run by Lucien Thomas, which also protected a pipeline constructed by Total and Unocal oil companies in Burma; and

- South African companies like MTS which secured a contract with the Botswana government that involved the training of pathfinders for its parachute troops.

Training of police, customs and excise, and immigration personnel

Governments could hire the full spectrum of modern police services from both EO and Sandline. The EO group acquired the services of both former and presently serving members of the South African Police Service to provide the following training interventions:[80]

- riot control;

- rapid deployment, SWAT services and hostage negotiation;

- marine, port and airport policing;

- counternarcotics, countercontraband and counterterrorist operations;

- corporate mineral field policing;

- electronic surveillance;

- covert operations to counter organised crime; and

- fire protection.

The training of dog and horse units is an interesting development. With the rise in organised crime in South Africa that is linked to global syndicates, such services are now popular. Both EO and MPRI tendered for a dog unit contract in Saudi Arabia in 1997.

Training of politically-allied paramilitary units

Where leaders of governments distrust their own security forces and political rivals are backed by armed forces, private militias are sought after. This is a controversial sector of private security, since it often exacerbates existing internal disputes and gives rise to further internal destabilisation. In Congo-Brazzaville, for example, political leaders armed themselves with foreign-trained personal militia who did not form part of the national forces. During Denis Sassou-Nguesso's rule, he hired the services of primarily French agencies to arm and train his personal Cobra militia. Lissouba, in turn, hired Israeli and South African forces to arm and train his Zulu paramilitary forces. Bernard Kolelas adopted the same strategy and built up a Brazzaville-based militia known as the 'Ninja's' who received military assistance from both South African and Belgian private military specialists.

In EO's case, the most comparable example would be the training, arming and military use of the Kamajors in Sierra Leone, described earlier in this chapter.

Other types of government contracts

Presidential and VIP protection contracts are common in Africa, especially where insecurity is increased and governments are weak. Kinshasa, in particular, has been a fertile ground for such business and both the head of state and members of government have traditionally bought personal protection packages from different agencies.

Demining and the removal of explosive ordnance is both a lucrative and popular sector of the private military industry. Saracen International is well-known in this respect and has recruited top SADF and SANDF experts to assist its mine-lifting and training operations. It has been hired by a variety of oil companies, as well as several UN departments, and has had contracts in Angola, Uganda, Bosnia and Mozambique. Mechem also provides such services and has worked with both Saracen and other rival firms.

Both Sandline and the EO group provide surveillance, countersurveillance and espionage services to government forces in a large number of African countries. Affiliated firms and the directors of both Sandline and EO have advised on weapons procurements and acted as arms brokers for governments. In addition to these services, both Sandline and EO have brokered arms deals and advised on weapons procurements for government clients.

The section of the private security market that provides strategic planning, threat analysis, risk consultancy and related services is where the largest number of consultancies can be found. It is also the most important and legitimate part of the industry. A vast number of private security and intelligence companies provide African situation reports and risk analyses to many governments, as well as to corporate clients. In Sierra Leone, EO was able to win support from the international community because it provided a number of embassies and aid organisations with intelligence on the unfolding war. In many parts of Africa where conflict is ongoing, reliable information is hard to access. Security and military firms with personnel in remote locations can provide useful security reports and risk analyses.

Corporate contracts

While deployed on military operations, EO has also provided personal, convoy and asset protection services to strategic resource companies. In Sierra Leone, EO led government forces in an offensive to liberate a large mining compound owned by Sierra Rutile Limited (SRL) that was held by rebel militia. EO subsequently established a base force of about twenty soldiers to protect the Sierra Rutile mining compound, owned equally by Consolidated Rutile Limited (CRL) in Australia and Nord Resources Corporation (Nord) in the US.[81] In both cases, payment was made by SRL. EO also provided helicopter transport and VIP protection to SRL executives who later visited the mining compound to assess the cost of repairs. There is therefore often an overlap of government and corporate contracts and military operations are sometimes fused with corporate protection contracts. EO also provided protection services to Lebanese diamond miners and conducted night patrols to stop nocturnal theft at diamond mines in Kono, near the Liberian border. EO and LifeGuard provided protection services to their affiliated mining companies, Branch Energy and DiamondWorks.

Using its military helicopters and small fixed-wing aircraft, EO can provide rapid reaction services, hot extraction, casualty evacuation and medical emergency services to private clients in Africa. It performed such operations in Sierra Leone and Angola and claimed to have performed hostage rescue operations in South America and Indonesia.

Industrial espionage services are provided by EO's affiliated companies, such as OPM Support Systems, one of the largest and most technologically sophisticated private companies operating in South Africa. OPM is also known to operate in Central and Southern Africa and has a client base that includes several large mining and energy corporations.

The EO group and private military firms can also protect and transfer mining equipment, general goods, cash and gems for corporations in high-risk territories. They can provide rapid reaction air transport to diamond miners when large gems are found – which presents an immediate security risk. These services have also been utilised by humanitarian and international organisations.

Other services that private military companies can provide for corporate clients include the training of security staff, risk assessment and threat analysis. In Sierra Leone, EO supplied risk assessment and conflict reports to several corporate clients. According to a confidential report,

"EO personnel were able to put together the most complete and up to date data on diamond production and recoverability figures covering many diamond producing areas across [Angola]. By extension they were able to monitor the quality of diamonds as well as gauge future production estimates, and were invariably better informed on diamond production figures than their Angolan government counterparts."[82]

There appears to be an increase in joint ventures with prominent local military, political and business leaders who become partners to foreign private security companies. For example, the local security companies in Angola – Mamboji, *Tele Service Sociedade de Telecomunicaçoes, Segurança e Servicos* (TeleServices) and Alpha 5 – all have Angolan shareholders who are either military or police leaders. The firms are managed by South African security experts and former SADF officers who are members of the EO group or other major security firms. The real partners are generally shadow partners.

A second trend is that government ministers and political leaders force foreign corporations to hire specific security firms from which they would benefit. If the corporation refuses and tries to bring in its own security company, government leaders could deny such a corporation access to its concessions. This has been reported in Liberia and Angola and has allowed several large, South African-managed firms to dominate the security business in some African states.

Finally, security executives increasingly attempt to negotiate cluster contracts that allow them to secure a number of non-security trade leases and mineral concessions that can be sold off to multinational companies.

Conclusion: Renaissance or disaster?

In its six years of existence as a corporate army, EO deployed fighting battalions and heavy artillery units, and undertook sophisticated airborne operations, protracted guerrilla warfare operations and air-to-ground bombardments. The EO/SRC/Sandline/Branch Energy complex of military and mining companies has offices around the globe – in the UK, the US, Canada, Singapore, Hong Kong, South Korea, Indonesia, China, Australia, and in over 26 African states. In Africa at present, through affiliated and front companies, it has personnel deployed in Angola, Uganda, Rwanda, the Democratic Republic of the Congo, Congo-Brazzaville, the Central African Republic, Sierra Leone, Liberia, Guinea, Senegal, Algeria, Kenya, Sudan, Mozambique, Namibia and South Africa. Through a wide number of affiliated companies, it provides a range of military, security and civil services. The latter include offshore banking services, tourism ventures, video productions, water drilling and purification, construction and air transportation. Companies in the complex use several offshore banks and have separate corporate accounts – a strategy that allows them to keep their total worth hidden.[83] In the spectrum of new corporate or mercenary armies, EO was the most visible and controversial.

As a result of their military conquests in African conflicts, organisations like the OAU and the UN have considered using the services of private military or security companies to facilitate regional peace-enforcing initiatives where the UN prefers not to be directly involved after its failures in Somalia and Rwanda.

It has been argued that the upsurge of South African mercenarism and the existence of EO as its most visible forerunner are not new or unexpected phenomena. EO has arisen in a post-Cold War and post-apartheid world as a result of historical and political factors that are hard to control or impede. It also has to do with what has been called the triumph of neo-liberal capitalism – unbridled commercialism. Currently, if a government wants control of its war-torn state, but does not have the means to do so, it must be prepared to both part with its sovereign jewels and sup with the devil, because there are no benign saviours to come to the rescue.

EO has claimed that it did not conduct mercenary activities – a claim that is clearly false, regardless of the semantic definitions one prefers. Hired foreign troops who conduct offensive operations and receive salaries from private contractors in excess of any national defence force's pay, are mercenaries. Admittedly, it was not a label that EO preferred and, in response, EO and Sandline attempted to coin a neutral term for themselves, such as 'contract soldiers', 'professional military advisors', or 'force multipliers' – a modern variant of the Italian Renaissance's *condottieri*.

EO representatives also claimed that the company was accountable to the rules of good business and to the foreign dictates of Britain, South Africa and the US. It claimed that EO adhered to international rules of military engagement. Yet, EO wore too many hats and juggled too great a diversity of political issues for an organisation whose business was war and whose operations would always be governed by laws of profit. Enrique Ballesteros, the UN Special Rapporteur on mercenarism, expressed his own fears about this:

"What worries me the most is the protection of human rights. Who can guarantee that a private company, which will protect mines in Zaire, or who are involved in armed conflict in South Africa, North Africa or South America, will not violate human rights in the absence of a tribunal which would have jurisdiction to judge them? Because what we are talking about are companies which come, do their job, and leave."[84]

There can be no lasting stability or legitimacy for a company such as EO without it being deployed under the full view of public scrutiny. As long as its business remains occluded and covertly sanctioned, Africa is at risk. A system is being created whereby power resides less with the governments of countries than it does with the new *condottieri* and their corporate kings who own multinational mineral and energy empires. If Western democracies and the international community continue to tacitly approve the involvement of private military companies like EO, they too should be accountable for the result.

The corporate conquest of EO has given rise to the proliferation in South Africa of smaller and less successful military companies. Many would like to apply the EO formula for success: secure a foreign military deal in Africa, grow trade relationships in the domestic and international arms industry, get mineral concessions, attract investors and build an empire. Not many will succeed. To improve their chances, some formed strategic alliances with EO and with competitors to increase space at the lucrative trough. They operate more as a loose network than as rivals. Private military companies are now arming and training numerous warring factions in Africa – a fact which is far more likely to exacerbate tensions and accelerate existing civil and regional conflicts than it is likely to bring stability and security to Africa. While companies like EO are able to secure strategic islands within conflict zones, their operations have not yet brought lasting peace to the continent. EO's initial success has also helped to activate a boom in the business of war.

Can Africa benefit from the strategy of allowing yesterday's apartheid warriors to become today's peace enforcers? Where will the proliferation of the storm-troopers for the global mineral and oil companies bring us tomorrow? In the case of the Italian *condottieri*, a new era of prosperity and learning developed in Europe after their feudal wars. Before this time, in the case of the free companies of the medieval era, the proliferation of mercenary armies brought chaos and destruction. The outcome in our contemporary case is still unclear. But already in 1998 and 1999, civil conflict has spread across Africa and started a transcontinental war.

Are the entities that constituted the private military industry and the EO group army stabilisers or destabilisers? The aftermath of EO's involvement in Sierra Leone and in Papua New Guinea argues for the latter. During 1998, EO personnel were redeployed in Sierra Leone through their affiliates, Sandline and LifeGuard. In Angola, troops are deployed under Luitingh – troops who are visible to visitors, but invisible to international eyes. The experiment goes on. Viewed through the lens of time, they will play either a constructive or destructive role in building the hesitant future in Africa. Hopefully, we will survive their executive outcome.

Endnotes

1   The information contained in this chapter is drawn from over a hundred interviews conducted during a period of more than three years. The author has interviewed about forty former SADF soldiers who were employed by Executive Outcomes between 1993 and 1998. Much of the information in this chapter can therefore not be attributed in an open manner.

2   See M Ashworth, *Africa's New Enforcers*, The Independent, 16 September 1996; D Shearer in a report by P Taylor, *Mercenaries Aren't All Bad – UK Think Tank Report*, Reuters News Agency, 26 March 1998; W Shawcross, *In Praise of Sandline*, Spectator, London, 1 August 1998.

3   H R Heitman, Personal Interview, Cape Town, 12 October 1998.

4   See A Mockler, Mercenaries, Macdonald, London, 1969, p. 44.

5   A Mockler, The New Mercenaries, Garden City Press, London, 1985, pp. 2-10.

6   Ibid., pp. 11-12.

7   A corporate army is here defined based on concepts borrowed from A Sampson and V Gamba.

8   Interviews with former special force trainers who worked with EO at the time.

9   In the early nineties, Barlow used Luther as a first name and Eben [sic] as a second name. Friends knew him as Eben. Later, his name was given as Eeben. 'Eben' is used throughout to avoid confusion.

10 Executive Outcomes, Special Training Programme Proposal, 1992-1993.

11 Ibid.

12 EO job quotes, marked 'secret', for *"... specialised [security] equipment"* were submitted to Anglo American Corporation at Marshall Street in Johannesburg in 1992. Invoices for electronic countersurveillance services were issued by EO in Kimberley and Johannesburg in 1993 and marked 'paid'. EO also carried out evaluation seminars for

security officials at the Debswana Diamond Company, a subsidiary of De Beers in Botswana. De Beers have denied that it had a direct relationship with EO. In a personal interview, De Beers' security chief, Vice-Admiral Sir Alan Grose (ret.) said that the group had hired a separate company that subcontracted the work to EO and that Anglo American and De Beers therefore did not have a direct relationship with EO. Documents in the author's possession show direct correspondence, addressed to EO, from Anglo American Corporation at Marshall Street.

13   See Chapter 8 on Angola.

14   Personal interviews with several mercenaries who were deployed in Soyo in 1993.

15   They were also told that the Angolan oil corporation, SONANGOL was paying a portion of the finances. A colonel was paid over R1 000 (then about $200) per day. At the signing of later contracts with personnel, Barlow and Luitingh reduced the salaries to $3 000 per month for normal soldiers.

16   Buffalo (32) Battalion was a Portuguese-speaking, light infantry unit staffed mostly by Angolans who had fought for the *Frente Nacional de Libertação de Angola* (FNLA) and was commanded by white South Africans.

17   Several ANC intelligence officers have admitted that they were approached by Barlow who offered to supply information to both the external and internal South African services. EO members subsequently provided the South African intelligence services with several briefings between 1993 and 1996. Personal interviews, Gauteng, 1996-1997. ANC intelligence and military officers also visited EO's operational Headquarters at the MPLA military base at Cabo Ledo, Angola in 1994. See K Pech, *UK Spies Link ANC Officials to Mercenaries*, Sunday Independent, 26 January 1997.

18   There is confusion over whether Buckingham or Barlow first registered EO Limited in London. Buckingham has denied reports that he registered EO in London. But a top secret UK intelligence document produced two years later stated that Buckingham and Mann registered the company in London. See K Pech & D Beresford, *Africa's New Look Dog's of War,* Weekly Mail & Guardian, Johannesburg, 17 January 1997.

19   Barlow and his second wife, Dorothy Harding are registered as the directors of EO (UK) Ltd.

20   Ibis Air named its clients as the governments of Liberia, Sierra Leone, Angola and Sudan, as well as EO, Sandline International and Renamo, the Mozambican opposition party and former rebel army and advertised its helicopter and fixed-wing expertise on the Ibis/Techline website in 1998 at <www.inter-plane.com/techline/prod02.htm>

21   Only two war correspondents, Jim Hooper and Al Venter, were allowed access to front-line operations.

22   Branch Minerals, Mineral Holdings Inventory, September 1996.

23   Ibid., p. 7.

24   All three had former experience with setting up or working for CCB front companies. In Palm's case, he was associated with a front company called Geo International Trading for which, as an explosives expert, he conducted *"... specific tasks during highly sensitive foreign operations."* See comments by former Special Forces chief, Major-General 'Joep' Joubert in newspaper reports in the Natal Sunday Tribune, late 1992.

25   Corporate documents in the author's possession.

26   Bank documents in the possession of the author dated up to 1995 reveal that about thirty of these companies fell under the full or partial control of EO directors at the time. These companies all shared directors, offices, personnel, contracts and clients.

27   Group corporate documents make this claim. See also Journeyman Pictures, EO: The Business of War, video documentary, 1997.

28   Personal interviews with former managers of EO-affiliated companies.

29 Although the directors of EO and Branch Energy have claimed that no formal relationship exists between the two groups, an internal memorandum at the Chelsea reception office of the London group of companies listed EO Ltd as a company operating out of the Plaza 107 offices in 1996.

30 S Correy, *Robert Friedland: King of the Canadian Juniors*, Background Briefing, Australian Broadcasting Corporation (ABC), 6 April 1997.

31 N van den Bergh, Personal Interview, EO offices, Wierda Park, May 1998. Stuart Mills no longer exists, since it was sold to Netcare, a private hospital group in South Africa.

32 According to Van den Bergh, Trans Africa Logistics was liquidated in 1997 and is no longer in operation; ibid.

33 The same strategy has been adopted by EO and Branch Energy in other African countries. In Sierra Leone, the group established a security company called LifeGuard, to protect their mining interests, which absorbed EO personnel and took over asset protection contracts when EO was forced to leave in early 1997. The group also tendered for marine fishing protection contracts and fishing concessions in Sierra Leone.

34 See Chapter 8.

35 K Pech, *Sierra Leone Battles to Pay SA's Former Stormtroopers*, Sunday Independent, Johannesburg, 7 July 1996; interviews with members of the former NPRC government, Sierra Leone, 1996.

36 The cost of EO's military operations was about US $1,5 million per month, according to a Branch Energy director interviewed in Sierra Leone in 1996.

37 Friedland quickly raised the stakes and *"... orchestrated a bidding war"* between two of the world's leading nickel producers, Inco and Falconbridge. Inco won, buying Diamond Fields for $3,1 billion in 1995. W Green, *Mining the Suckers*, Forbes, 10 March 1997.

38 Ibid.

39 In 1990, Friedland earned the name of 'Toxic Bob' when his first gold mining venture leaked cyanide into Colorado rivers and resulted in the largest toxic spill in North America. He abandoned the mine in 1992, leaving the Environmental Protection Agency to repair the damage – at an estimated cleanup cost of $148 million. R Moody, *The Mercenary Miner: Robert Friedland Goes to Asia*, The Multinational Monitor, Washington, 18(6), June 1997.

40 John Woods in Correy, April 1997, op. cit.

41 Canadian Securities Exchange, Prospectus for DiamondWorks, 1996, p. 55.

42 Correy, April 1997, op. cit.

43 They sold their first parcel in October 1997 for US $3,1 million. See DiamondWorks press releases, <www.diamondworks.com>, October 1997.

44 Ibid., May 1997.

45 Ibid.; Correy, April 1997, op. cit.

46 *Profile: Timothy Spicer – Dog of War with his Tail Between his Legs*, Sunday Times, Johannesburg, 30 March 1997.

47 M Smith, *Big Business for Officers of Fortune*, International News, 27 March 1997.

48 Information provided by a London-based security analyst who had interviewed Sandline.

49   K Silverstein, *Privatizing War: How Affairs of State are Farmed out to Corporations beyond Public Control*, The Nation, New York, 1997.

50   Press statements made by EO and Sandline representatives at the time.

51   *Agreement for the Provision of Military Assistance between the Independent State of Papua New Guinea and Sandline International,* 31 January 1997; see <www.pactok.net.au/docs/nius/9704141.htm>

52   Correy, April 1997, op. cit.; transcript from the judicial inquiry.

53   Interview with EO personnel, Sierra Leone, 1996.

54   Interviews with EO soldiers and Kamajors, Sierra Leone, February to April 1996.

55   How the Kamajors were financed during the rule of the military junta remains unclear. The ousted President Kabbah could not afford this cost and certainly the Kamajors have no money to speak of. Training and support that continued after EO left Sierra Leone in early 1997 were conducted through LifeGuard. Interviews with EO personnel, 1998.

56   Ibid.

57   Van den Bergh, op. cit.

58   Confidential interview.

59   Interview with former EO employees still under contact with the military group, November 1997 and January 1998.

60   Interview with informant who had been consulted by EO regarding Algeria. These operations are run out of the London office.

61   Confidential interviews

62   Remarks in Parliament, Cape Town, 26 February 1998.

63   Van den Bergh, op. cit.

64   Security informants have reported that a number of new companies have surfaced in Central Africa, but so far their links to EO have not been confirmed.

65   Van den Bergh, op. cit.

66   Interview with L Nathan, Executive Director, Centre for Conflict Resolution, Cape Town, 1997.

67   Van den Bergh, op. cit.

68   Ibid.

69   SAFM news report, South African Broadcasting Corporation (SABC), 4 January 1999.

70   For example, when approached to train and deploy dog units in Angola, senior members of both EO and Saracen International consulted experts in South Africa who supply such services to the local police and defence force. Interview with consultant to the private defence industry, January 1998.

71   D Isenberg, Soldiers of Fortune Ltd.: A Profile of Today's Private Sector Corporate Mercenary Firms, Center for Defense Information Monograph, Washington DC, November 1997, <www.cdi.org/ArmsTradeDataBase/control/SmallArms/mercenaries>

72   Ibid.

73   See Sandline contract with Papua New Guinea government.

74   Not all former EO staff who are deployed into new companies retain formal links with EO and it would be useful, given EO's reputation, to describe oneself as attached to EO in order to secure contracts.

75   P Thornycroft, *South African Arms Going to UNITA*, Weekly Mail & Guardian, Johannesburg, 25 June 1997.

76   See Chapter 6 on MPRI.

77   Silverstein, op. cit.

78   Ibid.

79   See Chapter 6.

80   Saracen unsuccessfully tendered for a contract to do dog training in Angola in 1996. EO also tendered with rival MPRI for such a contract in Saudi Arabia in 1997. Interviews with former EO personnel, October 1997; documents in the possession of the author.

81   Sierra Leone has one of the largest known deposits of rutile – a rare, strategic metal that is used in the production of titanium and its alloys. The SRL mine used to produce 25 per cent of the world's rutile and was the cornerstone of Sierra Leone's mining industry and economy prior to the start of civil conflict in 1992.

82   Confidential corporate report produced for a mining corporation by a Johannesburg-based strategic analysis company, May 1997.

83   According to a UK informant, in 1994 – barely one year after they first began – they were already said to be worth $43 million. Interview, October 1996.

84   E Ballesteros, UN Special Rapporteur, to S Correy, *We Don't Do Wars*, Background Briefing, Australian Broadcasting Corporation (ABC), 15 June 1997.

Chapter 6: The military as business –
Military Professional Resources, Incorporated

Jakkie Cilliers and Ian Douglas

Introduction

*T*he United States is the unrivalled military superpower at the close of the 20th century, its share in global deliveries of major conventional weapons having increased to 43 per cent.[1] Even more significantly, US military research and development spending was more than seven times that of France, its nearest competitor, in 1997. It is this strategic investment as much as the size of the US military that will ensure its military dominance into the next millennium. It is only natural that US dominance in global military terms also impacts upon the private security industry.

During the Vietnam War, US 'private military activity' was probably epitomised by the operations of the Vinnell Corporation, which began as a southern Californian construction firm in 1931. The company's involvement in military and intelligence work came at the end of World War II when it shipped military supplies on contract from the US government to Chiang Kai-shek's Nationalist Army in China. It continued with contracts to build military airfields in Pakistan, Japan, Taiwan, Thailand and South Vietnam throughout the 1950s and '60s. In return for serving as a cover for operatives of the Central Intelligence Agency, the CIA helped Vinnell to win construction contracts on oilfields in Libya and Iran. During the American war in Southeast Asia from 1965 to 1975, Vinnell became directly involved in military and intelligence operations. At the height of the war, it had more than 5 000 employees in Vietnam. In his study of Vinnell, Gaul quotes a Pentagon official who described Vinnell as *"... our own little mercenary army in Vietnam ... We used them to do things we either didn't have the manpower to do ourselves, or because of legal problems."*[2]

Vinnell subsequently fell on hard times, but in 1975 landed a US $77 million contract to train the National Guard of Saudi Arabia – a contact that has expanded since and remains Vinnell's most profitable venture. The current contract is worth US $163 million. The Saudi National Guard has a separate command chain and serves, effectively, as the palace guard to the ruling royal family, ensuring the survival of the present regime and a strategic US ally in the Middle East. This is achieved not at the cost of the US, but out of the Saudi national purse and at a much lower political risk than the use of US military services would incur.[3]

Vinnell and other companies such as Betac, DynCorp, Ronco and Science Applications International Corporation (SAIC) have undertaken 'military training missions' in Sri Lanka, Angola, Peru, Rwanda, Taiwan and Sweden. The activities of these companies have not been the subject of significant academic research, nor is information readily available on the industry.

Military Professional Resources, Incorporated (MPRI) is, of course, not Vinnell. Yet, from humble beginnings less than a decade ago, MPRI has probably become the best-known and largest current US private military company. Initiated, nurtured, and led by the élite of retired US military personnel, it has taken a prominent place in the lucrative market offered by the outsourcing of many former military functions. MPRI is similar to Vinnell in that it is encouraged to undertake profit-making military ventures that are aligned with the national security interests of the US, but does so overtly.

Until now, MPRI has not been a major factor in Africa. Despite what appears to have been a direct request by President Clinton to Angolan President dos Santos to consider the employment of MPRI to train the Angolan armed forces, there is, as yet, no confirmation of the company's involvement in that country. MPRI and companies similar to it are undoubtedly destined to play an important role in national, regional and even global security affairs in the future.

The company

According to the MPRI website, *"[t]he centre of mass of the company's US defence effort is in doctrinal development, force management, and activity based costing. New equipment training for active and reserve components, Army Staff support, wargaming, test and evaluation, and War College support are other sizeable MPRI efforts ... MPRI's current international efforts are centred in the Balkans, where the company conducts Democracy Transition Assistance Programs, Long Range Management Programs, and Military Stabilisation Programs involving the training and equipping of armies in transition. As part of these programs, MPRI established and runs a Battle Simulation and a Combat Training Centre."*[4]

MPRI was established nine years ago and has its corporate headquarters in Alexandria, Virginia, in the US. By the end of 1998, it had more than 400 employees with a turnover of US $48 million for 1997. The company is quite clearly a product of the post-Cold War defence downsizing and the reduction in the size of standing military forces, the US Army in particular. As in the case of most other armed forces, the US Department of Defense has tried to protect the central warfighting capability of its military by focusing resources on operational field formations and by outsourcing and privatising non-warfighting activities such as administration, logistics and even training.

The domestic market for MPRI's services within the US is therefore mainly the privatisation of appropriate military support functions. One example of the close relationship between MPRI and the US military and the extent of outsourcing that is occurring within many of the armed forces of the developed world is that MPRI took over the management and conduct of the Reserve Officer Training Corps (ROTC) in June 1998. As part of this contract, MPRI will provide 73 retired colonels to perform this task. By comparison, the US Army has only sixty colonels serving in its ten regular field divisions.

Typical of the defence industry in general, economies of scale have dictated that MPRI look towards the international market to reduce unit costs. By December 1998, MPRI had twenty contracts worth more then US $90 million of which only three were international, and not for the US government. While the greater number of MPRI's contracts are domestic, the split between domestic and international business in dollar terms is about even. The international marketplace is clearly more lucrative than the domestic one, and the company has embarked upon an aggressive international expansion programme.

The MPRI resource pool consists of more than 7 000 retired soldiers and officers who span the spectrum from general officer to infantry squad leader. MPRI includes more than 200 general or flag officers in its pool of those available for 'duty.' In his personal message on the MPRI website, Major-General (retired) Vernon B Lewis, President and Chief Executive Officer, is forthright:

"We are owned and operated by retired senior military professionals and/or their families. We work throughout the United States and in far-flung corners of the world, doing important things. If you have military or other skills that would be of value to our diverse, wide-ranging customers, we invite you to add your name to our database through this web site ... and be considered for future employment."[5]

MPRI's activities span the spectrum from teaching simple soldier skills to the production of the highest level of doctrine and teaching of the US and other forces – from grade school to post-graduate work. In its prospectus, MPRI defines its mission and vision as follows:

"MPRI's mission is to gather and employ the experience and talent of the top of the national resource of former military professionals, primarily in defence related areas, for the US government, and to assist foreign governments in converting their military into western models that support democratic institutions ... The MPRI Vision is to create a company of high quality professionals – tapping the cream of former/retired military – that sets the standard for quality performance, contract flexibility, business ethics, and management integrity, a company that makes a positive difference for those with whom it works, a company that grows in revenue and reputation; a company with world wide recognition and respect."

While MPRI does provide 'soft' services focusing on civil-military relations in a democracy, the vast majority of its activities are hard-core defence-related: fielding new weapons systems and conducting new equipment training, strategic and tactical military planning, simulation and wargaming, logistics management, doctrinal development, test and evaluation, operations research and analysis, force design and management, combat development, special operations, security assistance, fire support, law enforcement, maritime operations, military intelligence training, explosive ordnance training, and so on.[6]

MPRI has not provided armed personnel for use in direct security duties and emphasises that, as a matter of corporate policy, members of MPRI are unarmed – although it is clearly ambivalent regarding arms for self-defence purposes in high threat situations. Until now, the company claims that it has had to arm its members only during contracts in direct support of US government policy, such as the Military Stabilisation Program in Croatia, which is described below.

Nor does MPRI consider direct participation in military combat similar to the arrangements made between the government of Sierra Leone and Executive Outcomes, and the contract signed by the government of Papua New Guinea and Sandline. The official MPRI response regarding involvement in military combat operations is: *"If you want Executive Outcomes you don't want MPRI."*[7] The distinction between direct participation in combat and advising and planning operations is, of course, spurious. The difference between the man who pulls the trigger and the operational staff who decided where to attack, when and with what, or the trainer who moulds units into effective operational units, remains debatable. In fact, the MPRI website states that *"... MPRI can perform any task or accomplish any mission requiring military skill ... short of combat operations."*[8]

The defining characteristics of MPRI contracts are those limitations set by US law and the requirement that the company obtains a US government licence for its activities. Corporate activities within the US are governed by numerous federal and state laws which are applied to all businesses. MPRI sees itself simply as another domestic company, vying for contracts with similar US companies.

The acceptance of international commitments in the field of defence-related activities is governed by the Arms Export Control Act of 1976 (as amended) which regulates all foreign sales of 'defence goods and services', and the International Traffic in Arms Regulations that flow from it. Application for a licence must be made to, and approved by the Political Military Bureau of the Department of State. In this regard, even while bilateral discussions are allowed to take place, no commitment may be undertaken without the approval of the State Department. Indeed, where considered necessary, the Department will dictate conditions that must exist before a licence will be issued. The US Department of Defense is part of the interagency review that vets all such contract applications to the State Department. As an example, the licence for MPRI to seek a contract with the government of Angola was delayed for a time by the Department of Defense. In this case, the Pentagon demanded that nine generals from the *União Nacional para a Independência Total de Angola* (UNITA) had to be integrated into the *Forças Armadas Angolanas (FAA),* as previously agreed to by that government, before the Department of Defense would approve the application. The nine were accepted and the reservation of the US military was subsequently removed. Although the licence was ultimately issued, it has apparently not been activated. There are also reviews of contracts in progress (so-called 'in progress reviews', or IPRs) and, if anomalies or violations of the prescribed conditions are detected, the Department reserves the right to cancel the licence.

The Democracy Transition Assistance Program
for the Republic of Croatia

One example of MPRI's operations is the Democracy Transition Assistance Program (DTAP) that it provides in Croatia.

On 24 March 1994, the Defence Minister of Croatia appealed to the US military for assistance. In his letter to the Pentagon, Gojko Susak wrote that Croatia's goal was the transformation of the Croatian military *"... to one which follows the model of the United States."* More to the point, the Croatian army had suffered defeat at the hands of the Serbs in

1991 and Bosnian Croat forces fought Bosnian Muslim forces in a bloody stand-off during 1993. Serb forces occupied more than thirty per cent of Croatia. Although Washington was sympathetic to what it viewed as a potential moderate ally in an unstable region, a United Nations arms embargo tied the hands of the US armed forces. Pentagon officials referred Susak to MPRI.[9]

The Croatian Embassy in Washington subsequently contacted MPRI asking for assistance. The Croatians stated at the time that, with the end of the Cold War, the democratisation of Eastern Europe, and the ultimate expansion of the North Atlantic Treaty Organisation (NATO), the structure of their military should be reviewed with a view to make it more compatible with its potential NATO partners. Sacirbey, the former Bosnian Foreign Minister, stated in an article in US News and World Report that he had selected MPRI from a handful of competitors because it was the next-best thing to official US military assistance. However, he remained disappointed that the US was not willing to train the new Bosnian-Croat Federation forces itself.[10]

MPRI organised a five-person survey team who visited Croatia, and completed an assessment of requirements. After this initial exploration, the company decided to apply the Democracy Transition and Assistance Program, which it saw as a generic programme for emerging democracies.[11] Programme goals were to educate military officers, non-commissioned officers (NCOs) and civilian officials of the Ministry of Defence in the areas of leadership, management, and civil-military operations. Once the general agreements had been worked out bilaterally, it then remained for MPRI to arrange the licence with the Department of State – but only after certifying that it would only provide instruction on such non-lethal subjects as leadership skills and the role of the military in an emerging democracy. Since the UN arms embargo also required the US to restrict the activities of private security companies, MPRI *"... could not provide direct military planning or intelligence services or advice on strategy or tactics to Croatia or any other party in the former Yugoslavia."*[12]

One specific requirement saw MPRI design a fifteen-year programme to re-establish a competent core of NCOs. This programme initially involved NCO courses being conducted by MPRI personnel, with a longer term view of turning over the programme to the Croatian forces. The initial course was of six weeks' duration and emphasised structure, management and leadership functions.[13] The first contract for this part of the programme started in 1994, was for two years and was subsequently renewed for a second two-year period.

Popular legend has it that the immediate effects of MPRI's involvement were impressive. According to Gaul,

"... the impact of the ... MPRI-Croatia contract was dramatic. Just months after MPRI was hired to conduct leadership seminars for top Croatian military officers, the Croatian army launched the stunningly successful Operation Ulja [Storm] against the Serb-held Krajina region of Croatia. In a fivepronged offensive, the Croatian commanders integrated air power, artillery and rapid infantry movements to target the Serb command and control networks, sending much of the Serb army into retreat."[14]

The mechanised, all-arms integration evident during Operation Ulja appeared in marked contrast to the Soviet doctrine that had previously characterised Croat operations. Naturally, MPRI was credited with these changes.

Yet, closer examination appears to contradict popular legend. In the months leading up to Operation Ulja, from late 1994 to mid-1995, MPRI's DTAP training cadre consisted of a former general officer, fourteen other personnel, three of whom were majors or captains, with the remainder being retired enlisted personnel.[15] During the same period, two IPRs of the programme were performed by two senior members of MPRI, both retired four-star generals. Collectively, these officers would not easily have been able to impact upon combat doctrine to the extent implied in the limited time subsequent to MPRI's deployment into Croatia. It therefore remains a matter of speculation whether MPRI violated the terms of the UN arms embargo. *"...[B]ut the results for the United States national security apparatus were clearly positive: without the involvement of a single American soldier or a single American dollar, the MPRI project strengthened Croatia's military and bolstered the nation's strategic position in the region."*[16] The fact that these developments were attributed to MPRI, however, did not harm the company's international promotional campaign.

In reality, a number of US (and possibly other) covert assistance programmes, predating and running concurrently with the MPRI contract in Croatia, had a much more direct impact upon ensuing battles.[17] MPRI may be a welcome scapegoat and may benefit from the resulting publicity, but the Croatian military successes were probably not a direct result of its contract with the Croatian Ministry of Defence.

Military Stabilisation Program for the Federation of Bosnia and Herzegovina

MPRI's Military Stabilisation Program (MSP)[18] was initiated in early August 1996 and is assisting the Federation of Bosnia-Herzegovina Armed Forces (FAF) with the fielding of military equipment, and the conduct of a broad-based training programme. The company's successful bid occurred in competition with various other US companies, for the training and support requirements that would allow for the integration of new and additional military equipment into the new armed forces structure of the Federation. MPRI's 'equip and train' programme is run for the US State Department's Office of the Special Representative of Military Stabilisation in the Balkans. The assistance was touted as part of an international effort, led by the US, to improve the Federation's military capabilities to deter further Serb aggression by establishing a military balance sufficient to permit NATO's Stabilisation Force (SFOR) to withdraw from the region. Politically, it also serves to eliminate the Iranian influence in Bosnia that resulted from the presence of several hundred *mujaheddin* fighters and the provision of Iranian military aid during the conflict in the former Yugoslavia. Indeed, a standard joke in Bosnia was that MPRI really stood for Military Professionals Replacing Iran!

The US government contributed approximately $100 million worth of equipment surplus to the needs of its downsized army which included 45 M60A3 main battle tanks, eighty armoured personnel carriers, fifteen helicopters, 840 light anti-tank weapons, 116 medium gun-howitzers and several thousand small arms and other equipment. These arms are supplemented by significant military equipment grants from the United Arab Emirates, Egypt, Kuwait, Malaysia and Brunei.

The linkage to clear domestic foreign policy goals – the withdrawal of US forces and countering the spread of Islamic fundamentalism – ensured that the contract had cross-agency backing from the US intelligence community, the Pentagon and State Department, as well as bipartisan congressional support. Yet, Washington's European allies viewed the introduction of significant additional arms into Bosnia with disfavour, despite the fact that the US-Bosnian arms package fell within the limits of Article IV of the Dayton Peace Agreement. According to The Washington Post, *"[p]ouring new weaponry and military instruction into the Balkans ... is an invitation to renewed conflict and undercuts enforcement of arms-control limits. Some European officials also worry that as tensions inevitably rise regarding refugee resettlement and other potential flash points the know-how and weapons could turn against peacekeeping forces."*[19] Advocates of the contract argue, however, that without a military balance within the region, there is little chance of stability.

The purpose of the contract was to provide the FAF with the military capability to deter armed aggression and, should deterrence fail, to defend the Federation's territory and population. Training and doctrine focused on defensive warfare in contrast to the offensive tactics that the Bosnians had previously favoured.[20] This is therefore a classic military training mission, not unlike some of the services that Sandline International offers and that Executive Outcomes claims to have provided to the armed forces of Angola and Sierra Leone. The big difference, of course, is that Executive Outcomes eventually participated directly in combat, as well as offering training, advice and assistance. There is, furthermore, a crucial distinction to be drawn between the amount of external oversight and leverage in Bosnia compared to Angola. In Bosnia, NATO monitors and literally controls the armed forces of the Federation, partly through the SFOR forces deployed in the field. As a result, NATO commanders in Bosnia monitor the programme closely, restricting where and when Bosnian units can train and what training is conducted. In this sense, the equipment and training provided to the Bosnia and Herzegovina forces are part of a comprehensive stabilisation programme, very different from anything attempted in either Angola or Sierra Leone where inadequate international and regional peacekeeping forces have not had the same resources or mandate. In Bosnia and Herzegovina, MPRI is part of a wide process to solidify the integration of the previously opposing Muslim and Croat forces into a single army, which until then existed only on paper.[21]

With a contract worth several tens of millions of dollars, and with more than 200 individuals in the field, representing myriad skills otherwise available only in the US Army, MPRI acts in the Federation of Bosnia and Herzegovina very much as a direct organ of US policy, with considerable domestic and foreign policy advantages. Not only do MPRI's activities not impact upon the warfighting ability of the US Army, but the bill to extend its foreign policy interests is being paid by someone else (the Muslim Brotherhood). For the US, this is a win-win situation to the benefit of the State Department, the Department of Defense and, of course, MPRI itself, without running the risks of the issue being exploited for domestic political capital.

Civilian observers

MPRI has also participated in the provision of unarmed civilians in 'observer' roles. The mission, analogous to a UN Observer Mission (UNTSO, UNMOGIP, etc.), was established by the International Conference on the Former Yugoslavia. It deployed civilian observers along the border of Yugoslavia (Serbia-Montenegro) and the Bosnian-Serb controlled portion of Bosnia and Herzegovina from November 1994 to April 1996. The US government agreed to supply some forty observers as its contribution to the multinational mission. The positions were to be filled by both the State and Defense Departments. While the Department of Defense immediately decided to outsource the commitment to MPRI, the State Department initially tried to meet the requirement with its own civilian personnel, but eventually also contracted MPRI. The nature of the company and its employees provided an immediate reaction ability that the State Department itself could not match. Since MPRI employees were on contract to the US government in terms of a mandate from the international community, they were provided with additional protection under US law and international conventions.

All indications are that MPRI executed the contract successfully. The major difference was that the US taxpayer paid the bill, though it is safe to assume that the cost was lower than it would have been, had professional military or foreign service members been used.

There can be little doubt that this is the first of many instances in which the US, for one, will seek to outsource classic UN observer missions.

Africa

MPRI maintains that it has never had any significant activity in Africa apart from a two-man, vehicle instructor contract with the US government to support equipment donated to Liberia. MPRI, however, has been pursuing a significant contract in Angola for some years. The US government played a direct role in pressuring the Angolan government to evict Executive Outcomes and lobbied hard on behalf of MPRI, although without success thus far.[22] Senior company representatives have visited Angola on a number of occasions over the past two years to negotiate the contract. Although the State Department has already approved a licence for the contract,[23] very few specifics of the nature of the contract are available, notwithstanding the fact that a team leader has been appointed and, one would assume, detailed preparations have been completed.[24]

The MPRI contract in Angola would probably duplicate, in general, some of the elements of its operation in Croatia and Bosnia, thereby including at least some sort of DTAP, officer and NCO training, as well as core military competencies. During an interview, MPRI Vice-President, Ed Soyster, stated that he had briefed the Angolan authorities on the company and its abilities. He outlined what contributions the company might make to an Angola free of civil war, faced with the task of rebuilding its armed forces in a democracy. He pointed to the obvious fact that a stable, well-trained and motivated national armed force would have a strong confidence-building role in the early phases of post-conflict reconstruction.

MPRI has also been contracted to assist with the implementation of the US capacity-building programme in Africa, the African Crisis Response Initiative (ACRI).[25]

The potential problems which will have to be faced in Angola by MPRI and the US government, in its role of managing the licence for such operations, are both interesting and dangerous from a business, ethical and foreign policy point of view. After two, almost three years of negotiations no contract has been signed. A particular problem during the negotiations with the Angolan government appeared to be specific irregular ways and methods of payment demanded of the company should it wish to be successful in its tender.

Conclusion

Isenberg[26] was one of many analysts who suggested that the hiring of MPRI to carry out the DTAP and 'train and equip' programmes circumvents "... *the need to take the issue to Congress or the American public.*"[27] The examples of 'Air America', the CIA clandestine airline of the Vietnam War, Vinnell and Contra-operations in the 1980s, have been used to draw parallels to the current relationship between MPRI and the US Administration. Although there is some validity to these arguments, the driving force behind US government support of MPRI appears to be that of outsourcing and the privatisation of US foreign and security policy, rather than as a mechanism to avoid congressional oversight. The fact remains that, while MPRI may be constrained in its operations by the very nature of its overt close relationship with the US government, this may not be the situation with other companies or organisations. Private military service contractors may readily go beyond government sanctioned operations in search of higher profits. And the central question remains whether a developed democracy should be able to side-step domestic or even international opposition to involvement in political hot spots by simply arranging for civilian contractors to be put in harm's way. This was clearly the practical, if perhaps unintended effect of MPRI's involvement in Croatia, since the US military was barred from the region when MPRI first entered the Balkans.

This, of course, does not reduce the requirement for mechanisms designed to provide the checks and balances essential when applying 'armed force' to foreign policy. Nor does it reduce the demand for public debate, or at least public knowledge prior to 'exporting' arms or armed force. These concerns again underline the need for an emphasis on corporate 'good governance' practices and for openness and transparency in this area – within the US and elsewhere. Despite the contribution by the UN and efforts by many non-governmental organisations, the global defence and security service trade continues virtually unchecked and the black market trade in arms and defence-related services continues to expand.

While press oversight and investigative journalism provide some protection against abuse, the lack of public information on the activities of private security contracts, in particular, ensures that only the most dogged of journalists manage to track events and glean information.

The challenge of appropriate US oversight over activities of companies such as MPRI reflects the hard-nosed realist spectacles through which US policy-makers and politicians alike generally view the world. At the risk of gross oversimplification, the US view of the international arena reflects a domestic capitalist ethos – an approach where 'own interest' and 'anything goes' predominate. Domestically, this environment is exemplified by competitor economics and politics. The system works because it is in balance – the result of a complex society that is at once diversified, complex and intensely competitive. When this approach is brought to bear in a very unbalanced and skewed international system, the result is often different from that intended.

During the Cold War, US foreign policy – including covert military assistance and arms exports – was aimed at supporting allies and undermining communist countries and their sympathisers. While the US executive branch has proven over the years that it is adept at finding loopholes in congressional oversight, there is a broad consensus between the US legislature and the executive regarding 'legitimate' security interests in countries such as Croatia and the Federation of Bosnia and Herzegovina – as well as on the means through which to support these interests. Gaul's view on MPRI appears spot on: *"Recent dramatic reductions in federal budgets for national security agencies, as well as sensitive political and diplomatic considerations have lead the US to increasingly rely on corporate enterprises such as MPRI to perform military and quasi-military functions abroad. These private military service contractors ... view military activity as a purely commercial enterprise."*[28] The privatisation of US foreign and national security policy is primarily driven by domestic commercial and economic trends to the benefit of both the Pentagon and the State Department.

In simple terms, if the US military or State Department does not wish to contribute, for whatever reason, to stability in war-torn African societies, commercial companies such as MPRI and others will do so. The only restriction is the ability of their customers to pay and the willingness of the State Department to licence such companies' activities outside the US. *"For the American government, soliciting retired officers to accept privately-financed military contracts that further American interests is extremely cost-effective."*[29]

There can be little doubt that the use of private military service contractors by the US in Africa will increase as a corollary to US withdrawal after the peacekeeping debacle in Somalia. Thus far, it has largely been Britain and France that have played similar roles in Africa, but on a bilateral, country-to-country basis. In the case of Britain, this has mainly occurred through its various British Military Advisory and Training Teams (BMATT). Britain currently has such teams in Zimbabwe for Southern Africa, in South Africa to assist with the integration of the South African National Defence Force, in Ghana for West Africa, and will also shortly establish a team in East Africa. One could speculate, for example, over the requirement to re-establish a competent and effective armed force in the Democratic Republic of Congo as part of a lasting regional peace settlement if Rwanda and Uganda's security concerns are to be met. Similarly, the requirement for the reprofessionalisation of the armed forces of countries such as Sierra Leone, Congo-Brazzaville, Lesotho and even Nigeria remains unfulfilled. Experience would indicate that these types of programmes require a single lead nation (or company) for practical doctrinal reasons rather than to rely upon a coalition of forces. The latter leads to confused doctrine, command and control practices and inevitably reduces the impact of the training and assistance that are provided.

There is undoubtedly a legitimate place in the development assistance activities of the international community to provide help for democratic military development and regional stability. This does not necessarily mean training only in military skills, but much broader programmes designed to assist and cohere civil control of the armed forces in emerging democracies. Inevitably, such projects may have unintended consequences. Few foreign policy initiatives can guarantee unequivocal results. US officials and civilians, for example, may experience reprisal attacks elsewhere in retaliation for what is perceived to be assistance to one side to a conflict by a company seen to be closely aligned to the US Administration, such as in the case of MPRI.

Given the reduced sizes and over-commitment of most Western armies, companies such as MPRI are an inevitable requirement today, one which will only grow in the future

In the light of the shortage of resources and the 'donor fatigue' which seems to be affecting the international community, one has to consider novel approaches to development assistance outside the accepted UN/NGO nexus which has existed to date. While major advances in good governance will still require management at the highest level of the international community, there appears to be a gap for skilled private organisations that can tackle the complicated, technical problems in the military, political and logistic affairs of emerging nations. Given a proper system of checks and balances, companies such as MPRI and Defence Systems Limited (DSL) may contribute to peace and development.[30] The questions of methods of payment and the nature of the contracts awarded, however, will require particular transparency and oversight. What is necessary is a code of ethics – established, maintained and properly monitored – which would see the delivery of military training, education, and professional development in the democratic mould without interference with the sovereignty of nations which make use of the service.

Endnotes

1   According to the Stockholm International Peace Research Institute (SIPRI).

2   This account of Vinnell is entirely based on that of M J Gaul, *Regulating the New Privateers: Private Military Service Contracting and the Modern Marque and Reprisal Clause*, Loyola of Los Angeles Law Review, June 1998.

3   Vinnell's parent company is BDM International.

4   See, <www.mpri.com/about/activities.htm>, 31 December 1998.

5   See, <www.mpri.com/welcome3.htm>, 31 December 1998.

6   See, <www.mpri.com/about/capabilities.htm>, 31 December 1998.

7   E Soyster, Personal Interview, Virginia, 15 October 1997.

8   See, <www.mpri.com/about/capabilities.htm>, 31 December 1998.

9   Gaul, op. cit.

10   *Private US Companies Train Armies Around the World*, US News and World Report, 8 February 1997, <www.mpri.com/current/nr020897.htm>, 31 December 1998.

11   Subsequent contract extensions were called DTAP I and DTAP II.

12   Gaul, op. cit.

13   During the IPR that was conducted after six months of the programme, a specific and detailed briefing on the course content was made by a former NCO of the US Army. The Chief of the General Staff (CGS) of the Croatian Army was very surprised by the calibre of the presentation and suggested that he had assumed that the briefer was a senior officer.

14   Gaul, op. cit.

15   Soyster, op. cit.

16   Gaul, op. cit.

17   Should such a connection have existed, it would have been in clear breach of the State Department licence which did not permit combat operations.

18   See T Arbuckl, *Building a Bosnian Army*, Jane's International Defense Review, August 1997, <www.mpri.com/nr897.htm>, 31 December 1998; B Graham, *Ex-GIs Work to Give Bosnian Force a Fighting Chance*, The Washington Post, 29 January 1997, <www.mpri.com/current/nrO12997.htm>, 31 December 1998.

19   Graham, ibid.

20   Federation forces are taught five tasks through a five-phase programme, namely hasty defence, deliberate defence, move to contact, limited counterattack and counterfire technology.

21   The two armies were allied early in the Bosnian war, then fought one another during 1993 and 1994 before resuming a loose alliance against the Bosnian Serbs.

22   US News and World Report, op. cit.

23   Soyster, op. cit.

24   According to the US News and World Report, *"US officials said that the plan calls for more than 100 former US military trainers and could cost as much as the operation in Bosnia."* US News and World Report, op. cit.

25   See, <www.mpri.com/current/personnel.htm#afms>, 31 December 1998.

26   D Isenberg, Soldiers of Fortune Ltd.: A Profile of Today's Private Sector Corporate Mercenary Firms, Center for Defense Information Monograph, Washington DC, November 1997.

27   Ibid., p. 18.

28   Gaul, op. cit.

29   Ibid.

30   The primary problem with the US arms export regime is that it requires congressional review of military service contracts only when a contract exceeds US $50 million and there is no differentiation regarding the nature of the service or the type of equipment that is provided.

Chapter 7: Gurkhas and the private security business in Africa

Alex Vines

Introduction

*T*he private security business in Africa in the 1990s is more sophisticated than it was in the 1960s and 1970s. At that time, it was mostly associated with mercenary activity in violent and bloody civil wars and the emphasis was often on the recruitment of men to serve in combat units. Although some security firms, such as Sandline International, have continued to try and do this, opportunities are increasingly rare. The variety of products now on offer are wider, ranging from supplying bodyguards for eminent people to providing security for oil and mineral installations, drawing up threat analyses and giving military advice and training.

The firms that engage in these activities are increasingly image conscious and deny that they engage in mercenary-type activities. But the line between providing bodyguards or security advice and engaging in mercenary activity remains thin, and ethical and responsible behaviour may be eroded by the need to make a profit. The skills used in security consultancy and bodyguard work, furthermore, are almost identical to those used for mercenary activity.

The 1990s have also seen a growth in the number of private firms offering a wide portfolio of security products. These firms are often run by a couple of individuals who maintain a list of 'contacts' available for security subcontracting or discreet deals. Such firms own few assets and are positioned to mobilise their contacts at short notice. A number of these firms have tried to use Gurkhas from Nepal in their operations in Africa, as their employment is considered to be more cost-effective.

Gurkhas

Gurkhas are soldiers from Nepal, and the Gurkha brigades in the British army are the closest in model to *La Légion Etrangère* (the French Foreign Legion).[1] The British, Indian and Nepalese governments are sensitive to claims that these Gurkha soldiers are mercenaries. They assert that the provision of Gurkhas in their armies is governed by a tripartite treaty between the three governments and is akin to an understanding between allies. The main motivation for the Nepalese government is the arrangement's ability to generate revenue. The British government pays some £30 million a year in pensions to former soldiers who have retired to Nepal. Gurkhas serving in the British military can also expect virtually the same wage as their British equivalents, although the redundancy terms offered to them are considerably less generous than those offered to their British counterparts.[2]

Following the British government's <u>Options for Change</u> defence review in 1991, the Gurkha regiments were reduced in strength by seventy per cent through compulsory redundancy.[3] The

UK has tried to soften its cuts by lobbying the UN to employ a Gurkha UN rapid reaction force. British former Prime Minister, John Major, presented the idea to the UN in 1991 with little success.[4] Because of the large number of retrenchments in British Gurkha units, a number of British-based private security firms tried to recruit and market former Gurkha soldiers for employment in the private security sector. One such firm, Gurkha Security Guards (GSG), markets the Gurkha in its sales brochures as:

"... a phenomenon ... unique among the world's fighting men. Bred in one of the most inhospitable landscapes in the world, he is tough, self-reliant and used to dealing with great hardship. The very word 'Gurkha' has become a byword for steadfastness, courage and integrity and their reputation has won them respect and renown throughout the world.

Since the end of the [Second World] war, the role of the Gurkha has increasingly shifted to the maintenance of internal security and guarding of major installations and strategic assets. They were used as a counter-insurgency force in the defeat of terrorism in Malaya [sic] and Borneo, and their presence guaranteed stability during the riots and disturbances in Cyprus and Hong Kong. During the partition of India and Pakistan, Gurkhas were invaluable as a truly neutral and apolitical force able to segregate rival factions without prejudice."[5]

GSG's management also argues that the *"Gurkhas are good in Africa, because they are used to hardship, don't get bored like Europeans, are courteous, disciplined and are not expensive. They are also apolitical, they serve their client and don't get involved in asking why?"*[6]

This is all part of a myth-making exercise which maintains that Gurkhas are better trained and dependable than locally engaged staff. In Africa, Gurkhas have elicited a range of opinions about their skills. In July 1993, a Mozambican official working with Gurkhas on mine clearance operations said: *"They work hard and rid us of mines. They cook well, they are friendly and respect our customs and leave our women alone. They are not what we expected from Indians [sic]."*[7]

But they can command fear, too. A former Revolutionary United Front (RUF) soldier in Sierra Leone remembered seeing them in 1995: *"Those Vietnamese [Gurkhas]. I remember them. They carried AKs and large knives. We knew if they caught us we would be eaten. Whites and Africans are easier, we know what they are and what they do."*[8]

They can also command resentment. In Angola, a government official justified the expulsion of Gurkhas working for the British private security firm Defence Systems Limited (DSL) in January 1998 by saying: *"They take jobs from our young men. We have years of war experience. Our demobilised need jobs. Angolans can do better work than these Gurkhas."*[9]

The work offered by GSG is also attractive to Gurkhas for financial reasons. For example, a Gurkha serving in Mozambique for the company in 1993 said:

"I am in Mozambique because I need to feed my family and get my children educated. There is little work in Nepal and my land is not enough to feed us all. I worked for the British Army

for many years seeing Hong Kong, Brunei, Belize and active service in the Falklands. So I know about war and landmines. I've been in Mozambique now for twelve months. I like it. People like us and show us respect. But when the job is over I will be happy to leave. I'm here to make money, do a job, not to enjoy myself. I do that in Nepal."[10]

Gurkha Security Guards

Gurkha Security Guards Limited (GSG) specialises in recruiting primarily former British Army Gurkha officers and soldiers for security services, and has operated during the 1990s in Angola, Mozambique, Sierra Leone and Somalia. GSG was formed in late 1989 and claims that it provides a *"... professional, cost effective, competent, solution to the security problems faced by commercial, industrial, diplomatic, and aid organisations operating in the more remote and hostile areas of the world."*[11]

GSG is a privately owned British company. Its original co-directors, and now its 'operating consultants', are Mike Borlace and Anthony Husher. Both men served in the British armed forces and fought in the Rhodesian war. Husher, a Canadian, served in the 1st Battalion of the Rhodesian African Rifles in Rhodesia and Borlace was in the Rhodesian Air Force and later in the Selous Scouts. Borlace was imprisoned in Zambia between 1978 and 1981 after being captured on a Rhodesian cross-border operation. Husher and Borlace met up again in Sri Lanka in 1985 doing contract work for the security firm KAS and then worked together from 1988 for a contract security firm in the UK. Major John Titley, a British Gurkha regiment officer, was the third director until 1994 and was GSG's main link with Nepal.

What GSG offers

In GSG's brochures, the company offers a number of services.[12] It undertakes the worldwide recruitment, selection, vetting, training, deployment and management of security officers, logistical support staff, and explosive ordnance disposal (EOD) and landmine clearance engineers. Specific services offered by GSG include:

- the provision and management of manned guarding services in hostile areas in order to safeguard personnel, installations, equipment, and vehicles;

- security training and the management of specialist security manpower;

- close protection of VIPs and persons under threat of their lives;

- supply of security equipment and materials;

- EOD operations, and unexploded ordnance (UXO) and landmine clearance, in both urban and rural areas, including: the location and disposal of buried ordnance; landmine and unexploded ordnance surveys; subsurface and deep subsurface searches; route clearances;

specialist training of indigenous personnel in the clearance of landmines and explosive ordnance; quality control inspections of clearance operations; and the supervision and control of local operations.

GSG claims to be able to deploy worldwide at short notice in order to respond *"... to sudden threats to life, limb, and property; or requirements for logistical support."*[13]

Recruitment procedure

GSG indicates that it has a number of offices with its head office in St. Helier, Jersey, in the Channel Islands. It also claims to maintain representative offices in Harare, Zimbabwe; Kathmandu, Nepal; and Ottawa, Canada. The latter are no more than commercial answering services or claimed alliances such as with the Canadian Association for Mine and Explosive Ordnance (CAMEO) which is starting up mine clearance projects in Africa.[14] Since 1995, GSG's directors on its company documents have been no more than names on letterheads, appearing for legal and tax purposes.[15]

The only permanent employees are the two former co-directors, Husher and Borlace, who maintain a network of 'contacts', who are mobilised if a lucrative contract or subcontract is won. GSG claims that it maintains rigorous recruitment procedures but, as in the case of many private security firms, recruitment is done on personal recommendation. There are no standard procedures for recruitment or operations in the field.

The recruitment of Gurkhas is carried out in Nepal. An agent puts an advertisement in a local paper, uses word of mouth and telephone calls, sufficient to attract several thousand applicants for the few posts on offer.[16] Although GSG insists that it hires former British Army Gurkha soldiers – all of whom left the service with 'exemplary' conduct certificates after at least fifteen years of service and that references and curricula vitae are obtained for all personnel employed – the standard of these recruits seems to vary. Competition for these jobs is intense and there is a tendency among Gurkhas to present 'gifts' of around US $2 000 to agents and local officials to ensure a place on the recruitment short list of fifty or so. Since the average monthly wage for a Gurkha in the security business is US $600-700 and the average contract lasts for six months, several months' wages are used just to earn the money to cover these 'gifts'. There is also an increasing trade in falsified 'exemplary' conduct certificates and a number of international security firms recruiting Gurkhas in Nepal have experienced problems with recruits not being as skilled as indicated in their documentation.[17]

GSG in Africa

GSG has concentrated its work in Africa, mainly because of the background and experience of Borlace and Husher and their contacts. Their most significant contract was in Mozambique where they were subcontracted by Lonrho, the British multinational corporation, to provide security services. Once GSG lost its Lonrho patronage, its fortunes declined rapidly.

Mozambique: The Lonrho connection

The expanding war in Mozambique made Lonrho's £53 million business interests in tomato, tea and cotton farming, gold mining, an oil pipeline and hotels increasingly unprofitable. By 1989, the difficulties of managing the farms and exporting agricultural produce were contributing to Lonrho's annual global losses. A £6 million contract from August 1986 to 1989 with the British private security firm, DSL, to protect its estates and convoys, had become too costly and had failed to ensure complete protection. After trying its own security management, Lonrho hired Gurkhas from GSG in 1990.[18]

Security outlays consumed thirty per cent of Lonrho's operating costs – about US $1 million a year – in addition to production losses caused by sabotage. In the Limpopo Valley, great triple stacks of concertina wire surrounded Lonrho's 2 000 hectare cotton farm at Chokwe. Watchtowers and tanks guarded the perimeter fence. The estate was protected by a militia of 1 400, supervised by Gurkhas. Despite the war, Chokwe's 2 000 hectares achieved 20 000 tonnes of cotton, Africa's highest yield in 1989. Lomaco, a joint venture with the government, also became the biggest tomato grower in the southern hemisphere.[19]

In early 1990, prior to GSG taking over company security, an attack by the National Resistance Movement of Mozambique (Renamo) on one of the Lonrho installations strengthened its board's belief that running militarised farms in a civil war was no longer feasible and that 'Tiny' Rowland's efforts to assist the peace process should be fully supported. Some 200 rebels attacked at dawn, driving a herd of cattle through a perimeter fence after a tree was hurled over the barbed wire. The rebels rushed in and blew up $500 000 of chemicals and irrigation pipes in a matter of minutes. Offices were torched and trucks doused with petrol. The expanding war in Mozambique made Lonrho's businesses there increasingly hazardous.[20]

Rowland, chief executive of Lonrho at the time, had been involved with Mozambique since the early 1960s when he negotiated the building of an oil pipeline between Beira and the then Rhodesia for Lonrho. The pipeline was opened in December 1964 and for the next three decades was Lonrho's primary asset in Mozambique. Because the pipeline required security, Lonrho established direct contact with Renamo from 1982. In June 1982, a Lonrho subsidiary signed a secret protection agreement with Renamo leader, Afonso Dhlakama, and his Secretary-General, Orlando Cristina, over the Beira oil pipeline.[21]

Despite these early problems, Lonrho maintained its connection with Renamo, initially through South African contacts and directly by the late 1980s. Regular payments into foreign bank accounts were arranged for some of Renamo's senior internal leadership, in exchange for an explicit understanding that they would not order attacks on the oil pipeline. Later on, additional agreements were reached over the tea estates in northern Mozambique and for a cessation of attacks along the railway line from Malawi to the port of Nacala. These payments continued until the Rome General Peace Accord in October 1992 and cost the company some US $5 million.[22]

It was agreed that some symbolic Renamo attacks would continue, but that these would not be serious. At times, however, Lonrho plantations and assets were attacked, but Renamo officials alleged that these incidents were the work of renegade groups operating outside their leaders' command. It is also possible that some of these attacks were designed as reminders to Lonrho that payment was due.

The secret protection payments to Dhlakama of the 1980s and early 1990s, brought temporary respites in some areas, but no lasting peace.

GSG provided fourteen Gurkhas to manage security on the Lonrho estates between 1990 and 1993. These men were responsible for the training, command and control of the locally recruited 120-strong militias maintained on each estate. These militias were armed by the government with AK-47s and RPG-7s. They were also responsible for managing the vehicle convoys carrying goods to the ports. The GSG teams were successful, and the standard and discipline of the militias improved. Despite a number of attacks on the Lonrho installations and vehicle convoys in the first eighteen months of GSG's contract, none were successful once the Gurkha teams were in place. Only one Gurkha was injured during these operations.[23]

Many of these farms and installations became small pockets of tranquillity in a war-torn environment towards the end of the conflict. Although GSG was to claim that the improved security situation was the result of its operations, it is likely that Lonrho protection payments were equally important in reducing the incidence of Renamo attacks.

During this period, GSG provided additional Gurkha teams for the protection of a geological survey team of the Irish firm Kenmare Resources in the Angoche area, and some VIP and goods convoy work. GSG was also requested to provide security cover for a number of Renamo officials during the peace negotiations in 1992.[24]

Landmine clearance

Lonrho was responsible for GSG winning a lucrative mine clearance contract in Mozambique. After the General Peace Accord of October 1992, the Mozambican government and Renamo agreed at a meeting of the UN's Supervisory and Control Commission (CSC) on 31 December 1992, to hire GSG, through Lonrho, to remove mines in central Mozambique. The agreement ended a dispute over who should be contracted: Renamo wanted to hire the South African security company Minerva (a front for Mechem), and the government favoured the Zimbabwean army.

At the end of January 1993, GSG began formal mine clearance operations (operations Electric and Lincoln) in Mozambique in co-operation with Lonrho. The programme was initially funded by the European Community (EC) and directed by the International Committee of the Red Cross (ICRC). The aim was to clear roads of mines and unexploded ordnance, to allow relief vehicles carrying food and other forms of aid to reach more remote regions. GSG's clearance efforts first concentrated on roads north of Beira. Its contract was extended in July 1993 for five months so that additional roads could be cleared for the World Food Program. When the project finished in February 1994, GSG had cleared 160 kilometres of road. Three hundred and forty seven items of explosive ordnance were destroyed, including six mines, at a cost to the EU of $1 683 000.[25]

Between July and December 1994, GSG provided another full Gurkha EOD team in Mozambique for Project Caminho, a $4,3 million contract awarded by the UN to clear priority roads. The contract was won by a consortium consisting of Royal Ordnance, UK, Lonrho and Mechem of South Africa.[26] GSG again profited from Lonrho patronage in winning this subcontract.

Angola

GSG has also operated in Angola. In 1991, it was contracted by Oderbrecht Mining Services Incorporated to provide a fully integrated security team of Gurkhas for the prevention of theft at its diamond mine in Luzamba in Lunda Norte province. Theft at the mine did decline during this period.[27] However, when Angola returned to civil war in late 1992, the mine was seized by UNITA and the Gurkhas and other expatriate staff were evacuated.

In mid-1994, during the 'third' Angolan war, International Defence and Security Limited (IDAS), a Netherlands-based firm with strong Israeli and US connections, approached GSG to assist in recruiting Gurkhas. IDAS chief executive officer, Michel Jean-Pierre, a former member of the French Foreign Legion, planned to provide as many as 2 000 Gurkha troops to pacify the Lunda Norte area which had fallen under UNITA control.[28] GSG claims to have ignored the request. The contract never materialised because the South African firm, Executive Outcomes, dominated the market in the Lunda's at the time. GSG continues to solicit business aimed at providing security services for the diamond industry in Angola.

GSG has also been involved in mine clearance operations in Angola. In 1995, the company provided Mechem with a team of Gurkha EOD engineers to assist the UN with route clearance in various parts of the country.[29] The project was successfully concluded in August 1996.

Sierra Leone

GSG attracted international attention primarily because of its work in Sierra Leone. The civil war that began in Sierra Leone in 1991, reached a crisis stage in late 1994 with the capture by RUF rebels of the country's diamond, titanium oxide and bauxite mines. By early 1995, the capital Freetown was threatened and the then National Provisional Ruling Council (NPRC) government approached a number of private security companies to provide assistance. J & S Franklin Limited, the British manufacturer of non-lethal military equipment and a weapons sales agent, subcontracted GSG to train the Republic of Sierra Leone Military Force (RSLMF). GSG arrived in January 1995 under the command of Major Bob MacKenzie, an American and veteran of Vietnam, the Rhodesian SAS, Bosnia and a contributing editor on unconventional operations for Soldier of Fortune magazine.[30]

GSG sent 58 Gurkhas and three European managers – MacKenzie, James Maynard, a former British Gurkha officer, and former British Coldstream Guard sergeant Andrew Myres – to set up a training base for the Sierra Leone special forces and later infantry officer cadets.[31] The

Sierra Leone Information Minister announced that, *"[t]hese people have come to assist in the training of our forces. We've had some problems in the military getting used to jungle tactics."*[32]

The Sierra Leone government had requested that GSG train their army officer cadets. *"It is extremely unusual for any nation state to entrust the training and welfare of their future military officers to a commercial company composed solely of foreigners,"* states GSG about this contract in its sales brochure.[33]

Nick Bell, GSG's accountant, also maintained at the time that the Gurkhas, *"... are not in Sierra Leone in an offensive role."*[34] In January 1995, GSG began to train the Sierra Leone military in counterinsurgency techniques, from hot pursuit, to ambushing and evacuation. Husher claims that, *"[w]e trained selected security units in the very basics of protecting their civilian population and economic assets from the depredations of armed bandits."*[35] He also denied that GSG trained in mine warfare. He stated:

"We most certainly did not conduct any form of training involving land mine warfare, and certainly would never have countenanced this; unless it was in the detection and destruction of landmines. I actually spent half an hour with the Army Chief of Staff in Sierra Leone talking him out of his wish to lay landmines in order to protect their borders and vital installations. While I could not get his agreement to destroy their land mine stockpile; he agreed not to permit any to be laid."[36]

GSG's team not only provided specialist training for the Sierra Leone army, but also safeguarded the strategic Camp Charlie military base in the heart of the country. After some initial skirmishes with the rebels, GSG was able to secure the base and ensure the pacification of the surrounding area.

Soon after GSG started their training programme, government forces supported by two Russian Mi-24 helicopter gunships with Belarussian mercenary pilots engaged in attacks on a number of RUF bases.[37]

However, disaster struck on 24 February 1995. While scouting the Malal Hills in search of a live firing training area, MacKenzie, Myres, five Gurkhas and a platoon of RSLMF infantry walked into an RUF training camp by mistake and a fire-fight ensued. At least 21 were killed, including Major Anbou Tarawali, President Strasser's aide-de-camp, MacKenzie and Myres. Most of the Sierra Leone troops fled from the scene leaving the Gurkhas, MacKenzie and Myres to fight. Many of the bodies were never accounted for.[38]

The US State Department wrote in its annual human rights report that, *"[i]n a February attack, the military aide to the Head of State, the expatriate commander of the mercenary advisory group, and several other individuals were killed by rebels in an ambush. None of the bodies was ever recovered, and reports indicated later that they were mutilated and put on display in rebel-held areas."*[39]

A former RUF fighter described the incident as an organised attack. He stated:

"It was morning time. We were listening to a radio message, to announce promotions. Then we were called out of the base, and then ordered back in. Two jets came to bombard. But we knew the air raid was not the thing, that ground forces would come, so we were ready. They told us they [Gurkhas] are coming. We began to fight seriously. It was not an ambush.

Did you see the Gurkha commander [MacKenzie]?

There was one white man. He had compass, camera, gun. He was hit, and then killed. We dragged his body back to camp. We saw he had a tattoo on his arm. They cut the arm off, to show the tattoo to identify the person, to prove to the government that he had been killed. We buried Tarawali. After that attack the commanders decided to move the camp. After one week the jets came to bombard but we had left the camp site by then."[40]

In <u>Mercenaries: Soldiers of Fortune</u>, a coffee table book sold in a number of British supermarkets during 1997, MacKenzie's death was glamorised.[41] The author Tim Ripley incorrectly wrote, "*... the veteran American mercenary Bob MacKenzie, who was on a freelance contract in the country in 1995, was shot by the government soldiers he was supposed to be leading and left to be captured by rebels, who reportedly ate him.*"[42]

After the deaths of MacKenzie and Myres, Borlace and Husher went to Sierra Leone to continue the training. Camp Charlie was in a hostile zone and came under four days of heavy attack. They initially had 36 officer cadets, who in effect found themselves in live training and held on to the base. By late March, the government had withdrawn all of its cadets from the programme.[43]

At the time, the British Foreign and Commonwealth Office feared that the rebels would interpret the presence of Gurkhas as a sign of direct British intervention which could lead to the execution of some British hostages then being held. It issued a statement in March saying, "*[w]e have not been giving any military assistance to the government of Sierra Leone. We have made this perfectly clear to the RUF, but if people who are no longer in the British Army decide to sell their services elsewhere we cannot stop them. They can do what they like with their specialist knowledge as long as they don't break British laws.*"[44]

During this period, GSG was urged by the NPRC to engage in operations directly against the RUF, but it stuck to its contract and refused to conduct offensive operations against the rebels. Because GSG refused such operations, and it was becoming clear that the RSLMF, in spite of training, would be incapable of retaking important mining assets without assistance, the mining firms of Sieromco and Sierra Rutile approached Special Projects Service Limited (SPS) in the UK to provide 400 former British military personnel to secure the mines. SPS held a recruitment reception in a hotel in Banbury, Oxfordshire, which some fifty former British Army soldiers attended, and offered US $2 000 a week to work for SPS in Sierra Leone.[45] The Ohio-based Sierra Rutile already maintained a force of some twenty former British soldiers guarding its assets during this period.

However, given the uncertainty about the course of the war and the estimated US $80 million cost of such an operation, both companies decided on a wait-and-see strategy. A number of other UK-based security companies were also directly involved in pursuit of business opportunities in Sierra Leone during this period, including DSL, Control Risks, Group 4, J & P Security Limited and Rapport Research and Analysis Limited.[46]

The departure of GSG from the country in April 1995 coincided with the arrival of a 100-man team from Pretoria-based Executive Outcomes, which immediately began training the RSLMF. EO had sent a representative to Freetown in March to negotiate a contract with the NPRC after having been approached by the Sierra Leone government. GSG had tried in March to form a joint venture with Sandline International to work with EO in Sierra Leone, but EO showed no interest. Husher of GSG later claimed that EO won the contract because it was prepared to undertake offensive action. *"Their costs were also much less than ours because they didn't offer their employees comprehensive insurance cover or demand an up-front fee from the government."*[47]

GSG continues to look at Sierra Leone as a potential market for its services.

Other GSG activities

GSG has also done other work in Africa. It provided a two-man team for security work in Somalia and has undertaken security consultancy work in South Africa and Zimbabwe.[48] In 1997, it was subcontracted to provide five Gurkhas as field supervisors in Bosnia for the Zimbabwean firm, Mine-Tech. This contract was won because Mine-Tech is run by former colleagues of Borlace and Husher from the Rhodesian war, Chris Pearce and Colonel Lionel Dyke.[49] However, following a spate of accidents caused by the Gurkhas, relations soured between Mine-Tech and GSG.[50] GSG is also seeking to pick up a landmine survey subcontract in Sudan from the Nairobi-based NGO, Operation Save Innocent Lives and Canadian CAMEO.

Immediately after the Gulf War, GSG provided Gurkha engineering teams to assist British weapons manufacturer, Royal Ordnance with landmine and UXO clearance of the British sector in Kuwait. GSG deployed three teams for seven months, during which they cleared 258 000 separate pieces of ordnance. GSG has also provided the Cambodia Mines Action Committee with a managed team of Gurkha EOD instructors for six months and conducted a survey of a route through Cambodia and Vietnam which cuts across the 'Ho-Chi Minh trail'.[51]

GSG splits

In March 1994, GSG split following a meeting in a hotel at Batumbeng in Nepal between Major John Titley, Matt Matulewicz, a consultant for Maggie Peacock Working Dogs Limited (MPWD) and Marc Ranson who decided to form a new firm, Special Gurkha Services Limited (SGS), with an office in Kathmandu. The dispute was over management practices, money and the choice of clients. Initially, SGS encountered difficulties in recruiting Gurkhas in Nepal, and Titley and Matulewicz were detained briefly by local officials.[52] In August 1995, the UN awarded a contract to SGS to provide five field-level supervisors for its Accelerated Demining Programme in Mozambique. In 1998, SGS had five Gurkhas employed in Mozambique, two in Laos and two in Angola. The company also won a $350 000 contract to clear landmines and other unexploded ordnance in Taiwan in 1998.[53] SGS is involved with the French NGO, Handicap International, in developing their 'proximity demining programme' in Mozambique.

GSG in trouble

GSG attracted much unfavourable publicity in the British press in early 1995 on account of its Sierra Leone contract. Husher and Borlace attempted to limit the damage by trying to transform GSG into a non-profit organisation. They also hoped that this would help to restore the legitimacy of the operation. In 1994, GSG claimed to support two charitable trusts, the GSG Trust and a Gurkha charity, the Goorkha Trust, which were to fund a variety of aid projects in Nepal. A percentage of the company profits were to be paid into these trusts annually, but the two initiatives remained dormant. In July 1995, GSG relaunched its GSG EOD Trust, naming several British-based development NGOs, such as the Jaipur Limb Campaign and Save the Children Fund, as recipients of donations made by the Trust from contracts awarded. Without their permission, these NGOs were also named in a GSG project proposal sent to the EU. All the NGOs subsequently requested that their names should be withdrawn from the proposal, a request that GSG adhered to.[54]

In September 1997, GSG issued a statement after the death of Diana, Princess of Wales, calling for international attention to the landmine problem in Angola. *"... [M]aybe now it is possible,"* the GSG spokesperson wrote, *"to mobilise the British public in a campaign to put a stop to this. It would be a way of providing a positive and practical tribute to Diana."* The statement attracted unfavourable comment from <u>The Observer</u> newspaper which remarked:

"Concern on the part of GSG would seem entirely laudable. Its job is to find employment for thousands of Nepalese Gurkhas who served in the British Army until they were pensioned off under the last government's Options for Change proposals. As many Gurkhas were trained in explosive disposal, they are ideally suited to the job.

If only GSG restricted itself to landmine clearance. Just over two years ago, it signed a contract to supply 58 Gurkhas to the military dictatorship in Sierra Leone under Captain Valentine Strasser ... Both GSG and the Sierra Leone government were non-committal about the role of the Gurkhas. But when troops attacked a rebel base deep in the jungle, putting at risk British hostages and killing a number of guerrillas, they were certainly in attendance."[55]

By 1998, GSG had failed to attract any significant business and remained *de facto* a 'letterhead company'. In December 1998, Husher sent an e-mail about the Canadian Association for Mine and Explosive Ordnance (CAMEO) stating that:[56]

"The Board of Directors of The Canadian Association for Mine and Explosive Ordnance (CAMEO) Security have asked me to express their particular pleasure and satisfaction at the excellent response CAMEO has received from all those with whom it has worked since its incorporation as a non-profit Society in May 1997 and its registration as a Charitable Organization by Revenue Canada."

Husher clearly saw more value in marketing CAMEO than GSG, which had continued to fail to attract any serious business since the Sierra Leone debacle. Meanwhile, Borlace appears to be working with the airwing of Sandline International in Sierra Leone.

Defence Systems Limited

Defence Systems Limited[57] was founded in 1981 by Alistair Morrison, a former SAS officer who was experienced in operating in hostile environments, and realised the demand for such services.[58] For much of the 1990s, DSL was associated with the Hambros Bank.

In April 1997, DSL was bought by a US firm, Armor Holdings.[59] The take-over transaction accounted for a pooling of interests valued at $7,6 million in cash for all preferred shares and $10,9 million in stock (Armor also assumed $7,5 million in debt). DSL's revenues for 1996 were reported at $33,1 million in annual pro forma revenue, and it had more than 5 000 employees worldwide throughout South America, Africa and Southeast Asia, of which only 100 had access to firearms.

Today, the company has over 130 contracts with 115 clients in 22 countries. The company is mostly composed of former British special forces officers. DSL claims that it *"... never gets involved in other people's wars. It's simply not an aspect of our business, and business is good."*[60]

GSG had a contract for several years to provide Gurkhas for DSL, but it was cancelled at the end of 1994.[61] DSL continued to work with Titley after the split within GSG, saying that he was their main contact and SGS, the company to which he was affiliated, was regarded as reputable.

DSL has used Gurkhas in a number of African countries, including Angola and Mozambique. It was approached in 1992 by the UN to deploy 7 000 Gurkhas to protect NGO relief convoys in Somalia from threats posed by the warlords. However, after an assessment mission, DSL decided that it could not successfully undertake the contract. It admits that the company's use of Gurkhas in Africa has not been a success. David Abbot, a director of DSL, said:[62]

"Gurkhas have not been a success in Africa. Culturally and otherwise they are not good. We have found that they are much more successful in the Gulf, which has a strong tradition of foreign personnel in the asset security business. We do not see much future in their deployment in Africa."

Unlike GSG, DSL is a leader in the wider private security market and the employment of Gurkhas was only a tiny part of its services on offer to clients.

DSL began providing security and logistical personnel to the UN mission in the former Yugoslavia in 1992, becoming the largest contractor to this mission with at least 430 personnel by February 1995. The firm was also approached by the Papua New Guinea government in the mid-1990s to assist in establishing a paramilitary police force for the country. The contract was never concluded due to a lack of funds on the part of the government, but DSL chairman, Alistair Morrison, recommended Sandline International to Papua New Guinea.[63]

DSL has been involved in protecting British Petroleum (BP) oil interests against guerrilla attacks in Colombia for a number of years. In the Democratic Republic of Congo (DRC), DSL protects installations belonging to the SOCIR oil refinery of Congo-SEP (the Belgian Petrofina's subsidiary), as well as the US Embassy. Other DSL clients in Africa have been De Beers (DRC), Andarko Petroleum (Algeria), Anglo American (Mali) and Chevron (Angola); as well as NGOs such as CARE and Goal. DSL claims experience in Angola, Algeria, Congo-Brazzaville, the DRC, Ghana, Mali, Mozambique, Nigeria, South Africa, Somalia and Uganda.

DSL's core business is to devise and subsequently implement solutions to complex security problems. It is contracted to the US State Department for the provision of security to high risk embassies, as well as to other diplomatic clients such as the British High Commission in Uganda. DSL has subsidiaries in Washington DC (US Defense Systems), Singapore (DSL Security Asia), Hong Kong (JSGS), Colombia (DSC), Peru (DSP), the Republic of Congo, South Africa (DSL Systems Africa), Russia and Kazakhstan (Gorondel Trading), and has offices in the former Yugoslavia, Uganda and Mozambique.

DSL and Angola

Although in limited numbers, DSL has continued to use Gurkhas. It ran a high profile operation in Angola from late 1991, where some 25 per cent of its clients had interests.[64] Its security personnel guarded embassies, oil and diamond companies and a number of NGOs. On 24 December 1997, the Angolan government issued a decree which ordered all foreigners working for DSL to leave the country, citing a law of 1992, which, according to the Interior Ministry, made it illegal to run security companies under an entirely foreign management. The ministry claimed that DSL had contravened the law relating to the registration of public enterprise security companies (PESC) by concluding contracts with foreign corporate nationals directly through London rather than through DSL's Angolan subsidiary.

DSL's chief executive in Luanda, Richard Bethell, requested clients in a letter dated 15 January 1998 to put contingency plans in place. The expulsion involved 103 expatriate DSL personnel, 45 of them Gurkhas. Luanda claimed at the time, that DSL and its Gurkhas were 'mercenaries' and were undermining the Lusaka Peace Accords.[65] The expulsion of DSL from Angola had been on the cards for some time. The company had made little effort to indigenise its workforce and management, or to find a strong local patron in government. It had been threatened with expulsion a number of times by senior government officials. It appears that senior Angolan officials believed they could profit from running a DSL-type operation themselves with Angolans and moved against DSL. The company initially attempted to transfer its assets to the South African-based firm, Gray Security Services, which had a joint venture training agreement with the registered public enterprise security *Tele Service Sociedade de Telecomunicaçoes, Segurança e Servicos* (TeleServices). This did not happen, and ISDS, a firm with links to Gray Security, took over the daily running of this operation as DSL-Angola with a management core composed of Israelis. DSL's loss of the Angolan business translated into US $12 million in revenue and approximately $1 million in gross profit.

DSL mishandled its operation in Angola, but it was also the victim of the domination of the private security business by a number of senior MPLA government military and security officials. There is fierce competition in the security market in Angola, with some security firms concluding joint ventures with Angolan partners – usually senior Angolan officials who are paid hefty dollar salaries to sit on the local companies' boards of directors.[66] There are about ninety registered security firms in Angola, of which two of them – TeleServices and Alpha 5 – dominate the market.[67] Both firms are controlled by senior Angolan officials and are able to divert police and officers of the *Forças Armadas Angolanas* (FAA) into their operations if it is deemed appropriate.

DSL threatened the expansion of this *de facto* monopoly and had to be evicted. Despite joint ventures, the quality of security protection has deteriorated in some cases and the costs have risen. The attack by armed insurgents on the Yetwene diamond mine in November 1998 was made easy by lax security and subsequent looting of the mine by TeleServices personnel responsible for the mine's security, aggravated the security situation in Angola even further.[68]

Conclusion

GSG was a typical example of a small private security firm dependent upon a limited number of key individuals. Its work for Lonrho in Mozambique appears to have been professional, although it was possibly assisted in its job by Lonrho's protection payments to high-ranking officials. Once GSG lost Lonrho as a patron, it quickly fell upon hard times. GSG's entry into mercenary activities in Sierra Leone followed the loss of Lonrho as a client and a destructive split in the company. A clear lesson from GSG is that small private security firms, with little capacity to see them through difficult financial circumstances, may be more inclined to engage in mercenary-type activity in order to remain viable.

GSG has damaged its reputation beyond repair and has failed to attract any serious work since. Its attempt to bury this episode and break into the more ethically-driven NGO market for mine clearance has also failed because of its negative image. By December 1998, GSG remained little more than a letterhead with Husher preferring to be seen as part of the Canadian mine clearance NGO, CAMEO, and Borlace working in Sierra Leone for Sandline International. GSG's offshoot, SGS has been more successful, setting itself up as a mine clearance and EOD specialist firm.

GSG's lack of commercial success, following its Sierra Leone debacle, is also the result of a number of other factors. Its loss of a significant patron hurt, and failure in Sierra Leone made it an unattractive proposition, compared to firms like Executive Outcomes. GSG is also attempting to compete in the wider security market where there appears to be increasing competition and less room for generalist expatriate firms offering a wide portfolio of services.

GSG's specialisation in deploying Gurkhas was a clear weakness as the emphasis is firmly on indigenisation in the late 1990s. Many African governments see this as a key indicator of positive social impact, especially as they downsize their militaries and experience serious unemployment crises. In such circumstances, the use of Gurkhas can be seen as patronising and possibly racist. The expulsion of DSL from Angola was partly due to its poor efforts to 'Angolanise' its staff and the Gurkhas were a high profile advertisement of this failure. The future trend is to have joint ventures with local partners where a small number of expatriate staff are involved. The challenge will be to ensure international standards and best practice in such ventures. Work for Gurkhas in Africa will become increasingly rare.

Endnotes

1   The Gurkhas first served with the British in 1816, after the East India Company was granted the right to raise local troops in Nepal to serve in the Company's Army. They served in two world wars and numerous colonial conflicts. After Indian Independence in 1947, the Gurkhas were split between the British and Indians, with four out of ten regiments remaining under British control.

2   The wastage rate of Gurkha recruits in the British military is almost nil, that for British recruits is between 25 and 34 per cent. The Gurkhas' level of fitness is also superior to that of the average British recruit.

3   J G H Corrigan, Major, Royal Gurkha Rifles, Letter, The Times, London, 5 January 1998.

4   US News and World Report, 121(26), 30 December 1996.

5   GSG, GSG Limited: International Security, brochure, no date.

6   M Borlace, Interview, London, March 1994.

7   Gurkha soldier, Interview, Mozambique, June 1993.

8   RUF former combatant, Interview, London, October 1997.

9   Angolan official, Interview, June 1998.

10   Gurkha soldier, op. cit.

11   GSG, brochure, op. cit.

12   GSG, GSG Limited: Company Profile, no date.

13   Ibid.

14   GSG also offers a range of other managed services such as road, bridge, and airfield reconstruction teams, and logistical support services in remote hostile parts of the world. It also advertises the provision of skilled and artisan personnel able to operate in a range of fields: pilots, paramedics, plumbers, bricklayers, heavy goods vehicle drivers, vehicle mechanics, electricians, water engineers, camp managers, heavy-plant operators.

15   GSG refused to provide these names when requested.

16   Gurkhas, Interviews, employed by GSG, SGS, and DSL, Beira, June 1994; Maputo, May 1997; Luanda, January 1996.

17   Ibid.

18   See A Vines, *The Business of Peace: 'Tiny' Rowland, Financial Incentives and the Mozambican Settlement*, <u>Accord: The Mozambican Peace Process in Perspective</u>, 3, 1998.

19   L Crawford, *When Managers Carry Guns*, <u>Financial Times</u>, London, 25 May 1994.

20   Ibid.

21   A Vines, <u>Renamo: From Terrorism to Democracy in Mozambique?</u>, Centre for Southern African Studies, University of York, and James Currey, Oxford, 1996, pp. 144-145.

22   Ibid.

23   Lonrho personnel, Interviews, Maputo, October 1994.

24   GSG, Profile, op. cit.

25   GSG, <u>GSG Ltd. Land Mine Clearance Mozambique Contract Completion Report</u>, 1994.

26   Human Rights Watch, <u>Still Killing: Landmines in Southern Africa</u>, Human Rights Watch, New York, 1997.

27   Oderbrecht, Information, July 1997.

28   *Gurkha-diamond Row Rocks Angola*, <u>Africa Analysis</u>, 14 July 1995.

29   V Joynt, Communication, Director, Mechem, Johannesburg, March 1998.

30   MacKenzie was also the husband of Sybil Cline, the daughter of a former director of operations at the US Central Intelligence Agency, Ray Cline. MacKenzie knew Borlace and Husher from their Rhodesian days.

31   A Husher, Interview, London, 16 December 1997.

32   *Would Diana Approve?*, <u>The Observer</u>, London, 5 October 1997.

33   GSG, Profile, op. cit.

34   J Hooper, *Nation to Ransom*, <u>The Sunday Telegraph</u>, London, 12 March 1995.

35   Husher, 1997, op. cit.

36   A Husher, Letter to Jaipur Limb Campaign, 11 August 1995.

37   Hooper, 1995, op. cit.

38   Husher, 1997, op. cit.

39   US Department of State, <u>Sierra Leone: Country Reports on Human Rights Practices for 1995</u>, US Government Printer, Washington DC, 1996, p. 232.

40   K Peters & P Richards, *Why We Fight: Voices Of Youth Combatants in Sierra Leone*, unpublished manuscript, Working Group on Technology and Agrarian Development, Wageningen Agricultural University, Netherlands, 1997.

41   T Ripley, <u>Mercenaries: Soldiers of Fortune</u>, Paragon, Bristol, 1997.

42   Ibid., p. 82.

43   Husher, 1997, op. cit.

44   J Sambona, *British Mercenaries Shore up Sierra Leone*, <u>New African</u>, June 1995.

45   Ibid.

46   J Hooper, *Sierra Leone – The War Continues*, <u>Jane's Intelligence Review</u>, January 1996.

47   Husher, 1997, op. cit.

48   GSG, Profile, op. cit.

49   L Dyke (retired Colonel), *Natural Born Soldiers: Interview*, <u>Moto</u>, Harare, June/July 1995.

50   C Pearce, Interview, Johannesburg, March 1998.

51   GSG, Profile, op. cit.

52   SGS staff, Interviews, London, December 1997.

53   *By Unearthing Mines, Taiwan Buries its Past*, <u>Asian Times</u>, 24 March 1998.

54   GSG, Letter to Jaipur Limb Campaign, 22 August 1995.

55   <u>The Observer</u>, 5 October 1997, op. cit.

56   A Husher, *New Premises for Cameo*, Email Communication, 6 December 1998.

57   DSL attracted controversy over its training of local police for BP in Colombia in 1996. BP had signed an agreement with the National Police units assigned to protect oil rigs. Members of these police units were suspected human rights abusers. See Human Rights Watch, *Colombia: Human Rights Concerns Raised by the Security Arrangements of Transnational Oil Companies*, <u>Human Rights Watch Short Report</u>, April 1998; see also *Corporations and Human Rights*, <u>Human Rights Watch World Report 1999</u>, Human Rights Watch, New York, 1998, pp. 456-457.

58   Morrison (55) made his name leading the famous SAS rescue of a hijacked Lufthansa plane at Mogadishu Airport in 1977.

59   Armor Holdings Incorporated is a leading provider of security products and services for law enforcement, government agencies and multinational corporations around the world. Founded in 1969 as American Body Armor & Equipment Inc., the company primarily manufactured armoured products until a controlling interest was acquired by Kanders Florida Holdings in January 1996. Since this time, Armor Holdings has made five strategic acquisitions which has broadened the company's product offering, expanded its distribution network, and facilitated entry into security services.

60   D Abbot, Interview, London, November 1998.

61   In 1993, GSG entered into an agreement with Jardines in Hong Kong under which GSG recruited, vetted and selected Gurkhas in Nepal and arranged for their travel to Hong Kong where Jardines took over. Over 400 Gurkhas were successfully employed in Hong Kong.

62   Abbot, op. cit.

63   S Dorney, <u>The Sandline Affair: Politics and Mercenaries and the Bougainville Crisis</u>, ABC Books, Sydney, 1998, pp. 105-106.

64   According to DSL, the profits from Angola were lower given the high operational cost there. DSL, Interview, London, 10 July 1998.

65   *Angola-Mercenaries*, <u>Sapa-DPA</u>, Lisbon, 16 January 1998.

66   <u>Monthly Review Bulletin</u>, February 1998.

67   Gray Security Services entered into a joint venture with Alpha 5 after an initial relationship with Saracen Security, a firm linked to Executive Outcomes. Gray's main market is South Africa, although it has expanded through joint ventures into Botswana, Mozambique, Namibia, Nigeria and Zimbabwe. It claims to operate under the code of practice of the International Standards Organisation, the body that sets standards for industrial enterprises.

68   I Gilmore & C Dignan, *Diamond Fever – British Victims of Africa's Billion Dollar War*, <u>The Sunday Times</u>, London, 15 November 1998.

Chapter 8: Angola – A case study of private military involvement

Sean Cleary

Introduction

*A*ngola has experienced more than its share of conflict in the past thirty years. The period prior to independence was characterised by violent clashes in which the major parties comprising the liberation movement – the *Movimento Popular de Libertação de Angola* (MPLA), *Frente Nacional de Libertação de Angola* (FNLA), and *União Nacional para a Independência Total de Angola* (UNITA) – fought against the Portuguese forces and each other. Following independence in November 1995, a brutal civil war ensued between the MPLA government and UNITA, progressively engaging the former Soviet Union, Cuba, the United States and South Africa and resulting in increasing levels of death and destruction, which stunted Angola's growth and ensured its underdevelopment.

Even the signature of the <u>Angolan Peace Accords</u>[1] by President José Eduardo dos Santos and Dr Jonas Malheiro Savimbi on 31 May 1991, following Namibia's independence and the withdrawal of Cuban combat forces from Angola, brought no lasting respite. Sixteen months later, after a tense interregnum that can be described as only relatively peaceful, Angola was again at war. The period of most intense violence in the country's history was between late October 1992 and January 1995. A private military company played a significant role during this episode of the conflict, influencing both its course and duration.

A tentative and uncertain peace[2]

On 9 April 1997, almost four and a half years after Angola's first multiparty elections, seventy UNITA nominees were sworn in as members of the National Assembly, giving that body its full component for the first time. Two days later, a Government of Unity and National Reconciliation (GURN) was inaugurated in the presence of African heads of state, the President of Portugal, and senior representatives of the United Nations, the US, Russia and other countries.

Those present at the inauguration appeared relieved that the ceremony had taken place at last. They would also have been conscious that, even as the Angolan war was being ceremoniously ended for the second time in a decade, Laurent Kabila's rebel forces were continuing their advance against the debilitated army of President Mobutu Sese Seko across the border in Zaire. All must have been aware that both the Angolan government and UNITA had forces in Zaire, the former in support of Kabila's Alliance of Democratic Forces for the Liberation of Congo (ADFL) and the latter attempting to help Mobutu offer enough resistance to justify a negotiated settlement. The question uppermost in many minds, therefore, was whether the inauguration of the GURN would bring peace to Angola.[3]

Historical overview

Policy-makers, economists, academics and commentators, whether concerned with African foreign policy issues and conflict management, or interested in advancing the integration of the Southern African Development Community (SADC), have long shared the frustration of those directly concerned with resolving the protracted and apparently intractable Angolan conflict.

Foreign engagement

Three South African National Party governments, the ANC (until Mr Mandela's assumption of office) and South Africa's first democratic government since then, have grappled with the challenges of Angola's transition from a Portuguese 'overseas territory' to an independent state at war. Nor were they the only ones engaged: Angola has played a major role in Portugal's modern history, eventually affirming the latter's identity as a European, rather than a Luso-African state. It defined and tested the limits of Cuba's commitment to socialist internationalism and afforded combat experience to many units of its armed forces. It represented a southern beachhead in Brezhnev's drive into the Third World to exploit US weakness after Watergate and Vietnam, at the height of Moscow's effort to advance the 'world revolutionary process' through the encouragement of the 'national liberation movement' in the non-industrialised world.

Washington's engagement with Angola, given the nature of its political process, was less consistent. It became an icon in the Ford Administration's efforts to reassert the President's authority to direct foreign policy. Under President Carter, the US government, desiring *détente* with Moscow, seeking friendship with 'black' Africa and convinced of Pretoria's moral turpitude, suggested that the Cubans were a stabilising force in Angola, deterring a South African invasion. Reagan's victory over Carter in November 1981 brought the Republicans back to power not only in the White House, but with a majority in the Senate as well. This set the stage for a modest, ostensibly covert, though widely discussed, military support programme for UNITA,[4] administered by the CIA. It continued until mid-1991 and was followed by an electoral support programme to help UNITA convert to a political party participating in national elections.

In addition to these direct interventions, Angola's modern history has also seen the engagement of the Organisation of African Unity (OAU), the UN, the Front-Line States (FLS), Morocco, Senegal, Côte d'Ivoire, the former Zaire and various Arab states committed to an anti-communist stance.

Angolan fissures

To suggest, however, that the Angolan civil war was driven exclusively by foreign ideological agendas would be to misrepresent the conflict and would fail to explain why a solution has proved elusive even after the withdrawal of Soviet, US, Cuban and South African support for the warring parties. This answer must be sought in Angola's experience of Portuguese rule. Portugal's subjugation of Angola's indigenous peoples was effected chiefly by conquest and fuelled by slavery. Between 1580 and 1680, some 1 500 000 slaves are said to have been exported from Angola to Brazil. The slave trade continued until 1878, by which time perhaps 3 000 000 Angolans had been transported abroad, and was followed by a system of indentured labour enabling metropolitan Portuguese who had settled on the rich farmland of Angola, to have access to workers at minimal cost.

Many of Angola's indigenous peasants were dispossessed[5] of their land and forced into contract labour, either as farm workers or unskilled industrial workers. Portugal's own capital shortage, however, precluded its engagement in effective capital formation in Angola, a function undertaken by other investors.

Over time, Portuguese private and corporate entrepreneurs established significant agricultural landholdings. A burgeoning manufacturing sector developed out of these activities, focused on food processing, textiles and clothing, with most surplus production being exported to the metropole.

Portuguese colonial possession thus resulted in the formation of three distinct classes among indigenous Angolans: a *petit bourgeoisie* comprising intellectuals and commercial traders,[6] a near-proletariat divided into industrial and agrarian components, and the residual peasantry whose members were engaged in subsistence agriculture and were seen as a source of contract labour by the industrial and agrarian bourgeoisie. Even in the last decade of Portugal's occupation of Angola, the government provided almost no education or health services for the indigenous people outside the main cities. Such services as were available for *indigenados* in rural areas were provided by missionaries (Catholic and Protestant) and private landowners.

The emergence of Angola's three 'liberation movements' in the 1950s and 1960s, reflected this pattern of colonial development.

- The MPLA was founded by the educated left-wing, urban élite concentrated in Luanda. Its leadership culture was (and is) Luso-African; its leading cadres were seminarians educated in Catholic schools, or other *assimilados*, with a high percentage of *mestiços,* some of whom received higher education in Portugal before independence and in Eastern Europe thereafter. Its limited rural base was essentially Kimbundu.

- The FNLA, out of which UNITA was later born, in its guise as GRAE (Revolutionary Angolan Government in Exile), was pre-eminently a Bakongo movement, led by Holden Roberto, the brother-in-law of Mobutu. The FNLA was originally rural in character, although many members later gravitated to the northern coastal cities, where they came to be reviled as *Zairenses*, envied for their trading skills and mistrusted for their good French, clumsy Portuguese and distinctive style.

- UNITA was founded in 1966 by Savimbi on a peasant, largely Ovimbundu base, although its founding took place in Chokwe territory and its leadership structures have always included Cabindans, Bakongo, Lunda-Chokwes, Nganguelas and others. Moreover, its support in Bakongo areas grew strongly in recent years, as that of the FNLA declined. Its institutional culture is rural-traditional African, in contradistinction to the MPLA's urban, Luso-African character.

The Angolan urban élite of the coastal corridor, many of whom are traditionally supporters of the MPLA, are the products of the Portuguese colonial administrative culture. The more promising *assimilados* were seen as the natural partners and, later, heirs of the Portuguese, succeeding them as cultural surrogates after Lisbon's disorganised withdrawal from Angola in 1975. Their sense of superiority to the Ovimbundu of the central plateau, whose economic roles were menial in colonial times and have continued to be since independence, is palpable even today.

Political mobilisation among the urban élite since 1975 has been a function of this feeling of superiority to, and fear of the *pretos/mutumbas* (pejorative terms for non-*assimilado* black Angolans), whose resentment of the domination of the *mulatos* and *Luandenses* has fuelled UNITA's campaign against the MPLA since 1975. It will be impossible to build a sustainable peace in Angola without confronting this core reality.

There is, as such, no Angolan nation. The élite of Luanda have an exclusive concept of their Angolan identity that is chillingly similar to that of the majority of South African whites a decade ago. UNITA's resentment of Luanda's domination has often boiled over into racist outbursts against *brancos* and *mulatos*. The antagonism of each side to the 'other', apparent when their diplomatic guards are down, can be frightening. The challenge of overcoming deep-rooted resentments, fears and suspicions, defining common visions, developing common values and building a nation, still lies ahead in Angola.

The Bicesse Accords

Angola's move toward peace in 1989-91 was not indigenously motivated. Neither side had a desire to reach out to the other. The peace accords were the product of a compact between the superpowers after Gorbachev's accession to the Soviet leadership, based on their understanding that their proxy confrontations were counterproductive, in Afghanistan especially, but also in Central America and Angola.

The first phase of the movement towards peace was thus the agreement in the trilateral talks between Angola, South Africa and Cuba, facilitated by then US Assistant Secretary of State, Chester Crocker, with the discreet assistance of the USSR, to link the withdrawal of Cuban combat troops from Angola to Namibia's independence. South Africa's withdrawal from Angola and Namibia and its cessation of military assistance to UNITA, were the *quid pro quo* for Castro's withdrawal of his Cuban combat troops and logistic specialists from Angola.[7]

The object of the New York Accord, signed on 22 December 1988,[8] was to bring Namibia to sovereign independence and progressively deprive the warring Angolan parties of the external resources that had sustained the civil war throughout the 1980s. Neither Washington, which had supported UNITA since 1985, nor Moscow, with its long ties to the MPLA, intended that its protégé should be defeated on the battlefield; both had agreed by then, in the interests of a wider *détente,* that a political solution was needed to the military conflict to which each had contributed.

In 1989, the Portuguese government, sensing an opportunity to play a decisive role in a territory of great economic and emotional importance to it, offered its services to both Angolan parties as mediator. The troika of observer nations were composed of the Portuguese mediator and representatives of the US and Russia, joined in an awkward endeavour to protect and advance their own national interests, while bringing an end to the Angolan war. These negotiations led to an agreement that a Joint Political-Military Commission (JPMC), comprising representatives of the Angolan government, UNITA and the three observer nations, would oversee the transition to elections after the cease-fire had taken effect.

The <u>Bicesse Accords</u> of 1991 relieved Angolans of the shocks of war for sixteen months between June 1991 and early October 1992. Deep-seated mutual suspicion, inadequate management of the challenges of the pre-electoral period, exploitation by both the Angolan government and UNITA of the inability of the UN observer mission to effect compliance with the provisions of the Accords, and electoral manipulation led to resumption of the civil war. <u>The Guardian</u> later described the disastrous performance of the international community as an attempt to *"… get peace on the cheap."*

The UN had a tiny team of military monitors (UNAVEM I) in Angola since early 1989 to observe the progressive withdrawal of Cuban troops. The UN, however, was drawn into the JPMC as an observer and charged to monitor the two Angolan parties' compliance with their undertakings. Until just before the elections, UNAVEM II's resources throughout Angola were limited to 350 unarmed military observers, 130 unarmed police observers and 100 electoral observers; the last increased to 400 during the actual elections.[9]

Second civil war

The second phase of armed conflict began at the end of October 1992 and lasted officially until 20 November 1994, when the <u>Lusaka Protocol</u> was signed in the Zambian capital on behalf of, but not by President dos Santos and Dr Savimbi, the latter fearing for his life if he left his safe haven near Huambo. Negotiating the Protocol had taken just over a year, following the announcement of UNITA's unilateral cease-fire in Abidjan on 14 September 1993, and was marked by the relentless energy of the new UN Special Representative, Maître Alioune Blondin Bêye from Mali; the introduction of a US Special Envoy with experience of both Southern African and Middle Eastern conflict, former Ambassador to Zambia, Paul Hare; and, on the margins, sympathetic interest by the ANC hierarchy in South Africa.

The success of these negotiations, after the failure of earlier attempts by the UN to broker peace – in Namibe in south-west Angola (November 1992), Addis Ababa (January and

February 1993) and Abidjan (April to May 1993) – was due largely to the frenetic persistence of Bêye, and the dogged serenity of Hare.

Following the signature of the cease-fire and the Protocol, however, the *Forças Armadas Angolanas* (FAA) – supported since September 1993 by former South African forces on mercenary contract (including elements of 32 Battalion and Koevoet assembled and led by field grade special forces officers) – continued their advances for several months against UNITA positions in Huambo and Uíge provinces in an effort to eliminate UNITA's military capability. Savimbi's decision to abandon the city of Huambo in November 1994 without offering resistance frustrated this attempt, leaving both FAA and FALA (UNITA's military wing) units largely intact and deeply suspicious of the intentions of the other.

Although one may be sceptical of the UN's lamentations early in 1994 that the new phase of the war was killing 1 000 Angolans every day, it is clear that more than 500 000 died during the two years of resumed hostilities: the ethnic cleansing of Ovimbundu and Bakongo citizens between November 1992 and January 1993; revenge killings by both sides of those suspected of supporting the other in cities which changed hands; as well as from landmines, starvation and disease. More Angolans died as a result of war in the two years between October 1992 and November 1994 than in the sixteen years of conflict before 1991.

The explanation for this lies in the technological sophistication of the newly imported weaponry of the FAA and, to a lesser extent, UNITA (with extraordinary profits and commissions characterising the purchase chains), and the superior efficiency of the private military forces which helped to plan and lead the FAA counterattack against UNITA after Savimbi had announced his unilateral cease-fire in September 1993.[10] Unwilling to accept a cease-fire when UNITA effectively controlled four-fifths of Angola, and relieved of the prohibition on arms sales to either Angolan party that had earlier comprised part of the Bicesse Accords, the government simply ignored UNITA's termination of hostilities, disregarded the ensuing peace negotiations in Lusaka and deployed its new weapons and better trained and led forces, along with mercenary special forces units, against cities occupied by UNITA, with devastating effect. Special forces teams were also used against logistical staging points and diamond areas in UNITA hands, providing the basis for the subsequent transfer of 'concessions' to companies associated with Executive Outcomes.[11]

Originally under instructions to defend themselves but not to attack, UNITA commanders, starved of weapons and fuel – the UN Security Council having imposed a prohibition on sales of these items to UNITA, but not to the government's forces – succumbed to pressure. The unilateral cease-fire collapsed and middlemen who were prepared to deal with UNITA made big profits – though on a smaller scale than those supplying the government – from exchanges of weapons, ammunition and fuel for diamonds recovered from areas under UNITA's control. The war became one of attrition throughout much of 1994, with each side systematically shelling or bombing cities held by the other.[12]

What little was left of Angola's economy after almost sixteen years of civil war was destroyed between 1992 and the end of 1994. The GDP declined by seventy per cent over three years;

total external debt, as a percentage of GDP, almost quadrupled, as did military spending, while social expenditure was halved.[13]

Civilian security companies and a private military company

A review of private military activities in Angola is necessarily dominated by an analysis of the performance of Executive Outcomes (EO). A number of other companies have also provided private security services in Angola: Defence Systems Limited (DSL), Gray Security Limited, *Alpha 5 Lda* and *Tele Service Sociedade de Telecomunicações, Segurança e Serviços* (TeleServices) being the most prominent among them. None of these companies, whose parentage differs from that of the EO family, appears to provide combat, military advisory, or military training services of the sort provided by EO; although TeleServices has the capacity to do so and Alpha 5 has been accused by UNITA of harbouring EO personnel[14] since the latter company ostensibly withdrew its military staff in January 1996.

Both TeleServices and Alpha 5 are registered public enterprise security companies (PESCs), controlled by Angolan military officials, able to divert FAA officers and men into these companies when deemed appropriate. They have had no reason to do this for military purposes, although TeleServices, assisted by Gray Security, provides site protection services at Soyo and in certain diamond areas, while Alpha 5, again with assistance from Gray Security, offers similar services in Luanda and at other diamond sites. DSL, a British company, was expelled from Angola in 1998 after many years of providing site and other asset protection services to foreign embassies and private companies.

DSL's expulsion was effected by Angola's Minister of the Interior, ostensibly because the company had contravened the law relating to the registration of PESCs by concluding contracts with foreign corporate nationals directly through London, rather than through DSL's Angolan subsidiary.

In a broadcast by America's Defence Monitor on 7 December 1997, Isenberg pointed to the proliferation of private security groups in Africa, alleging that there are over 100 on the continent of which about eighty are in Angola.[15] Other commentators make similar estimates, but few of these other companies are known outside their immediate circle. Moreover, as far as can be established, the PESCs registered there, including DSL, have provided only 'asset protection' services: guarding and protection services for embassies, hotels and corporate premises, warehouses, diamond fields, oil refineries and terminals, and of cash-in-transit.

While there is no doubt that retaining a significant number of former military personnel, some of whom carry modern arms, gives a private security company the ability to influence events in microcosm, and that such activities need to be regulated and monitored carefully, it is not these companies that have attracted attention in Angola. Although control of companies like TeleServices, Alpha 5 or DSL might enable their owners to displace others from control of economic assets, for example, and secure the control for themselves, these companies have not undertaken such tasks to date in Angola. Angolan security forces have been used when the government wished to clear diamond fields, whether of *garimpeiros*,[16] or of UNITA elements, although private companies such as TeleServices and Alpha 5 have subsequently been charged to protect the resource for its owners.

What distinguishes EO in Angola, therefore, is not that it was a private security company. It was, in fact, a private military company, capable of delivering private, specialised, military forces, thus providing services that no civilian security company is equipped or licensed to provide. In a recent paper, Shearer offers an interesting definition of 'private military companies':

"Their essential purpose is to enhance the capability of a client's military forces to function better in war, or to deter conflict more effectively. These companies are distinct from organisations operating in other areas of the security industry in that they are designed to have a strategic impact on the security and political environments of weak states facing a significant military threat."[17]

Howe has drawn a further distinction between EO and other similar companies. He speaks of three layers of 'private military groups' operating in Africa:

"One layer is that of training [and] maybe guarding military installations, fairly benign operations. The second might be combat support; for example, ferrying troops up to the front in transport helicopters. And then the third layer is actual combat. Executive Outcomes is an incredible, what we call 'force multiplier'. It can do all three of those. Most other organizations can do only one, or perhaps two, of the three."[18]

Others providing combat services

Foreign mercenaries

EO is thus not simply a species of the same genus as the civilian security firms providing asset protection services in Angola. What distinguishes it is that it provided **combat** services to the Angolan government in its military campaign against UNITA. Although EO appears to have been unique in providing such corporate services in the last five years in Angola, however, mercenary services antedate the 1990s in the Angolan conflict, as elsewhere in Africa.

In November 1975, FNLA President Roberto, suddenly deprived of Western support after the passage of the <u>Clark Amendment</u>,[19] and faced with the retreat of the Zairian forces provided by Mobutu, recruited mercenaries in Britain, the US and the Netherlands.[20] Bridgland writes:

"The quality of the mercenaries was exceptionally low ... They were the new young unemployed of the mid-1970's, and for the most part they were the most socially ill-equipped of their generation – poorly educated and from poorer homes, many of them real intellectual innocents ... Most had very little combat experience. Some had no military training at all, and two were London street sweepers recruited with the lure of $US300 a week and sent from their jobs straight to Angola."[21]

These mercenaries were unable to assist the FNLA in avoiding defeat. The psychopathic behaviour[22] of Costas Georgiou, whose *nom de guerre* was Colonel Callan, became notorious. Callan and twelve other mercenaries were captured after the FNLA's rout on the border with the former Zaire in the north-west of Angola on 6 February 1976. The ten Britons and three US citizens were brought to trial for war crimes before a People's Revolutionary Tribunal by the Angolan government in June and convicted in July. Three Britons and one American were executed by a firing squad on 10 July 1976. The others were imprisoned.

Congolese Katangans and Angolan Bakongo

The MPLA used Katangan forces[23] in the battle for the control of Luanda in 1975,[24] and later to invade the Shaba province of Zaire in 1977 and 1978. These forces, approximately 4 000-strong, originally comprised part of the Katangan *gendarmerie* which had fought under Moise Tshombe for Katanga's secession in 1961 and 1962, and fled to Angola after their defeat by UN forces. The Portuguese military authorities thereafter exploited the *Katangenses'* resentment of Mobutu, who had assumed the presidency of the Congo for the second time in 1965, and mobilised a Katangan unit against the FNLA forces[25] commanded by Roberto. These *Katangenses* were later incorporated into the armed forces of the Angolan government, where they gained a reputation as one of the most effective fighting units.

On the other side of the Angolan conflict between 1976 and 1989, many members of the defeated FNLA forces were brought south to Namibia by Colonel Jan Breytenbach of the South African Defence Force (SADF), and constituted as 32 Battalion. This battalion, known colloquially as 'Buffalo Battalion', was frequently used as an element of the SADF's support operations for UNITA in southern Angola. Barlow, who later founded EO, served as the second-in-command of the reconnaisance wing of 32 Battalion in the early 1980s.

This activity, while involving foreign forces (the Katangans), or indigenous forces under foreign command (32 Battalion), does not constitute **private** military support. Both the Katangans and the former FNLA troops in 32 Battalion were deployed as units of national military forces.

Did UNITA use mercenaries?

Since the outbreak of the 'second civil war' in October 1992, General João de Matos, Chief of Staff of the FAA, and other persons have accused UNITA of making use of mercenaries. General Matos was cited in January 1995, as saying that *"... some 300 South African mercenaries serve with the government forces and slightly less with UNITA ..."*[26]

Venter wrote late in 1995: *"Savimbi, too, is recruiting mercenaries and transport pilots in South Africa. Specialists from Belgium, Israel, Morocco, France, Germany and Zimbabwe are training UNITA forces in northern Angola near the Zaire border and in Zaire itself, which is his main conduit of supplies. Many of these professionals are employed to teach special forces-tactics to counter the FAA accent on dislocating enemy command and control centres."*[27]

Human Rights Watch/Africa claimed that EO was providing assistance to UNITA on contract until April 1993, and observed that, *"... in the first quarter of 1993, EO employees found themselves assisting operations against each other."*[28]

This remarkable assertion seems to relate to a vague reference in the report of Ballesteros, the UN Special Rapporteur on the use of mercenaries, to the UN Economic and Social Council on 12 January 1994:

"... the South African firm Executive Outcomes, headed by Esben [sic] Barlow ... [recruited] ... former members of South Africa's 31st and 32nd Battalions as security guards at Angolan oil refineries and installations, who are alleged to have fought in Huambo alongside the UNITA forces ... Three mercenaries ... were wounded in fighting in Huambo and evacuated on a clandestine Propilot flight to South Africa on 11 March 1993."[29]

Ballesteros appears misinformed: the three EO employees were injured in the attack on Soyo by EO.

Ballesteros makes a number of other references to UNITA's use of mercenaries. In the same report, he notes *"... reports [on] the presence of foreign mercenaries in the ranks of UNITA, most of them from South Africa and Zaire ... UNITA's control of the eastern provinces reportedly facilitated the arrival in Angola of mercenaries from Zaire to fight alongside the rebel forces ..."*[30]

Ballesteros also cites other reports of mercenary activity in support of UNITA, and refers to clandestine flights from Durban and Johannesburg to Mucusso and Jamba, transporting mercenaries and equipment. Unfortunately, he offers no particulars of the companies involved in any of these, or dates that would permit further investigation. He refers to a warning by the Chief of the SADF on 11 September 1993 about the illegality of mercenary service, but seems not to understand that this related to EO's recruitment activity.[31]

No further information on the identity of the mercenaries allegedly supporting UNITA is thus available. Companies and individuals domiciled in Belgium, Zaire/DRC, South Africa, Namibia and perhaps elsewhere, undoubtedly provided logistical support to UNITA in the course of the war. This included deliveries of weapons and petroleum products, both of which were prohibited in September 1993 under a UN Security Council resolution. Arms deliveries to any Angolan party were also prohibited, after April 1991, in terms of the 'triple-zero' prohibition in the <u>Angolan Peace Accords</u>. This ban was effectively lifted by the Security Council, in respect of the government of Angola, in September 1993.

Even the FAA, which has supplied details of companies providing logistical support to UNITA and of aircraft violating Angola's air space to the UN, the US, Russia, Portugal and the South African government since 1993, has apparently not been able to gather particulars on the identity of mercenaries said to be assisting UNITA.

EO would thus appear to have had the field essentially to itself, in the provision of battlefield support in Angola's 'second civil war'.[32]

Executive Outcomes in Angola

Did EO provide 'mercenary' services and to what effect?

If EO is the only private military group known to have had a strategic impact on the security and political environment of Angola, certain questions must be addressed:

- What was the objective character of its role there? Were the men in EO's employ in Angola between 1993 and 1996 'mercenaries', within the scope of the technical meaning of the term according to international law?

- What were the effects of their engagement, firstly on the enhanced efficiency of the FAA, and secondly on contemporary efforts at international conflict resolution in Angola?

The first question is relatively easy to answer. Three international conventions provide definitions that offer a framework for analysis. To qualify as a 'mercenary', there must be:

- recruitment for, and direct participation in hostilities in an armed conflict;

- in a country of which the person is neither a national nor a resident, nor a member of its national armed forces, or of the armed forces of another country sent to the country in conflict on active duty;

- by a person who *"... is motivated to take part in these hostilities essentially by a desire for private gain ..."*;

- who *"... is promised ... material compensation substantially in excess of that promised or paid to combatants of similar ranks and functions in the armed forces of that party ..."*[33]

Mercenary activities are regarded as undesirable and illegal.[34] The legal scope of the prohibition against mercenarism, however, is unclear, particularly whether the provision of such services to recognised governments in civil wars falls foul of the prohibition.[35] If one leaves aside the technical debate – which is explored elsewhere – the nature of EO's activities and the capacity in which they were performed, are clear.

Detailed descriptions of incidents involving EO units, based on interviews with EO personnel by journalists such as Venter[36] and commentators such as Howe and Shearer, make it clear that they saw combat in Angola and were intended to do so. They were not simply advisors or trainers. Similar evidence – albeit from wives (or widows)[37] and other family members of persons admitted lost in combat – and gruesome photographs released by UNITA of the uniformed corpses of EO employees, prove the same point.

These former SADF soldiers from the Reconnaissance Regiments and 32 Battalion, airmen from the fighter and helicopter squadrons of the SAAF, and members of Koevoet and perhaps MK, did what they were trained to do, notwithstanding the formal denials by company spokesmen.[38] Their senior officers helped to plan the campaigns against UNITA with members of the FAA General Staff:[39] their pilots flew reconnaissance, support and operational missions including aerial bombardment of towns held by UNITA; small special forces units undertook independent operations, as well as others in company with Angolan special forces personnel.[40] On at least one occasion, a senior officer commanded a joint armoured assault on a UNITA logistics base.[41] In addition, officers and especially non-commissioned officers (NCOs), trained Angolan personnel to fight better and taught them the tactics that they had earlier taught UNITA, in order to neutralise them more effectively.[42]

With Russian and Portuguese training on offer and a history of both in the FAA, and with Portuguese former commandos readily available, the FAA would not have turned to a group of former South African specialists – many of whom had fought in support of UNITA while in the SADF – in their hour of greatest need, and paid them very large sums of money,[43] if the South Africans had refused to use their skills on the battlefield. Nor would EO have deployed at least 500 men[44] – mostly former private soldiers drawn from 32 Battalion and paramilitary forces from Koevoet who were not known for their training skills – if the purpose was merely to advise and train. There is thus no doubt that the company, and at least many of its recruits for service in Angola, were *"... specially recruited ... in order to fight in an armed conflict ... [and took] ... a direct part in hostilities ..."*[45]

Neither EO[46] itself, nor the most senior EO personnel were nationals of, or resident in Angola when they were recruited between 1993 and 1995. Many men from 32 Battalion, and perhaps Koevoet, however, may have been Angolan nationals.

There is no doubt that their motive was financial. Barlow and other EO spokespeople repeatedly made it clear that they were motivated by money, while ideology played no role.[47] The officers and men recruited for Angola were offered exceptionally high remuneration, far higher than that available to serving members of the South African National Defence Force (SANDF) or the FAA.[48]

EO's actions in context: Angola's second civil war

Analysing the effects of EO's operations in Angola poses a different challenge. Human Rights Watch and to a lesser extent <u>Africa Confidential</u>, as well as Venter, have provided a partial chronological account of the firm's activities between 1993 and 1996.[49] The Angolan peace process, the elections in September 1992 and the early stages of the war that followed them, have likewise been the subject of several overlapping accounts. A number of people have written personal memoirs of the events which led to the resumption of the war at the end of 1992.[50] These diaries are often at odds on key questions, however, and the diversity of the writers' experiences makes it difficult to understand elements in the causal chain leading to the resumption of the war and its subsequent prosecution.

In order to understand the context of EO's involvement in the war and in efforts to resolve the Angolan crisis, it is necessary to summarise the events between the resumption of conflict at the end of October 1992 and the cease-fire proposal by Savimbi in August 1993, shortly before EO's formal engagement by the Angolan government

Angola's first democratic elections were held on 29 and 30 September 1992 and were characterised by the enthusiasm and commitment of millions of voters. Tensions arose within a short time after the close of the polls, however, when government media began to broadcast results, not released by the National Electoral Commission (NEC), reflecting victories for the MPLA and President dos Santos in many constituencies. Five small opposition parties, as well as the FNLA and UNITA, protested to the NEC, UNAVEM and the troika, citing catalogues of irregularities, documented with varying degrees of accuracy.

Savimbi broadcast to UNITA supporters on VORGAN, its radio station, on 3 October, suggesting that UNITA would not tolerate electoral fraud. He withdrew from Luanda to his personal house at Huambo shortly thereafter, on the advice of ministers of the government of Côte d'Ivoire,[51] who suggested that his life was at risk in the capital. In an effort to force the NEC to address the alleged instances of fraud, UNITA general officers in the FAA issued a statement demanding that these should be investigated and declaring their intention to abandon the FAA until this had been done. Other UNITA officers and men began to leave the camps where forces had been concentrated before the elections and fanned out into neighbouring municipalities.[52]

The intervention of South African Foreign Minister Pik Botha and members of the troika, and the arrival of a UN team despatched by the Security Council, persuaded UNITA, which had by then presented a detailed list of serious irregularities, to await the results of the UN investigation called for by fourteen opposition parties. When UN Representative, Margaret Anstee, declared victory for the MPLA, however, and a plurality for Dos Santos – requiring a second presidential ballot in elections that, despite irregularities, were said to be generally free and fair – tensions rose alarmingly. Clashes multiplied between UNITA units and members of the paramilitary riot police, into which most members of Angola's special forces units had been transferred before the elections, with each side accusing the other of aggression.

In an effort to avert a crisis, negotiations were arranged in Luanda in the last week of October between teams representing the government and UNITA. The two sides exchanged position papers containing proposals to end the clashes, restore the peace process and govern the country until the second round of presidential elections could be held.

Between 31 October and 2 November 1992, however, while negotiations to resolve the crisis were still under way,[53] the riot police and other FAA units attacked and destroyed all UNITA's residences and party offices in Luanda, leading to the death of many and the capture of almost all its military and civilian cadres in the capital.

UNITA's troops had by now occupied many more *municípios*, as well as the strategically important towns of Uíge and Negage. A number of international diplomatic initiatives were launched at the end of November and the first half of December in an effort to staunch the ominous slide to war.

On 18 December, UN Secretary-General Boutros-Ghali reported to the Security Council that *"... UNITA forces continue to occupy up to two-thirds of the municipalities in Angola ..."*[54] Government emergency police, army troops and government-armed vigilantes (*fitinhas*), meanwhile, had concentrated on destroying UNITA's party offices and killing its putative supporters in Angola's main cities. At least 10 000 Ovimbundu and Bakongo were reported to have been killed in these purges within a few weeks. Maier notes that *"... the battle for Luanda ignited a wave of urban clashes and massacres of unarmed civilians [by government forces] that continued for the next three months and saw UNITA crushed in key cities such as Benguela, Malange and Lubango."*[55]

Just one week after the Security Council called for a resumption of political dialogue between the government and UNITA,[56] and Savimbi had accepted Boutros-Ghali's proposal for a meeting with Dos Santos in Geneva, government forces began a concentrated drive on 29 December to cleanse Angola's main cities of UNITA supporters. UNITA offices and other positions at N'dalatando, Caxito, Dondo, Lubango, Benguela, Lobito, Namibe and Cuíto had been attacked by 6 January 1993.

McGreal reported on 8 January 1993, that *"... the Government has made it clear that it has no intention of halting its push against the rebels until they are cleared from Angola's main cities."*[57]

Reporting on events in Benguela, Catumbela and Lobito, McGreal noted a week later: *"In all three towns the fighting was heavy. UNITA offices were blown apart, spewing party membership cards onto the pavement amid smashed glass and rubble. Once the UNITA soldiers and officials had been dealt with, government forces, led by the police, turned on the rebels' civilian sympathisers."* He suggested that some 1 000 to 2 000 were killed in this way and cites a relief worker from *Médecins sans Frontières* as saying: *"They didn't just kill men, they killed families."*[58]

Savimbi had seemingly been traumatised by the events in Luanda in which many of his senior officers and party leaders were killed or captured. He was unexpectedly compliant with UN and troika demands throughout November and December. After an air and ground attack on Huambo between 9 and 11 January had destroyed his personal house near the airport, as well as much of the surrounding area, however, he advised Portugal's President Soares, among others, that he was obliged to *"... put on my General's uniform, or we shall all be killed."*[59]

Savimbi's assumption of command turned the tide. UNITA regrouped its forces and counterattacked in Huambo, Cuíto, Menongue, Cuíto Cuanavale, M'banza Congo, Saurimo and Soyo.[60]

When UN Special Representative Anstee convened peace negotiations in Addis Ababa at the end of January, the UN estimated that UNITA controlled 105 of the country's 164 municipalities.[61] Although both sides sent delegations to the Ethiopian capital, the talks did not result in a cease-fire. By 3 February, the Christian Science Monitor was quoting diplomats in Luanda who said that UNITA controlled *"... between 60 and 70 per cent of the country."*[62] The same report cites UN officials estimating that 2 000 people died in Benguela alone and about 1 500 in Lobito, as a result of killings (of suspected UNITA supporters) by armed civilians and special police, with fears of more to come.

Anstee sought to convene a second round of peace talks in Addis Ababa at the government's request, between 26 February and 1 March, motivated partly by Luanda's desire to avoid defeat in Huambo, the recapture of which had become a matter of honour for Savimbi. UNITA did not send a delegation from within Angola, but two representatives from abroad. Savimbi's aim was evidently not to be distracted from a victory in Huambo.

By 6 March, after 55 days of bloody clashes,[63] UNITA had recaptured Huambo and Savimbi gave a seminal speech,[64] opening a window on one side of the fear and antagonism that had driven the Angolan civil war.[65] On 11 March, however, the UN Security Council adopted Resolution 811, condemning UNITA for its violation of the Angolan Peace Accords and demanding an immediate cease-fire.[66]

Washington took the initiative to arrange talks in Abidjan with delegations representing the Angolan government and UNITA. On 28 March, US Deputy Assistant Secretary Jeff Davidow announced that both Angolan parties seemed ready to meet under UN auspices before 12 April, to discuss a cease-fire and a means of restoring national reconciliation, *"... with broadened participation by UNITA in the government at the national, provincial and local levels."*[67] UNITA's Political Commission confirmed its willingness to attend and issued a statement proposing a suspension of hostilities by troops on the ground, followed by a cease-fire that was premised on the formation of a single national army.[68]

Three principles – a cease-fire, resumption of the Bicesse Accords and *"... national reconciliation, to include broadened participation by UNITA at the national, provincial and local levels ..."* – were adopted as the basis for the negotiations between 12 April and 21 May 1993 in Abidjan, convened under the auspices of Anstee. These principles echoed those which had provided the framework for the negotiations in Luanda in October 1992 when the government decided to crush UNITA in the capital.

The Abidjan talks failed after almost six weeks because UNITA was not prepared to withdraw and quarter its forces until a UN peacekeeping force had been deployed in Angola. In a letter to the Daily Telegraph, Anstee wrote:

"... there might have been agreement on a new cease-fire during the six weeks of negotiations at Abidjan, Ivory Coast, if I had been able to commit to the UN providing a small symbolic force of 'Blue Helmets' to oversee it from the outset. However, I was told that even if a cease-fire were agreed, no UN troops could be available for six to nine months ... because of all the other peacekeeping calls on the UN and the difficulties of obtaining more troops ..."[69]

In the light of subsequent events, UNITA's demand that a UN peacekeeping force should be put in place before its troops were confined to cantonment areas seems understandable.[70] The Clinton Administration, reflecting profound frustration at what it saw as UNITA's intransigence, however, extended immediate diplomatic recognition to the Angolan government, thereby estranging UNITA.

The UN Secretary-General described the breakdown of the talks as *"... a major and tragic setback to the peace process."*[71] The Security Council, in response, adopted Resolution 834 of 1 June 1993, holding UNITA *"... responsible for the breakdown of the talks and for thereby jeopardising the peace process ... [demanding that] ... it immediately cease [its] ... actions and armed attacks."*

When UNITA returned to the offensive in the aftermath of the Abidjan talks and the US' recognition of the government, African peace initiatives moved to centre stage. In August and September, discussions were proposed between the two Angolan leaders and UNITA also invited a senior OAU delegation to Huambo for talks. Nothing came of these proposals, however.

EO's entry and subsequent role:
Inducing Savimbi to negotiate or prolonging the war?

Although EO apparently signed its first contract with the Angolan government in September 1993, a small contingent had been in the country for at least six months before that. News reports[72] suggest that EO began recruiting men who had served in the SADF Reconnaissance Regiments and 32 Battalion in February. There are conflicting reports on the origin of the initiative. A British subject, Anthony Buckingham, seen to be representing either Ranger Oil, a Canadian company, or Heritage Oil,[73] reportedly approached Barlow to assemble a team of special forces operatives to recapture Heritage assets overrun by UNITA at Soyo. The fact that Ranger's and Heritage's petroleum interests at that time, were apparently concentrated 120 kilometres south of Soyo,[74] gave rise to a belief that Buckingham was acting either for a consortium of international oil companies, or for the Angolan government.[75]

Whatever the origin of Buckingham's mandate, the first contingent of between eighty and a hundred EO troops, deployed under the leadership of Luitingh, and *"... backed by two Angolan battalions ..."*, recaptured Soyo in May 1993, though UNITA retook the town after the EO contingent withdrew.[76] In August 1993, the Angolan government, apparently encouraged by the South African group's success at Soyo, began negotiations for a contract under which EO was to train 5 000 troops from the FAA's 16th Regiment, as well as thirty pilots, and to direct front-line operations against UNITA. This agreement was concluded in September 1993.[77]

EO's engagement for two periods of twelve months, from September 1993 to September 1995, and for a further three months thereafter, until January 1996, undoubtedly contributed significantly to the FAA's subsequent military ascendancy.[78] The company multiplied the effect of other factors – including major new weapons purchases and the dynamic leadership by General de Matos – in turning the tide of the Angolan civil war in 1994 and 1995, by enabling the FAA to recapture a great deal of territory from UNITA's forces.

EO has also claimed, however, that its intervention in Angola forced Savimbi to the negotiating table.[79] This impressive claim has been carelessly repeated by some commentators[80] and, if accurate, would enable the company to argue that it made a positive contribution to the resolution of the Angolan conflict. Other interpretations of the influence of EO's intervention are also possible, however.

On 11 August 1993,[81] before it was known that the government was negotiating with EO, Savimbi proposed a cease-fire in a radio broadcast from Huambo. The proposal was rejected by Luanda.[82] On 3 September, Savimbi phoned President Soares, repeating his proposal for a cease-fire and the resumption of negotiations. He made similar calls to Boutros-Ghali and US Assistant Secretary of State, George Moose on 4 September. Soares, in response to Savimbi's call, sought unsuccessfully to have talks resume between the Angolan parties before the UN Security Council meeting scheduled for 15 September, at which the possibility of lifting the arms embargo against the Angolan government by imposing a new ban on oil and arms sales to UNITA alone, was to be decided.

In response to Savimbi's call to Moose, Washington pressed UNITA for detailed proposals. After a visit to Luanda (but not Huambo) by Robert Cabelly of the US State Department to explore possibilities, Savimbi sent specific proposals to Moose in a letter on 10 September.

UNITA's Chief of Staff, General Arlindo Chenda Pena 'Ben-Ben', met President Soares, as well as members of the Portuguese and European parliaments in Lisbon just after this. It seems that he intended to meet the troika there as well – the observers having assembled in Lisbon in preparation for the UN Security Council meeting – and to announce UNITA's cease-fire proposal. As the troika (and the Portuguese government) were 'unable' to meet the UNITA delegation, however, it apparently decided to make its announcement in Abidjan.

On 13 September, General Pena issued a formal statement at a media conference in Abidjan, after consultations with the Ivorian government, announcing that UNITA would observe a unilateral cease-fire from midnight on 20 September. As a result, Bêye flew to Abidjan to meet the UNITA delegation on 14 September; Boutros-Ghali encouraged the UN Security Council to postpone the imposition of oil and weapons sanctions against UNITA for ten days until 25 September, to allow time for a cease-fire to take effect. Washington sent Ed Brynn, the new senior Deputy Assistant Secretary for African Affairs, to Abidjan to discuss the agenda for a new round of talks, and King Hassan II of Morocco travelled to Lisbon on 20 September to consult with President Soares on means to advance a negotiated solution.

On 20 September at 11:00, in a broadcast over UNITA's VORGAN network, Savimbi confirmed General Pena's earlier announcement by formally declaring *"... the implementation of a unilateral cease-fire throughout the Angolan national territory, beginning at 24:00 on Monday, September 20 ..."*[83] This would permit the evacuation of foreign nationals from Cuíto[84] and the resumption of humanitarian aid deliveries as demanded by the UN Security Council, as well as the resumption of talks on the basis of the Abidjan principles.[85]

Unlike the Angolan armed forces, Bêye responded positively to this proposal. On 21 September, following a telephone conversation with Savimbi, he announced a meeting, scheduled for 23 September on São Tomé and Principe, between the Chiefs of Staff of the FAA and UNITA, with Lieutenant General Garouba, head of the UNAVEM II military mission, and the military attachés of the troika. UNITA's General Pena attended, accompanied by four officers. General de Matos sent his regrets at the last moment.[86]

Although the UN Security Council's oil and weapons embargo on UNITA became operative on 25 September, as no cease-fire between the two sides had come into effect,[87] UNITA's Political Commission reaffirmed its acceptance of the 1992 electoral results certified by the UN, pledged to maintain the cease-fire, and to work with Bêye in seeking a peaceful solution on 6 October.[88]

On 7 October, Bêye issued the following statement in response:

"One cannot help but welcome UNITA's wish to maintain the cease-fire contained in its declaration of 20 September 1993. One must also acknowledge with satisfaction that UNITA accepts the validity of the Bicesse Accords, reiterates its acceptance of the September 1992 elections, as well as considers that the Project of Abidjan constitutes a serious basis for negotiation."[89]

On 8 October, the US State Department issued a press advisory statement in reaction to UNITA's statement of two days earlier: *"UNITA's communiqué goes a long way in removing lingering obstacles to the peace process. We believe the Government must take advantage of this opportunity for peace."* [90]

On 9 October, however, President dos Santos issued a remarkable statement, calling on FAA troops to stand up to UNITA. Two days later, he 'demanded' that UNITA clarify *"... ambiguities and, in some respects, contradictions in its positions ..."* taken on 6 October.[91]

On 18 October, the UN Special Representative called for a meeting between the Angolan parties in Lusaka to clarify points in the UNITA statement required by the government, and to lay the foundations for serious peace talks. Talks began on 25 October in Lusaka and continued until 31 October, but the government delegation refused any direct contact with UNITA members. On 15 November 1993, however, the Lusaka peace talks were formally convened by Bêye. These talks eventually gave rise to the signature of the Lusaka Protocol by representatives of both leaders on 20 November 1994.[92]

Nothing in this chronology supports the proposition that EO played any role in inducing Savimbi to negotiate. The Lusaka peace talks were initiated by a cease-fire proposal made by Savimbi on 11 August 1993, approximately one month before EO's first formal twelve-month $40 million contract was signed with the Angolan government.

EO's impact on the FAA's military capability and on efforts to resolve the conflict by peaceful means

Savimbi's call for a cease-fire in the second week of August 1993 is intelligible only in the context of the African efforts at mediation that began after the failure of the Abidjan talks. He had frequently said that Anstee did not understand the issues at stake and that only an African could facilitate resolution of the crisis. He had thus welcomed Bêye's appointment when Anstee stepped down.

But it was not only the fact that he expected a better hearing from Bêye and the Africans then engaged that had an influence. Other factors contributing to his cease-fire proposal no doubt included the realisation that the war had reached a stalemate; pressure from the US in the aftermath of the failed Abidjan talks; the move afoot in the UN Security Council to permit arms sales to the Angolan government, formerly forbidden under the 'triple-zero' provisions of the cease-fire included in the Bicesse Accords; and the announcements by the British and Russian governments that arms sales to the Angolan government would be resumed.

By 20 September, when Savimbi's cease-fire took effect, the government could only claim control of the coastal plain from Ambriz in the north to the Namibian border, and the interior cities of Malange, Saurimo and Luena. UNITA controlled a significant part of the rest, with the larger part of the country, however, either hotly contested, or not seen by either side as being of strategic importance. UNITA was besieging Cuíto, pounding it with artillery fire with seemingly as little regard for human life as the government's forces had displayed when attacking Huambo.

FAA units, already strengthened by General de Matos' restructuring programme, Portuguese training, and the consignments of new weapons received from former East-bloc countries and Brazil, were advancing on Huambo along four routes – from Waku Kungo, Lubango, Cubal and Balombo. UNITA's forces had checked their advance from the coastal plain to the west, shortly after the climb up to the central plateau had begun. The Angolan Air Force was conducting regular bombing raids on Huambo.

Certain well-informed and prescient observers outside the UN understood both the risk and the opportunity in September 1993. Former US Assistant Secretary of State for African Affairs, Chester Crocker, had written a trenchant opinion piece in October 1993:

"Today a new stalemate may be emerging. UNITA is stronger on the ground and better organised … But the MPLA holds Luanda, the revenue from some 500,000 barrels of oil per day output and universal diplomatic recognition. Washington, Lisbon and Moscow, meanwhile, have dropped a key restriction from the 1991 package, thus enabling the MPLA government to return to the world arms market with the means to attract mercenaries, contractors and assorted hired guns from around the world."[93]

The purpose of EO's engagement was to recover the territory captured by UNITA between January and August 1993, and to shift the balance of military power in the Angolan government's favour. The principles of the peace embodied in the Lusaka Protocol – a cease-fire, resumption of the Bicesse Accords and *"… national reconciliation, to include broadened participation by UNITA at the national, provincial and local levels …"* – had been settled in Abidjan in April 1993, and were almost identical to those introduced in the crisis negotiations in October 1992 in Luanda. The Angolan government, having been freed formally from the restraints of the triple-zero arms sale ban[94] and having secured the services of EO, preferred to seek military victory.

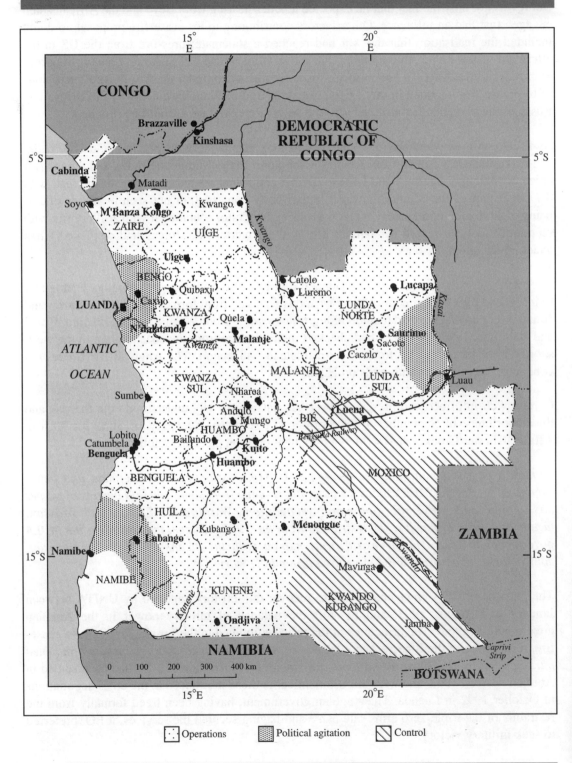

Areas of UNITA operations, control and influence: September 1993

CONGO

Brazzaville
Kinshasa

DEMOCRATIC
REPUBLIC OF
CONGO

5°S

Cabinda

Matadi

Soyo
M'Banza Kongo
ZAIRE

Kwango

UIGE

Kwango

Uíge

Catolo
Luremo

Luçapa

BENGO

Quibaxi

LUANDA
Caxito
KWANZA

Quela

LUNDA
NORTE

Saurimo
Saçote

N'dalatando
Kwanza
Malanje

Cacolo

ATLANTIC

OCEAN

KWANZA
SUL

Nharea

MALANJE

LUNDA
SUL

Luau

Sumbe

Andulo
Mungo

BIÉ
Luena

Benguela Railway

Lobito
Catumbela
Benguela

HUAMBO
Bailundo
Kuito
Huambo

MOXICO

ZAMBIA

BENGUELA

HUÍLA
Kubango
Menongue

15°S

Labango

Namibe

Mavinga

NAMIBE
KUNENE
Ondjiva

Kwando

Jamba

Caprivi
Strip

NAMIBIA

0   100   200   300   400 km

BOTSWANA

15°E

20°E

:·: Operations   Political agitation   Control

The government therefore refused to accept the cease-fire even after the peace talks had begun in Lusaka in November 1993. EO was given a chance to show its mettle. The approximately 500 men initially deployed by EO in Angola had a significant effect on the overall operational efficiency of the FAA from an early stage. By helping the FAA General Staff define their requirements for armour, artillery, fighter and bomber aircraft and special *accoutrements,* and acquiring specialised materiel for them on world arms markets,[95] EO was able to engage and permit its trainees to fight with state-of-the-art equipment. Drogin's estimate of US $2 billion spent on new equipment by October 1994 is not far off the mark, to judge by the catalogues of armaments actually imported.[96]

Secondly, EO's delivery of tactical advice, training and combat capability[97] rendered UNITA – whose forces maintained the cease-fire[98] for perhaps three months after 20 September, despite severe provocation and loss of territory previously captured – especially vulnerable to FAA attacks. By October 1994, "*... EO ha[d] trained 4,000 to 5,000 government troops and about 30 pilots ... at three camps, located in Lunda Sul, Cabo Ledo and Dondo ... reportedly ... [in] basic fighting techniques, weapons maintenance, signals, engineering and specialised skills such as reconnaissance.*"[99] HRW/A also recorded its training of the FAA Reconnaissance Regiment and Special Tactical Units. Furthermore:

"*EO also maintains two 'Special Units' of its own, which since February 1994 have been active in front-line operations against UNITA. One was deployed in Uige province, the other in Lunda Norte province in August 1994. Human Rights Watch has been told that three ex-SADF helicopter pilots regularly transport both EO employees and Angolan soldiers, including in combat situations.*"[100]

The decisive role of EO units in ground combat and aerial bombardment in this period has already been highlighted. HRW/A cites the somewhat more circumspect account of the mercenaries' contribution to the capture of Cafunfo in July 1994, provided by Brummer in the Weekly Mail & Guardian, alleging that "*... about 20 Executive Outcome 'advisers' had been spread through the column, from platoon to command level, and air support had been given by Executive Outcomes-trained pilots.*"[101] Venter's detailed accounts of more extensive engagement are more persuasive.[102]

Shearer (1998) offers a useful thumbnail sketch of EO's activities in 1994:

"*In January 1994, the FAA's 16th Regiment was airlifted to N'dalatando, a key town south-east of Luanda, and retook it with tactical assistance from EO. The Cafunfo diamond fields in Luanda [sic] Norte province were captured in June 1994 in an operation in which EO personnel participated directly. In August the FAA regained Soyo and took the provincial capital Uíge, and, in September, the key town of Huambo fell to government forces.*"[103]

The following map, reflecting the situation in February 1995, illustrates, by comparison with that for September 1993, the FAA's successes with EO's help.

It is arguable, therefore, that the effect of the heightened capability afforded to the FAA was not to shorten, but to prolong the war.[104] Without better capacity – at least in prospect – there

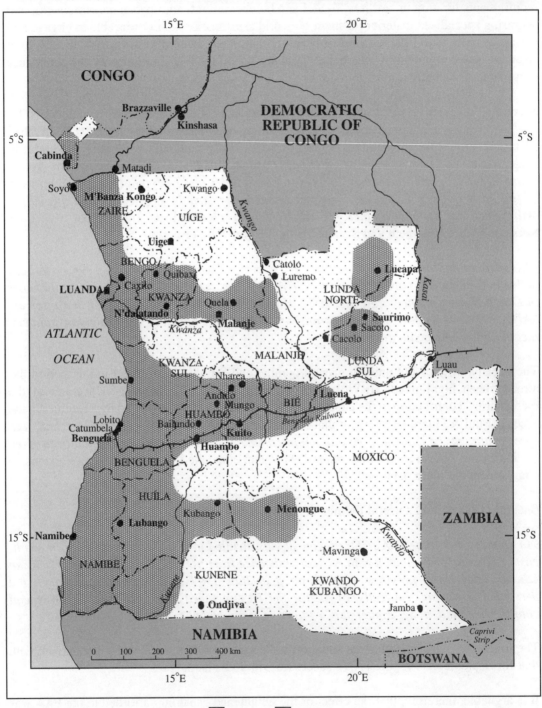

is every reason to believe that the Angolan government would have responded favourably to the cease-fire proposal made by Savimbi in August 1993, and implemented unilaterally by UNITA on 20 September. The government had sent representatives to negotiate in November 1992 and January, February and April 1993. It was only from August that it no longer had any interest in a cease-fire.

The government's hard-line

EO's continued availability and efficiency – together with substantial arms deliveries from several countries – gave the Angolan government reason to believe that the FAA could continue to disregard the cease-fire throughout the Lusaka talks.[105] Drogin observed late in October 1994: *"As a result [of international legitimacy and superior military capability], government hardliners insist that Savimbi can now be beaten, or at least pushed back into the bush. They want to force UNITA from diamond-producing areas and cut its supply lines to Zaire."*[106]

Angolan government ministers and FAA military commanders made no secret of this in private discussions. Even after the initialling of the <u>Lusaka Protocol</u> on 31 October and formal signature of the truce provided for in the Protocol on 16 November 1994, the FAA military attack, assisted by EO, did not end.[107]

Huambo fell to government forces on 6 November, after Savimbi abandoned the city rather than take the casualties that defence would have entailed. Uíge was captured on 17 November after a night of intense aerial bombardment; FAA troops then moved on Negage. Cuíto Cuanavale was captured on 19 November. The FAA continued to move against UNITA positions in strength until 22 November 1994 and then, for at least two months, in a more discreet way with its Special Forces, with EO support, to recapture territory from UNITA.[108]

EO's engagement and the FAA's progressive advance continued less visibly until December 1995, when President Clinton, in the course of President dos Santos' first official visit to Washington, brought pressure to bear on the Angolan President to instruct EO forces to withdraw.[109] EO senior officers, however, boasted privately after the company's formal withdrawal of 178 men on 15 January 1996, that their withdrawal was stage-managed by agreement with the Angolan government, and that sufficient forces for essential tasks were retained within Angola.

Diamond interests contaminate the equation

Control of Angola's rich diamond fields was another factor in prolonging the war. In further payment for EO's services, substantial concessions were granted to Branch Energy, Buckingham's company,[110] which were transferred to Carson Gold (later converted to DiamondWorks Limited) through Hansard Management Services Limited and Hansard Trust Company Limited, in exchange for shares in DiamondWorks.[111] Numerous concessions were also secured by FAA generals and other senior officers. Capture and occupation of these areas for personal benefit were important goals for the combatants.

Likewise, of course, UNITA occupied and exploited the diamond areas under its control, to give it the resources needed to continue fighting. Many of these alluvial fields were worked by South African and other fortune-seekers. UNITA's income from its diamond operations has been estimated at between $300 million and $600 million per year. Enormous damage has been done by parties on both sides to the alluvial diamond fields by bulldozers and amateurish incompetence.

Results of the prolonged war

EO unquestionably helped the FAA to achieve its military objective, but at a terrible cost. When the second contract was signed in September 1994, the determination of the government and EO to continue the war despite UNITA's unilateral cease-fire, had cost the lives, in that year alone, of perhaps 200 000 Angolans,[112] destroyed most of the remaining national infrastructure, and fractured the Angolan economy.[113] Social and economic

Angola: Selected indicators: 1991-2000

Index	1991	1992	1993	1994	1995	1996	1997	2000
GDP ($ million)	12 127	8 702	6 645	4 706	5 529	5 896	6 248	7 728
Exports[1] ($ million)	3 630	3 796	3 005	3 113	3 625	3 840	4 139	
Oil exports ($ million)	3 238	3 573	2 826	2 896	3 400	3 588	3 869	
External Debt[2] (% of GDP)	67,3	106,1	149,7	233,8	193,8	152,3	140,1	101,1
Debt service ratio[3] – %	60,6	47,1	63,8	53,6	47,8	35,2	34,2	
Overall BoP (% of GDP)	-12,4	-15,4	-25,9	-28,1	-18,9	-10,9	-8,4	-2,7

1 Exports of goods and non-factor services
2 Excludes some oil company debt (data not available)
3 Ratio of debt service obligations to exports before debt relief

Composition of government spending
(percentage of GDP)

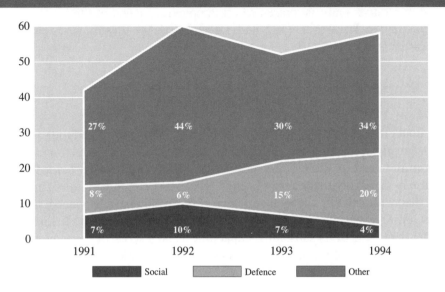

Gross domestic saving
(percentage of GDP)

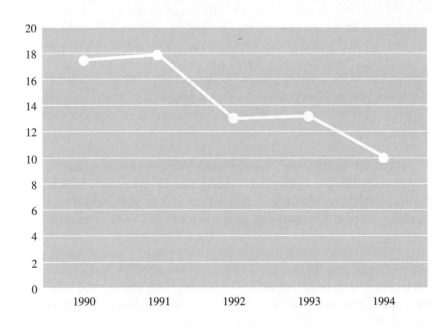

conditions in Angola were markedly worse in September 1995, when EO signed a contract for the third time.

The IMF's comparative analysis, presented on the previous page, of the key features of the Angolan economy in December 1992 and December 1994 illustrates the impact of the prolonged war most effectively.[114]

Current assessment

There is no doubt that EO's engagement by the FAA in 1993 contributed to the prolongation of the war – greatly worsening the suffering by Angola's civilian population.[115] It diverted attention from the need to address the root causes of the conflict and helped to create an Angolan military capability that has not been wisely used in regional affairs since then. This is not to say that, without EO's engagement, none of this would have happened; nor, of course, that it bears all, or even most of the blame. There is, however, a causal link between its activities after deploying of its substantial capabilities, and a series of consequences apparent in Angola and other parts of Central Africa today. At the least, EO contributed to the results.

Worse yet, peace is still not at hand in Angola, or its surrounding region, in part because the Angolan government, just as the old South African government, appeared to believe that it could resolve its domestic challenges by internal suppression and military pressure on its neighbours.[116] Savimbi's failure to overcome his (likely well-founded) fear of assassination if he travelled to Luanda, led to his refusal to demobilise his troops and, indeed to his rearming them against the likelihood of attack. UNITA's response to provocation by those in Angola's security services who believe that a final confrontation is inevitable, has thus contributed to the inevitability.

Persons associated with EO, in whatever corporate guise thereafter, were still engaged in the Angolan government's efforts to resolve the conflict by military means in 1998, albeit that they provided services that could not fall foul of the definition of 'mercenary'. Training of special forces units were undertaken by South African specialists, to the great satisfaction of the FAA General Staff, at the training unit in Huambo, and South African pilots flew the King Air electronic reconnaissance aircraft and other Angolan Air Force craft, that intercepted aircraft on illicit flights to supply UNITA in contravention of the UN Security Council resolution prohibiting such flights.[117]

These services were not intrinsically objectionable. What gave rise to concern was the fact that they were provided in the context of a rising tide of tension in Angola, which, many seasoned observers believed, presaged a new round of war with serious consequences for neighbouring states, despite the ostensible progress made in 1997 in implementing the peace accords.[118]

This insight proved prescient. In the face of evidence that UNITA had not disarmed and had in fact rebuilt its army in expectation of a FAA attack, FAA forces, under instructions from President dos Santos, moved against UNITA-controlled Andulo and Bailundo early in

December 1998, thereby formally beginning Angola's third civil war. UNITA seems, moreover, to have learned from the FAA's book. Recent reports suggest that it has recruited Ukrainian and South African mercenaries, some formerly employed by EO,[119] to train its troops and provide advisory services on the battlefield.

Another round of war in Angola, however, will offer no solution. Indeed, in the face of wider regional conflict, encompassing both the Democratic Republic of Congo (Kinshasa) and the Republic of Congo (Brazzaville), where Angolan belligerents have fought proxy wars in recent years, a new war can only contribute to the economic exhaustion of the region. Both Angolan parties should be dissuaded from war with all the capacity at the command of the international community.[120] It stands to reason that there is no place for the sale of private services which encourage one side, or the other, to believe it can benefit from further violent military clashes.

ENDNOTES

1   The <u>Bicesse Accords</u>, after the location on the outskirts of Lisbon where the signing ceremony took place.

2   Adapted from S M Cleary, *Angola: Prospects for Peace*, <u>South African Yearbook of International Affairs 1997</u>, SAIIA, Johannesburg, 1997.

3   It did not. As of the date of publication of this book, Angola is again embroiled in civil war.

4   C A Crocker, <u>High Noon in Southern Africa</u>, W W Norton and Company, New York, 1992, pp. 293-296.

5   <u>Decree No 58470</u> (1901), reviewed in 1919, abolished by <u>Decree No 42894</u> (1961). See C M de Sousa, <u>Angola Libre?</u>, Gallimard, Paris, 1975; Makidi-Ku-Ntima, *Class Struggle and the Making of the Revolution in Angola, Proletarianization and Class Struggle in Africa*, <u>Contemporary Marxism</u>, 6, Spring 1983, pp. 119-141.

6   The *petit bourgeosie* comprised whites, persons of 'mixed race' and acculturated black Angolans.

7   Crocker, op. cit., pp. 120 and 425-446; see also South African Department of Foreign Affairs, <u>Namibian Independence and Cuban Troop Withdrawal</u>, Pretoria, May 1989.

8   UN, <u>Agreement among the People's Republic of Angola, the Republic of Cuba and the Republic of South Africa</u>, UN Security Council document S/20345, New York, 22 December 1988.

9   M Anstee, *Letter to the Editor*, <u>Washington Post</u>, 10 June, 1993.

10   VORGAN radio broadcast, 11:00, 20 September 1993.

11   B Grill & C Dumay, *Der Söldner-Konzern,* <u>Die Zeit</u>, 4, 17 January 1997.

12   Huambo and surrounding towns suffered most under FAA bombardment; Cuíto (Bié) under that of UNITA.

13   IMF calculations based on Angolan government data, unpublished IMF data, September 1995.

14   While this is not impossible, no independent confirmation of UNITA's allegations could be found.

15   America's Defence Monitor, *Conflict Inc.: Selling the Arts of War*, broadcast on Private Security Groups, 7 December 1997. Isenberg is a Senior Research Analyst, Center for Defense Information, Washington DC, and author of <u>Fortune</u>

Ltd: A Profile of Today's Private Sector Mercenary Firms, Center for Defense Information Monograph, Washington DC, November 1997.

16   'Illegal' diamond miners, recovering stones without a concession.

17   D Shearer, Private Armies and Military Intervention, Adelphi Paper 316, International Institute for Strategic Studies, London, February 1998, p. 23. Shearer is explicit about EO's direct engagement in combat in Angola: see pp. 46, 48, and 66.

18   America's Defence Monitor, op. cit.

19   Prohibiting US support to any Angolan party in the conflict.

20   J Stockwell, In Search of Enemies: A CIA Story, Andre Deutsch, p. 224; Baltimore Sun, 3 February 1976; New York Times, 3 February 1976.

21   F Bridgland, Jonas Savimbi: A Key to Africa, Macmillan, London, pp. 177-178.

22   Ibid., p. 178

23   Surviving members of these forces and their descendants now comprise a large part of the 40th Brigade of the armed forces of the DRC, after their repatriation in the wake of Mobutu's demise in 1997.

24   M Meredith, The First Dance of Freedom, Hamish Hamilton, London, 1984, p. 295.

25   Ibid.

26   See SAPA-AFP-Reuter, Angola: Many SA Mercenaries Here, Citizen, 11 January 1995, p. 19.

27   A J Venter, Mercenaries Fuel Next Round in Angolan Civil War, Current Conflicts: Jane's International Defence Review, 1996.

28   Human Rights Watch Arms Project, Angola: Arms Trade and Violations of the Laws of War since the 1992 Elections, Human Rights Watch/Africa, New York, November 1994, p. 30.

29   E B Ballesteros, Report to the Economic and Social Council, E/CN.4/1994/23, United Nations, New York, 1994, para. 41.

30   Ibid., para. 40. This report of mercenary activity seems less plausible. The Bakongo straddle the borders between Angola, Zaire (as it then was, now the DRC) and the Republic of the Congo, and members of the same families belong to UNITA and owe allegiance to Kikongo chiefs, while Mobutu provided all types of assistance to UNITA, and earlier to the FNLA. None of this fits the description of mercenary activity, and it is unlikely that UNITA would have paid soldiers for such support. It did 'pay' for Mobutu's support in other ways, such as percentages of the proceeds of diamond sales from UNITA-controlled areas where such stones were sold through Zaire.

31   Ibid., para. 59. Ballesteros says that he "... has been informed that foreign mercenaries are training members of the Angolan rebel UNITA forces at Kamina ... which is also reportedly being used for the transport of weapons and equipment of the Angolan rebels. It has also been reported that South African mercenaries have settled in the area of Moanda, Zaire, and that the territory of Zaire is being used for the transport of South African and other mercenaries, weapons, equipment, medicines and food, on clandestine night-time flights, to the areas of Angolan territory under UNITA control." Regrettably, he provides no names of companies, or dates, or allegations of participation in particular actions. EO and Propilot are the only companies named in connection with Angola in the 1994 report, making one cautious about offering definitive statements on the basis of such unsubstantiated, information.

32   The possibility that individuals may have decided to fight with UNITA cannot be ruled out, although there is no evidence of recruitment efforts, or an identifiable group being involved in combat.

33   The 1977 Additional Protocol I to the Geneva Conventions, 12 August 1949, article 47(2); the International Convention against the Recruitment, Use, Financing and Training of Mercenaries, 4 December 1989; article 1; the OAU Convention for the Elimination of Mercenarism in Africa, 1977, which combines some elements of each of the other conventions; see Chapter 10.

34   Article 47(1) of 1977 Additional Protocol I prescribes that *"... a mercenary shall not have the right to be a combatant or a prisoner of war."* Articles 2 through 6 of the 1989 Convention define the following as offences for the purpose of the Convention: acting as a mercenary, using, financing or training mercenaries; attempting to commit one of these offences; or being the accomplice of any person who commits, or attempts to commit one of these offences. The government of the then People's Republic of Angola became a signatory to the 1989 Convention on 28 December 1990.

35   Shearer, op. cit., p. 19, asserts that Article 47 of 1997 Additional Protocol I *"... does not ... apply in a civil war ..."*, and secondly, that, *"... if companies work only for recognised governments, as most [private military companies] argue that they do, then they are exempt from terms of these conventions ..."* Ballesteros, though harshly critical of mercenary activities, observes that *"... the legal framework for mercenary activities is ... not clear and specific enough ... the contracts which private military **advisory, training and security** companies conclude with States and the personnel working for them, even when they have a military background and are highly paid, cannot be strictly considered as coming within the legal scope of mercenary status as defined in the reference material."* Emphasis added. See E B Ballesteros, Report to the Economic and Social Council, E/C no 4/1997/24, 20 February 1997, p. 23 para 106. See also Sandoz's extensive arguments in Chapter 10.

36   Especially A J Venter, *Combat Group Bravo*, Penthouse, date unknown; A J Venter, *Targets of Opportunism*, Soldiers of Fortune, April 1996.

37   See L Smerczak, *Soldiers of Misfortune*, Fair Lady, 10 March 1996.

38   EO's original contract with each person recruited for service in Angola provided that, while the duties he is to perform may be extremely dangerous and may lead to death, the contracting party will forfeit his salary and pay an amount of R100 000 as liquidated damages to EO, if he breaches an undertaking *"... not to divulge any information relating to this contract or his duties to any person or body."* See HRW/A, op. cit., p. 33; ibid., p. 54.

39   See, for example, Venter, April 1996, op. cit., pp. 61-62.

40   See, for example, A J Venter, *Africa's Forgotten Jungle Air Wars*, World Airnews, November 1995, pp. 23-24; A J Venter, *South Africans in Russian Planes Turned the Tide on Their Old Ally, UNITA*, Sunday Independent, 21 January 1996, p. 6; also T Cohen, *Executive Outcomes and Thereafter*, Associated Press, 24 March 1997.

41   See Venter, April 1996, op. cit., pp. 56-61, 82-85; H Howe, *South Africa's 9-1-1 Force*, Armed Forces Journal International, November 1996; *We're the Good Guys These Days*, The Economist, 29 July 1995, p. 32.

42   See Venter, ibid., p. 61; S Brummer, *Investing in the Bibles and Bullets Business*, Weekly Mail & Guardian, 16-22 September 1994.

43   Estimates of the sums paid vary. See, for example, Brummer, ibid.; F Rosetti, Interview with Eeben Barlow, *Folha de São Paulo,* 15 September 1994, p. 3; S Brummer, *Distrust as SA 'mercenaries' leave Angola*, Weekly Mail & Guardian, 19-25 January 1996, p. 4; A Rake, *Dangerous Dogs of War*, New African, 35, November 1995; *Reining in the Dogs of War*, Africa Express, 20 May 1997.

44   Again, estimates vary, as did numbers employed at different times in the period between September 1993 and January 1996. See Brummer, ibid.; Africa Express, ibid.; Rake, November 1995, op. cit.; Howe, op. cit.

45   International Convention against the Recruitment, Use, Financing and Training of Mercenaries, op. cit., Article 1(1)(a); see also Chapter 10.

46   It would appear to have been a closed corporation at the time the original contract was concluded. Barlow refers to having registered the 'company' in 1989, but details seem to differ. See, for example, A Johnson, *Broker of War and*

Death, <u>Weekly Mail & Guardian</u>, 28 February – 6 March 1997; Brummer, September 1994, op. cit.; B Drogin, *Hired Guns Turn the Tide in Angola War,* <u>Los Angeles Times</u>, 30 October 1994. The registered number of Executive Outcomes (Pty) Ltd is 95/02016/07, indicating that it was only registered in 1995.

47   See Drogin, op. cit.; E Rubin, *An Army of One's Own,* <u>Harpers Magazine</u>, February 1997, p. 55. EO's now defunct website, <www.eo.com>, also emphasised the 'a-political' [sic] nature of their services.

48   Estimates vary, but the most frequently quoted range for Sierra Leone is between US $2 000 and $7 000, with top pay in other contracts reaching about $10 000 a month. See, for example, Cohen, op. cit.; Rubin, op. cit.; Drogin, op. cit.; HRW/A, op. cit., p. 31; Smerczak, op. cit., p. 54; Howe, op. cit., p. 39; F de Lange, *UK Oil Company is Hiring Mercenaries,* <u>Citizen</u>, 4 March 1993, p. 11; I Capraro, *Die MPLA Werf in SA, Toon Pak Foto's,* <u>Beeld</u>, 2 March 1993, p. 1; E Gibson, *Onderneming Lewer net 'n Diens – Hoë,* <u>Beeld</u>, 20 August 1996, p. 5.

49   HRW/A, op. cit.; <u>Africa Confidential</u>, various issues, 1993 to 1995; Venter, November 1995, op. cit.; Venter, January 1996, op. cit.; Venter, date unknown, op. cit.; Venter, April 1996, op. cit.; also, A J Venter, *SA Mercenaries in Thick of Battle in Sierra Leone,* <u>Sunday Independent</u>, 27 August 1995; A J Venter, *Not RUF Enough,* <u>Soldiers of Fortune</u>, December 1995.

50   M Anstee, Angola: <u>Orphans of the Cold War</u>, Basingstoke, London, 1996; M Bredin, <u>Blood on the Tracks</u>, Picador, London, 1994; Human Rights Watch Arms Project, <u>Angola: Arms Trade and Violations of the Laws of War since the 1992 Elections</u>, Human Rights Watch/Africa, New York, November 1994; K Maier, <u>Angola: Promises and Lies</u>, William Waterman, Rivonia, 1996; J Matloff, <u>Fragments of a Forgotten War</u>, Penguin, London, 1997; J Patrício, <u>Angola-EUA, Os Caminhos do Bom-Senso</u>, Publicações Dom Quixote, Lisboa, 1998; F Roque, <u>Em Nome da Esperança</u>, Bertrand, Lisbon, 1993.

51   Personal communication of members of the Government of Côte d'Ivoire.

52   See Roque, op. cit.

53   See Anstee, op. cit.

54   B Boutros-Ghali, Letter to the President of the UN Security Council, 18 December 1992.

55   Maier, op. cit., p. 124.

56   Statement by the President of the UN Security Council, 22 December 1992.

57   C McGreal, *Luanda Threatens to Ban UNITA Rebels Unless They Disarm,* <u>The Guardian</u>, 9-10 January 1993.

58   C McGreal, *Vanquished Rebels Flee Angola's Killing Fields,* <u>The Guardian</u>, 18 January 1993.

59   Personal communication by a member of Soares' staff.

60   This is the context of HRW/A's remarkable claim that EO was providing assistance to UNITA on contract until April 1993. See HRW/A, op. cit., p. 30.

61   Ibid., p. 20.

62   J Battersby, *Violent Cleansing Part of Angola War, Aid Workers Say,* <u>Christian Science Monitor</u>, 3 February 1993.

63   According to a UNITA press release datelined Huambo, 6 March 1993. HRW/A gives the date as 8 March; HRW/A, op. cit.

64   The speech addressed three themes: a definite, though defensive, celebration of African culture (*ubuntu*) contrasted with domination by what he disparagingly called the 'creole culture of the mulatos'; an attempt to regain Ovimbundu unity

as a building block for national unity, rejecting secession while calling for administrative decentralisation on a regional basis; and expression of a desire for peace and national reconstruction in a Government of National Unity, coupled with a warning that UNITA had the strength to do serious damage to any force seeking to harm it.

65   The other side is the fear of the élite in Luanda of the consequences of the *pretos*/Bailundos/*kwachas*, represented by Savimbi and UNITA, coming to power. There are echoes of earlier white fears of emergent black power in South Africa in all this.

66   This resolution was prompted chiefly by anger at Savimbi's determination to recapture Huambo after its loss to the FAA and emergency police units in January, and his failure to support the cease-fire talks in Addis Ababa in late February.

67   J Davidow, Transcript of Press Conference, Deputy Assistant Secretary of State, Bureau of African Affairs, Abidjan, 28 March 1993.

68   UNITA, *Conversações sobre a paz em Angola*, Abidjan, 12 April 1993

69   M Anstee, *Why the UN has Failed Angola*, Daily Telegraph, 7 September 1993.

70   UNITA's persistent demand for a far larger UN presence with a mandate to keep the peace also supports Roque's assertion that it feared its troops would be massacred in the camps if they remained there in October 1992; Roque, op. cit.

71   B Boutros-Ghali, Further Report of the Secretary-General on the United Nations Angola Verification Mission II (UNAVEM II), United Nations, New York, S/25840, 25 May 1993.

72   R Kennedy, *Pretoria Troops to Fight UNITA*, The Times, 1 March 1993; Capraro, op. cit.; De Lange, op. cit.

73   He is recorded in the DiamondWorks Limited preliminary prospectus, 11 February 1997 as Director: International New Business Ventures, Ranger Oil Limited, Calgary, Alberta prior to being Founder and Director of Heritage Oil and Gas Limited, London, since 1992. Heritage Oil was apparently formed by Buckingham's Branch Energy with Premier Consolidated – then headed by Roland Shaw – and Fleming Mercantile Investment Trust to acquire and develop proven hydro-carbon reserves in developing countries.

74   Economist Intelligence Unit, map of Angolan exploration and production areas.

75   De Lange, op. cit., p. 20; Capraro, op. cit.

76   K Pech & D Beresford, *Africa's New-look Dogs of War*, Weekly Mail & Guardian, 24-30 January 1997, p. 24; Shearer, op. cit., p. 46.

77   See Brummer, January 1996, op. cit., p. 4; Shearer, op. cit.; Pech & Beresford, op. cit.; S Laufer, *Mercenary Group Recolonising Africa*, Business Day, 17 January 1997, p. 9.

78   Shearer, ibid., p 46.

79   See Venter, December 1995, op. cit., p. 76; *South Africans go to war in the jungles of West Africa*, Sunday Independent, 27 August 1995; A Brown, *You Can Take Men Out of War, but Not the War Out of All Men*, The Star, 8 August 1995.

80   See Howe, op. cit.

81   See F Sousa, *Savimbi apela ao fim dos combates*, O Público, 12 Agosto 1993; F Sousa, *Savimbi quer fim dos combates*, Diario de Notícias, 12 Agosto 1993.

82   UNITA proposed a formula for a cessation of hostilities, followed by a cease-fire on 12 April 1993. The Angolan government did not permit publication of this proposal by Savimbi in Angola; see *Mesagem de Jonas Savimbi não foi*

difundida no país, O Dia, 13 Agosto 1993; *Apelo Indeferid'o,* O Público, 13 Agosto 1993. General de Matos responded on 14 August that the Angolan government rejected the cease-fire proposal and that the FAA would continue with air strikes against Huambo.

83   UNITA, *A Window of Opportunity for Peace in Angola,* Free Angola Information Service news release, Washington DC, 20 September 1993.

84   UNITA was laying siege to Cuíto, resulting in one of the greatest tragedies of the war.

85   This refers to three principles – a cease-fire, resumption of the Bicesse Accords and *"... national reconciliation, to include broadened participation by UNITA at the national, provincial and local levels ..."* – set as the basis for the inconclusive negotiations between 12 April and 21 May 1993, in Abidjan, under the auspices of UN Special Representative Anstee.

86   The purpose of the meeting was *"... to analyse the strategy of a bilateral cease-fire in Angola as well as studying other means to implement an effective cease-fire."* C Garuba, Extract from a Letter to the Chiefs of Staff of both Angolan parties, UNAVEM II military commander, 21 September 1993. Translated from Portuguese.

87   It is clear that the Angolan government had no incentive to agree to a cease-fire, as this would have prevented the embargo against UNITA – and in effect, the government's release from the ban on weapons sales to all Angolan belligerents under the 'triple zero' provisions of the Bicesse Accords – from coming into effect.

88   *"... After exhaustive discussions, the Political Commission decided to: ...2. Reiterate [the Political Commission's] acceptance of the validity of September 29 and 30, 1992 electoral results while still considering them fraudulent ... 5. Maintain the ceasefire unilaterally declared by UNITA on September 20, 1993 and requests its verification by United Nations observers ... 4. The UNITA Political Commission takes note of the United Nations Security Council Resolutions and reiterates its readiness to co-operate with the United Nations Secretary General [sic] Special Representative in Angola, Alioune Blondin Beye in the search for genuine and durable solution to the Angolan conflict."* Extracted from the English of the *Final Communiqué of an Extraordinary Meeting of UNITA's Political Commission,* Huambo, 6 October 1993.

89   UNAVEM II, Media Release, Luanda, 7 October 1993. (Translated from Portuguese.)

90   US Department of State, press advisory, Washington DC, 8 October 1993

91   Secretariat of the Angolan Council of Ministers, *Posição do Governo da República de Angola a respeito do comunicado da UNITA datado de 6/10/93,* Luanda, *aos 8 de Outubro de 1993.*

92   Manuvakola, then Secretary-General of UNITA, signed for Savimbi under full powers issued by fax on 19 November after Savimbi had refused to travel because of an ongoing attack on Huambo by government forces; Foreign Minister de Moura signed on behalf of President dos Santos, who was present in Lusaka.

93   C Crocker, *Angola: Can this Outrageous Spectacle be Stopped?,* Washington Post, 13 October 1993.

94   This provision of the Bicesse Accords reflected an obligation on the US, the former USSR and third parties not to provide any further war material to either of the two armed parties in Angola.

95   See Chapter 5.

96   Drogin, op. cit.; see also IISS, The Military Balance 1995/96, International Institute for Strategic Studies London, 1996.

97   Including night bombing and fighting capability; see Drogin, ibid.

98   J Muekalia, Update on the Peace Process: The Unilateral UNITA Cease-fire, Free Angola Information Service, Washington DC, 24 September 1993.

99   According to the estimates of HRW/A, op. cit., pp. 31-32.

100   Ibid., p. 32.

101   Brummer, September 1994, op. cit.

102   Venter, April 1996, op. cit., pp. 59-61 and 82-85, based on interviews with Blaauw.

103   Shearer, op. cit., p. 48.

104   See Venter, 1996, op. cit.

105   This initially caused confusion and frustration in Washington, which believed in January 1994 that an agreement would be achieved by mid-February. Personal communication, US Department of State.

106   Drogin, op. cit.

107   Venter, April 1996, op. cit.

108   EO's combat role continued far longer, according to Venter, 1996, op. cit.

109   Shearer, op. cit., p. 48.

110   See DiamondWorks, Preliminary Prospectus, 11 February, 1997, pp. 9, 15-21; Pech & Beresford, op. cit.; also Grill & Dumay, op. cit.

111   Buckingham appears to control all the shares owned by the two Hansard entities, but the prospectus indicates that "... under the terms of a discretionary trust, Anthony L.R. Buckingham may become a beneficial owner of up to 12,750,000 common shares." DiamondWorks, ibid., p. 55.

112   Estimates of the death toll vary, though UN Special Representative Bêye's claim that 1 000 Angolans were dying each day, may be excessive.

113   The explanation for this destruction is the vastly greater spending on armaments by the government forces and the greater destructive efficiency that EO brought to its application. See Drogin, op. cit.; also Venter, November 1995, op. cit., pp. 23-24.

114   International Monetary Fund, unpublished reports, 1995; material sourced from Angolan government and IMF data.

115   See HRW/A, op. cit. pp. 2, 34.

116   Santos' enthusiasm in helping to effect Mobutu's overthrow in Zaire, followed by that of Lissouba in the Republic of Congo, in 1997 proved misplaced. Kabila was no more reliable in curbing UNITA, and the retention of Sassou-Nguesso in power in Brazzaville became too demanding and expensive for Angola's troops.

117   R Ndovala, *Envolvimento secreto de sul-Africanos,* Folha, 8, 24 February 1998.

118   There is evidence of links between UNITA and Hutu Interahamwe units and other refugees who fled into UNITA-controlled areas of Angola ahead of Kabila's Tutsi army, former FAZ troops, Lissouba's and Kolelas' militias from Congo-Brazzaville and dissident groups from Burundi – an alliance of the dispossessed – seeking to reverse the setbacks of the past eighteen months.

119   Which, according to media reports, has since closed its doors and reportedly no longer provides military support services.

120 Licklider, paraphrased by Stedman: *"... in civil wars fought over identity issues, negotiated settlements tend to be less stable than military victories; two-thirds of negotiated settlements fall apart within five years, and only twenty-one percent of wars that end in military victory see a resumption of fighting in the same time frame ..."* See S J Stedman, *The Consequences of Negotiated Settlements in Civil Wars, 1945-1993*, <u>American Political Science Review</u>, 89(3), September 1995, pp. 681-690. Stedman also notes his finding that *"... in civil wars over identity issues, genocide was carried out in nineteen percent of military victories ..."* (p. 687). The evidence of this tendency in Angola is already available. Outsiders surely ought not to facilitate the destructive capacity of either side. That is the spirit that underlies the prohibitions on mercenarism.

Chapter 9: Fighting for diamonds –
Private military companies in Sierra Leone

Ian Douglas

Introduction

*T*he story of private military intervention in the affairs of Sierra Leone goes back a considerable time, and is intimately connected to attempts by either the state or other political and economic actors to exploit or control the country's mineral resources. As will become apparent, it is often difficult to draw a distinction between the public and private roles of key players, with the result that the line dividing private security interests from those of the state also becomes blurred, as do the motives informing certain actions. Equally so, the predatory interests of a regime such as that of former Nigerian President Sani Abacha suggests the requirement for at least as much scrutiny of the Nigerian intervention in Sierra Leone, eventually under the auspices of the Economic Community of West African States Monitoring Group (ECOMOG), as that of mercenary companies such as Executive Outcomes and Sandline International.[1]

Much of the following account centres upon the richest of Sierra Leone's mineral prizes, the Kono diamond fields, and the commercial activity, licit and illicit, associated with this area. That Koindu, the centre of the region, is all of 500 kilometres from the capital Freetown, but only eight kilometres from the border with Liberia, and three from that with Guinea, adds an international complication to the quest for control and security – just as it enhances the opportunities and rewards for a trade in contraband. The six properties/concessions that the company DiamondWorks[2] admitted to owning in Sierra Leone in 1997, include diamond resources of almost 6,5 million carats in the proven, probable, or inferred category of resources. At an average price of US $300 per carat, this translates into US $2 billion to be gained from these concessions alone.

The origins of the war

In 1966 at independence, the British handed the country's administration to the Sierra Leone People's Party (SLPP), headed by Milton Margai. Sierra Leone's modern and troubled history, and its legacy of problems, started with Siaka Stevens breaking from the SLPP and forming the All Peoples Congress (APC), winning a contested and controversial election victory in 1967. Following a brief spell of military government, the army restored civilian power in 1968, with Siaka Stevens and the APC assuming control. Yet, neither Stevens nor his handpicked successor, General Joseph Saidu Momoh managed to stem the continued downward spiral of the economy.

The crisis in Sierra Leone started in March 1991[3] when the Revolutionary United Front (RUF), led by Corporal Foday Sankoh,[4] crossed the border from Liberia to launch its rebellion against the government of President Momoh. Since then, the war between the government and the RUF has claimed at least 20 000 lives and has forced more than half the country's population to flee their homes.

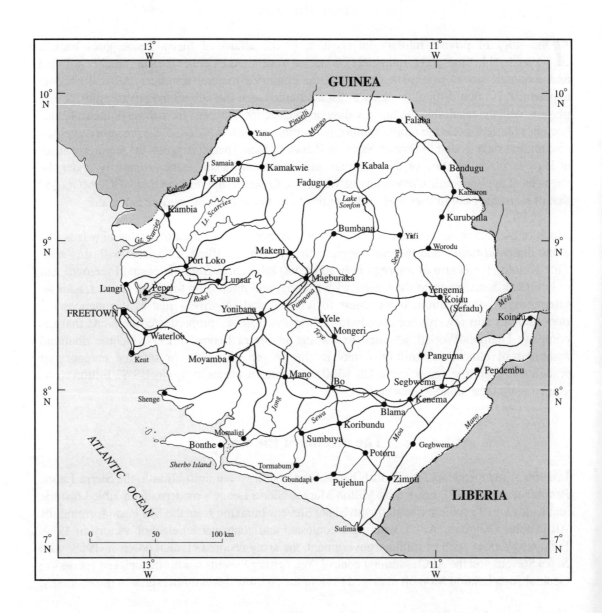

The manifesto of the RUF called, in typical fashion, for "... *national salvation and liberation ... the historic responsibility of each patriot ... for a national democratic revolution involving the total mobilisation of all progressive forces.*" It also stated that, "*[t]he secret behind the survival of the existing system is our lack of organisation. What we need then is organised challenge and resistance. The strategy and tactics of this resistance will be determined by the reaction of the enemy forces – force will be met with force, reasoning with reason, and dialogue with dialogue.*"[5] As time would prove, the cannibalism and brutality of the RUF has few parallels, even in war-torn Africa.

Sankoh and other vanguard elements of the RUF had originally received guerrilla training in Benghazi, Libya, where he had met Charles Taylor (former warlord, now President) of Liberia. Taylor would subsequently use the remote areas of south-eastern Sierra Leone to train and stage attacks of his own against the then Liberian president Samuel Doe. After deposing and killing Doe in 1990, Taylor provided arms and fighters to the RUF, as part of its war against Sierra Leone's President Momoh. Taylor hoped that his support of the RUF would impair Freetown's ability to assist the military effort of ECOMOG in Liberia.

The RUF launched its military campaign with less than 100 men who crossed the Liberian/Sierra Leone border in the area of the Kailahun 'finger'. The operations of the RUF, which envisaged it working in the supportive framework of peasant society, and indeed recruiting from it, quickly fell apart. The barbarity and cruelty seen in Liberia in operations of the National Patriotic Front of Liberia (NPFL) were mirrored in RUF operations, and sometimes blamed on Liberians, but evidence and testimony indicated that there was more than enough blame to go around. The particularly brutal practice of hacking off limbs to terrorise and subjugate the population, has subsequently been documented in numerous books and horrific television news coverage. Given the choice of joining or dying, the decision for many new recruits was easy. Desertion was punishable by death. Yet, despite its barbarity, the RUF could feed off the hatred against the government and its cruel and vindictive oppression of the population

Even after Momoh's government was overthrown in April 1992 by a group of rebellious officers under Captain Valentine Strasser who called themselves the National Provisional Ruling Council (NPRC), the RUF continued its campaign of random violence in the forests of the south and east. Hailed as saviours, the NPRC had no political leaders, knowledge or indeed an agenda, but simply carried on governing as they had witnessed and experienced it being done in the past. As a result, the change in leaders did little to aid the ailing economy or to end the civil war. For their part, the rebels remained a mysterious force with no coherent ideology and a constantly changing composition, and they persistently refused to enter into negotiations with Strasser's regime, denying its legitimacy and demanding the withdrawal of Guinean and Nigerian troops assisting the Sierra Leone government.

It appears at about this time, however, that soldiers at the front realised the immense profits to be made from the war situation, both through the illegal mining of diamonds and the looting of civilians.

There is no great military tradition in the Republic of Sierra Leone Military Forces (RSLMF). While dissatisfied activists plotted and planned, the army lived in relative comfort largely as a ceremonial force, receiving its patrimonial handouts, which included a rice subsidy on top of wages. Dissatisfaction only became a problem within the RSLMF when a plummeting economy halted the payment of wages and the receipt of other benefits.

RUF operations continued to grow until the NPRC, in panic, initiated conscription. This move saw youths being taken off the street, equipped with some rudimentaries and, with only a few days training, sent to the front – wherever that might have been. Army successes in the field dropped even further.[6] Indeed, as the war progressed, the RSLMF acted less and less like a military force and more like groups of bandits. Rumours of military collusion with the rebels abounded. There certainly seemed to be a commonality of purpose between the RUF and the RSLMF early in the war when the NPRC overthrew the APC, against which the RUF had initiated the campaign in the first place. It also seems as if the NPRC, in the early days, had agreed to create a government of national unity that would include the RUF. Subsequent power struggles within the NPRC, and the progress of the war, caused this plan to be abandoned. However, stories of collaboration between the RSLMF and the RUF in the field are numerous.[7]

The plummeting economy, a lack of foreign aid and a severe cash flow problem forced the army outside of Freetown to exist, as did the RUF, in a foraging mode and thus to spend less time pursuing the war. The legend of the 'sobel' – soldier by day, rebel by night – came from this period. Both the RSLMF and the RUF existed by foraging and looting, each trying to blame the excesses thus committed on the other.

By 1994/95, the RSLMF had become a bloated, ill-trained organisation, which had become very much a part of Sierra Leone's problem.[8] For its part, the RUF was allowed to reconsolidate its position and, by the end of 1994, began a series of raids from its forest camps into virtually all parts of the country, reaching areas close to Freetown by the beginning of 1995. Not only were the alluvial diamond fields of the south, east and north-east overrun by the RUF, but the areas of bauxite and rutile mining were also captured, production had stopped, and thus most of the foreign exchange revenue essential to government operations was not available. The depredations of the rebels were aided and abetted by the army, and the continuation of the war provided an excuse to prolong the military's profitable tenure of power.

Operationally, the RUF was roughly organised into six battalions, each of which operated from jungle camps, using classic guerrilla tactics. Units sought to acquire the uniforms of the armed forces of Sierra Leone and identity documents to fake 'sobel' attacks, and thus to divide civilians and RSLMF troops. While research on the RUF is limited, and evidence is in some cases anecdotal, it seems as if the RUF had an overall strength of three to four thousand with a hard core of five to six hundred soldiers.[9] Sankoh also established an efficient radio network consisting of about twenty radio stations throughout the country. An office in Abidjan, Côte d'Ivoire, which was part of the radio network, dealt with international relations, and was controlled by Sankoh's brother.[10]

Strategically, the RUF depended upon outside support from Libya, Guinea and Liberia, while tactically, it depended upon guerrilla tactics, foraging, and the capture of arms and equipment from the RSLMF which was weak, poorly led and seemed prone to flee on contact.

With the RUF literally knocking on the doors of Freetown by 1995, Strasser first looked to the outside world for military and security aid. Seeking to ensure a continued flow of revenue, Britain introduced him to a private military company employing Gurkhas to assist in securing the country's principal diamond and titanium oxide mines against the raiders. The Gurkha Security Guards (GSG) contingent was commanded by Major Bob MacKenzie and was supposedly composed of former 'crack' troops from that most famous of British mercenary sources – the Gurkhas of Nepal. As discussed in greater detail in Chapter 7 by Alex Vines, a number of questions and uncertainties surround the role of GSG in Sierra Leone. The commonly accepted story is that they were hired to train the RSLMF and not to conduct combat operations. The battle that caused the eventual departure of GSG from Sierra Leone apparently happened by accident. MacKenzie and a reconnaissance team were evidently seeking a remote jungle area to be used for the conduct of field firing exercises. During the reconnaissance, the group stumbled upon an RUF camp, a firefight developed during which MacKenzie and others of his team were killed. The story has it that MacKenzie was dismembered and his arm, with tattoo intact, was held as proof of his demise.[11] In any case, GSG departed in May 1995. By this time, Strasser was negotiating with another organisation – Executive Outcomes.[12]

By early 1995, the NPRC was in a desperate situation, since its primary source of revenue – mining companies such as Branch Energy and Sierra Rutile – had ceased to operate, and its military, the RSLMF, had become part of the problem.

Strange bedfellows

Executive Outcomes was introduced to Strasser by Michael Grunberg and Anthony Buckingham of the mining company Branch Energy. When asked why he and Buckingham would represent EO in the negotiations with the government, Grunberg stated[13] that Branch Energy and the government had a common security problem, and as EO was an organisation that could solve this, "*... ownership of the company, EO or Branch, is irrelevant ...*"

The EO contract with the government was financially complex, due in part to the government's lack of resources. Despite the obvious collaboration, it is difficult to prove that there was a formal business link between EO and Branch Energy. Clearly, the connection was used to finalise the contract, and there can be little doubt about the 'common security problem' and the co-operation that this might engender. Yet, the exact manner of payment, given the parlous state of government finances, remains unclear – in particular, the issue whether shares in Branch Energy, based on mining concessions that had been granted by the government, were used as collateral to pay EO. Whatever the contractual relationship, there was clearly a close personal and professional connection between the management of EO, Branch Energy and Sierra Rutile.

The Branch Energy agreement with the government called for different leases and agreements. The largest of the six leases – for Koindu with potential reserves valued at US $1,2 billion – was finalised shortly after the EO contract with the government had been negotiated by senior management of Branch Energy in July 1995. On the assumption of a 2,7 million carat reserve, a 25-year lease was granted to Branch Energy. The general conditions of the contract call for an investment, in the short term, of US $6 million, and a further $80 million to be invested once a feasibility, or 'due diligence' study has been completed. Given these conditions,

"Branch Energy and government of Sierra Leone ... agreed in principle ... that a decision is made to go into production, they will establish a corporate entity to commercially exploit the Koindu property in which Branch Energy will hold 60%, government of Sierra Leone will be granted a free carried 30%, and the remaining 10% interest will be made available to local business interests in terms to be negotiated."

All development costs and the risk for failure rested with Branch Energy which carried the risk to re-establish the operations.

Branch Energy[14] also negotiated the contract for the provision of security services between EO and the government of Sierra Leone. This contract required EO to provide 150 to 200 soldiers, fully equipped and with helicopter support, mandated to support the RSLMF with training and other forms of assistance, while aiding in prosecuting the war against the RUF. For this, EO would be paid US $2 million per month. Since the government had no ready cash, the partners to the agreement agreed that fifty per cent of the tax revenue from Sierra Rutile, once it was able to operate, would be used to pay the EO bill. As it transpired, Sierra Rutile did not reopen and EO was not paid. It later became apparent that the Sierra Rutile tax revenue would only amount to US $15m per year, and would therefore not have been sufficient to cover the costs of EO.

Military operations

During May 1995, with the RUF offensive having reached the outskirts of Freetown, fifty soldiers from EO arrived in Sierra Leone. This was the lead contingent, with a further 130 or so arriving six months later as the Angolan operations of EO drew to a close. The EO historical synopsis states that, over the period April 1995 to January 1997, the company was contracted to provide "... *military advisory and support services ... to the NPRC of Sierra Leone.*" This obviously includes the services provided to the Sierra Leone Peoples Party (SLPP) which replaced the NPRC in March 1996.

The first item of business was a restructuring exercise, directed by EO, which saw the reorganisation of basic and specialist training along the lines in the accompanying table. Given the urgency of the situation, a crash course for individual soldiers and rifle companies was conducted at the same time to deter the immediate threat to Freetown.

The requirement to lift the RUF siege on Freetown dictated the establishment of a Joint Headquarters between EO and the RSLMF, subsequently set up at Cockril Barracks in Freetown, the headquarters of the RSLMF. While the training of rifle companies for the impending operation was going on, EO supplied the RSLMF with the essential, though less visible functions of information and intelligence gathering, command, control and

Course schedule for training in Sierra Leone by Executive Outcomes, 1995-1996		
Basic Training	60 students	Sep, Oct 1995
Basic Training	310 students	Nov, Dec 1995
Rapid Reaction Force	120 students	Dec 1995
VIP Protection Training	30 students	Dec 1995
Basic Training	300 students	Apr, May 1996
Mortar Training	30 students	May 1996
Section Leaders	60 students	Jun, Jul, Aug 1996
Retraining	150 students	Jul 1996
Basic Training	150 students	Aug 1996
Security Guards	60 students	Sep 1996
Section Leaders	60 students	Sep 1996
Junior Commanders	30 students	Aug, Sep 1996
Mortar Training	12 students	Oct 1996
Infantry	90 students	Oct 1996
Basic Base Protection	28 students	Oct 1996
Close Protection	16 students	Oct, Nov 1996
Battalion Mortars	30 students	Oct, Nov 1996
Infantry Protection	60 students	Oct, Nov 1996

communications, helicopter support, and finally a guarantee of both logistic and fire support for operations.

At this stage, the RUF had been seizing mining properties, the main government source of hard currency and an obvious first priority for EO, Branch Energy and the government to reclaim. The Joint Headquarters devised a three-phase operational strategy beginning with the immediate problem of the siege of Freetown. The rebel force besieging Freetown worked out of a base to the east of the city in a location known as Ma-Sherwe. The RSLMF battalion-level combined operation was supported by two BMPs (Soviet-built armoured personnel carriers), two Land Rovers with mounted machine guns, and two Soviet-built helicopters (one Mi-17 and one Mi-24). This was the first battle of the war in which the government troops had achieved positive results, with fifty rebels killed within two days, and the siege of the city lifted in ten days. By this time, about 200 rebels had been killed and there were more than 1 000 deserters, most of the latter having been enlisted as unwilling conscripts and employed, among others, as porters and general labourers. Within ten days, the RUF had withdrawn 100 kilometres into the interior. After this operation, the trained companies that had been formed by EO were subdivided and the synergy and effectiveness of bonded, cohesive subunits was lost.

The second phase of the joint government/EO operational strategy was to stabilise the alluvial diamond area around Koindu by removing rebel forces from the area. This operation started in June 1995, with the same support group of armoured vehicles, but with two additional rifle companies. Within a few days, and without much resistance, Koindu was recaptured and 'area' (clearing) operations were conducted in the Kono district. The government decided to retain a presence in the area to provide mining companies with the necessary security, and to allow mining operations to recommence. Once the diamond area of Koindu was cleared, the government requested EO to clear and occupy the area of Sierra Rutile – an operation essential to the payment for EO's services.

The third objective was to locate and destroy the RUF headquarters. Air reconnaissance indicated the presence of a large enemy base approximately eighty kilometres east of Freetown which was attacked on 5 December 1995. Follow-up intelligence indicated that this was formerly the main springboard for operations against Freetown.

By late 1995, the main objectives of the government/EO strategy had been achieved. The siege of Freetown had been lifted and the RUF had suffered a series of defeats. The Koindu diamond area had been liberated and was once more open for operations. The RUF headquarters east of Freetown had been destroyed. Finally, the Sierra Rutile area was secured and ready to resume production. Concomitant with this strategy, efforts were made to develop a psychological warfare and a strong public relations programme.

These operations were characterised by the effective use of helicopters and co-ordinated fire support. In classic air-mobile operations, EO sought to find, fix and destroy. They first found the RUF, using electronic warfare and good intelligence; then fixed them in place using direct fire from helicopters and indirect fire from mortars flown into position; and, finally destroyed the enemy by using helicopter-borne assault troops. Using these tactics, EO and the RSLMF elements involved, suffered very few casualties while RUF losses were extremely high.

The retaking of the mining areas demonstrated that a cohesive, well-trained organisation, with appropriate intelligence and firepower, had the ability to defeat a force that outnumbered it significantly. The success of small unit operations by the RSLMF, up to company level, increased. This was particularly true when the organisation had been trained by, and bonded with similar EO elements. EO provided hard, combat-oriented training programmes, supplemented with knowledgeable leadership – and leaders who lead from the front, not the back. There was evidently nothing wrong with the soldiers and junior leaders of the RSLMF that some serious training, motivation and leadership could not solve. However, while the RSLMF was organised to assault and capture objectives, it could not be trusted to occupy them. After the RUF had been driven out of the mining areas and concessions, EO occupied these specific financial vital points which were eventually turned over to LifeGuard Security.

In the process, EO had begun to co-operate with local rural militias and self-defence units to curb the excesses of rebels and soldiers alike. The best known and most formidable of these militias were the Kamajors,[16] a Mende group from the south-east of the country, based on traditional hunter guilds and skilled in bushcraft, which EO supplemented by providing additional training in counterinsurgency. The use of the Kamajors grew from the efforts of a retired army officer, Captain Hinja Norman, to mobilise a local militia force for the defence of Tetu Bogor, a chiefdom south of Bo of which he was the regent chief, during 1994.[17] Chief Norman's activities saw the Kamajor militia grow to two to three thousand strong. By virtue of captured weapons, and co-operation with EO, the Kamajors became the bulwark of a regional defence force. Familiar with the jungle and sworn enemies of the RUF, the Kamajors became the eyes and ears of EO, reporting the movements and locations of rebel units. They became fiercely loyal to the South Africans, whom they and the majority of the population regarded as liberators. As time progressed, regional defence and the protection of civilian life and property became more and more the recognised role of the Kamajors, versus the self-serving efforts of the RSLMF and the RUF.[18]

The Kamajors provided information and intelligence to EO and, in some cases, acted as guides for assault operations. While the EO/RSLMF team achieved the three objectives of the 'operational strategy', regional protection operations in the remainder of the country were conducted by the Kamajor militia. The areas of Bo and Kenema, south and west of the diamond fields, are good examples of this, and, while the Kamajors could not eradicate the RUF presence in the area, they were able to keep the towns free of the RUF and secure.

As the war progressed and the NPRC, through the RSLMF, became less and less capable of pursuing the war effort against the RUF, the Kamajor militia grew in influence and capability. The Kamajor was subsequently structured and formalised as the Civil Defence Force of Sierra Leone. The schism between the RSLMF and the NPRC widened as responsibility and credit for success were increasingly heaped upon the Kamajor militia who expanded their numbers by instituting recruiting quotas for towns and areas.

While EO's military efforts did not destroy the RUF, they forced them out of the vital diamond and rutile-producing areas, compelling them to seek sanctuary in the deep forest. By April 1996, the combined efforts of EO and the Kamajor caused Sankoh and the RUF to seek a cease-fire. However, it was another seven months before a peace agreement was finally signed in November. The final major joint thrust against the RUF occurred during October 1996 when Sankoh, having failed to observe the agreed upon cease-fire which he had requested, saw his headquarters attacked. The fire support for this operation included medium and close support artillery. A number of senior RUF commanders were killed and the headquarters facilities effectively destroyed.

EO had temporarily defeated the RUF in the field, that staved off further loss by entering into negotiations. When overt hostilities ceased, EO, supported in the countryside by the Kamajors, controlled the mining centres.

As negotiations dragged on and peace talks became bogged down, the small EO force continued to provide security to financial vital points and became a 'security guard force' as opposed to a warfighting unit. An uneasy calm developed as the RUF hid in its deep bush camps, foraging for survival, while the RSLMF was doing exactly the same thing from its barracks and temporary camps along the road network. During this period, the lack of logistic support by the government soon neutralised the army's effectiveness and allowed the RUF to re-occupy areas it had previously controlled. There was no doubt that, if the newly elected government were to succeed, it desperately needed the profits from its mining industry which, in 1996, could only be guaranteed by EO and its subordinates.

In the meanwhile, the government's financial position continued to worsen. No bills were paid during the period May to November 1995. As a result, EO Sierra Leone was being carried on the financial shoulders of EO Angola – and the bill was growing.[19] In December 1995 with the promised elections approaching, and another military *coup* threatening, EO stated that, without a firm payment plan, it was going to leave.

The subsequent agreement between EO and the government, that was reached at the end of December 1995, called for the 1995 debt to be consolidated at US $15,9 million, with $2,4 million being written off and a debt of $13,5 million to the government of Sierra Leone remaining. Of this amount, $3 million would be paid during January 1996, with the remainder paid off during the year in monthly instalments of $1,6 million. A further protocol (secret – as it involved an additional 200 soldiers) was also agreed upon at a cost of $2 million per month. The soldiers would provide an increased security presence during the elections for two and a half months, thus incurring a further potential bill for $5 million.

Under severe domestic and foreign pressure to proceed with the promised transition to civilian rule, Strasser eventually announced that the elections would be held on 26 February 1996. On 16 January, he was overthrown by his deputy, Brigadier Julius Maada Bio, and exiled to Guinea. This was undoubtedly an attempt by the military to deflect the threat posed by the forthcoming elections, although Bio was at pains to refute this and even called on Sankoh to hold talks with the government. Less than a week later, the RUF announced a unilateral cease-fire and offered to talk to Bio's government unconditionally, save for a demand that the elections should be postponed. If there had been any doubt about the concurrence of interests between the rebels and the soldiers, this act in itself should have dispelled it. At about this time, it also came to light that Bio's elder sister, Maada, was part of the RUF high command. The electoral commission and other elements of civil society pressed on with their demand for elections, and had the support of the donor community.

In the countdown to the elections, EO received warnings that the RUF was planning a major attack in the vicinity of Bo. When the Kamajors reported and confirmed a rebel presence in the Mokanji Hills, the RUF suffered yet another massive defeat. The air-mobile tactics used by EO were so devastating that Sankoh offered a $25 000 reward for the destruction of an EO helicopter. An additional bounty, paid in diamonds, was also offered for any captured EO employee.

Talks between the military government and the RUF began in Côte d'Ivoire on 22 February 1996. Central to the discussions was the rebels' sudden insistence that they would only deal with Maada Bio, and would refuse to acknowledge the outcome of the elections, which they aimed to disrupt. What transpired in secret between the two delegations is open to conjecture, but in the event, it was the army rather than the rebels who appeared to do the most to intimidate the electorate on 26 and 27 February.

After two rounds of voting in which the regional nature of party support became apparent, Ahmad Tejan Kabbah of the Sierra Leone People's Party (SLPP) emerged as president in mid-March. There were few commentators who believed that he would have an easy task in restoring a ruined economy and asserting his control over a disaffected army. Kabbah was a lawyer, with some twenty years of working in the United Nations, but no political experience or claims to personal charisma. Nor were the results of the parliamentary and presidential elections uncontested, and even the electoral commission admitted that irregularities had occurred. Nevertheless, there was a general sense of relief when the military regime handed over power to the elected president.

The transformation, indeed metamorphosis, of the Kamajor militia into the recognised military arm of the country, was formalised when Chief Norman was appointed Deputy Minister of Defence (Kabbah held the defence portfolio in addition to the presidency). Norman's public disrespect for the RSLMF and his support for the Kamajors during 1996 and early in 1997, would serve to further weaken and antagonise the RSLMF.

Large areas of the national territory remained essentially under the control of the RSLMF, operating virtually as a force unto itself. In mid-March, the rebels initialled a two-month cease-fire and, in late April 1996, held talks with the new Sierra Leone government in Yamoussoukro, Côte d'Ivoire. A peace agreement seemed in prospect. The RUF insisted, however, that all foreign troops, including those of EO, should be withdrawn from the country before the process of encampment and disarmament of forces could begin. The talks stalled at this point, and the cease-fire began to look increasingly fragile.

In the meantime, the formal diamond sector had begun to stage a minor recovery, largely because of the protection afforded by EO to DiamondWorks properties. EO was also reportedly providing logistics and security for at least one foreign aid agency, and had assisted the government with helicopter transport. Nevertheless, the international community expressed its disquiet about the activities of the mercenaries.

When President Kabbah was consulted on the contract with EO, allegedly only in April, he stated that the country did not have the resources to meet the contract agreed to by his predecessors. After some haggling, Kabbah agreed in May to monthly payments of US $1,2 million beginning that month, with April being provided free of charge, and the contract terminating in December. These payments were reduced to $900 000 in September, thus incurring a further $300 000 per month in arrears. A subsequent unilateral decision by the finance department of the Sierra Leone government reduced the monthly payments to $700 000. While EO initially balked at this last proposal, it eventually agreed, thus "... *helping the government of Sierra Leone through a difficult period.*"[20] In fact, Kabbah had a cash-strapped EO over a barrel.

In June 1996, Sankoh hired at least two Belgian mercenaries tasked either with training the RUF or shooting down EO helicopters. 'Henri' and 'Michael' left after three days, apparently disillusioned with the RUF's lack of organisation and discipline.

In September 1996, a number of officers were arrested on suspicion of plotting to murder the president. This came only a few days after 26 senior officers and 155 non-commissioned officers had been retired in a major purge of the army. It was a clear indication of dangerous disaffection in the military, many of whom were becoming alarmed at the prominence of the Kamajor militia, and at the prospects of retrenchment, as the army's strength was to be halved. Clashes between army and Kamajor elements were reported on a number of occasions.

The cease-fire agreement notwithstanding, Sankoh ordered the resumption of RUF attacks against both the civilian population and the RSLMF. Kabbah immediately put EO on the offensive – once again with devastating effect. The EO attack on Zagoda in the Kenema district destroyed the base, killing a number of Sankoh's most trusted lieutenants and the majority of the RUF founding vanguard. Within days of the Zagoda attack, the remnants of the self-styled RUF 6th Battalion was discovered fifty kilometres east of Freetown and virtually annihilated. 'Libya', another important RUF camp near the border with Liberia was pinpointed and destroyed. Within a matter of weeks, Sankoh had lost more than 500 of his most experienced fighters. When Sankoh signed the peace accord in Abidjan on 30 November 1996, EO was preparing to destroy the remaining RUF base at 'Burkino' near the border with Guinea.[21]

The peace agreement provided for the cessation of hostilities to be monitored by a neutral monitoring group, the withdrawal of EO and other foreign forces five weeks after signature, and the establishment of the RUF as a political party. During negotiations, Sankoh specifically demanded the expulsion of EO and ECOMOG, in particular the Nigerians, whose Alpha jets had regularly provided tactical air support to EO operations against the RUF. Exactly how tenuous this agreement was, became evident when two more *coup* plots were uncovered in the following two months, apparently by disgruntled RSLMF officers whose illicit diamond trading was threatened by the installation of the new government.

There has been much conjecture that the IMF forced President Kabbah to end the contract with EO and to expel its employees from the country. This has been convincingly rejected by sources close to the IMF who stated that the Fund had pressurised the government to reduce its deficit, but had not suggested how. It seems as if Kabbah had responded by suggesting an increase in the tax on rice, and a reduction of the rice subsidy to the RSLMF. While these measures would have raised revenues and indeed reduced the deficit, the proposal was unrealistic given the poverty levels in the country. It was perhaps at this time, in September 1996, that the unilateral decision to reduce payments to EO was made. EO was seen as an anomaly, 'the dog of war once more loose in Africa' and President Kabbah was clearly being pressured from all sides to break relations with the company.

Whatever substance there may have been to objections to EO's presence in the country, its subsequent withdrawal during January 1997 left Kabbah dangerously exposed, although LifeGuard Security Sierra Leone, an offshoot of EO, was still protecting DiamondWorks' assets with a much reduced presence. EO considered that it had only received US $15,7 million out of a total contract value of $35,3 million and identified the arrears as a 'sovereign debt' of $19,5 million.[22] As predicted by EO on its departure, Kabbah was soon to be overthrown in a *coup*.[23]

By February 1997, a cease-fire was in place, the international community had returned, an internationally monitored election had been held, and the new civilian government was constituted. During March, Sierra Leone and Nigeria signed a defence pact and 900 Nigerian troops arrived in Freetown as partial replacement of EO. While UN agencies were formulating plans to meet their own specific mandates, World Bank teams were negotiating with the government of Sierra Leone on the longer term aspects of the peace and development process, while the new Ministry of Natural Reconstruction, Rehabilitation and Resettlement was organising and preparing to implement the disarming and demobilisation function essential to the process. The British government was on hand with seed money to initiate the process. A broad and long term approach seemed to be followed in dealing with the problems of the peace process by all concerned. The foreign perspective on Sierra Leone was positive, a country on the verge of peace.

The view from inside Sierra Leone was less optimistic, however. While some of the politicians were new, the bureaucrats were not. An old hand perhaps explained it best when he said that there would be no operational decisions or actions taken, regardless of the urgency, until the vital problem of cars, secretaries, office space, and hierarchy was settled. The opportunities offered by the cease-fire and the democratic elections, slipped away as time was wasted and the essential elements of the 'emergency stabilisation stage' of the peace process were ignored. Patrimonial-type bureaucracies were designed, and offered as models for the new ministries. Security, safety and stability declined in the countryside as both the RSLMF and RUF continued to forage, pillage and kill. The government of Sierra Leone had no trust in the RSLMF, believing that the Kamajors were protecting the people of the interior.

For their part, the Kamajors believed that they were strong enough to take on the army and executed several armed attacks against the RSLMF.

The 25 May 1997 *coup*

The *coup* of 25 May 1997 was led by Corporal John Gborie who, with a number of his colleagues, succeeded in overpowering the Nigerian-manned presidential guard, compelling President Kabbah to flee to Conakry, Republic of Guinea, from where he beseeched Nigeria to intervene militarily to restore his government to power. The *coup* was accompanied by twelve hours of shelling in Freetown and an orgy of looting, murder and rape in which as many as 200 people died. This was coupled with acts of extreme cruelty and atrocities especially against women, which generated fear and distrust in the minds of many. The Former Foreign Minister of Sierra Leone, Abass Bundu, summarised the situation as follows:

"Although the military junta must take the blame for what happened to the civilian population on the day of the coup, *having started the rebellion, it was plain that they were heavily assisted in perpetrating the atrocities by the underclass of Sierra Leone society, consisting largely of unemployed youths. From their conduct, these youths appeared to be pointing an accusing finger ... at other sections of society as if they were to be held responsible for their deplorable condition and therefore believed that they could vent on them their deepening sense of frustration and despair."*[24]

The plotters released hundreds of prisoners from the central jail, including Major Johnny Paul Koroma and several other officers due to stand trial the following day for the *coup* attempt in September 1996. Koroma subsequently emerged at the head of the Armed Forces Revolutionary Council, which justified its actions partly by referring to the marginalisation of the army by the Kamajors. Koroma, a relatively uneducated young officer with a reputation for rebellious behaviour, had been close to Strasser and his erstwhile deputy, Major S A J Musa, who shortly joined the new regime from exile in Britain.

Sankoh had managed to retain leadership of the RUF despite his arrest in Nigeria in March 1997, and announced that the RUF was allying itself with the new junta in a People's Revolutionary Army. Senior members of the RUF were subsequently appointed to senior positions in the administration.

Once more, governance of Sierra Leone descended into chaos as Koroma, with the RUF as partner, took over the reins of power, suspended the Constitution, dissolved parliament and banned political parties. In the ensuing chaos, a Nigerian force (nominally under the auspices of ECOWAS) was dispatched to reverse the *coup* and maintain law and order. While the international community condemned the junta, there was little if anything in the way of concrete support for the duly elected government. As the dust settled on the events of 25 May 1997, the junta controlled Freetown and its environs. The Nigerian forces maintained control of Lungi Airport with a beachhead on the Freetown side of the bay. The upcountry communities relied even more on the Kamajors, and private security companies attempted, with financing from concession holders, to protect the infrastructure and equipment of the mining companies.

Despite the dangers involved, the public in several towns displayed their anger at these developments, and stay-aways were organised. Western governments voiced their disapproval, evacuated their citizens and imposed sanctions on the military junta in Freetown.

In the meanwhile, the Kabbah government-in-exile was busy with its own plans through the Kamajor-based Civil Defence Force, headed by former Deputy Minister of Defence, Hinja Norman. Norman headed the War Council and normally operated out of a field headquarters in Liberia where he was supported by ECOMOG. The Nigerian troops on the ground in Sierra Leone, and their control of Lungi Airport and a bridgehead near Hastings Airport, provided a staging point for future operations.

Before the end of May, an additional 700 Nigerian troops had arrived in Freetown to reinforce the 900-strong contingent already deployed in the country. The Nigerians soon gave notice of their intentions, shelling the junta's headquarters from warships on 2 June, killing hundreds of civilians in the process. The accompanying ground operations proved disastrous: 300 Nigerians were captured, while many civilians were killed in fighting around Freetown. In the aftermath, companies such as DiamondWorks and the Toronto-based Rex Diamond Mining Corporation halted work and withdrew their personnel to neighbouring Guinea.

The Nigerian warships withdrew on 21 June, but troops continued to hold the international airport at Lungi and a base at Jui, just outside Freetown, which they reinforced and re-equipped. Nigeria had, in fact, acted unilaterally during this period. The regional sanction for ECOMOG intervention was only forthcoming at the Abuja ECOWAS Summit of 29 August, and despite the Security Council commendation of ECOMOG in its July 1998 resolution establishing UNOMSIL, the UN military observer mission, explicit UN authorisation for ECOMOG's intervention, in terms of Article 53[25]of the UN Charter, never materialised. In the interior, clashes continued between junta/RUF forces and the Kamajors.

Enter Sandline International

Shortly after these events, Kabbah made contact with Sandline International, a company closely associated with EO and DiamondWorks. Sandline claimed close contact with the British government and had a less offensive international profile than EO, but there was little to choose between the two organisations. The purpose of the contact was to negotiate the provision of military expertise and planning for the eventual return of the Kabbah government-in-exile to Sierra Leone by force, if the international community did not provide a satisfactory solution. According to the account of events later released by Sandline's lawyers, the initial contact was made by Kabbah at the suggestion of Peter Penfold, the British High Commissioner to Sierra Leone, who was also sheltering in Conakry. Kabbah had arranged for funding for the Sandline operation through Rakesh Saxena, a banker and Indian national wanted for embezzlement in Thailand, then out on bail in Vancouver pending charges of travelling on a false passport. Saxena was evidently anxious either to protect or extend his own diamond operations in Sierra Leone and was promised that, in return for his financial assistance, a restored government would grant him certain concessions.[26] In exchange, Saxena would finance the military operation in two tranches: an initial $1,5 million for personnel and start-up costs, and a further $3,5 million for military support equipment and its transfer to the area of operations.[27] By the middle of July, Tim Spicer, the head of Sandline, had flown to West Africa to see Kabbah (using an initial $70 000 provided by Saxena) and ECOMOG. Spicer's subsequent proposal provided:

- contingency plans for possible military operations;

- co-ordination arrangements between the Civil Defence Force and ECOMOG; and

- liaison between the Kabbah government in Conakry, ECOMOG in Sierra Leone, and ECOMOG and the Civil Defence Force.

Details of the role that Sandline was to play, remain unclear, but the training of the Kamajors was mentioned, as was the supply of weapons to rearm the force. Sandline also appears to have been involved in co-ordinating the planning of the campaign to unseat Koroma, the provision of logistical support, control of ECOMOG air operations, including the services of two helicopters, and intelligence gathering.

By the end of July, Koroma was feeling confident enough to abort talks with other West African leaders in Abidjan and assert his intention of staying in power until 2001. On 6 August, the UN Security Council issued a statement indicating that, in the absence of a satisfactory response from the junta, it was "... *ready to take appropriate measures with the objective of restoring the democratically elected government.*"[28] It was another two months before it adopted a British-sponsored resolution imposing oil, arms and travel sanctions on Sierra Leone.

At the time of the Abuja ECOWAS Summit in August 1997, it was obvious that Kabbah and his government had lost hope that they would be restored to power through the force of arms of the international community. ECOWAS reflected the opinion of the international community when it opted, as the subregional body, to follow the course of trade and other sanctions to defeat the junta.[29]

The Nigerian-led ECOMOG forces and the Kamajors, by this time, had exerted enough pressure on Koroma for him to consider negotiating a peaceful solution, though he was eager to have Sankoh, who was still in Nigerian detention, participate in the discussions. At the end of August, ECOMOG was authorised to enforce the economic embargo on Sierra Leone. It did this in a characteristically controversial way, by shelling ships at harbour in Freetown, and shelling and bombing the vicinity of the harbour and other centres – inflicting several civilian casualties over the next few months. These actions drew international criticism, however, without prompting a more determined attempt by other powers to oust the Koroma regime, which was later described in the Guardian[30] as "... *a truly appalling gang of brutal kleptocrats.*" Nor was the irony of the situation lost upon the Nigerian pro-democracy movement when it learned in October that the Abacha regime was committed to the restoration of democracy in Sierra Leone. Writing in the <u>Guardian</u>, Ken Wiwa, son of the late Ken Saro-Wiwa, had earlier said:

"The Nigerian military is an old hand at meddling in the affairs of its neighbours in West Africa. The horny hand of its various despotic regimes has, among other things, sponsored or plotted coups *in Gambia and exacerbated the terrible troubles in Liberia. On each occasion, this meddling has been called peace-making ... If the experience of Sierra Leone is anything to go by, then military intervention,* coup *plotting and 'restoring democracy' are lucrative businesses for those involved. That the British government might have found itself feeding this food chain, wittingly or not, has made a mockery of Robin Cook's ethical foreign policy."*[31]

By late October, with Britain making unusually strong gestures of support to Kabbah's government-in-exile, Koroma was induced to conclude a peace agreement in Guinea with ECOWAS. This provided for Kabbah to return to office before the end of April at the head of a broad-based government of national unity. The deal also gave immunity from prosecution to the leaders of the *coup*. All parties agreed to an immediate end to hostilities and the initiation of a programme of disarmament, demobilisation and reinsertion of combatants. Certain details still needed finalisation, however, and the position of the RUF in the bargain was unclear, as was the prospect of Sankoh's return to Sierra Leone.

By the beginning of November, it appeared that the jubilation which accompanied the peace agreement might have been premature. Koroma insisted that Nigerian troops should be excluded from the ranks of the new ECOMOG monitoring force. He also voiced reservations about the nature of the unity government, and added a demand for Sankoh to be released. By 11 November, Koroma was insisting that, as the national army, his troops should be excluded from the disarmament process. From Liberia, President Charles Taylor added his objections to ECOMOG's activities against the junta.

On 27 November, a report appeared in Toronto's <u>The Globe and Mail</u>,[32] detailing the relationship between EO, LifeGuard, Sandline International and a number of mining companies, including DiamondWorks. It alleged that members of these companies were engaged in planning a counter-*coup* in Sierra Leone to restore Kabbah. By the end of November, DiamondWorks shares had declined by 25 per cent to $1,55 each since June. The article failed to generate much response, but by the middle of December, ECOMOG and the Kamajors stepped up their air and ground offensive along the Liberian border. Throughout January 1998, as Koroma continued to procrastinate, the Kamajors began to retake certain of the diamond towns from the junta/RUF forces. On 27 January, junta and ECOMOG troops clashed in Freetown for the first time since the peace agreement, and it was clear that both sides were preparing themselves for renewed war.

During this period, Sandline had acquired LifeGuard Security which nominally severed its formal association with EO, South Africa. LifeGuard was now guarding key income generating areas such as Sierra Rutile and Kono and was headed by the former commander of EO's military contingent in the 1994/96 operation.[33] LifeGuard was therefore able to transfer individuals with appropriate technical qualifications to Sandline's efforts and also employed former EO personnel. These circumstances would later help Sandline operations significantly.[34] Sandline had also prepared a concept of operations but, more importantly, had developed the logistic and equipment requirements to support the operational plan.

The five-phase Sandline plan included the Civil Defence Force as the lead element of the operation, with support from ECOMOG, and co-ordination provided courtesy of Sandline's communications and aircraft. The plan included:

- Phase I: isolating cities such as Bo and Kenema through control of the inner road network, for example, by ambush;

- Phase II: encircling key cities;

- Phase III: conducting simultaneous attacks;

- Phase IV: exploiting the capture of vital points; and

- Phase V: returning the Kabbah government.

By Christmas/New Year 1997/98, the operation had begun. The first $1,5 million had been received and Kabbah had co-ordinated action with Nigeria. Command, control and communications facilities were set up by Sandline with personnel transferred from LifeGuard. On 27 January 1998, the Civil Defence Force reported that phase I was complete, but that phase II was not quite ready to launch. The required arms had not yet arrived. It was at this stage that problems started to surface.

As he was about to hand over some $3,5 million, the second contract instalment, Saxena was arrested on passport charges by the Royal Canadian Mounted Police. This exacerbated Sandline's problems, which was trying to get an exemption to the UN arms embargo on Sierra Leone. Sandline eventually provided the money itself, believing that ECOMOG and Kabbah was exempt from the embargo, based on discussions with the US, the UK and ECOMOG authorities.

It would seem as if the subsequent ECOMOG offensive, which started on 26/27 January 1998 out of the Freetown side bridgehead, was premature and initiated without proper co-ordination and support. As a result, the Nigerian offensive only broke out of its positions outside Freetown on 6 February and a week later could claim to have control of the capital. Two days later, well-armed Kamajor forces took the major towns of Bo and Kenema. Though the war front remained flexible, it was clear that Koroma and the RUF were retreating towards their positions in the north-east of the country. As they fell back, they committed numerous atrocities against the civilian population who, in turn, exacted revenge on captured soldiers for earlier wrongs.

ECOMOG declared Freetown secured on 12 February 1998. An interesting sidebar to the main operations was the escape by helicopter of the junta, possibly including Kromah, apparently with a number of Ukrainian mercenaries. The helicopters, originally the property of EO and then Sandline, were forced down in Liberia by ECOMOG on 13 February 1998 and, despite loud protestation by the Liberian government that wished to keep them, returned to Sandline crews on 14 and 16 February 1998. By January 1999, 'Bokkie' – as the one helicopter had become known – was the only remaining one in service with ECOMOG, piloted by a South African.

While the battle was raging up-country, and a scantily armed Civil Defence Force was making do with what it had, 28 tons of small arms arrived in Sierra Leone from Bulgaria on 23 February 1998 through the offices of Sandline.[35] The arms were never to be distributed, but were impounded by ECOMOG and held at Lungi. In any event, a 'country-wide' push was ordered for 27 February 1998 which resulted in a consolidation of effort and the establishment of an ECOMOG/Civil Defence Force line of Bo, Kenemo and Zummi, but did not include areas of Koindu/Kono and Kailahun. At this stage, operations became more static.

On 10 March 1998, President Kabbah returned to Freetown in triumph. By early April, he could claim to control about ninety per cent of the national territory, but sporadic junta/RUF outrages continue to be reported from the deep interior. By April, a stalemate seemed to have developed, with the RUF and its allies settling in the alluvial diamond areas, their rear secured by the Liberian border and supported by Charles Taylor's government in Liberia. During May, ECOMOG announced that it had captured close to 100 'mercenaries' from Liberia either behind the front-lines, in combat or in various towns and villages in the interior. According to one captured member of the NPFL, "*President Taylor could not integrate us into the Liberian army and I thought coming to Sierra Leone to fight, could have helped me out.*"[36]

At least three more articles appeared in the international press in March about the role of Sandline in Kabbah's restoration, including one in <u>Africa Confidential</u>, but it was not until May that questions in the British parliament revealed that a customs investigation was being mounted into the provision of arms to ECOMOG, in possible violation of the UN embargo. This, in turn, focused the attention on the question whether the British government had been aware of the role played by a private military company in the Sierra Leone conflict.

The initial official reaction to the claim that the British government had condoned or even connived at the involvement of 'mercenaries' in a counter-*coup* to oust the military junta of Koroma, and the sale of weapons to Kabbah, was one of outraged innocence. The Foreign Office minister responsible for handling African affairs denied angrily that his government would associate with 'hired killers' and dismissed the allegations as irresponsible rubbish. He was subsequently supported by the Foreign Secretary, though it was soon apparent that senior officials and diplomats had enjoyed prior knowledge of Sandline's involvement. Indeed, Sandline's defence of its position was rather more expert than the disingenuous one mounted by Whitehall. Its lawyers detailed meetings with senior British and US officials, in some of which actual plans had been shared by the company. Sandline claimed with some justification that it had every right to believe that its operations enjoyed the support and approval of London and Washington.

While much of the lively debate in the British press concentrated on the ministers' possible lack of control over their officials, or the failure of the Foreign Secretary to pay sufficient attention to detail, the broader ironies implicit in Cook's defence also drew comment. On 8 May, <u>The Times</u> carried the following:

"Had President Kabbah not turned to the private sector, he would still be in exile. He had universal verbal backing; but during and after last year's coup, *the only force Western governments used was to evacuate their nationals; Nigerian troops had tried to overthrow the plotters and failed ... Since the wrath of the 'international community' had not the slightest impact on the regime, a rational observer might have expected the British Government to be quietly pleased that unorthodox methods had worked. It certainly professed itself delighted at the result. Instead, Sandline has been placed under criminal investigation and Robin Cook, the Foreign Secretary, has flatly condemned the operation ..."* [37]

This was not to be the full extent of the Foreign Office's embarrassment about its handling of the affair. UN Security Resolution 1132 – that, among others, prohibited the supply of arms to Sierra Leone – was drafted in large part by Sir Franklin Berman, chief legal advisor to the ministry. The Order in Council giving effect in British law to the Resolution was also drafted by Berman's staff. Berman's interpretation was that the embargo applied equally to all parties in the conflict and that, on these grounds, Sandline may have been breaching the law. But by the end of May, the UN lawyers appeared to have changed their minds, arguing, as had Sandline, that since the Resolution had as its purpose the restoration of the elected government in Sierra Leone, ECOMOG, which was working towards that end with the encouragement of the UN, must enjoy an implied partial exemption from the ban. During October, it would eventually emerge, as was suspected, that MI6 had been deeply involved in the whole matter and, in fact, had encouraged Sandline to break the UN embargo. Eventually, the fuss over who-said-what-when-to-whom would simply underline Britain's extreme sensitivity to evidence of its collaboration with Sandline, whatever its degree of concern may have been for the desperate plight of Sierra Leone. In Freetown, in a spectacle not seen for many years, the people of Sierra Leone converged to the central cotton tree during May to chant their support for British High Commissioner Peter Penfold and Nigerian despot Sani Abacha – those that had brought some stability to Sierra Leone. The Legg report that investigated the linkage between Sandline and the British government and published during July, effectively downplayed the matter, accusing the British Foreign Office of incompetence, and ignoring the role of MI6.

Stability had not returned to Sierra Leone, however, as more and more forces and companies were drawn into the conflict. During July, Nigeria transferred more than 4 000 troops from Liberia to Sierra Leone, at a time when LifeGuard and Defence Systems Limited were providing security to UN relief operations. Earlier in April, *Tele Service Sociedade de Telecomunicaçoes, Segurança e Servicos* (TeleServices) began to support LifeGuard at Branch Energy properties in Koindu. The US company ICI provided protection to businessmen, interests and aid workers in the south. [38]

In October, Sankoh, in detention in Freetown, was sentenced to death for treason as a result of his role in the May 1997 *coup*, but appealed against his sentence.

By Christmas 1998, West African countries opened emergency talks on the civil war in Sierra Leone with the US and Nigeria accusing Liberia of supporting the junta/RUF in renewed fighting as the rebels pushed the ECOMOG forces back. Apparently with the help of mercenaries from the Ukraine, rebel forces had already regained control of the diamond fields. A few days earlier, Nigeria had rushed an extra 600 troops to Sierra Leone to bolster ECOMOG as the rebels claim to have captured the key northern town of Makeni, 185 kilometres from Freetown, and were threatening Freetown itself. These reinforcements boosted ECOMOG to about 12 000 troops with more to follow – all to replace the hundred or so mercenaries that had previously brought a large degree of stability to Sierra Leone. The Committee of Six (composed of involved ECOWAS countries) held an extraordinary meeting in Abidjan on 28 December, appealing to the rebels to stop fighting, lay down their arms and recognise Kabbah as president. In the light of the deteriorating security situation, the Committee also pressed for additional troops, as well as a resumption of the Abidjan Agreements and the Conakry Peace Plan.

By January 1999, fighting had erupted in Freetown as the rebel forces under Sam Bockarie continued to advance. Kabbah had taken refuge at the Lungi airport town and offered to release Sankoh. Britain committed £1 million of financial and logistic support to ECOMOG. Anton la Guardia commented on the state of affairs in Sierra Leone:

"... the exclusive reliance on the 15 000 ECOMOG intervention force by Nigeria ... has turned out to be a political failure and a tragedy for the country's civilians. Within 12 months, the victorious Nigerian troops have been pushed back to their starting point ... the West's hopes that Nigeria could preserve stability in West Africa by acting as a regional policeman were clearly unrealistic, particularly when Nigeria is preoccupied by its own transformation to democracy."[39]

By 22 January 1999, Sam Kiley wrote in The Times: *"Whether or not Sandline was implementing British policy then, it is quite clear that it should be now ... The redeployment of mercenaries in this blighted nation would be an act of genuinely ethical foreign policy."*[40]

Conclusion

The per capita annual income of $200 per person in Sierra Leone is half of that of poverty stricken sub-Saharan Africa. Life expectancy is less than forty years and the government is effectively run from Lagos. Had Executive Outcomes and Sandline International not been involved, the savage war in this country would not have raised much public interest in Britain, where it was basically a party-political issue, nor in South Africa, where the government has made an implicit connection between EO, the 'third force' and resistance to the new order.

The guilt of foreign countries is not that of short term complicity, but of long term complacency. Against the backdrop of the murder, mayhem and chaos in Sierra Leone, much domestic interest in a country such as Britain was focused on the political embarrassment for Robin Cook, the Foreign Secretary, who had loudly and repeatedly committed the Blair administration to the pursuit of an ethical foreign policy.[41] As the story broke, it appeared that Sandline might have violated the UN arms embargo on Sierra Leone by supplying weapons to forces loyal to Kabbah, with the knowledge of officials or ministers in the British government. There was also the question of how the government would attempt to reconcile its ethical position with the essential role played by Nigeria in the affair, which was suspended from the Commonwealth because of its abuses of human rights and doubts about its commitment to the restoration of civilian rule.

There is nothing unusual in this ambivalence. If Britain had grown weary of the white man's burden, it still did not find it easy to disengage. Under the eleven-year sway of Baroness Chalker, the Foreign and Commonwealth Office had consistently supported military actions to the incoherent but vicious rural rebellion gripping its former colony of Sierra Leone. In 1994, Britain helped to bring in 58 Gurkha troops from GSG to assist in the fighting. At the same time, Britain was instrumental in bringing about the 1996 elections and, subsequently, in introducing Sandline to Kabbah. Assistance was also forthcoming to the extent of repairing Sandline helicopters from the frigate HMS Cornwall in Freetown harbour. All these efforts were in vain, as Liberia's support for the hostilities in Sierra Leone continued unabated and the civil war in the country degenerated in a macabre orgy of bloodletting.

It is difficult and dangerous to apply Western assumptions about the nature of state security in many African countries where concerns for state survival are often subordinate to those for the personal security and well-being of the incumbent leadership. Countries such as Liberia, Nigeria and Sierra Leone have seen the creation of a parallel political authority, where personal ties and controls replace failing institutions. In this 'shadow state', alternative extrastate power networks underpin political and economic privilege. So potent and pervasive are these networks that, by manipulating the vestiges of state power, they are able to frustrate and bend interventions by the international financial and donor community designed to undermine the informal sector and strengthen the structures of the state for their own purposes. It is against this background and in this context that the military activities and interventions of state, regional and private security forces have to be analysed.

In a country such as Sierra Leone, the military is not a stable bulwark against chaos and instability. The RSLMF has never hesitated in the past to replace leaders or governments that did not please it. The use of private security forces such as EO can allow responsible decisions, such as military or civil service downsizing, to take place without fear of interference. Indeed, Reno states that "... *EO prevents chaos.*" In the context of military strongmen overruling political decisions in such countries as Liberia and Somalia, "*[r]ulers in Sierra Leone and Angola avoid this fate by privatising violence and [guaranteeing the] accumulation of wealth to reliable foreigners, and contracting out the task of disciplining wayward politicians and social groups.*"[42] The argument that real sovereignty comes from the unfettered ability to make unpopular but necessary decisions flies in the face of those who, in arguing against the use of private security, hide behind a false and self-centred definition of sovereignty. The other side of the coin is portrayed by Doyle[43] who presents the "... *arrival of powerful foreigners as a consequence of efforts of elite factions to recruit outside help to deal with local rivals who have their own foreign connection.*" Doyle calls this 'imperialism by invitation', and suggests that each case should be judged on its own merits. Foreign intervention is not necessarily bad or good, but judgements should pragmatically depend upon the reasons giving rise to such an intervention.

The situation in which the government of Sierra Leone found itself after the 25 May 1997 *coup* was completely different from the euphoric conditions that existed in February 1997 in the wake of the elections. Instead of being the internationally recognised government of a sovereign state-in-exile, enjoying the support of the international community, the Kabbah government found itself expelled, destitute, and dependent upon a neighbouring country for asylum. While the international community wrung its collective hands helplessly, the elected government could only sit on the sidelines and watch the country regress into a state of despotic anarchy under the thugs of the junta. To whom could Kabbah turn? Since Executive Outcomes was politically unacceptable, Kabbah would eventually turn to Nigeria and Sandline International.

EO's initial task was to reopen the alluvial diamond fields and other sources of revenue. In the process, it had brought short term stability to Sierra Leone, a cease-fire was agreed to, and a peace process started. It was this process, regardless of how sporadically and incompletely it was understood and applied, which allowed the elections and improved the prospects for peace.

The Kabbah government was brought down in 1997 by a combination of factors, including the destabilising role of the RSLMF, which was perhaps aided by strongmen elements in the bloated bureaucracy functioning in the vacuum that developed when EO left.

The Kabbah government was brought back into power in February 1998 by private deals made between what was essentially two private military organisations – Sandline International and Nigeria. Ironically, Sandline was more transparent in its affairs than the then government of Nigeria, with the latter being the source of extensive human rights abuses and criminal activity in a country such as Liberia.

Given that ECOWAS did not initially sanction military action to eject the junta and reinstate the government, but rather adopted a policy of trade and other sanctions, the use of Nigerian troops was a private deal between Sierra Leone and Nigeria. While the designation 'ECOMOG'[44] is used to characterise the Nigerian soldiers who originally represented ECOWAS, it would seem as if the Nigerian forces in the battle against the junta were just that – military forces hired by the government of Sierra Leone. In this context, an examination of President Kabbah's dalliance with Nigeria will show that the post-25 May 1997 activities were much more complicated, with possibly dangerous consequences to a free, sovereign and democratic Sierra Leone, than the use of EO in 1995/96. If history holds any lessons, it may be that Kabbah may have had a much harder time ridding himself of Nigerian troops than he would have had with either of the two private security companies previously engaged. Sierra Leone may only have been saved from Nigeria by the death of Abacha and the tenuous democratisation process in Nigeria.

Under military rule, Nigerian hegemony had spread across West Africa. The two Anglophone countries in the region, Liberia and Sierra Leone, that are the richest in natural resources besides Nigeria itself, were effectively influenced, if not controlled by a country run by a clique of self-serving despots who plundered their own country's oil resources as effectively as they did the natural riches of others. Writing about the role of ECOMOG some years later, Ofuatey-Kodjoe would summarise it thus:

"The notion that a group of states headed by military dictatorships have the right to intervene in another state in order to establish a democratic regime is grotesque; and the notion that these states can in fact achieve that objective by the application of outside force may be only an exercise in wishful thinking."[45]

The Sierra Leone experience has demonstrated how a small, private security force can impact positively and strongly upon a chaotic, destabilised state, and potentially establish the conditions for economic rejuvenation at minimal cost. Impartial, private organisations can marginalise the traditional strongmen of previous government models. Given the resource shortages of the UN and 'donor fatigue', the controlled use of private security companies, as demonstrated in Sierra Leone, presents opportunities that justify further analysis.

According to this analysis, the use of private security forces should perhaps be considered as one possible solution to the problems of security in weak, emerging democracies.

Commenting on the release of the Legg report during July, the Financial Times made three sensible points.

"First, sanctions imposed by bodies like the UN need to be better drafted ...once decided, they at least need to be properly implemented ... Second, mercenaries are being increasingly used by governments. But they are a double-edged sword and need careful handling ... Last but not least is the realisation that Africa needs more diplomatic attention than it has been getting. It may account for an ever diminishing share of the world's wealth, but it also, sadly, generates an increasing ration of the world's conflicts."[46]

Endnotes

1 Prior to the Abuja ECOWAS Summit of 29 August 1997, ECOMOG had no legal mandate in Sierra Leone. See A Bundu, *ECOWAS: Conflict Management and Resolution in the Sierra Leone Crisis 1997*, in J N Garba (ed.), Militaries, Democracies, and Security in Sub-Saharan Africa, papers read at a conference in Abuja, Nigeria, 1-4 December 1997, p. 146.

2 DiamondWorks, Prospectus, Vancouver BC, Canada, October 1997.

3 On the twentieth anniversary of the execution of Brigadier Bangura, 23 March 1991.

4 Sankoh was a former corporal in the Republic of Sierra Leone Military Forces (RSLMF). He served under Brigadier John Bangura who was executed by Siaka Stevens in 1971.

5 Revolutionary United Front, Footpath to Democracy, undated.

6 A J Venter, *Sierra Leone's Mercenary War, Battle for the Diamond Fields*, International Defence Review, 11/96, London, 1996, pp. 65-70.

7 I Douglas, Personal discussions in the field, Sierra Leone, July-August 1996.

8 RSLMF estimated strength in 1996 was about 15 000 soldiers in uniform.

9 The six battalions, of about 4-500 fighters each, were organised as follows: Vanguards (hard core trainers/leaders); Special Forces (Liberian migrants); Lumpen (most commanders came from this group); Salong Wosus (rank and file,

pressed into service); Standbys (pressed into service, under training, unarmed); and Recruits (fresh intakes). At the height of the war in 1995, the RUF had deployed throughout the country with: Zogoda Base Camp – RUF HQ; Western Battalion – Malal Hills; Eastern Battalion – Giema; Peyeima Battalion – Peyeima; Sendumei Jui Group – Menima; Sulima Group – Camp Libya; Northern (Sixth) Battalion – Kangani Hills. Reintegration of War Effected Youth and Ex-combatants, Report to the Ministry of Resettlement, Rehabilitation and Reconstruction, 1966, Chapter 2, pp. 13-17.

10   Venter, op. cit., pp. 65-70.

11   C Dietrich, *Altered Conflict Resolution: EO in Sierra Leone*, unpublished thesis, Princeton University, 1977, pp. 68-69.

12   There is one account, which cannot be confirmed, that besides GSG and EO, a contingent of fifteen former British Special Air Service (SAS) soldiers were employed by Strasser following MacKenzie's death and GSG's departure. A possible reason for this brief appearance, if it happened, is that this group was reported to be a very expensive organisation, charging $22 500 (US) per man per month. Venter, op. cit., p. 66. Also see Chapter 7 on GSG.

13   M Grunberg, Telephone conversations with I Douglas, November/December 1997.

14   Ibid.

15   Various interviews with EO personnel conducted by I Douglas.

16   Historically, Kamajors learned their skills through apprenticeships, and through acquisition of various powerful and expensive medicines (it is suggested that many of these medicines would prevent harm, even from firearms, to the Kamajors using them). Tradition has it that founders of pre-colonial Mende towns were often esteemed hunters, famed for having driven off the natural 'lords of the forest' (the elephants) so holding open a protected space for human occupancy. This tradition has served as the cornerstone for the development of a militia which, while no longer made up of the new 'lords of the forest', has used the mythology and, where possible, the skills of the hunter, to guard local or regional interests.

17   Dietrich, op. cit., p. 31.

18   Ibid., p. 32.

19   It is not verifiable whether EO accepted shares in Branch Energy in lieu of cash.

20   Dietrich, op. cit.

21   J Hooper, *Peace in Sierra Leone – A Temporary Outcome?*, Jane's Intelligence Review, 2, London, 1997, p. 91.

22   EO's figures reflect that the average fee per man per month, including all equipment and administration, was $11 500.

23   DiamondWorks, op. cit. EO had given Kabbah 90 days before he would be overthrown in a *coup*. The *coup* happened after 85 days.

24   Bundu, op. cit., p. 145.

25   Article 53 states that "... *no enforcement action shall be taken under regional arrangements or by regional agencies without the authorisation of the Security Council.*" The only lawful embargo against Sierra Leone is that passed by the Security Council under Resolution 1132 (1997) on 8 October. It is limited only to arms and ammunition, petroleum and petroleum products, and travel restrictions against members of the junta and their families.

26   The Toronto Globe and Mail, Toronto, Canada, 1 August, 1997. According to The Times, the Memorandum of Understanding between Kabbah, Spicer and Saxena stated: "... *the Grantee (Saxena) agrees to give economic and other assistance, to the value of $10,000,000 US to the Grantor (Kabbah) for ... restoration of the Constitution.*" See, *UK Firm to Escape Action over S Leone Arms*, The Times, London, 17 May 1998.

27 There was at least one other offer to support the military operation. An Israeli entrepreneur offered financial support, but the government stuck with Saxena's offer.

28 E Leopold, *UN Threatens Sanctions against Sierra Leone Junta*, Reuters News Service, United Nations, 6 August 1997.

29 ECOWAS Summit, Abuja, Nigeria, August 1997.

30 *The System Goes Wrong – But Sierra Leone Isn't Iraq*, Guardian, London, 8 May 1998, p. 26.

31 K Wiwa, *Opportunity Knocks*, Guardian, London, 13 May 1998, p. 20.

32 M Drohan & K Howlett, *DiamondWorks' African Site at Risk*, The Globe and Mail, Toronto, 27 November 1997.

33 Bert Sachse.

34 See, for example, P Sherwell, *International Dogs of War Stand Guard over Land of Diamonds*, Daily Telegraph, London, 21 May 1998.

35 The arms came from the company Arsenal and were flown to Sierra Leone by Sky Air Cargo Services.

36 *Liberian Mercenaries Support Ousted AFRC*, Inter Press Service, 1 May 1998.

37 *Cooked Up – The Foreign Secretary has Rushed to Judgement Prematurely*, The Times, London, 8 May 1998, p. 25.

38 *Militias and market forces*, Africa Confidential, London, 23 October 1998.

39 A la Guardia, *Sandline 'Should Have Been Left to Finish the Job'*, Daily Telegraph, London, 14 January 1999, p. 18.

40 S Kiley, *Send in the Mercenaries, Mr Cook*, The Times, London, 22 January 1999.

41 Cook's successful campaign to embarrass the previous government over the 'arms-to-Iraq' scandal marked him as a prime target for the opposition.

42 W Reno, *African Weak States and Commercial Alliances*, African Affairs, 1997, pp. 165-185.

43 M W Doyle, Empires, Cornell University Press, Ithaca, NY, 1986.

44 Liberians cynically state that ECOMOG stands for 'Every Car Or Moving Object Gone.'

45 W Ofautey-Kodjoe, *An Evaluation of the ECOWAS Intervention in Liberia*, in Garba (ed.), op. cit, p. 101.

46 *Legging it*, Financial Times, London, 28 July 1998, p. 19.

Chapter 10: Private security and international law

Yves Sandoz

Introduction

Mercenaries and mercenarism have been debated for a very long time. While there is a relatively strict definition of the status of a mercenary and mercenary activity, 'private violence' which becomes protracted or is assisted by private companies, reflects a much broader topic. In recent years, a host of private companies emerged that provide various 'security services'. These services are often offered amidst situations of internal strife or armed conflict. It is therefore not merely the issue of mercenaries in the context of international law that requires investigation. Equally important is the significance of a much broader range of security services, their compatibility with international law, and the requirements that companies providing such services have to meet within the more precise framework of international humanitarian law.[1]

This chapter starts with a general discussion of international humanitarian law, before presenting an overview of the debate on mercenarism within the United Nations. Against this backdrop, a closer investigation of the lawfulness of the relationship between a recognised government or a dissident authority on the one hand, and the private entities that provide it with military support on the other, can be undertaken.

A second issue that is examined, is the relationship that develops between those companies that provide security services and others that benefit from or contract them, such as multinational mining companies or even humanitarian organisations.

The responsibility of the states within whose territory the headquarters of private security companies are located, or that allow those organisations to set up logistic or administrative bases on their territory, is also considered. From the point of view of international humanitarian law, the issue at stake appears to be the rules relating to state responsibility and, in time of war, the rules governing neutrality.

International humanitarian law

The purpose of international humanitarian law is to preserve a measure of humanity during the conduct of war. When first developed, this body of law was consistent with the prevailing order of international relations, which did not rule out the possibility of war. Subsequently, it evolved to respond more effectively to the humanitarian problems engendered by war, but was gradually relegated to the sidelines with the move to 'outlaw' war, most prominently through the adoption of the UN Charter.[2]

The UN did not succeed, however, in fulfilling the ambitions of its founding fathers, particularly on account of the tension that existed from the outset between the Soviet Union and the other members of the Security Council. The Cold War that followed, led to the failure of negotiations on the implementation of Article 45 and the provisions of the UN Charter which were envisaged to enable the organisation "... *to take urgent military measures*" where international peace and security were breached. The proceedings in the Security Council were soon paralysed by the systematic exercise of the right to veto. Once it was clear that the UN would be unable to prevent war, states agreed to reopen the debate on international humanitarian law. The result was the four Geneva Conventions which were adopted in 1949 and which are still in force today. At the time, the atrocities committed during World War II were still fresh in the public mind and there was a strong moral impetus to support the conventions.

The boost given to human rights by the adoption in 1948 of the Universal Declaration of Human Rights provided another impetus behind the 1949 Geneva Conventions. The internal affairs of countries were no longer considered to be out of bounds. Albeit still very cautiously, states started to accept the idea that international humanitarian rules could be established to be observed in the conduct of internal conflicts.[3]

International humanitarian law therefore provides safeguards – a last bastion against the excesses associated with an outbreak of violence that could not be avoided. In order to be effective and respected by the combatants, whom it primarily affects, international humanitarian law must meet three conditions.

- It must be rooted in absolute fundamental rules or 'first principles' that command universal respect. The violation of these first principles must place the perpetrators beyond the pale, so to speak, of the international community. This is particularly important during internal conflicts, since the dissident party may wish to distance itself from international obligations incurred by the government that it is opposing.[4] Once these rules form part of customary international law, their application no longer depends on the formal commitment made by the government.[5] A dissident party must therefore be left with no practical possibility of rejecting the obligations arising under international humanitarian law without discrediting itself in the eyes of the entire international community.

- Respect for international humanitarian law should not detract from the effectiveness of military action. It is unlikely that parties that have decided to go to war, often in defiance of international law, would be willing to lose the struggle for the sake of observing humanitarian rules. It is important to demonstrate that the requirements of international humanitarian law do not undermine military effectiveness.[6] This presupposes that certain limits to the use and application of force, relating to the 'public conscience'[7] and the demands of international security, are recognised and observed. First and foremost among these is the notion that the aim of war is not the complete annihilation of the enemy, since the wholesale use of weapons of mass destruction against enemy armed forces would obviously be 'effective' in such a case.

- International humanitarian law, although subsidiary law, should apply alongside general international law, without any cause-and-effect relationship. In other words, belligerents should be judged under humanitarian law only in terms of their behaviour in conflict and not in terms of the cause they are defending. Humanitarian law may be breached in pursuit of a good cause and respected in pursuit of an unjust cause. This aspect is particularly important at the level of the individual soldier, who cannot be held accountable for the political decisions taken by his government, but who must be held responsible for breaches of basic and widely recognised humanitarian rules.

This does not mean that everyone is absolved of all responsibility under general international law. But it does mean that responsibility for political or strategic decisions lies at another level and, above all, that the two aspects must be kept separate.

This interpretation of humanitarian law has certain limits, however, particularly in the context of internal conflicts. In an international conflict, a captured combatant can be punished only if he has committed war crimes or other breaches of international humanitarian law. If he has not, he may not be punished, but only 'neutralised', and his internment should serve that purpose only, with all kinds of guarantees to ensure this. But this is not the case in internal conflicts. Indeed, the law does not prohibit the punishment of a combatant on the sole grounds that he took up arms against the government, regardless of his behaviour as a combatant – unless, of course, the government recognises the existence of a state of belligerence.[8] Such a recognition would confer a status on combatants and prisoners of the adverse party, similar to that which they would enjoy in an international conflict. But there has been virtually no instance of this kind of recognition in recent times.

It follows that the governments of states involved in internal conflicts must be convinced on a case-by-case basis of the continuing importance of differentiating between the illegality of the act of rebellion, on the one hand, and acts of war that are illegal in themselves, on the other. It is therefore generally recommended that convictions on the sole grounds of having taken up arms should be 'frozen', as it were, until the end of the conflict, and that irreversible measures, such as the death penalty, should be avoided. Besides, the soldiers of a government that resorts to measures of this kind during hostilities are unlikely to be treated much differently if they were captured by the dissident party. The upshot is almost inevitably a spiral of reprisals and counterreprisals during which all humanitarian rules are thrown out of the window.

International humanitarian law therefore draws a distinction between the justification of the use of force, which lies outside its scope, and the manner in which military action is conducted, which is its primary concern. It is within this context, therefore, that the question of 'private violence' must be addressed.

The debate on mercenarism within the United Nations

The contemporary image and concept of mercenarism only came into focus during the process of decolonisation. It was not so much the phenomenon itself that came under attack as the support that was given by mercenaries to colonial governments intent on remaining in place – and hence opposed to the struggle for national liberation.

Resolution 3103, adopted by the UN General Assembly in 1973, aptly illustrates this situation, particularly in paragraph 5:

"The use of mercenaries by colonial and racist regimes against the national liberation movements struggling for their freedom and independence from the yoke of colonialism and alien domination is considered to be a criminal act and these mercenaries should accordingly be punished as criminals."

The use of the phrase 'these mercenaries' and not 'the mercenaries', clearly shows that mercenary activity was identified with opposition to liberation struggles.

At the same time, efforts were being made to enhance the status of 'liberation movements' by placing 'wars of liberation' on the same footing as international conflicts. This was finally achieved in Protocol I of 1977 additional to the 1949 Geneva Conventions.[9] Although the rules of international humanitarian law that are applicable in such conflicts ultimately remain the same for each of the belligerents – a vital prerequisite if the law is to have any prospect of implementation – many people were far more amenable to the idea of giving foreign aid to liberation movements than to the governments that opposed them.

The generally negative image of the role of the mercenary also stemmed from the idea that, since the right of peoples to self-determination acquired the status of a human right in the two International Covenants adopted by the UN in 1966,[10] the very fact of taking up arms on a government's side in such circumstances could be viewed as a violation of human rights. This further strengthened the perception that mercenaries were combatants who disregarded all such rights.

Since then the situation has changed considerably. The greatest fear at present, is the prospect of destabilisation of newly independent countries, or even covert recolonisation through the control exerted by big multinational companies over a large part of the national economy. Although governments still generally take a dim view of mercenaries – not only because of their willingness to make war for money, but also because of their role during the decolonisation process – many governments have recourse to private firms offering services similar or related to those previously provided by mercenaries. This relationship does not trigger a violently negative reaction, precisely because the purpose is to strengthen the post-colonial government and not to weaken it.

Security services provided to a public entity

Military assistance, even private assistance, to a government in office generally elicits less negative reaction than assistance to the dissident party in an internal conflict. Since such assistance is requested by the government, it does not pose – on the face of it – a threat to national sovereignty. Indeed, a government might claim that it helps to preserve such sovereignty.

The fear expressed by some is that the need to resort to private companies betrays the weakening of the state. This perception is not unjustified. In soliciting such support, a government is accused of 'selling its soul to the devil' and could subsequently have to make concessions that would undermine national sovereignty. Obviously, this will also depend on the nature and the ethics of the private organisation selling its services.

The question whether security services[11] furnished to a public entity are lawful or unlawful ultimately depends on the legitimacy of the entity concerned, the origin of the services provided, the framework in which they are provided, their nature, and the manner in which they are provided. Each is discussed in turn.

The nature of the public entity

When security services are requested or commissioned by a government, the sovereignty being protected in terms of international law is not that of the government, but that of the state. Needless to say, the government must be established in a recognised state and must be the legitimate representative of that state. Both are complex issues in themselves that require separate analyses beyond the scope of this chapter. Suffice it to state that current international law is not precise, nor effective with regard to the requirements relating to legitimate states and governments. As has been noted,

"... an irregular change of government does not automatically have a direct impact on a State's participation in international organisations: the principle of the continuity of the State runs counter to the possibility of using this political turn of events as a pretext for expulsion or readmission. [In practice,] ... the principle of effectivity prevails over that of legitimacy."[12]

This was most vividly illustrated during 1997 when an armed campaign deposed former President Mobutu in Zaire, installing Laurent Kabila as the head of the government of the newly named Democratic Republic of Congo (DRC). The extent of the regional and indeed global relief at the end of a notorious dictatorship translated a *de facto* transfer of power almost immediately into legal recognition.

The international community has consistently been trapped between the need to protect the national sovereignty of states, on the one hand, and the right of people to self-determination, on the other. In fact, the balance between the two is contested and has shifted markedly in recent decades. It is useful to note, for example, that,

"... while it was necessary in the historical circumstances of decolonisation to recognise that peoples enjoyed certain rights in order to facilitate their attainment of independence, there was no question of the new States sharing with peoples the powers and rights traditionally exercised by States alone. Once the State was established, it confiscated the rights formally recognised as pertaining to peoples."[13]

Moreover, the situation with regard to existing political borders is not definitive – new states can and are being created. Recent examples include the disintegration of the former Soviet Union and the former Yugoslavia, and the partition of Czechoslovakia and Ethiopia, all of which were members of the UN. In these developments, there was no *a priori* arbitration and the role of the International Court of Justice remains modest. It is the material existence of these new states that gives them a recognised place in the international community. In effect, it is the success of a secessionist struggle that endows such a state with legitimacy *a posteriori*.

The international community constantly veers between the need for absolute protection of the national sovereignty of every state on the one hand, and respect for peoples' right to self-determination, which may lead to changes in state borders, on the other.[14]

It is difficult to assess the lawfulness of any support given to a government in terms of the latter's nature and 'legitimacy' under international law. Only in extreme and exceptional cases does the international community call the legitimacy of a government into question. The concern to maintain stability in international relations undeniably favours governments, even though there has been some degree of tolerance, in cases such as the civil war in the former Zaire, for support to rebels opposing a government that has lost a large part of its credibility, if not its legitimacy.

Thus, a private company can lawfully provide support for a struggle against a government only if, within the framework of the UN, both the illegitimacy of the government and the legitimacy of those engaged in the struggle are indisputably acknowledged. If that were not the case, the very act of entering the territory of a state without the consent of the government will be a violation of sovereignty, whatever the reasons for such an action. Even international humanitarian relief operations conducted in the context of internal armed conflicts require the consent of the government. Admittedly, such relief actions cannot legitimately be refused if the aid they bring is indispensable, but the principle of consent does exist and is the crux of all the discussion generated by the *droit d'ingérence* (right to intervene).[15] If this restriction is disputed in the case of those who claim to be bringing humanitarian aid in full compliance with the principles of impartiality and neutrality, it is easy to understand that states would not consider recognising a 'right' to provide military support – whether directly or indirectly – by a dissident entity, except pursuant to a decision of the Security Council.

The reluctance shown by the UN to rule on the legitimacy of governments, or of struggles undertaken in the name of the right of peoples to self-determination, does not entitle a private entity (or, indeed, a state acting individually) to substitute itself for the international community and decide unilaterally whether any of its support activities on behalf of an entity involved in a struggle against a government are lawful or otherwise. This has been confirmed by the International Court of Justice, notably in its judgement of 27 June 1986 on 'Military and Paramilitary Activities in and against Nicaragua'. In specifying the scope of the prohibition on direct or indirect interference in the internal or external affairs of another state, the Court stressed, in particular, that

"... the element of coercion, which defines, and indeed forms the very essence of, prohibited intervention, is particularly obvious in the case of an intervention which uses force, either in the direct form of military action, or in the indirect form of support for subversive or terrorist armed activities within another State."[16]

Indeed, the Court had specified much earlier, in the Corfu Channel case, that an alleged right of intervention "... *cannot, whatever be the present defects in international organisation, find a place in international law.*"[17] While it is true that international law does allow for certain exceptions (state of distress, state of necessity), these are strictly limited.[18]

International law has been strict in its judgement that the means cannot justify the ends. For that reason, there is little room for exceptions, and "... *any derogation to the prohibition on interference must be subject to strict interpretation.*"[19]

Can a private company lawfully provide military assistance to a UN sanctioned government even if that government's legitimacy is hotly disputed? Placing the obligation on private entities to separate the wheat from the chaff is obviously an impossible burden. However, in situations of stabilisation there is a clear limit – the private military services provided should in no way hinder or restrict peacekeeping or peacemaking measures mandated by the UN.

Moreover, "... *the principle concerning the duty not to intervene in matters within the domestic jurisdiction of any State, in accordance with the [UN] Charter,*"[20] and not to "...*interfere in civil strife in another State.*" does imply restraint in the assistance offered to a government. A case could therefore be made that this principle applies to those individuals or organisations providing private military services to governments. While some would argue that such assistance to governments is also interference in civil strife, others could interpret the principles as parameters that limit the undermining of a government's authority.

Operationalisation of this principle could take the form of a transparent and coherent approach taken by the UN and in particular the Security Council. This would shed a new light on the provisions of Chapter VIII of the UN Charter and the role of regional organisations.

Origin of the services rendered

International humanitarian law is only concerned with recourse to private entities in the context of armed conflict in relation to mercenaries and not in relation to other security services. But the definition of a mercenary given in Article 47 of Protocol I sets out five requirements, in addition to the definition of the service rendered, which must be fulfilled. To be considered as a mercenary, a person who takes a direct part in the hostilities:

- must be specially recruited to fight;

- must be motivated essentially by the desire for private gain and, in fact, be promised remuneration in excess of that paid to those of similar rank or function in the armed forces of the party to the conflict that uses his services;

- must be neither a national of a party to the conflict nor a resident of territory controlled by that party. It should be noted in this connection that the fourth Geneva Convention prohibits the enforced enlistment of a national of occupied territories, with such an act actually being considered as a war crime.[21] To avoid any danger of abuse, it was nevertheless deemed necessary to specify that a resident of occupied territories could not be considered as a mercenary under any circumstances;[22]

- must not be a member of the armed forces of a party to the conflict; and

- must not have been sent on official duty by another state.

The last two conditions are obviously incompatible with the notion of 'private' violence.

In the final analysis, the decisive factors are, on the one hand, the degree of involvement in the hostilities, which will be considered below, and, on the other, the purely financial motivation. The definition of a mercenary therefore places us at the core of the current debate, the key question being the extent to which the involvement of private individuals (as opposed to members of armed forces) is acceptable in a conflict.

The context in which private violence occurs

In formal terms, international humanitarian law only deals with mercenaries in the context of **international** armed conflicts, although Protocol I extends the definition of an international armed conflict to include wars of liberation.[23]

However, the matter is not restricted to international conflicts in either the 1989 UN International Convention against the Recruitment, Use, Financing and Training of Mercenaries,[24] or in the 1977 Convention for the Elimination of Mercenarism in Africa of the Organisation of African Unity (OAU).[25]

Security services furnished outside of situations of armed conflict are therefore not covered by international humanitarian law, but are obviously directly relevant in the present context, where private security companies provide training of military personnel, the delivery of arms, training in the handling of high-technology weapons, contributions to police operations, and the like. The fact that there is no article on mercenaries in Protocol II of 1977 is actually of no great significance, in view of the purpose of the provision in Protocol I. The aim of Article 47 of Protocol I is to discourage mercenarism by penalising mercenaries, that is, by denying them the protection enjoyed by prisoners of war. In an international conflict, as already mentioned, prisoners of war can be held during the conflict for purposes of 'neutralisation', but cannot be convicted merely on the basis of having taken part in the conflict. There is no such immunity for combatants captured in an internal conflict, the context within which most modern mercenaries operate.

In practice, a combatant captured in an internal conflict – as long as it is not a war of liberation that has the status of an international conflict – can be punished under domestic law on the sole basis of having taken up arms. There is nothing to prevent lawmakers from prescribing a more severe penalty for a foreign combatant motivated by the prospect of gain.

On the other hand, there can be no question of denying a mercenary the protection afforded by Part II of Protocol II (Humane treatment). The three constituent articles – Article 4

(Fundamental guarantees), Article 5 (Persons whose liberty has been restricted), and Article 6 (Penal prosecutions), stipulate that all captured persons shall be treated humanely. These articles lay down minimum requirements for the treatment of detainees and set forth principles to be observed in criminal proceedings (prosecution, trial, conviction). The prohibition of the death penalty contained in Article 6, paragraph 4 – for acts committed by a person who was under the age of eighteen years at the time of the offence – would also be applicable to a combatant who might be described as a mercenary.

These articles contain fundamental and universal guarantees that, among others, should prevent an individual from being falsely described as a mercenary. Mercenaries cannot be excluded from the protection afforded by these provisions. Moreover, these guarantees are consistent with the appropriate approach to international conflicts inasmuch as Article 75 of Protocol I, listing similar fundamental guarantees, is applicable to all persons having any connection with an armed conflict, including mercenaries.

Nature of the services rendered

The nature of the security service that is provided, is a crucial issue, since it is decisive in determining whether or not the term 'mercenary' is appropriate. It is, in fact, the key issue in the current debate on companies providing security services. It is therefore useful to revert to international humanitarian law and its definition of a mercenary. Of the six components of the definition of the term in Article 47 of Protocol I, only one concerns the services rendered: the mercenary must *"... take a direct part in the hostilities."*[26] It is thus essential to determine what this phrase means. The commentary published by the International Committee of the Red Cross (ICRC) states that the services of military advisors and technicians are not seen as mercenary activities:

"The increasingly perfected character of modern weapons, which have spread throughout the world at an ever-increasing rate, requires the presence of such specialists, either for the selection of military personnel, their training or the correct maintenance of the weapons. As long as these experts do not take any direct part in the hostilities, they are neither combatants nor mercenaries, but civilians who do not participate in combat."[27]

The commentary on Article 43 (Armed forces), states more specifically: *"Direct participation in hostilities implies a direct causal relationship between the activity engaged in and the harm done to the enemy at the time and the place where the activity takes place."*[28]

To sum up, the unlawfulness of the 'services' rendered, relates only to direct participation in the hostilities, which implies actual involvement and would exclude the provision of advice, services or support. Even though some individuals do take an active part in the hostilities, they are in a minority. This was, in fact, the case under an agreement for the provision of military assistance signed on 31 January 1997 between the government of Papua New Guinea and Sandline International. One may therefore ask, on the one hand, whether this criterion is still valid today and, on the other, whether it is the only criterion to be taken into account.

Manner in which the services are rendered

The primary aim of international humanitarian law is to prevent the excesses that are perpetrated during hostilities. From the perspective of this body of law, therefore, it is far more important to know **how** mercenaries behave, or indeed how any participants in the hostilities behave, than to determine whether they are really involved in the hostilities or whether they earn a great deal of money. There can be no denying that the negative connotations of the term 'mercenary' are based on prejudices that need to be investigated. The Special Rapporteur of the Commission on Human Rights did not avoid prejudging the matter when he said:

*"Mercenary activities are a form of violence which has been used in the last 40 years to hamper the exercise of the right to self-determination of peoples **and to violate human rights.** Mercenaries tend to be present mainly in armed conflicts, where they offer their services to one or more parties to the conflict in exchange for payment, **causing serious damage to the people and territories that are victims of their actions**."*[29]

The basic question that arises from the standpoint of international humanitarian law is whether a person who takes part in hostilities for financial reasons acts *a priori*, contrary to the principles of international humanitarian law and human rights law. The definition of a mercenary contains no condition relating to behaviour, probably because of a reluctance to imply that there can be 'good' mercenaries in terms of their compliance with the rules of international humanitarian law. At the same time, the fact cannot be overlooked that the conduct of certain 'regular' combatants can certainly be worse than that of mercenaries. Recent events and indeed history have amply demonstrated that combatants driven by ideological, ethnic or religious fanaticism are capable of far worse behaviour towards the general population than that of persons popularly depicted as mercenaries.

Security services rendered to private corporations

Those services on offer to private business concerns are central to the current debate. There is a general trend towards the curtailment of public authority and state control over several sectors of society in certain parts of the world. The doctrine of privatisation and outsourcing has gained particular popularity in areas such as education and health. In the area of human rights, a variety of watchdogs and advocacy organisations have sprung up and serve to supplement and augment the responsibility of states in the implementation of human rights. This raises a particular question regarding the delegation of state responsibility in the area of security. What responsibility is devolved to private companies that *de facto* perform tasks that are usually incumbent on the public authorities?

This issue will be at the heart of future discussions. As far as international humanitarian law is concerned, the problem is most acute in the context of armed conflicts taking place in situations where state structures have been weakened or are disintegrating.[30]

Private security is an increasingly widespread phenomenon. Passive security measures involving increasingly sophisticated protective installations are often accompanied by the services of armed guards. Private security in this form can occur on a very large scale in the case of major facilities, such as an industrial plant or mining operation.

Normally, such security services are administered and regulated by the state through licensing systems such as those regarding the carrying of firearms. The weaker the state and the more chaotic the situation, the less effective this type of control and the more extensive the direct security services provided by private bodies. In conflicts marked by the virtual disintegration of state structures, such licensing by the authorities is frequently sullied by corruption, or the licensing system itself may simply no longer work.

In most cases, private security companies are employed to protect particular economic interests. Such protection may be quite extensive, involving security measures that cover large parts of the territory. An example would be the protection of mining or oil installations, which would also require that access routes and links with ports or other communication centres are safeguarded. Measures of this kind may therefore affect a large number of people and may be geographically expansive.

When these privatised security measures occur within the context of an armed conflict, they may lead to acts related to the conflict. If they do, responsibility for such acts must be clearly determined in terms of international humanitarian law. Companies that provide security services for major private corporations must do so within the legislative and administrative framework established by the state. When this framework has practically disappeared and the security companies take on increasingly large-scale assignments, they assume some of the responsibility incumbent on the state. Is this necessarily undesirable where the international community has taken no other action to remedy the situation? This is essentially a political question that merits an examination of the principle involved and that needs to be assessed on a case-by-case basis.

Moreover, the manner in which security is provided, is not beyond the scope of human rights obligations or, in situations of armed conflict, of obligations arising from international humanitarian law. To what extent is this responsibility borne by the security company or by the corporation which enlists its services? The general rules governing criminal and civil responsibility should offer guidance in such cases. As far as sanctions for violations of international humanitarian law are concerned, the rule of individual responsibility and that defining the responsibility of superiors apply.[31]

But who is to ensure observance of those rules? The fact that responsibility for the punishment of breaches of international humanitarian law lies primarily with each party to a conflict in respect of offences committed by its own combatants, is all too frequently overlooked. The responsibility of a private company becomes so much greater in this regard if it is no longer subject to the control of the public authorities. But how can the company exercise the responsibility it has incurred? It may have recourse to administrative sanctions such as dismissal, but it is still hard to imagine a private company assuming the power to dispense justice. Serious cases would have to be referred to the courts in the company's country of origin or even to an international criminal court.

The problem takes on a new dimension in the event of grave and repeated violations of international humanitarian law – as opposed to occasional transgressions. In such a case, primary responsibility must be sought at the highest level, either of the corporation that hired the security company, or of the security company providing the service. But who is going to do this?

A peculiarity of the 1949 Geneva Conventions is that they assign collective responsibility to all states party to the Conventions for ensuring compliance with their provisions.[32] This means that states cannot remain indifferent to such problems and must at least examine the possibilities for taking practical action. In the hypothetical situation described above, one might feel that states could at least agree to investigate, prosecute and, if appropriate, try cases in which their own nationals are alleged to have committed war crimes. The states on whose territory private security companies are located, or on whose territory corporations are located who pay for private security services, should be particularly vigilant. They should not hesitate to investigate serious cases involving such companies or even, where necessary, to bring charges against senior management.

The establishment of an international criminal court[33] will give fresh impetus to this collective responsibility of the international community, since the court will have every reason to pay particularly close attention to situations in which the public authorities are incapable of shouldering their responsibilities.

Responsibility of the state on whose territory a private security company is based

The question of the responsibility of a state in relation to a security company that is based on its territory, or uses its territory as a logistic base for providing security services, can be viewed from two angles. Firstly, there are services that are unlawful in themselves, and secondly, violations of human rights law or international humanitarian law may have been committed in providing such services, whether the latter are intrinsically lawful or unlawful.

Services unlawful in themselves

The services provided by a security company will be regarded as unlawful in themselves if they contravene the international instruments concerning mercenarism or, as a general rule, if their object is to support an entity engaged in a struggle with a legal government. The question here is the responsibility of a state in relation to those services emanating from its territory. The reply to this question must be sought in the rules governing the international responsibility of states.

The draft articles on state responsibility drawn up by the UN International Law Commission specified that "... *every internationally wrongful act of a State entails the international responsibility of that State.*" It sees the state as being responsible for the conduct of its organs, whatever the authority on which they depend, and for other bodies empowered to exercise the prerogatives of the government authority. On the other hand, it does not bear direct responsibility for the conduct of private companies: *"The conduct of a person or a group of persons not acting on behalf of the State shall not be considered as an act of the State under international law."* The state is not released from its responsibility, however, *"... if any ... conduct which is related to that of the persons or groups of persons ... is to be considered as an act of State."* It is therefore important to establish the nature of the link that actually exists between the company concerned and the state on whose territory it has its headquarters, or which agrees to the company conducting its activities on and from that territory.

However, even if the act that is unlawful in itself, except in the eventuality mentioned above, is not considered as an act of the state, the latter could be criticised for failing in its duty of 'due diligence'.[34] An act of the state which is unlawful under international law is a 'behaviour' which amounts to a violation of an international obligation binding on that state, and behaviour attributable to the state under international law may be *"... an act or an omission."* As Max Huber mentioned in the decision of the arbitration board in the Palmas Island case, territorial sovereignty *"... has as its corollary a duty – the obligation to protect, within the territory, the rights of other States, in particular their right to integrity and inviolability in time of peace and in time of war."*[35]

In fact, the state is not responsible for the acts of the private company in such cases, but for its own agents' lack of vigilance. A distinction will therefore be drawn between the case of a company which has its headquarters in a state and in whose affairs the state can play a decisive role by withdrawing its licence to operate, and the situation where a company uses the territory of a state without the formal agreement of the government. In the latter case, all that can be required of the government is a high degree of vigilance.

In a situation of armed conflict, the law governing neutrality must also be taken into account in assessing the acceptable limits of 'security' services. According to this law, *"... corps of combatants cannot be formed nor recruiting agencies opened on the territory of a neutral Power to assist the belligerents."*[36] The question here is thus whether the 'security services' that are rendered, involves the recruitment or training of combatants. On the other hand, the combatants who are recruited or trained, do not have to meet all the criteria included in the definition of a mercenary, particularly the financial requirement, for there to be a breach of the law of neutrality. Moreover, the state cannot be absolved of its responsibility by claiming that the activity is carried out by a private company. It is clearly responsible for making sure that such an activity does not take place.

In a situation of internal conflict, support for a government in office does not constitute a breach of the law of neutrality. As discussed earlier, there are two exceptions to this rule:

- where the conflict is a 'war of liberation' according to <u>Protocol I</u>, in which case it is 'elevated' to the rank of an international armed conflict in terms of international humanitarian law; and

- where there is 'recognition of belligerence' (see above), which has a similar effect.

However, these two exceptions are more theoretical than practical, since they have not arisen in any of the conflicts that have occurred in recent years.

The provision of private security services to private business organisations or the use of such services by organisations in situations where state structures are no longer functioning, must be judged in the light of the prevailing circumstances. If an internationally recognised government still exists, its position will be decisive. Harbouring the headquarters of a company that provides or uses such services may be viewed as an infringement of national sovereignty if the government in office is opposed to those services. If there is no longer a government that is internationally recognised, notably by the UN, as representing the country concerned, the acceptability or otherwise of such services should be determined primarily by the Security Council on the basis of a general assessment of the situation as it affects the maintenance of international peace and security.

Violations of international humanitarian law

Another issue to be considered is that of violations of international humanitarian law, regardless of who the beneficiary of the security services is. The state in which a company that uses or provides security services has its headquarters, would not appear to bear direct responsibility for the results of such violations. In this regard, mention may be made of the judgement of the International Court of Justice on 'Military and Paramilitary Activities in and against Nicaragua', in which the Court expressed the view that a state would incur legal responsibility for the results of violations only if it "... *had effective control of the military or paramilitary operations in the course of which the alleged violations were committed.*"[37]

On the other hand, if the acts in question amount to war crimes in particular, the state should ensure that the culprits are found and punished by compelling the company's management to take the appropriate action. This stems from the international obligation to punish war criminals or to make sure they are punished[38] and, more generally, from the duty to ensure respect for international law under all circumstances.[39]

National legislation

A number of people have been convicted under the rules relating to mercenaries, the best-known instance being the trial of thirteen mercenaries in Angola in 1976.[40] Elsewhere in Africa, the issue of mercenaries had already attracted attention, notably during the civil war in Nigeria. The code of conduct drawn up at the time stated that, *"[f]oreign nationals on legitimate business will not be molested, but mercenaries will not be spared: they are the worst of enemies."*[41]

In principle, countries should have adopted internal legislation to punish mercenaries, in order to meet the obligations set out in international humanitarian law and in the specific conventions on mercenarism. Although no exhaustive study has been carried out on the subject, this is obviously not the case.

However, several countries of the former Soviet Union have recently examined the matter and have incorporated the relevant provisions in their penal codes. The new <u>Penal Code</u> of the Russian Federation, adopted on 17 June 1996, includes punishment for a number of violations of international humanitarian law, and makes no distinction between offences committed in international conflicts and those committed in internal conflicts. The Code punishes, on the same basis, not only the use of mercenaries (four to eight years' imprisonment), but also recruitment, funding and training. The use of minors is an aggravating circumstance (seven to fifteen years' imprisonment). Taking part in a conflict as a mercenary is punishable by three to seven years' imprisonment. The <u>Kyrgyz Penal Code</u> contains similar provisions, but defines the use of an official position for the commission of such acts as an additional aggravating circumstance. It seems that such rules are also included in the codes of Georgia and the Ukraine.

Although there are other countries whose penal codes contain comparable provisions, there does not appear to be a very strong commitment to an absolute ban on mercenarism. In fact, such rules intend primarily to protect national sovereignty. As has been pointed out, "... *there are powerful proscriptions against mercenary activity which could jeopardise the neutrality or interests of home states, and less concentration on the absolute abolition of mercenary activity*."[42]

The inclusion of specific provisions relating to mercenaries in penal codes, however necessary, does not therefore answer all the questions raised by the growing phenomenon of private companies selling security services.

The new South African <u>Regulation of Foreign Military Assistance Act</u>, in particular, is interesting because it goes further than most other examples in this regard. Indeed, companies offering security services were only partially covered by the law in force before the adoption of this legislation in 1998. Section 121A of the <u>Defence Act</u> prohibits members of the South African armed forces from serving as mercenaries, but this law does not apply to all South African nationals. The 1980 <u>Keypoints Act</u>, the 1987 <u>Security Officers Act</u> and the second amendment of the <u>Penal Code</u> of 1992 contain provisions applicable to security companies operating on South African soil. In particular, such companies may not use firearms or explosives, and may not train their personnel in certain types of military or paramilitary operations.

The <u>Regulation of Foreign Military Assistance Act</u> expands on these limitations, especially with concern to controls, through the strengthening of the powers of the National Conventional Arms Control Committee (NCACC) set up in 1995. Under the terms of the Act, foreign military assistance would be subject to an approval procedure before such services could be offered. Moreover, prior authorisation is required before contact can be made with a third party in order to offer such services, similar to the South African arms export control regime.

The South African legislation has adopted a broad definition of foreign military assistance. Indeed, foreign military assistance includes not only direct combative participation in armed conflict, but also military assistance to a party to an armed conflict in the form of advice or training; personnel, financial, logistic, intelligence or operational support; recruitment; procurement of equipment; and even, surprisingly, medical or paramedical services. This list is supplemented by a general clause referring to "... *any other action that has the result of furthering the military interests of a party to the armed conflict.*" Finally, the definition of foreign military assistance encompasses not only the rendering of the services mentioned above, but also "... *any attempt, encouragement, incitement or solicitation to render such services.*"

The provision concerning those receiving such assistance is also broad in scope. It covers all parties to a conflict – the armed forces of foreign states involved in an international or non-international armed conflict, dissident forces opposing government forces in an internal conflict, and non-governmental armed groups fighting among themselves in an internal conflict – and also applies to security services for the protection of individuals involved in armed conflict or their property.

On the other hand, the definition of foreign military assistance seems to be strictly limited to armed conflicts, which raises certain questions. Indeed, services of the type listed above could be offered for preventive purposes, notably in situations where internal strife, that has not yet reached the intensity of an armed conflict, prompts a government to seek such services in order to restore public order. Should these services be subject to no rules at all? What happens when internal strife escalates into armed conflict and services covered by the <u>Regulation of Foreign Military Assistance Act</u> are already being rendered?

It is also interesting to examine United States legislation as several companies offering security services are based in that country. The principal rules relating to the matter are to be found in the amendments to the <u>International Traffic in Arms Regulations</u>.[43] Without going into the minutiae of these very detailed regulations "... *any person in the United States or otherwise subject to US jurisdiction who is in the business of brokering transfers of defence articles or services is required to register and pay a fee.*"[44] 'Defence services' are defined as follows:

"*(1) The furnishing of assistance (including training) to foreign persons, whether in the United States or abroad, in the design, development, engineering, manufacture, production, assembly, testing, repair, maintenance, modification, operation, demilitarisation, destruction, processing or use of defence articles;*

(2) The furnishing to foreign persons of any technical data controlled under this subchapter, whether in the United States or abroad; or

(3) Military training of foreign units and forces, regular or irregular, including formal or informal instruction of foreign persons from the United States or abroad or by correspondence courses, technical, educational, or information publications and media of all kinds, training aid, orientation, training exercises and military advice."

Defence services in excess of $50 million may furthermore not be concluded until the Office of Defence Trade Controls notifies the service provider through the issue of a licence or other approval that Congress has not enacted a joint resolution prohibiting the rendering of the service. Any person who engages in brokering activities in this sphere is required to register with the Office of Defence Trade Controls, with certain specified exemptions. Activities conducted for close allies of the US – members of NATO and a few other countries – are not subject to this constraint, except in the case of some specifically sensitive activities such as the provision of fully automatic firearms or nuclear weapons strategic delivery systems. Brokering activities are prohibited in respect of certain countries, in particular those under US embargo and those subject to special regulations for reasons of national security.

Thus, the system does not rule out the activities of organisations providing security services, but subjects them to restrictions which have more to do with US foreign policy than with the provisions of international law. This is clearly illustrated, especially in the diverse treatment meted out to different countries and the fact that no distinction is drawn *a priori* between services rendered to a government and those rendered to irregular forces.

The United Kingdom is also home to a number of companies offering security services. The Foreign Enlistment Act of 1870 prohibits British subjects from recruiting for or enlisting in the armed forces of a foreign state. The Diplock Report[45] – on the issue of mercenaries, requested after the trial of British mercenaries in Angola – concluded that preventing British citizens from working abroad as mercenaries was an unjustified infringement of individuals' personal freedom. It recommended that a legal system should be established whereby the government could draw up a list of countries in which British nationals were not permitted to enlist by reason of the country's international relations. To date, there has been no change in the law, with the result that security companies can operate out of the UK with very little restriction.[46]

Private violence and humanitarian organisations

The problem of armed escorts

Humanitarian action is particularly difficult in situations of armed conflict in which state structures are weak or have disintegrated. In these circumstances, humanitarian organisations face a major security problem. They no longer have recourse to anyone who is in a position to make and enforce commitments regarding the delivery of humanitarian aid and, in particular, the movement of numerous food aid convoys.

Of course, the basic condition is still that humanitarian assistance should be publicised and accepted by all the combatants. Every means of communicating information about such assistance to the various combatants have to be used. In Somalia, for instance, extensive use was made of radio broadcasts. In circumstances where there is no assurance that all the combatants have agreed to the provision of humanitarian assistance, practical working methods have to be identified which would reduce the exposure of humanitarian personnel to danger. One possibility that may be considered, and that has been utilised in the past, is the use of armed escorts.

For the ICRC, the concept of a humanitarian organisation using armed escorts to impose humanitarian action on parties against their will is untenable. Should a party to the conflict oppose humanitarian action – thereby withholding aid from people who urgently need it – humanitarian organisations have no choice but to report the situation to the international community, in particular the Security Council. It is then up to the Security Council to take the appropriate corrective steps. In these circumstances, the challenge clearly exceeds the responsibility and authority of the humanitarian organisations. The role they may subsequently play in the event of action by the Security Council or regional organisations is another matter, which falls outside the scope of this chapter.

The issue at stake is the question of limited armed protection – not for the purpose of imposing anything on a party to the conflict – but in order to protect humanitarian action, particularly convoys, against banditry attacks in circumstances in which the weakness of the public authorities has led to a very sharp increase in criminal activity. It should be borne in mind that international humanitarian law itself does not preclude medical personnel from bearing light weapons, precisely for the purpose of protecting hospitals or convoys of casualties from looting and attacks.[47]

After investigating this challenge, the International Red Cross and Red Crescent Movement did not entirely rule out the use of armed protection of humanitarian conveys in exceptional circumstances,[48] but viewed it with great misgivings and extreme caution. The ICRC justifies this approach on a number of counts. The most serious is the risk of tarnishing the image and hence the general acceptability of Red Cross or Red Crescent organisations in the event of untoward incidents, should an individual member of an armed escort use his weapon without proper justification. The following also have to be considered:

- the questions of insurance and responsibility, which are extremely complex in such circumstances;

- the continuing security risks involved – if the escort is inadequate, the convoy may come under attack anyway, with the use of greater firepower and the attendant danger of escalation; and

- the ambivalent link that may be forged with those supplying the escorts – for example, they may exert pressure or even threaten reprisals, possibly to demand more money, especially if the humanitarian organisation concerned wishes to terminate the contract.

The use of escorts from outside the country is also a matter requiring careful consideration. In some cases, troops involved in peacekeeping operations have played this role. It is a relatively understandable option in the case of genuine peacekeeping operations that were launched with the consent of the protagonists in terms of Chapter VI of the UN Charter. But experience has shown that these operations are very frequently of a mixed nature, i.e. including limited Chapter VII powers. By virtue of its responsibility for the maintenance of international peace and security, the Security Council can impose appropriate measures or even take coercive action in terms of Chapter VII of the UN Charter. That being so, an armed escort consisting of UN forces projects a composite image of political measures and humanitarian action which the ICRC views as undesirable. Depending on the particular situation, and the mandate and actions of the UN forces, the humanitarian organisation under escort will be closely associated with the actions of the world body. In the case of enforcement actions, this carries the risk of being unacceptable to one or more of the parties to the conflict or peace agreement. Where a major UN agency is involved, this option has been used in the past and cannot be ruled out in extreme circumstances. But there is still a need for a detailed assessment of the advantages and disadvantages that such measures entail.

The situation is entirely different when no UN soldiers are involved. Should humanitarian organisations contemplate training permanent armed guards? It is extremely difficult to envisage this course of action, as it would lay humanitarian workers open to suspicion of a lack of impartiality and make their presence less acceptable. One wonders, therefore, whether humanitarian staff should or could enlist the services of security forces hired out by private companies in certain circumstances. In this regard, the Special Rapporteur referred to statements made by the managing director of Executive Outcomes, who admitted that men attached to his company "... *had taken part in some military action in Sierra Leone, but had done so at the request of humanitarian agencies which wanted food aid to reach the interior of the country.*"[49] This approach is problematic, since humanitarian organisations that use such services would incur responsibilities and risks extending far beyond their terms of reference and would be likely, in the long run, to taint all humanitarian organisations.

To sum up, there are no simple answers to this problem. Every effort must be made to ensure that the work of humanitarian organisations is universally respected. A far better way of going beyond the limits of what is possible in difficult circumstances, is to improve the working methods and the quality of the services provided by the humanitarian organisations through careful staff selection and appropriate training, and to ensure a strictly ethical approach in their activities.[50] The ambition to 'do more' by relying on locally available armed forces is liable to divest the organisations of their credibility and to offer cogent arguments to those who distrust all international humanitarian aid agencies and organisations. The use of private security companies by humanitarian organisations is therefore likely to prove a 'step too far' and should be discouraged.

It is clear, moreover, that a private organisation that accepts 'security' or even military assignments in a particular country cannot hide behind a contract with a humanitarian organisation. Such a company must assume direct responsibility *vis-à-vis* the country concerned, whose government would be quite justified, if necessary, in accusing it of a breach of sovereignty.

The responsibility of the International Committee of the Red Cross to ensure compliance with international humanitarian law

The Geneva Conventions of 12 August 1949 and their Additional Protocols of 1977 entrust the ICRC not only with a broad right of initiative, but also with the authority to offer its services as a substitute for Protecting Powers in armed conflicts in which such Powers have not been designated.[51] This role involves ensuring that the parties to armed conflicts fulfil their obligations under international humanitarian law, specifically the humane treatment of all persons under their control, observance of the rules pertaining to occupied territories, and compliance by their armed forces with the restrictions relating to the conduct of hostilities.

The Protecting Powers system does not really function in practice[52] and does not apply formally in non-international conflicts, which account for the vast majority of conflicts today. On a pragmatic basis, however, the ICRC plays its role as "... *guardian of international humanitarian law*"[53] in a large proportion of ongoing conflicts. Moreover, this general role has been confirmed in the <u>Statutes of the International Red Cross and Red Crescent Movement</u>, of which the most recent version was adopted in 1986.[54]

The first and most important aspect of the ICRC's role in this regard, is the establishment of a dialogue with the conflicting parties to jointly examine the situation and to inform them of the ICRC's findings, with a view to encouraging compliance in the areas outlined above. The involvement of large numbers of delegates in humanitarian work and the ICRC's presence in the field, in prisons, occupied territories and hospitals, generally gives the organisation a clear picture of the problems in humanitarian terms, and this carries significant weight in the dialogue.

It may also happen, where the parties to a conflict display negative attitudes or are incapable of taking the necessary steps, that the ICRC appeals to the international community. Both the <u>Geneva Conventions</u> and their <u>Additional Protocols</u> place all states party to them under an obligation not only to respect, but also "... *to ensure respect for*" the <u>Conventions</u>.[55]

The presence and use of private security companies in armed conflicts and potentially volatile situations, and the potential impact of such involvement, call for the ICRC's very careful scrutiny, in a given context, of the short term practical and humanitarian implications. In light of the ICRC's own mandate, it also calls for close consideration of the long term implications for international humanitarian law as its mandate includes the task to "... *prepare any development thereof.*"[56]

Since the ICRC "... *work[s] for the faithful application of international humanitarian law,*"[57] it endeavours to contribute to the training of all those involved in armed conflict to ensure full respect of humanitarian rules pertaining to engagement. In peacetime, it contacts the armed forces in different countries, urging them to incorporate humanitarian law in their programmes of instruction and, if necessary, helping to plan the content of the courses themselves.

Should private security companies come to play a greater role in armed conflict, the question arises whether an ICRC-led dialogue with such companies should be instituted in order to ensure that their staff are familiar with and abide by international humanitarian law. The answer is clear that in a conflict situation, where all combatants have to be taken into account, such a dialogue is indispensable. The ICRC has always sought to secure compliance with humanitarian rules by all those involved in armed hostilities. Such contact has never implied the endorsement or approval of any issue related to the conflict in question. This would also appear to tip the scales in favour of such an ICRC-led dialogue with private security companies in times of peace.[58]

Conclusion

The expansion of private security services is a matter of direct concern to the international community. By agreeing to 'delegate' the maintenance of order, a government endangers the very essence of public authority. Such a danger also exists when various non-state armed factions are formed, criminal activity of all sorts flourishes, not to mention situations in which the military seizes power. Is the international community justified in applying stricter standards to private security services than to the armed forces of governments of doubtful legitimacy? A security company can hardly be blamed for helping a government in office, however doubtful its democratic legitimacy, if that government is accepted by the UN. It would be more logical for the UN to apply stricter standards to its own members than to hold private security companies hostage to the lack of discretion by the international community. This is unlikely however, although the establishment of an International Criminal Court may have a salutary effect in this regard.

Most private security companies have understood the situation and restrict themselves to assisting governments in office. But in doing so, they endorse the preference of the community of states for order rather than justice. There are just struggles against governments, but who is to decide what is just? A trend is emerging whereby the states in which security companies are based, decide where those companies may operate. Such decisions are based on the judgement – or interest – of the state concerned and do not necessarily restrict the companies' activities. In so doing, these states *de facto* take over the role that should be entrusted to the UN. By agreeing to – or even encouraging – the activities of security companies, one could argue that such states assume the power to decide what is just and what is not, or what deserves to be defended and what does not.

It is therefore important for the UN to strengthen its role, as entrusted to it by Article 1 of the Charter, namely, "*... to bring about by peaceful means, and in conformity with the principles of justice and international law, adjustment or settlement of international disputes or situations which might lead to a breach of the peace.*" The UN has a duty to preserve international peace founded on the respect for international law, and hence to clarify the meaning of this law, if necessary, by having recourse to the International Court of Justice. Without such clarification, the risk exists that people can and will do as they see fit. In such cases, the strongest are likely to prevail and, by so doing, confuse selfish interests and justice.

The need for clarity is even more important today, as the end of the Cold War has given new hope to entities which, rightly or wrongly, feel entitled to exercise peoples' right to self-determination. It can be argued that clarification of such entities' range of action and aspirations – whether it is the creation of a new state, conferring a status that preserves a degree of autonomy, or enhanced protection of the rights of minorities – could prevent a great deal of bitterness and suffering, and perhaps conflict. In any event, private security companies cannot be asked to perform the task of deciding for themselves which causes are just or not. It is also dangerous to leave such decisions to individual states who may not always respect democratic principles and the rule of law.

Furthermore, it would seem that the international community should conduct a more thorough examination of the problem of private security companies taking measures on behalf of public authorities to undertake, pursue or develop security activities in their respective countries. In weak states, such situations may undermine international peace and stability. It may therefore be concluded that the topical issue of 'new mercenaries' must be approached from a different angle than in the past. Indeed, how can the international community react without calling the principle of state sovereignty into question?

The issue of the 'new mercenaries' should be addressed by placing it in the flawed context of international relations as they stand today. There can be no hesitation in affirming that, in the spirit of international humanitarian law, any action of a military nature has to comply with the principles of that body of law. This obligation is further binding on anyone directly or indirectly involved in armed hostilities. The key question is deceptively simple: should we tolerate the provision of private security services to governments or industry in situations threatening anarchy in an attempt to save what can be saved, or rather, do we severely regulate a phenomenon which, in the long term, could erode the very foundations of an international system based on national sovereignty? This should be the crux of the debate, particularly within the UN, as it reflects on its own weaknesses.

Endnotes

1   Reflection on this topic only began recently. See, in particular, J C Zarate, *The Emergence of a New Dog of War: Private International Security Companies, International Law, and the New World Disorder*, Stanford Journal of International Law, 34(1), Winter 1998.

2   On the history and development of international humanitarian law, see, in particular, F Bugnion, Le Comité international de la Croix-Rouge et la protection des victimes de la guerre, ICRC, Geneva, 1994, pp. 345-457; K J Partsch, *Humanitarian Law and Armed Conflicts*, Encyclopedia of Public International Law, 2, Elsevier, New York, 1995, pp. 933-936.

3   See article 3 common to the four 1949 Geneva Conventions. This provision was the first to lay down rules applicable during non-international armed conflicts.

4   J Pictet (ed.), Commentary on the Geneva Convention relative to the Protection of Civilian Persons in Time of War, ICRC, Geneva, 1958, pp. 37-38.

5   The ICRC is currently conducting a study of customary law for the 27th International Conference of the Red Cross and Red Crescent, due to take place in 1999.

6   This was an important element of the debate on the use of anti-personnel mines: see ICRC, Anti-personnel Landmines: Friend or Foe? A Study of the Military Use and Effectiveness of Anti-personnel Mines, ICRC, Geneva, March 1996.

7   On this notion, see, in particular, H Strebel, *Marten's Clause*, Encyclopedia of Public International Law, 3, Elsevier, New York, 1997, pp. 326-327.

8   See, in particular, J Crawford, The Creation of States in International Law, Clarendon Press, Oxford, 1979, p. 255; C Zorgbibe, *Sources of the Recognition of Belligerent Status*, International Review of the Red Cross, 192, March 1977, pp. 111-127.

9   Protocol I of 8 June 1977 additional to the Geneva Conventions of 12 August 1949 (hereinafter Protocol I), article 1, para. 4: "*The situations referred to in the preceding paragraph include armed conflicts in which peoples are fighting against colonial domination and alien occupation and against racist régimes in the exercise of their right of self-determination, as enshrined in the Charter of the United Nations and the Declaration on Principles of International Law concerning Friendly Relations and Co-operation among States in accordance with the Charter of the United Nations*". See also D Schindler & J Toman, The Laws of Armed Conflicts, Martinus Nijhoff/Henry Dunant Institute, Dordrecht/Geneva, 1988, pp. 621-68; Y Sandoz et al. (eds.), Commentary on the Additional Protocols of 8 June 1977 to the Geneva Conventions of 12 August 1977, ICRC/Martinus Nijhoff, Geneva, 1987, pp. 41-56.

10 International Covenant on Economic, Social and Cultural Rights, article 1, and International Covenant on Civil and Political Rights, article 1.

11 'Security service' means any service associated with state security, whether it amounts to direct military involvement, protection, intelligence, or law and order functions, or not.

12 N Q Dinh, P Dailler & A Pellet, *Droit international public*, Librairie de droit et de jurisprudence, Paris, 1992, No. 375, p. 540 (ICRC translation).

13 Ibid., No. 272, p. 398 (ICRC translation).

14 This is reflected in the definition of 'aggression' annexed to Resolution 3314 (XXIX) of the United Nations General Assembly and in the Declaration on Friendly Relations and Co-operation among States in accordance with the UN Charter (hereinafter Declaration on Friendly Relations) annexed to Resolution 2625 (XXV) of the same body.

Article 1 defines aggression as "… *the use of armed force by a State against the sovereignty, territorial integrity or political independence of another State,*" and acts of aggression are enumerated in Article 3. Article 7, however, specifies: "*Nothing in this Definition, and in particular article 3, could in any way prejudice the right to self-determination, freedom and independence, as derived from the Charter, of peoples forcibly deprived of that right … particularly peoples under colonial and racist regimes or other forms of alien domination; nor the right of those peoples to struggle to that end and to seek and receive support, in accordance with the principles of the Charter …*"

In the Declaration on Friendly Relations, the same contradiction is particularly evident when one considers two of its provisions. On the one hand, the duty to provide support for peoples seeking, in the framework of their right to self-determination, "… *the establishment of a sovereign and independent State, the free association or integration with an independent State or the emergence into any other political status freely determined …*" is stipulated under the heading *The principle of equal rights and self-determination of peoples*; but, on the other hand, the section entitled *The principle of sovereign equality of States* contains the reminder that "… *the territorial integrity and political independence of the State are inviolable.*"

However, some attempt to resolve the tension between the two requirements is made in another passage of the section entitled *The principle of equal rights and self-determination of peoples*. Although it is specified that the duty to provide support to a people, if necessary even to enable it to establish an independent and sovereign state, must not be "… *construed as authorising or encouraging any action which would dismember or impair, totally or in part, the territorial integrity or political unity of sovereign and independent States,*" this restriction is tempered by the enumeration of certain requirements that the state and government to be preserved, must meet. The state concerned must conduct itself "… *in compliance with the principle of equal rights and self-determination of peoples as described above and thus [be] possessed of a government representing the whole people belonging to the territory without distinction as to race, creed or colour.*"

These requirements relating to states and governments are interesting in that they set timid limits within which a state must remain if it is to preserve its legitimacy, and hence a limit to the right of every state "… *freely to choose and develop its political, social, economic and cultural systems*" laid down under the heading *The principle of sovereign equality of States.*

15 See, among others, Y Sandoz, *'Droit' or 'devoir d'ingérence' and the Right to Assistance: The Issues Involved,* International Review of the Red Cross, 288, May-June 1992, pp. 215-227.

16 *Military and Paramilitary Activities in and against Nicaragua,* (Nicaragua v. United States of America), Merits, Judgement of 27 June 1986, ICJ Reports, 1986, para. 205.

17 *Corfu Channel Case,* Merits, Judgement of 9 April 1949, ICJ Reports, 1949, p. 35.

18 See Dinh et al., op. cit., p. 734 (ICRC translation).

19 Ibid., p. 870 (ICRC translation).

20 As set out in the Declaration on Friendly Relations, op. cit.

21 Article 147 of the Fourth Geneva Convention.

22 See Protocol I, op. cit., article 47, para. 2(d).

23 The relevant article in Protocol I that deals with such conflicts, does not appear in Additional Protocol II. The latter deals only with non-international conflicts.

24 International Convention against the Recruitment, Use, Financing and Training of Mercenaries, 4 December 1989, United Nations General Assembly Resolution A/RES/44/34.

25 Convention for the Elimination of Mercenarism in Africa, Organisation of African Unity, Libreville, 3 July 1977, CM/817 (XXXIX), Annex II, Rev. 3.

26 Protocol I, op. cit., para. 2 (b).

27 Sandoz et al., op. cit., para. 1806, p. 579.

28 Ibid., para. 1679, p. 516. The terms used in the 1989 International Convention against the Recruitment, Use, Financing and Training of Mercenaries are slightly different. According to this Convention the mercenary must be recruited "... *to fight in an armed conflict*" and, further on, must "... *take part in the hostilities.*" Taking the two expressions together leads one to conclude, however, that there is no divergence regarding this particular condition. The 1977 OAU Convention for the Elimination of Mercenarism in Africa combines the two notions, explicitly taking up the requirement of 'direct' participation: the mercenary is an individual "... *who is specially recruited locally or abroad in order to fight in an armed conflict*" and "... *who does in fact take a direct part in the hostilities.*"

29 E B Ballesteros, Report on the Question of the Use of Mercenaries as a Means of Violating Human Rights and Impeding the Exercise of the Right of Peoples to Self-determination, United Nations Commission on Human Rights E/CN.4/1997/24. Author's emphasis.

30 See in particular *Armed Conflicts Linked to the Disintegration of State Structures,* preparatory draft document, First Periodical Meeting on International Humanitarian Law, ICRC, Geneva, 19-23 January 1998.

31 See, in particular, Protocol I, op. cit., article 85 ff.

32 Article 1 common to the 1949 Geneva Conventions and article 1 of Protocol I. See also, in particular, Pictet, 1958, op. cit., pp. 15-16; Sandoz et al., op. cit., paras. 35-51, pp. 34-38; L Condorelli & L B de Chazournes, *Quelques remarques à propos de l'obligation des Etats de 'respecter et faire respecter' le droit international humanitaire 'en toutes circonstances',* Studies and Essays on International Humanitarian Law and Red Cross Principles in Honour of Jean Pictet, ICRC/Martinus Nijhoff, Geneva/The Hague, 1984, pp. 17-35.

33 The role which the International Criminal Court could play in repressing war crimes was raised at the <u>First Periodical Meeting on International Humanitarian Law</u>, ICRC, Geneva, 19-23 January 1998.

34 *Report of the International Law Commission on the Work of its 48th Session*, General Assembly, Official Records, 51st Session, Supplement No. 10 (A/51/10), 6 May-26 July 1996, pp. 121-132.

35 Island of Palmas (Netherlands *v.* United States of America), 4.IV.1928, *Recueil des sentences arbitrales.* ICRC translation.

36 <u>Convention (V) respecting the Rights and Duties of Neutral Powers and Persons in Case of War on Land</u>, The Hague, 18 October 1907, Art 4.

37 <u>ICJ Reports</u>, 1986, op. cit., para. 115.

38 Articles 49/50/129/146 of the four <u>Geneva Conventions</u>, respectively.

39 See note 28.

40 See M S Hoover, *The Laws of War and the Angolan Trial of Mercenaries: Death to the Dogs of War*, <u>Case Western Reserve Journal of International Law</u>, 9(2), 1997.

41 <u>Operational Code of Conduct for Nigerian Armed Forces</u>, article 4(m). (ICRC Archives and Advisory Service on International Humanitarian Law).

42 Zarate, op. cit.

43 See *Rules and Regulations*, <u>Federal Register</u>, 62(247), 24 December 1997, pp. 67274 – 67278.

44 Ibid., p. 67275.

45 <u>Diplock Report of the Committee of Privy Counsellors Appointed to Inquire into the Recruitment of Mercenaries</u>, London, Cmnd. 6569, 1976.

46 On this subject, see Zarate, op. cit., pp. 137-138.

47 See, in particular, article 22 of the <u>First Geneva Convention</u> of 1949 and J Pictet (ed.), <u>Commentary on the Geneva Convention for the Amelioration of the Condition of the Wounded and Sick in Armed Forces in the Field</u>, ICRC, Geneva, 1952, pp. 202-205; <u>Protocol I</u>, article 13, para. 2; and Sandoz et al., op. cit., paras. 557-574, pp. 176-180.

48 Resolution 9 adopted by the Council of Delegates at its session of 1-2 December 1995, Geneva, Switzerland: *Armed Protection of Humanitarian Assistance*, <u>International Review of the Red Cross</u>, 310, January-February 1996, pp. 150-151.

49 Ballesteros, op. cit., para. 52.

50 On the question of security for humanitarian organisations, see, in particular, *Respect for and Protection of the Personnel of Humanitarian Organisations,* preparatory draft document, <u>First Periodical Meeting on International Humanitarian Law</u>, ICRC, Geneva, 19-23 January 1998.

51 Articles 10/10/10/11 of the four <u>Geneva Conventions</u>, respectively; Pictet, 1952, op. cit., pp. 112-125; <u>Protocol I</u>, op. cit., article 5, para. 4; Sandoz et al., op. cit., paras. 205-224, pp. 83-87.

52 G Raub, *Protecting Power*, <u>Encyclopedia of Public International Law</u>, 3, Elsevier, New York, 1997, pp. 1147-1153.

53   Y Sandoz, *Le Comité international de la Croix-Rouge gardien du droit international humanitaire*, <u>Jugoslovenska Revija za Medunarodno Pravo</u>, 43, 1996, pp. 357-389.

54   <u>Statutes of the International Red Cross and Red Crescent Movement</u>, adopted by the 25th International Conference of the Red Cross in Geneva in October 1986, article 5, in: <u>Handbook of the International Red Cross and Red Crescent Movement</u>, ICRC/International Federation of Red Cross and Red Crescent Societies, Geneva, 1994, p. 422.

55   See note 32.

56   <u>Statutes</u>, op. cit., article 5(g).

57   Ibid., article 5(c).

58   See article 3 common to the 1949 <u>Geneva Conventions</u>, which relates to non-international armed conflict: *The Application of the Preceding Provisions Shall not Affect the Legal Status of the Parties to the Conflict.*

Chapter 11: Africa – From the privatisation of security to the privatisation of war?

Jakkie Cilliers and Richard Cornwell

Introduction

*I*n 1986, the noted Kenyan scholar, Ali Mazrui wrote that the African state, since independence, has been subject to two competing pressures: the push towards the militarisation of politics and the pull towards the privatisation of the state; and the competition between capitalist greed and the quest for naked political power.[1] Mazrui argued that Western-style imported political institutions in Africa had established shallow roots. Africans internalised capitalist greed through colonialism, but failed to internalise free market discipline. In the process, Western consumption patterns were much more effectively transferred than Western production techniques. Western tastes were acquired more quickly than concomitant skills. The profit motive was adopted without the efficient calculus of entrepreneurship. As a result, *"... in a technologically underdeveloped society in the twentieth century, ultimate power resides not in those who controlled the means of production [as postulated by Marx], but in those who controlled the means of destruction [captured by the soldier/bandit with an AK-47]."*[2] Africa has therefore been *"... torn between the forces of anarchy on the one side, in the sense of decentralised violence, and the forces of tyranny, on the other side, in the sense of orchestrated centralised repression."*[3]

While there is much to gain from Mazrui, he is wrong in one crucial respect. The analysis reflected in this book would indicate that the trend towards the militarisation of politics and the privatisation of the state, in fact, have become mutually reinforcing in Africa. The expansion of the private security industry, including the role of mercenaries, has exemplified this trend. As African state collapse has continued through the 1980s and 1990s, access to political power has increasingly constituted a way to monetary reward. Hence the phrase 'the privatisation of the African state' – the political and commercial subjugation and exploitation of the state and the general populace in the interests of élite commercial, often criminal, gain.

The years since Africa attained general independence have seen the modern legitimisation of African military involvement in the affairs of neighbouring states, either through the transfer of arms, support or acquiescence to neighbouring dissidents, direct invasion or raids. While the academic discourse is dominated by the repetition of the fallacy that conflict in Africa has become more intrastate than interstate in character, the reverse is true. In a continent characterised by soft and unclear borders within which state control often does not extend beyond the end of the urban sprawl, military and political interference in the affairs of neighbouring countries is the norm. At the last count, nearly a third of sub-Saharan Africa's 42 countries were embroiled in armed conflict, and more and more African rulers are seeking military solutions to political problems. At least thirteen have sent troops to neighbours' wars. Tensions have erupted in war between Ethiopia and Eritrea. Elsewhere, Senegal is helping to squash a rebellion in Guinea-Bissau, as did South Africa in Lesotho, while Namibia,

Zimbabwe, Rwanda, Uganda, Chad and others are all embroiled in the conflict in the Democratic Republic of Congo.

By the late 1990s, non-indigenous hired military assistance had become endemic to a country such as Sierra Leone without having brought any greater degree of stability. In fact, instability was a function of their continued employment. Following the termination of an earlier contract with the Gurkha Security Guards (GSG), the South African company, Executive Outcomes (EO) had initially brought a sense of security to the conflict-torn, diamond-rich country. During May 1997, at a time when President Kabbah was deciding between a new contract with EO[4] or placing his trust in the Nigerian-led peacekeeping forces in Freetown, he was ousted in a bloody *coup d'état* by a group of young, middle-ranking officers of the Sierra Leone Military Forces.[5] Some months later, EO's sister mercenary company, Sandline International[6] played a central role in the reinstatement of Kabbah as president. Sandline provided intelligence, logistical and air support during the Kabbah operation, as well as 35 tons of military equipment from Bulgaria to the Nigerian-led forces of the Economic Community of West African Monitoring Group (ECOMOG), which did most of the fighting. None of these efforts appeared to have brought long term stability to Sierra Leone, as the Revolutionary United Front rebels were battling ECOMOG for control of Freetown itself by January 1999.[7]

While the apparent collaboration between the British government and Sandline International has seen the issue investigated and debated vigorously in Britain, the co-operation between private military companies and a regional grouping such as ECOMOG is a development that has attracted almost no comment or interest from the academic community. At the level of the United Nations, the debate about outsourcing military-type services is pursued vigorously, yet subregional enforcement structures such as ECOMOG have much less compunction about such alliances. Sandline assisted ECOMOG in 1998 in a direct supportive role. Its helicopters ferried ECOMOG commanders across the country, at one point rescuing ECOMOG commander, Brigadier Maxwell Khobe and UN officials from an RUF fire-fight. In the same year, 1998, Sandline was engaged in a disastrous operation in Papua New Guinea, largely on behalf of Branch Energy and Heritage Oil and Gas. The company had subcontracted EO for the provision of military instructors, but the operation failed when the Army commander publicly objected, having been paid off by a competitor.[8]

In a similar vein to the co-operation between ECOMOG and Sandline, the security services that LifeGuard Security provided to UN relief operations in and around Freetown have not raised much controversy – despite the fact that both LifeGuard, Sandline and EO personnel are drawn from the same recruitment pool.[9] Although not discussed at any great length here, this trend is certain to expand and grow in the years that lie ahead. Some may also question the real difference between Sandline's support to ECOMOG and the alleged use of French or South African helicopter pilots under contract by ECOMOG.[10]

But one must balance this version of events with a healthy dose of pragmatism. Western governments and large multinational corporations do not want to be associated with political conflict in their operating environments and have every reason to end such conflicts – preferably on terms which are to their own advantage. Many of the countries in Africa where large multinational companies operate, are politically unstable – civil war, political turmoil and corruption rage unabated. Democratic governments may expect serious political problems at home should evidence of too direct a role emerge. Shareholders may feel equally uncomfortable about the means used to ensure the continued extraction of minerals in far-flung and hostile countries such as Angola, the Democratic Republic of Congo, Sierra Leone and Liberia. Yet, if conflict cannot be ended and appears to be endemic, the opportunity to exploit the situation for commercial gain, if the pickings are rich enough, is difficult to resist.

At the conclusion of this study, three areas require comment. The first, and most crucial evidence that has been led in this study relates to the nexus between the twin processes of the privatisation of the state in Africa, central to the structural adjustment agenda, and the response to privatisation by many of the post-colonial African élite. It will be argued that it is this nexus between these trends that currently provides space for the expansion of private military activity in Africa. The second area deserving comment relates to the debate around the legitimacy and efficacy of such involvement. It is essential that these issues are satisfactorily resolved if national governments and the international community are to find appropriate mechanisms of oversight and transparency to deal with this rising phenomenon. The final section contains a number of tentative policy proposals.

The African state and the privatisation of security

From an African perspective, it has to be questioned whether peace is to be kept only at the cost of African states placing their natural resources in pawn. By extension, one might ask whether those countries lacking the necessary and conveniently exploitable unassigned assets are by implication excluded from such assistance by the private sector. Of course, it may also be argued that these resources can only be exploited and the proceeds taxed to benefit the general good, if relative security is established.

It does seem evident, however, that companies and entrepreneurs – if they can command reliable private military assistance – will be in a better position to negotiate concessions than other businesses without such connections. Is the time that far off when private companies will do battle, literally, for access to the natural wealth of Africa, as did the chartered companies of yesteryear? Should this happen, it will be because the international community have ceased to regard Africa as a continent entitled to the consideration of the community of nations and African problems as a vital threat to their own growth and tranquillity.

Another, potentially more worrying question must also be raised, however. It is one that may not have occurred either to those who deplore the use of private military companies and mercenaries or those who see this as an inescapable necessity given the reluctance of the major players in the international community to assist in the risky business of peace enforcement in remote and relatively unimportant areas. It has to do with the nature of the African state: in part, its weakness, but also the matter of its essence and *raison d'être*. It also raises the tricky question of the difference between a recognised state and a legitimate state.

What distinction are we to draw between the security and survival of the state and the security and survival of its present ruling élite? In so many cases, it appears that the latter, rather than the former consideration, actually dictates policy. In this respect, the 'privatisation of war' takes on another, rather more sinister meaning, as heads of state deploy the instruments of sovereignty for personal and private ends. More worrying is the tendency of the diplomatic community – which has its own interest in preserving the myth of abstract and disinterested sovereignty – to ignore this reality, at least in public. Under such conditions, it is hardly likely that the mainspring of African, and other foreign and domestic politics will be correctly identified, surely a prerequisite for considered international intervention.

In a recent draft paper on the criminalisation of the African state,[11] the Gorée Institute argues that, while donor governments and organisations have extolled the virtues of structural adjustment programmes for some years and have introduced the concept of 'good governance' which, in their view, should enhance the process of the democratisation of African political systems and the strengthening of civil society, other processes were rather more in evidence. The widespread demand for democracy, which had weakened the grip of dictatorships and single-party states, had been largely contained by countermeasures implemented by the holders of power themselves. The process of democratisation has been co-opted and used to legitimise and disguise the continuation of the same political and economic order. Even in cases where a change in government has taken place, the Institute argues, this had often proved insufficient to cause any profound break with the entrenched political-economic systems. On this basis alone, the much vaunted democratisation of Nigeria, Africa's most populous state, must be questioned. How strong are the democratic forces in Nigeria when faced with an entrenched military-economic élite – and how relevant are they to the majority of people of that troubled country?

Structural adjustment programmes were intended to eliminate unproductive forms of economic behaviour and rent-seeking corruption, as well as to reduce the influence of political interests in economic life and decision-making. The results, however, have been varied. The privatisation of public companies and banks and the promotion of a minimum state at the instigation of aid donors have led to the privatisation of many of the sovereign functions of the state including tax collection, customs services, the issuing of banknotes, the maintenance of internal security and shortly, national defence. Driven by the neo-liberal agenda, the commercialisation and outsourcing of the powers of weak, unconsolidated governments have created new opportunities for private security companies and other actors. The apparent loss of the coherence of the state has also encouraged the emergence of new forms of power relations, notably between the central government and local actors, and of new institutions, such as vigilante groups and private militias. The creation of new economic and financial opportunities has seen the emergence of national and transnational actors who are directly implicated in criminal economic activities such as drug-trafficking, trade in stolen cars, general smuggling, and more. In short, the outsourcing and commercialisation of state functions in unconsolidated states have not proven to be a panacea for the lack of capacity, corruption and poor delivery that have characterised the post-colonial state.

The current fashion of privatising services that, for up to a century ago, were the sole preserve of the state, has seen the commercial sector move into areas such as the provision of domestic and professional security, including armed response, and even the running of prisons.

There has also been a growing tendency on the part of defence ministries, eager to reduce their recurrent budgets and to divert their resources to the 'sharp' end of their establishments, to outsource certain of the administrative and logistical tasks that increasingly assume a complexity for which civilian skills are better suited. This form of privatisation has taken on global dimensions with Africa also participating, albeit in a way dictated by the confines of its meagre resources. At the international level, the United States has been at the forefront of the effort by northern powers to downsize the UN through the modernisation of its management, the cutting of costs and a reduction in waste, commensurate with global business trends. The agenda has primarily been to modify UN mandates and *modus operandi* in line with 'northern' priorities and practice that have gained credence with the fall from favour of leftist economic policies. While these economic policies have generally proven successful in developed societies, the verdict with regard to developing societies in Africa in particular, is not yet out.

As police forces fail to cope with petty and violent crime that emanate from a society in which gross inequalities of wealth and opportunity prevail, and where the sanctity of life is mocked by the misery in which most are compelled to struggle for an existence, those with properties to defend have to pay for this service. When the comparatively well-off attempt to secure their possessions and personal safety against would-be criminals, the result in Africa and often elsewhere, has been a proliferation of private security companies, and the apartheid of security described in this book by Lock. Ironically, the growth of the private security industry thrives upon the creation and deepening of a climate of anxiety and fear among the relatively wealthy, so that insecurity and security form an ever-accelerating spiral of subjective impressions.

It has also been shown how the globalised economy, particularly international corporations, have wrested important assets from African state control in many instances. This economic vulnerability has eroded the ability and competence of the state to survive, while insecurity and rising poverty within the state have led to an increased ethnic awareness and the development or resumption of a variety of forms of identity politics. These, together with Africa's cross-border ethnic communities, have therefore further softened borders that were already porous and unenforceable.[12]

The results and characteristics of these challenges have recently been recognised as part of the growth in organised crime in much of Africa – to the extent that writers such as Bayart, Ellis and Hibou have taken to refer to the 'criminalisation of the African state'.[13]

Organised crime is traditionally viewed as group activities with hierarchical relationships that permit the leaders to earn profits or control territories or markets, internal or foreign, by means of violence, intimidation or corruption, both in furtherance of criminal activity and to infiltrate the legitimate economy.[14] Many of the elements of this definition apply equally to the way in which business is done between multinationals and the domestic political-military élite in weak African states – hence, the phrase 'the criminalisation of the African state' – the invasion of the political arena by criminal practices.

Seen through this prism, criminality remains a wide concept, but clearly includes

"... economic and financial practices that are generally considered to be forms of theft or fraud such as the diversion of foreign aid, the illegal export of capital, the looting of capital and natural resources, the large-scale forgery or falsification of foreign-branded consumer goods, systematic tax evasion and money-laundering; or types or economic activity that are regarded as illegal according to the laws of virtually every country in the world, such as currency forgery. A further example is the illegitimate use of the coercive resources of the state or the use of violence which is private and, hence, illegitimate."[15]

"Far from being a tendency peculiar to the political life of Africa, the criminalisation of the state and of the economy can be properly understood and apprehended only in the context of globalisation. In as far as Africa is concerned, this process of criminalisation expresses the re-negotiation by African societies of their insertion into the international system far more than it represents the marginalisation of the continent. Furthermore, criminalisation is not the outward sign of a decline, collapse or dislocation of the state but is one of the modes in which it is formed. It is therefore quite possible that, in the long run, this proves to be quite compatible with the process of democratisation."[16]

For example, sub-Saharan Africa has witnessed a spectacular increase in the occurrence of widespread fraud in recent years – a wave of duplicity and deceit which affects medical and pharmaceutical products, foodstuffs and products for human consumption, fertilisers, and much more.

There can be little doubt that the activities of private security companies, acting on behalf of and in collusion with multinationals and the local élite are aimed at securing certain benefits for their paymasters – to provide a particular value-added service. Sometimes, this may be to enable mineral exploitation to the exclusive benefit of certain companies or groups. Seen in isolation, little fault can be found with such endeavours. The private security industry is wide-ranging, and involves billions of dollars, with the greatest part of its business probably being entirely legitimate and conducted in accordance with generally accepted business practices, norms and standards. Companies are entitled to seek legitimate business. Governments must establish mechanisms for oversight and regulation, both individually and collectively – where they exist and can do so.

Yet, the trend is part of a larger one – the recent growth in the predatory exploitation of economic resources across large swathes of Africa. Evidence of these practices include the development of quasi-military poaching and hunting, of armed raids, cattle-rustling and vehicle theft, the unregulated cutting of hardwood – the expansion of a trend consisting of soldier/rebels and policeman/criminals. This trend is also reflected in the rise of African warlords who are motivated by ethnic survival, political ambition and personal gain to control those areas where the government writ no longer holds sway. It is this trend that sees armed rebels halt the famous Dakar rally during January 1999, search the participants for valuable goods and hold them to ransom in defiance of the local security forces.

The legitimacy and efficacy of the use of private military companies

The British debate on the involvement of a private military company in the reinstatement of President Kabbah of Sierra Leone, referred to above, casts an interesting light upon the public and private attitudes towards this form of private military activity. On 5 May 1998, in a leading article entitled *Double-edged sword — The case for a pragmatic assessment of mercenary forces*, The Times expressed its amazement at the Foreign Office's handling of the affair, which seemed designed to deny itself any credit in achieving the restoration of the legitimate government of Sierra Leone, despite numerous indications that this was an important aim of British policy in Africa. Moving on from the unfathomable ways of politicians, the writer focused on a less ephemeral aspect of the involvement of Sandline International in Sierra Leone.

"This is a 'scandal' to be kept in perspective. But it raises a wider question, about what relationships governments should have with the private military companies that have become a fixture of the post-Cold War world. Mercenaries have been used down the ages, often openly and effectively ... They could have a modern role. When national armies are being cut back and publics will not stand for casualties, the choice may be between limited privatisation of peacekeeping, or no action at all. The manpower engaged in UN peacekeeping has been cut by 70% since its peak in 1994. The answer is not to criminalise operators who have skills the world needs, but to develop a coherent framework to make them more transparent and improve accountability. That, if the moralists permit, is the main lesson that policymakers should draw from this affair."

Tim Spicer, the retired Scots Guards officer who heads Sandline International, published a comment piece in the Sunday Times of 24 May. After sketching some of the gratuitous atrocities inflicted by the rebels upon the civilian population, he reiterated his opinion that Sandline was proud to have played a part in restoring a responsibly elected government.

"I sometimes wonder if the people who have talked so disparagingly of 'mercenaries' from the comfort of their armchairs in recent weeks have any idea of what a dangerous world it is out there. Since the end of the cold war smouldering ethnic conflicts have broken out all over the globe. In the old days, one or other of the superpowers would have snuffed them out. Now, the forces of the traditional 'policemen' are depleted. Most have neither the resources nor the political will to involve themselves in faraway conflict, particularly if it is not nationally significant. Local armies can't always deal with conflict. So how can countries create a safe, stable environment for peaceful existence and economic growth? Often they can't and are left on their own with catastrophic results. That's where private military companies (PMCs) come in.

Sandline and other PMCs are part of a wholly new military phenomenon. Could things have been different in Burundi or Rwanda if an effective military force had been deployed quickly? The answer is yes. Thousands of lives could have been saved, but nobody went."

Spicer proceeded to make a number of points about the sensitivity of his company in accepting contracts, with due consideration of the client's legitimacy, honesty and regard for human rights.[17]

The same sentiments are reflected on the Sandline International website, which also states, as a matter of policy that "... *the company only accepts projects which, **in the view of its management,** would improve the state of security, stability and general conditions in client countries. To this end the company will only undertake projects which are for:*

- *Internationally recognised governments (preferably democratically elected);*

- *International institutions such as the UN;*

- ***Genuine, internationally recognised and supported liberation movements;***

- *And which are ...[w]here possible, **broadly in accord with the policies of key western governments** ..."*[18]

The contradictions evident in such a policy statement, while understandable at the corporate, competitive level, are truly breathtaking at the international level. Ten years ago, the *União Nacional para a Independência Total de Angola* (UNITA) was considered a genuine, internationally recognised and supported liberation movement in most Western capitals, while the African National Congress (ANC) of Nelson Mandela was branded a bunch of terrorists by more than one Tory cabinet member some years earlier.

The fact that upmarket companies, such as Sandline and Executive Outcomes, were not prepared to work for anything but 'recognised governments' does not mean that other, more shady companies with no public relations division, website and brochures will not do so.

The question is 'who decides'. Clearly, this cannot be purely left to the management of a private military company, hired by multinational corporations with clear commercial interests, or to clients consisting of the narrow élite governing countries and approved by intelligence agencies of 'key Western governments'. To do so would be to abrogate any whiff of international law and accountability to commercial interests and to leave peace and security to the jungle of unregulated predatory corporate exploitation.

Spicer has criticised the rogue elements that, by public association, damage the reputation of the respectable parts of this particular service sector, and has urged in favour of the introduction of regulatory legislation instead of outlawing the mercenary industry as did South Africa in 1998. However, there are some who might cavil at the assumption that the human rights record of Kabbah's government was quite as good on his return to Freetown. In fact, some 2 000 suspects were rounded up as collaborators with Koroma's junta, and many found themselves facing the prospect of being tried for their lives. Others were even less fortunate and were summarily executed by the militias or mobs. A related concern has to do with Sandline's apparent enhancement of the Kamajors' military effectiveness, which may impact upon the domestic politics of the country for some time to come.

Kadir Jasin, writing in Malaysia's <u>New Straits Times</u> on 26 May 1998, gave the issue a different perspective. He pointed out that the end of the bipolar Cold War conflict had reduced the incentive for outside powers to ameliorate or end conflicts in areas of remote interest. *"To the rest of the world, it means a new form of extra-territorial intervention is taking shape – the so-called 'privatised peacekeeping' when big powers 'franchise' their foreign military operations to mercenaries, renegades and international gun-runners."*[19]

The question was echoed by <u>Africa Confidential</u> in its issue of 29 May 1998[20] when it asked to what extent the British government could or should entrust the making and implementation of foreign policy to private military and mining companies, even in countries of little strategic importance. However successful the Sierra Leone project was in restoring the rule of a legitimate government, and possibly also in containing the regional hegemonic goals of Nigeria, some members of the Commons' Foreign Affairs Committee were understandably hesitant to approve of this kind of precedent.

What has been the concern of this volume, however, has not been so much the private security companies – though these do impinge on the military security arena, as seen in the case of Angola – but on the role of companies purveying military services even as far as participating in combat operations. In this, it appears, Africa may be 'leading the field'. This is not to say that mercenaries have not been contracted to participate in other wars – it is an established and continuing phenomenon – but they seem to be attaining new levels of professionalism and organisation in and from Africa. This is the trend towards 'private military companies' or PMCs that Sandline's CEO, Spicer so boldly proclaims.

The problem often facing government commanders is how to augment their forces, to regain a significant, if not decisive, advantage in the field over their irregular opponents. Often, there is little to choose between the quality of government forces and rebels. The response of companies such as EO and Sandline International has been to revert to classic counterinsurgency doctrine – mobilise and arm sympathetic sectors within the local population against the rebels. As a result, communities such as the Kamajors were trained, armed and used against the RUF by both Sandline and EO in Sierra Leone. Similar to the indiscriminate arming of the population of Luanda by the MPLA some years earlier, when UNITA appeared to threaten the capital city, the independent observer must ask what contribution this irreversible militarisation of society makes to future peace.

On the broader international front, the downsizing of conventional forces in the aftermath of Russia's economic collapse and the disbanding of the Warsaw Pact left a sudden surfeit of weaponry and men-at-arms on the world market, neither of which were as readily converted to pacific usage as the peace dividend optimists had hoped. In Africa, the end of the Cold War removed many of the external restraints upon incipient conflicts and slow wars, and the withdrawal of the patronage of the great powers left the continent's fragile state structures exposed to challenge in a way unprecedented since independence.

In South Africa, the redesign and reorientation of the SANDF prompted many of the most skilled exponents of counterinsurgency warfare to seek private employment in their chosen field, at precisely the time when their skills were likely to be most in demand.

The need to employ private security and military companies also relates to the nature of African forces and their changing relationships with the former colonial and other external powers. In the aftermath of the Cold War, there is less appetite among overseas powers to donate equipment and expertise to maintain or enhance the operational capability of the forces of client states. Even France has indicated that it can no longer afford to mount costly military interventions each time trouble erupts in Francophone Africa, nor can it maintain garrisons in Africa on the same scale that it had done previously.[21] Certainly, there have been exceptions to this, with attempts to instil Western traditions of military professionalism, partially in the hope that these will dissuade African militaries from intervening in the political arena. There have also been a number of initiatives to improve the peacekeeping capabilities of African militaries, though it remains uncertain whether the use of such skills will be limited to the narrow field for which they were intended, as seen in the case of the Ugandan deployment into the Democratic Republic of Congo.

Unable to trust that the UN Security Council would accord Africa the priority to which its states were entitled – especially as problems in areas of greater strategic and global importance required attention from the cash-strapped world body – Africa's leaders turned perforce to the more robust of the private military companies that could assist their weakened security forces.

The future of regulation and oversight

The international community has long been unwilling to concede and discuss the structural collapse in many African societies that have been described in this volume, nor the fundamentals that underlie the trend. The whole structure of diplomacy and international recognition rests on the state as the cornerstone and building block of international law and international relations. Heads of state, in little more than the titular meaning of the word, participate in, and are accorded, the same status, in practice and in law, as elected leaders of consolidated democracies, while many of the policies of the traditional donor countries and the structure of the global financial system condemn the poorest of the poor to remain locked in apparent eternal poverty. The result is a façade and a sense of inviolability in the nature of state borders while leaders conceal or simply refuse to acknowledge the extent of state collapse. International law has never objected to other states helping to prop up a weak state, but has little room for a private company helping to secure sovereignty. Elsewhere, warlords such as Charles Taylor capture the power in a feeble state with a firm resolve to seize and exploit those valuable assets still remaining for their own use.[22]

Since any regulatory system must inevitably rely first on national regulation and oversight, and then on international agreement and co-operation, the reality of a rampant superpower that believes in the sanctity of its own laws alone, as well as an unconsolidated and unequal international state structure and state collapse are therefore particularly difficult challenges to overcome in confronting the issue at hand: how to regulate and oversee the activities of private security and military companies in weak African states.

It has already been illustrated that the links between private security companies, mining companies, governments and individuals are complex and obtuse. In some cases, such as between Military Professional Resources Incorporated (MPRI) and the US government, the links are overt. In these cases, companies tender for work on a competitive basis and are paid in accordance with standard and accepted commercial practices. With other relationships, such as that between Sandline International and the British government, the links are less overt, but are clearly revealed during events such as those that occurred in Sierra Leone during 1998. In these latter cases, there is generally little transparency with regard to payment, shareholding and, indeed, the process of awarding contracts to a company like Sandline whose profitability and veritable survival depend upon absolute confidentiality.[23] As a result, analysts such as Pech and Vines point to the vested interests of the Canadian company DiamondWorks in Sierra Leone, where it owns the Koidu diamond mine, the Sewa diamond concession, and the Sierra Rutile titanium mine, its close links to Sandline, and the role the latter played in restoring Kabbah to power.[24]

There is no clarity about the exact relationship between governments, such as Britain, and private security companies, such as Sandline. In its own interest, the former publicly distances itself from the latter, while the latter publicly associates itself with the former. Unable to penetrate the hidden world of interaction between the Foreign and Commonwealth Office, MI6, Sandline, DiamondWorks and Kabbah – and to distinguish reality from public pronouncement – the analyst and observer can only guess at the truth.

Many companies argue in favour of 'corporate good practices' as part of a system of oversight over private security companies. Following the introduction of value-added financial statements and a greater sense of corporate social responsibility that is evident among Fortune 500 companies, there is, undoubtedly, some usefulness to be gained from such practices.[25] However, it must be acknowledged, at the same time, that these practices are often restricted to the national boundaries of developed societies where intense competition, not some inherent sense of social obligation, has seen corporations adopting a social responsibility ethos to advance their competitive edge in the market. In the rough justice that is Africa, where business can literally be of a cut-throat nature, Generally Accepted Accounting Practice (GAAP) has little, if any, impact. Leaving the market to regulate itself, in this instance as in so many others, will provide little comfort – or real oversight. Asking competitive companies operating in an unregulated, brutal and corrupt marketplace to apply 'First World' business practices, is to ask the bottom line to challenge the corporate sense of social responsibility, where the latter often does not even apply.

The global community has embarked upon various initiatives to control illegal and harmful practices, many of which were discussed in the chapter by Sandoz. Yet, the efficacy of these measures are varied and lacking. For example, Britain, while publicly deploring the use of mercenaries, has no legal means of curbing mercenary activity other than the obsolete Foreign Enlistment Act of 1870. No one has been tried under the provisions of this Act for more than a hundred years. France and Belgium have also banned the recruitment of mercenaries, but have not enforced these laws in recent years. The US Neutrality Act of 1937 prohibits the recruitment of mercenaries in that country (but not being a mercenary *per se*), as does the Australian Foreign Incursions and Recruitment Act of 1978. The United Kingdom, along with most other European Union and G8 countries, have not signed the 1989 UN Convention against the Use, Training and Recruitment of Mercenaries, because they regard the

<u>Convention</u> as legally unenforceable. As pointed out by Abraham, the legal impact of the <u>Convention</u> is rendered tenuous by the fact that five of the sixteen signatories had either hired or dealt with mercenaries (Angola, the Republic of Congo, Nigeria and the former Zaire) or was a significant source of mercenaries (the Ukraine).[26]

The failure of the international community and of international law to address this problem, has much to do with the difficulty of having to define the nature of the service that is to be outlawed. Thus far, this debate has revolved around unsuccessful attempts at defining mercenarism. Indeed, this was why the Diplock Committee of Privy Counsellors that was appointed to inquire into the recruitment of mercenaries in the UK chose not to regulate 'mercenaries' in 1976. A precise definition of such services is particularly essential, since individuals will potentially be deprived of important rights as a consequence of falling into a prescribed category.[27] The Diplock report concluded that:

"... any definition of mercenaries which required positive proof of motivation would ... either be unworkable, or so haphazard in its application between comparable individuals as to be unacceptable. Mercenaries, we think, can only be defined by reference to what they do, and not by reference to why they do it."[28]

It could well be asked to what extent the infatuation with the term 'mercenary' has become an obstacle rather than an aid to oversight and regulation. An approach that seeks to regulate all types of foreign security services, including military and paramilitary services, would arguably be much more fruitful.

Clearly, some type of common position among the members of the European Union, which include countries with a long history of mercenary involvement in Africa such as France, Britain and Belgium, could go a long way in curbing the activities of private military companies. Such measures, however, will not affect the new sources of mercenaries in Africa, increasingly consisting of former soldiers from the Federal Republic of Yugoslavia (Serbia and Montenegro), Bosnia and Herzegovina, and the Ukraine, often with arms from Yugoslavia and Bulgaria.

South Africa, which has shown much less compunction with respect to the practical implementation of well-intended government policy, boldly enacted the <u>Regulation of Foreign Military Assistance Act</u> in 1998. The Act aims to outlaw mercenary activity and regulate the provision of 'foreign military services' in similar fashion to the system regulating arms exports. Yet, by January 1999, there had apparently not been a single application under the Act to the National Conventional Arms Control Committee (NCACC), charged with the implementation of the legislation. The fact that the leading department in legislative terms is the South African Department of Defence, undermines the effectiveness of this legislation without a greater role for a department with the information (the intelligence agencies), motivation (Department of Foreign Affairs) or means (Department of Justice) to act. Abraham holds that,

"[t]he legislation was rushed through parliament without sufficient thought being given to the problem of definition. If the object was to avoid the pit-falls of defining mercenarism in terms

of motivation, a more effective definition of what constitutes mercenarism could, instead, have looked to the purpose for which the mercenary is employed. Ordinarily, the legitimacy of that purpose is reflective of the legitimacy of the employer. And, of all, it is purpose that is of ultimate concern. However, simply to define mercenary activity as 'participation ... in armed conflict ... for private gain' is to render the definition meaningless."[29]

Whatever the real or potential ability of the South African government to enforce the provisions of the Act, the fact remains that EO closed its doors three months after the Act came into effect, leaving more than one commentator speculating on the causal relationship. The South African precedent should therefore serve as a spur for developed countries, who have many more means to enforce what was, in South Africa's case, probably largely symbolic legislation. At the same time, the ability of a company whose major asset is a well-managed database of former military personnel and the right connections to relocate to a different country, to mutate and change or conceal its identity, must serve to sober too enthusiastic an analysis.

For the international community, particularly for agencies that operate within what has become known as complex emergencies, the establishment of a roster of 'accredited' private security companies that are vetted and trained to accompany aid convoys, protect humanitarian relief workers and even provide limited traditional peacekeeping duties, is probably a minimum requirement. Such companies would have to apply for certification that would be endangered by transgressing a set series of standards. Admittedly, this would only apply to a limited number of companies, and then only to those who are interested in operating within a legitimate environment. Both the UN and individual governments may also wish to deploy a much smaller observer team – alongside a private company engaged in peacekeeping duties – as an independent check on activities in the field. But these companies would probably not include the 'classic' private military companies such as Sandline.

Until the international community can come up with a clear legal response to what constitutes illegal private military involvement, as opposed to mercenary activity, conventions such as the International Convention Against the Recruitment, Use, Financing and Training of Mercenaries will remain toothless and useless. International conventions on mercenaries and that of the Organisation of African Unity (OAU) both contain definitions that focus on acts aimed at overthrowing or undermining the constitutional order and territorial integrity of the state. Working for a recognised government therefore clouds the legal basis for the classification of activities as mercenary.

Generally, attempts at regulating international private military and security activities, human rights standards and those conventions dealing with organised crime and mercenaries should be strengthened. For example, the monitoring of cross-border movements of cash and appropriate negotiation instruments between countries are generally well established within the developed world, but absent in much of Africa. The same argument could be used with regard to bank secrecy and the availability of records and extradition agreements. Similarly, existing war crimes statutes provide for legal action against personnel who have participated in committing atrocities – provided that proof of such actions can be found and that the legal client, the supported government, wishes to extradite and proceed with legal steps. The well-known principle which is followed in cases of international crimes is 'extradite or prosecute'. A similar approach should be adopted to deal with atrocities committed by private security and military companies.

The proposed <u>Protocol Against the Illicit Manufacturing of and Trafficking in Firearms, Ammunition and other related Materials</u>, as part of the draft <u>Convention on Transnational Organised Crime</u>, offers the opportunity to advance international co-operation and co-ordination in terms of the control and investigation of the activities of private security companies that overstep the mark. Although in itself insufficient, this measure will provide additional resources to regulate international private military activity.

Conclusion

A change in the debate regarding foreign private security companies seems to be emerging. Whereas the debate was obsessed with mercenaries and all the emotive and ideological baggage that accompanied this term until recently, much of the contemporary writing and thinking are moving away from the unhelpful and often sterile attempts to judge actions as being mercenary or not. In a perceptive paper, Clapham underlines the need to objectively confront the internal security dilemma facing many African states. He points to "... *two basic criteria by which any security system needs to be judged: its efficiency in maintaining some kind of order on the one hand, and its accountability to those people whose security is at stake on the other.*" In similar vein to many of the arguments evident in this volume, he argues that the

"*... emergence of 'mercenary' forces, which have prompted much of the concern about the privatisation of security in modern Africa, is far more the result than the cause of the underlying problems of African security: and rather than being inherently or necessarily evil, such forces need to be assessed alongside other would-be solutions to the African security dilemma, each of which – supposedly 'national' armies most definitely included – has its own elements of privatisation.*"[30]

Many of the trends discussed in this chapter can be illustrated by events in Luanda where the private security company TeleServices dominates and virtually controls the market along the coast and oil areas (as does Alpha 5 in the diamond areas). According to Vines, the main shareholders of TeleServices are the chief of staff of the armed forces, the commander of the army, the head of intelligence, the Angolan ambassador to Washington and the Interior Minister (who received a 25 per cent stake, apparently as a reward for helping to evict Defence Systems Limited (DSL), the rival company).[31] In this manner, senior Angolan government officials have outsourced core government functions to private companies for personal gain and further eroded an already weak state. Such actions can surely only serve to undermine the remaining legitimacy of the MPLA government in the eyes of foreign investors and local inhabitants alike. In January 1998, Ballesteros, the UN Special Rapporteur on the use of mercenaries, wrote that private security forces were "*... incapable of replacing those agencies responsible for the State's inherent and pre-emptory role to protect life and* *security ...”* and blamed the collapse of President's Kabbah's government in Sierra Leone on the regime's dependence on EO.[32]

The question whether this incestuous collaboration constitutes organised criminal activity is a moot point. In fact, the relationship between organised crime, the international arms bazaar and the private military industry is a key area that has not been the subject of vigorous investigation. Thus far, the international debate has been driven by the focus on arms trafficking in attempts to track and evaluate global defence equipment flows. Little, if any, attention is paid to tracking the various services that accompany such deliveries or that create the demand for such deliveries.

The activities of the private security industry have, in fact, not been the focus of significant research, although there has recently been an upsurge in interest. There remains a clear requirement for the collection and sharing of much more information on this industry in a much more concerted manner than was the case in the past. There are, as yet, no common definitions, standards and methodologies that can be used – illustrated by the problems in even defining the concept 'mercenary'. There has similarly been little attempt at analysing trends in a country such as South Africa which has seen a veritable explosion in the private security industry in recent years. At a global level, little effort has been made to gain a greater understanding of the nature and impact of the private security industry as a global force with its own significance. The one important exception is provided by the reports and activities of the UN Special Rapporteur who has significantly and consistently added to the body of knowledge on the industry throughout recent years. His is an endeavour that should continue and even be expanded.

Whatever point of departure is used, there are a variety of political and economic reasons for the upsurge in the activities of private security companies in Africa. On the political front, some of these organisations have assisted governments in their struggle against opposition groups and have propped up dictators – often at the behest of corrupt leaders or for commercial gain. The mining and oil industries often have to provide their own security to protect fixed investments worth millions of dollars. As a result, giants such as Lonrho, Rio-Tinto Zinc, Anglo American and Barrick have utilised the services of security organisations such as DSL,[33] Keeny-Meeny Services (KMS),[34] the Control Risks Group[35] and Kroll Associates. Shell, British Petroleum (BP), Mobil and Texaco have been known to utilise private security organisations for a variety of services from guarding oil installations and fields to augmenting the security forces/military of host governments. Texaco used EO in Angola, while the Israeli company International Security Consultants (ISC) or the US company, AirScan has provided services for Chevron in Cabinda.[36] Yet, the unbridled expansion of the activities of foreign private military companies, even foreign private security companies cannot be envisaged in Africa. Only a few African countries have exploitable minerals and valuables of sufficient short term return, such as oil and diamonds, to provide the revenue streams required to pay the hefty fees that are charged. Tea, cocoa and coffee are high volume, low price commodities that tend to degrade as a country's infrastructure collapses. Extracting copper, ferrochrome, gold or asbestos requires massive capital injections that are difficult to justify to shareholders in a world characterised by falling base commodity prices.[37]

Private security companies that want to operate more or less like regular businesses, with a sustainable and growing market share, a marketable corporate identity and the possibility to trade profitably on international stock exchanges, such as DSL, will only engage in failing African states at their own peril. Working for international organisations such as the UN High Commissioner for Refugees (UNHCR), the World Health Organisation (WHO) and CARE within African states is, however, an entirely different manner and both legitimate and potentially lucrative.[38]

With no vital or strategic interests at stake in Africa, the Permanent Five Security Council members have proven increasingly reluctant to risk their soldiers' lives in Africa. The stated preference is to build African capacity to deal with Africa's crises. Given the immense gulf in equipment and training that separates them, it seems inevitable that the result will be the development of a two-tiered system of global peacekeeping – one set of standards for the developed world and another for Africa. And different criteria may open the doors for less scrupulous players who rely on force of arms and coercion rather than a careful mandate from the UN Security Council. In this scenario, the primary goal of enduring foreign and domestic private security companies will be to protect international aid organisations that deliver emergency food and other aid, and to replace the armed forces of developed countries in retraining and professionalising those of the countries of Africa.

After Somalia the disinclination of even heavily armed American-led NATO forces in Bosnia to undertake any activity that might risk casualties – much less to engage in actual warfighting – also stands in marked contrast to the role of the Nigerian-led peacekeeping forces in Liberia and, especially, Sierra Leone. Similarly, African leaders such as Dos Santos (Angola), Nujoma (Namibia), Museveni (Uganda), Mugabe (Zimbabwe) and others are prepared to have their armed forces sustain casualties in neighbouring countries to a degree that is unthinkable in the developed world. It thus seems that, at least in environments where high-technology weaponry is no substitute for the common foot soldier, the developed world has ample armaments and little stomach for their use, while African peacekeeping forces lack not the will, but sometimes the tools.

What capacity do Western governments really have to control the activities of private companies, whether they are engaged in mining, mineral exploration or private military security? And what political will could democratic governments garner from their electorate and from their domestic political opponents to regulate such activities? This study has focused on the current phenomenon of foreign private security companies as a clear symptom of the malaise of the crumbling African state, and as part of the response of weak African states to globalisation.

But it should be borne in mind that, in the case of a country such as Angola, war is both made possible by, and is a competition for the spoils of Africa's curse of abundant and extractable natural resources. While the multinational oil companies continue to pump oil for Western consumption in Angola – handsomely benefiting the private pockets of the senior MPLA élite in Luanda, who are free to mortgage future oil concessions and profits to fuel the war – and while UNITA is able to extract and sell untraceable rough diamonds, hard wood and other resources in neighbouring countries, there can be little chance of an end to the war. The developed world can regulate private military companies and avoid overt involvement in the slaughter that is Angola at the start of 1999. But this will neither make any difference to the MPLA and UNITA, who can fund their campaigns through profits from the sale of minerals, nor to the population at large. Thus, both the activities of companies such as EO and corporations like Chevron, EXXON, Agip and Elf Acquitaine will have to be curtailed if the international community is serious about ending the war in Angola. Doing the one without the other will make very little difference, except, of course, if all you really intend to do, is to avoid being seen too close to where the trigger is pulled, while you are passing on the ammunition from the shadows.

Endnotes

1   A A Mazrui, The Africans: A Triple Heritage, BBC Publications, London, 1986, p. 15

2   Ibid., p. 16

3   Ibid., p. 20

4   To provide a 500-man combat and small intelligence unit.

5   In one sense, EO had never left Sierra Leone. Their presence was assured by the company LifeGuard which guarded a variety of installations belonging to the mining company Branch Energy and its subsidiaries. See K Pech, *Too Late for the Mercenaries*, Weekly Mail & Guardian, 30 May 1997.

6   Based in London's Chelsea district, but registered in the Bahamas.

7   In a press release dated 5 August 1997, EO denied that it had any business links with LifeGuard Ltd. See <www.eo.com/presrel/pressrel.asp?series=21>, December 1998.

8   The head of the armed forces blew the whistle on Sandline, in part because he had been accepting payments (some £31 000) from a rival company, the UK-based J & S Franklin Corporation. Franklin has a long history of supplying military equipment to Africa and introduced GSG to Sierra Leone. See A Vines, *Mercenary Operations in African in the 1990's: Trends, Issues and Problems*, paper read at the conference on The Privatisation of Security in Africa, South African Institute of International Affairs, Johannesburg, 10 December 1998, p. 12.

9   *Militias and Market Forces*, Africa Confidential, 38(21), London, 23 October 1998, p. 1

10   Reported in *ECOMOG Troops Surround S Leonean Rebel Forces*, The Citizen, Johannesburg, 22 January 1999. It is unclear from the report whether the pilots were from a private company or on contract from the French military.

11   Gorée Institute, *Draft Concept Paper on Criminalisation Project*, Gorée Island, February 1998, p. 1.

12   J Mackinlay, *War Lords*, RUSI Journal, London, April 1998, p. 26.

13   J Bayart, S Ellis & B Hibou, The Criminalisation of the State in Africa, James Currey, Oxford, 1999.

14   Loosely taken from the Draft United Nations Convention against Transnational Organised Crime, Buenos Aires, September 1998.

15   Gorée Institute, op. cit. p. 2.

16   Ibid., pp. 2-3.

17   See <www.sandline.com/company/index.html>, 31 December 1998.

18   See <www.sandline.com/company/index.html>, 31 December 1998, p. 1. Emphasis added.

19   A Kadir Jasin, *Big Power Adventurism Poses New Kind of Threat to Weaker Nations*, New Straits Times, 26 May 1998.

20   *Private Armies, Public Relations*, Africa Confidential, 39(11), 29 May 1998, <www.africa-confidential.com>

21   Paris has closed two bases in the Central African Republic (CAR) and reduced its standing force in Africa from 8 500 to 6 300 troops who are stationed at its five remaining African garrisons. France has also cut its financial assistance to African armed forces by Ffr 23 million to US $139 million in 1998. See J A C Lewis, *France Reviews Commitment in Africa*, Jane's Defence Weekly, London, 6 January 1999, p. 18.

20   Charles Taylor of Liberia has been particularly successful at exploiting the local timber and diamonds to become France's third largest supplier of tropical hardwoods. See Mackinlay, op. cit., p. 27; and J Herbst, *Contemporary Efforts at Regulation: A Local and International Perspective*, paper read at the conference on The Privatisation of Security in Africa, op. cit., pp. 2-3.

21   See, for example, the emphasis on client confidentiality in the material on the Sandline International website at <www.sandlines.com/home/index.html>

22   Vines, op. cit., p. 15; see Chapter 5.

23   This is acknowledged by Sandline: *"PMC's must be willing to open themselves up for inspection beyond the requirements of company law ... This is an essential factor in establishing acceptability and credibility in the eyes of the world community."* See, *Should the Activities of Private Military Companies be Transparent?*, <www.sandline.com/company/index.html>, 31 December 1998, p. 5.

24   G Abraham, *The Contemporary Legal Environment*, paper read at the conference on The Privatisation of Security in Africa, op. cit., p. 20.

25   Ibid., p. 4.

26   Quoted in ibid., p. 17.

27   Ibid., p. 24.

28   C Clapham, *The Changing Nature of Mercenary Activity in Africa: An Historical Analysis*, paper read at the conference on The Privatisation of Security in Africa, op. cit., pp. 2-3.

29   Vines, op. cit., p. 21.

30   Quoted in Herbst, op. cit., p. 2.

31   The company was founded in 1981 and comprised former British special forces personnel. The company was taken over by a US firm, Armor Holdings, in April 1997. It has provided security services to oil and gas, surveying and mining companies in Algeria, the DRC, Angola and Mozambique. It was also involved in mine-clearing, refugee camp security and related security and protection services for the UN, the Red Cross and a variety of aid agencies and NGOs. Among its clients, DSL can count the UN mission in the former Yugoslavia in 1992. In Angola, its clients included Angolan parastatals Sonogol (oil) and Endiama (diamonds), along with a cement factory, four embassies (including the US Embassy) and the main hotels in Luanda. In the DRC, DSL's subsidiaries, USDS and Sapelli SARL, protected installations belonging to the SOCIR oil refinery of Congo-SEP (the Belgian oil company Petrofina's subsidiary) and the US Embassy. Other DSL clients include De Beers, Shell, Mobil, Amoco, BP and Chevron; CARE and GOAL; and several UN agencies and missions. The company claims experience in Algeria, Botswana, Kenya, Malawi, Mozambique, Rwanda, Somalia, Sudan and Uganda. Its French subsidiary, CIAS, is now trying to get a contract to protect the projected 1 100 km pipeline between the southern Chad oil fields and the port of Kribi in Cameroon. In

supporting the missions of such organisations as the UN and the World Bank, DSL has gained gradual respectability. See K O'Brien, *Freelance Forces – Exploiters of Old or New-age Peacebrokers*, Jane's Intelligence Review, August 1998, p. 42. During the eighties, DSL acquired other formed Special Air Service companies such as Intersec and Falconstar.

32   A British company that employs former special forces soldiers.

33   Control Risks Group provides security services mainly to oil and oil industry-related corporations in Algeria. Its South African operation is believed to have been virtually closed down.

34   A list of some of the other more well-known security firms that operate in Africa would include the following. **Saladin Security Limited** who provided bodyguards and security advisors in Algeria and the Yemen. In the past, it has offered training for security forces and (in South America) has provided interventionist forces. **Eurisc Limited** operated in the DRC, Angola and South Africa and attempted to establish itself in Nigeria. **Alpha** is a Russian company founded in 1991 by former KGB special forces personnel. Alpha apparently has agreements with DSL. **Gray Security Limited** is a South African based security firm that operates in South Africa and, more recently, Angola. Gray Security is apparently linked to **TeleServices**, also active in Sierra Leone. In 1994, the Israeli company **Lev'dan** signed a $50 million contract with the government of Congo-Brazzavile to train the local army and presidential bodyguard. **Rapport Research and Analysis Limited** is a small, new organisation that has operated successfully in the former Zaire and Rwanda, since early 1997, providing security cover and liaison for NGOs. **SP International**, based in Paris, is a small security and information company that provides security staff in a number of Francophone countries. According to Africa Confidential, op. cit., **Alpha 5** was founded jointly by the *Forças Armadas Angolas* Chief of Staff, General João de Matos and Executive Outcomes. **Riscon (Kenya)** provides security advice, personnel and equipment in Kenya, Zimbabwe and Tanzania. It is also able to provide a useful service in Mozambique and Uganda. **Secrets** is a French company active in Cameroon. Another French company active in Togo is **Service and Security**. **Eric SA** is a French company competing on behalf of DSL to win oil installation security contracts in Algeria., O'Brien alleges that the French government used **Geolink** as a cover for the provision of mercenary forces in support of former Zairian president Mobutu during the final stages of his regime. **Alpha Bravo Associates Limited** provided security services in Nigeria, Ghana, Liberia, Côte d'Ivoire and in remote areas of Sierra Leone. It also has operatives with on-the-ground experience in Algeria, former Zaire, Somalia, Somaliland, Kenya, Uganda, Rwanda, Congo-Brazzaville, Cameroon, Angola, Namibia and South Africa. **Stability Control Agencies (Stabilco)** is South African-based and run by Mauritz le Roux, and was involved in the former Zaire. The US, Florida-based, company **AirScan** has had the contract to protect the oil installations in Cabinda since 1995. Of these, DSL is probably the most important, enduring and legitimate with some 130 contracts for 115 clients in 22 countries.

35   Herbst, op. cit., p. 12.

36   Ibid., p. 13.